T0285112

DECADENT WOMEN

DECADENT WOMEN
Yellow Book Lives

Jad Adams

REAKTION BOOKS

For Julie

Published by
Reaktion Books Ltd
Unit 32, Waterside
44–48 Wharf Road
London N1 7UX, UK
www.reaktionbooks.co.uk

First published 2023
Copyright © Jad Adams 2023

Printed and bound in Great Britain
by TJ Books Ltd, Padstow, Cornwall

A catalogue record for this book is available from the British Library

ISBN 978 1 78914 789 6

CONTENTS

PART ONE
Fin de Siècle

IT WAS IN THE company of Ernest Dowson that I first learned to walk the streets of 1890s London. One thing I felt was deficient in my work on Dowson was the absence of women's voices. It was not an absence of women in his life, for he was not short of love objects, muses and sexual partners. They were decorative, they inspired love, sometimes they had sex; we know they sighed and moaned, and they were hymned in verse, but what did they say?

Women made little or no appearance in such accounts of the period as *Men of the Nineties* or *The Beardsley Period*, yet the most cursory examination of contemporary material showed that women were everywhere writing novels, short stories and poems, selling and being reviewed and bought at the same level as the men.[1] A third of the writers of the *Yellow Book*, the outstanding literary and artistic journal which published in the middle years of the 1890s, were women. Soon after writing *Madder Music, Stronger Wine: The Life of Ernest Dowson*, I opened a file called 'Lost Girls' and started gathering material to identify them and research their lives.[2] This book is the product of that research in many archives, libraries and personal collections.

For the first time in history, at the end of the nineteenth century, large numbers of women were able to take charge of their own destinies. This is the story of the cohort of them who assailed the gates of literature in the late Victorian and the Edwardian periods. Their dress, their speech, but most of all their behaviour, was outrageous. *Decadent Women* is the story of the first generation to choose their own names, to work for themselves, to seek out their own places to live and their own sexual relationships.

The battles of earlier generations of women for the right to economic freedom had been partially won by the 1890s, allowing them to venture off alone to challenge further restrictions. *Decadent Women* is about what they did with those freedoms when the massive expansion of the print media meant there were more publications – books, magazines, newspapers – than ever before, to be fed by an army of hungry freelance writers. *Decadent Women* follows some of the women who first came to public notice in the pages of the *Yellow Book*.[3] They ranged across aristocrats, political activists, the desperately poor, the academically well connected and the fashionable. This is the story of their struggles with work, love and sex and, for some of them, with childbirth and disease. They were pioneers of a new style, living lives of lurid adventure and romance and, not infrequently, of squalor and lies. The consequences of error or failure were terrible: unwanted pregnancy, infection with incurable diseases and poverty to the point of starvation.

'Decadent' was a catch-all term for challenges to the establishment consensus. 'New', 'modern' and 'decadent' were all used to describe these gender-challenging anarchists whose behaviour was taken as evidence of the degeneration of a hysterical society. Decadence was taken to be the dissolution of the staid and stoical Victorian values that had gradually become the consensus of correct behaviour as Great Britain's power and influence had advanced through the century. These values related to the fixed order of things: heterosexuality, patriarchy and a woman's place in the home.

Decadent Women's perspective is a deliberate challenge to those who think of social change as caused by political parties and committees. Most change is in fact brought about by people choosing to live their lives differently and defending their right to do so. Only one of the women whose lives are delineated here was a great campaigner for the feminist cause; two were socialists; the rest were busy making a living, getting on with their friendships and loves and writing about their lives and those of their friends.

The structure of *Decadent Women* is to take the group of women from their first strivings towards independence. The first half of this book, '*Fin de Siècle*', covers that time up to the end of the nineteenth century or the very beginning of the twentieth. The second, '*Commence de Siècle*', follows their lives and adventures up to their deaths over many decades of the twentieth century.

1

The Launch

The Hotel d'Italie was in a back street away from the main thoroughfares of central London. Old Compton Street was known as a meeting place for exiles, particularly after the suppression of the Paris Commune in 1871; the poets Paul Verlaine and Arthur Rimbaud had frequented pubs there. This was where guests at the launch of the *Yellow Book* came on 16 April 1894, past the fried fish shop, butcher, newsagent, grocer and Admiral Duncan pub.

Arthur Waugh, a somewhat sour observer, said the restaurant was in a 'very Bohemian back street' and 'it really seemed unnecessary to choose such a smelly, ill-favoured place.'[1] In fact, if he did not already know, it was because John Lane, the *Yellow Book* publisher, was notoriously cheap where entertaining was concerned.

An odd assortment of people ascended the stairs to an upstairs dining room; there was a wide age range and varying standards of dress, though all had made an effort. Writer and musician Elizabeth Pennell felt it was 'free of formality' and noted that the men were in dress suits or tweeds as they chose, the women in evening or tailored gowns. She wrote,

> I can still see the animated faces and hear the animated voices of Mrs Harland and John Oliver Hobbes (Pearl Craigie) and Ménie Muriel Dowie and Kenneth Grahame and George Moore and John Lane and Max Beerbohm, and all the brand-new writers prepared to shock, or to 'uplift' or to pull down old altars and set up new ones, or any other of the fine things that were to make the *Yellow Book* a force and famous.[2]

More people seemed to have come than were expected. Arthur Waugh said, 'The room was as full as it could be and Harland was everywhere at once, introducing those who had not met before.' The table arrangement was a trilith with the top table at the middle of the cross section. There sat the small and somewhat pudgy publisher John Lane, who reputedly published more verse than anyone else in London and was, despite his personal timidity, one of the most forward-looking publishers in the country. By his side was Ménie Muriel Dowie, the tall, beautiful and adventurous woman who had made her name as a travel writer and stayed in the public eye through frequent mentions in celebrity gossip columns; the novelist Berta Ruck described her as 'a French fashion-plate of a woman'.[3] Elizabeth Pennell sat between the editor Henry Harland and the art editor Aubrey Beardsley. She thought them 'as nervous as debutantes at a first party. Shrinking from the shadow cast before by their coming speeches.' They paid scant attention to their meals, or to her: 'all about me was talk and laughter . . . But each editor had to make a speech and both were bracing themselves for the ordeal.'[4] Both of them were consumptive to such an extent that Charles Lewis Hind, editor of *The Studio*, which had favourably covered Beardsley's work, said, 'I used to look at Harland and Beardsley, wondering which would die first.'[5] At the time of the dinner, Beardsley had four years to live, Harland eleven.

At least Waugh, if not others, thought Elizabeth Pennell was out of place: 'Why our good friend Elizabeth Robins Pennell was elevated in the boss-place to the exclusion of *Some Emotions and a Moral* [referring to Pearl Craigie by the name of her most successful novel] I don't know, but she bore it bravely and smiled to everyone.' Pearl Craigie was in fact sitting next to George Moore, who ordered champagne which he shared with her. Waugh described the scene: 'George Moore was radiant: on either side of him was a lovely woman; he alone drank champagne with them: his hair grew wild and his eye merry. He left early with the ladies. Then we smiled.' Craigie, one of the few women who wrote in the epigrammatic style of Oscar Wilde, was being wooed by Moore, who had been engaged in a 'literary collaboration' with her. This was his usual method of seduction, by which he ensured he could legitimately spend long periods alone with a woman when they were supposedly polishing a manuscript. He also proposed a 'literary collaboration' with fellow *Yellow Book* contributors Ella Hepworth Dixon and Lena Milman and with novelist Gertrude Atherton.[6] Hepworth Dixon wrote, 'For some obscure reason George Moore was set on collaborating with the present writer on a novel of modern life, which was to appear in the *Lady's Pictorial*.'[7] Of course, she knew very well what the reason was; the disingenuous humour is typical of that in her book about contemporary mating, *My Flirtations*.

The other 'lovely woman' was Olivia Shakespear, whose first sight of W. B. Yeats was at this gathering. He was at this time not a major celebrity but certainly a poet to look out for. She was beautiful and reflective, and locked into a loveless marriage. Moore, as a fellow literary Irishman, knew Yeats but was disinclined to introduce them, presumably so he could monopolize Shakespear's attention, as well as that of Craigie. Shakespear was her friend rather than his; her first novel, *Love on a Mortal Lease*, to be published later that year, was dedicated to Craigie.

Elizabeth Pennell felt she had been elevated in place of her husband, the writer, illustrator and artist Joseph Pennell, who had to be away on a commissioned project in Dalmatia. She noted, 'The editors were disappointed not to have him at the dinner to celebrate its launching at the Café d'Italie in Soho. They accepted me as his representative and did it gracefully by placing me in the seat of honour between them at the high table.'[8] She was self-deprecating, though she had every credential to be present in her own right.

Waugh drew a map of the seating arrangements for Edmund Gosse, who could not be present. He noted the seats of forty people (though he says just under fifty attended); he did not know the names of fourteen of them. It is reasonable to imagine him more likely not to know the names of women than men; he twice makes a point: 'a female – name unknown' and 'a lovely lady!' It is not possible to tell whether the places marked with a cross as unknowns on his plan were those of women. He describes most women by their relationship to their husbands, including Mrs (Aline) Harland, the *Yellow Book* editor's wife, and Mrs (Grace) Rhys, who was the wife of Ernest Rhys, a founder member of the Rhymers' Club, which had an all-male membership including Yeats, Ernest Dowson, John Davidson and Lionel Johnson, all of whom were present at 52 Old Compton Street that night in 1894.

The women Waugh notes as being present were perhaps known to him only because they had connections with men who were already significant in the literary world. Olivia Shakespear was Lionel Johnson's cousin; Ménie Muriel Dowie was the wife of Henry Norman, literary editor of the *Daily Chronicle* and a leading journalist. Egerton Clairmonte is the only guest who is defined by his wife: 'husband of George Egerton [née Mary Chavelita Dunne]', who was unwell but Clairmonte still came. 'I am he! She is mine!' He mocked Clairmonte's evident pride in his wife's achievements; it was a matter for droll humour for Waugh, who, if he wished to use a technical term, would describe such sentiments as uxorious.

One missing woman, who was nonetheless present in conversation, was Ella D'Arcy, a writer of Irish extraction related to no one noteworthy, who was destined to be important to the *Yellow Book*. Another important *Yellow Book* character, Netta Syrett, was away because of the death of a 'dear relative', in fact her grandfather who had died the day before.[9] It is very typical of the sort of self-sacrificing character who often appears in her fiction that Syrett should be denied the experience of the *Yellow Book* launch dinner because of a family event. It is rather typical too of her dogged determination that she would be the only one of the *Yellow Book* women still publishing more than fifty years later. Evelyn Sharp was not present, as she was just this year trying her fortune in London. Her first novel, *At the Relton Arms*, was yet to come out and she was not well enough known to have been invited.

Dinner in the noisy, low-ceilinged room, as Waugh described it, 'was bad, bad, bad; but everyone talked to his heart's content'. The speeches about which Harland had been nervous came and he made a creditable effort, reciting some verses written by Gosse (the recipient of Waugh's letter about the event). Artist Walter Sickert made a witty speech looking forward to the time when authors would be put in their places by being compelled to write stories and poems around the pictures supplied to them by artists.

The Bodley Head office in Vigo Street, *c.* 1896 and present day.

The only speech by a woman was by Ménie Muriel Dowie, an indication of her celebrity and her skill at public speaking. Waugh noted she
'talked about the women and said that Ella D'Arcy was a discovery to be
proud of'. It is clear therefore that the women's contribution to the *Yellow
Book* was part of the event.[10]

After the party, Elizabeth Pennell went with Aline and Henry Harland,
Lane and Beardsley to Lane's nearby shop next to where he lived in the
Albany, 'to which he took us all that we might see the place from which
the *Yellow Book* was to be published'.[11] They admired the display described
by the office junior John Lewis May, with evident pride in his role in cre-
ating it, as 'such a mighty glow of yellow at the far end of Vigo Street that
one might have been forgiven for imagining for a moment that some awful
portent had happened, and that the sun had risen in the West'.[12] Elizabeth
Pennell thought, 'to me the bright yellow-bound volumes meant youth,
gay, irresponsible, credulous, hopeful youth.'[13]

Not everyone was so impressed with May's window dressing. Katharine
Bradley and Edith Cooper (who wrote as Michael Field) wrote in their
journal on 17 April that they had gone to the Bodley Head to buy a copy
of the *Yellow Book*:

> We have been almost blinded by the glare of Hell . . . As we came
> up to the shop we found the whole frontage a hot background
> of orange-colour to sly, roistering heads, silhouetted against it and
> half-hiding behind masks. The window seemed to be gibbering,
> our eyes filled with incurable jaundice . . . One felt as one does
> when now and then a wholly lost woman stands flaming on the
> pavement with the ghastly laugh of the ribald crowd in the air
> round her. One hates one's eyes for seeing! But the infamous window
> mocked and moved and fizgiged, saffron & pitchy, till one's eyes
> were arrested like Virgil's before the wind of flame.

They felt no more comfort when they had the book in their hands:

> It is full of cleverness such as one expects to find in those who dwell
> below light & hope & love & aspiration. The best one can say, of
> any tale or any illustration, is that it is clever – the worst one can
> say is that it is damnable. But George Egerton does not even deserve
> damnation, but something weightier – crushing out silence.[14]

There is a coda to this out-and-out condemnation by a couple of poets who had been featured in the prospectus, and so had presumably been approached by Harland pre-publication. He had accepted a poem from them for the *Yellow Book* but they wrote to him on 17 July 1894,

> I must request you to return my typed copy of 'Rhythm'. I dislike the *Yellow Book* both in its first and second number & greatly regret that in a sudden rashness of sympathy I proposed to contribute to it – it has all been my fault, & I should not ask you to return an accepted paper if your delay in printing had not convinced me that you feel M.F. [Michael Field] is not an ingredient in the *Yellow Book* broth.[15]

They had, therefore, submitted a poem and withdrew it only when it was not published fast enough and their pride was piqued. Their disdain for the *Yellow Book* only reached the tipping point of rejection when they perceived the limited value the publication had for them.

Despite their smaller numbers at the launch party, women were an essential part of the *Yellow Book* project. The need for a regular anthology of new writing and art had emerged with the success of John Lane's *Keynotes* series, launched with George Egerton's book of that name. Its origin was in 1893 when a parcel of short stories arrived at John Lane's offices. They were the work of Chavelita Clairmonte, who wrote as George Egerton. She had been living in some poverty, to such an extent that she was unable to pay the rent and was preparing to sell her possessions. As a desperate attempt to make enough to live on, she wrote six stories in ten days, called them *Keynotes* and sent them to magazines, where on a second attempt the reader was positive but suggested she try a publisher. Heinemann sent them back with a letter saying they were 'mediocre', which enraged Egerton.[16] She posted them to John Lane 'and we prepared to auction and trek'.[17]

When he received the stories Lane passed them on to Richard Le Gallienne for a reader's report. He reported in 'glowing terms and strongly urged their publication'. The publisher wrote making an offer of acceptance but the letter was returned 'Gone away. Address not known.' There was nothing Lane could do but wait for the author to contact him. Chavelita (Egerton) had arrived in London but was crossing the city in search of cheaper and cheaper lodgings as what little money she had declined. Office assistant John Lewis May wrote, 'Weeks or it may have been months went by, when at last, one summer morning, the door opened and admitted, together with a flood of sunlight, a very attractive young woman, slim, dark-haired and dressed all in white. She spoke with vivacity and charm.' May heard her and was so intrigued he stepped down from his high stool at the sloping clerk's desk and pretended he had to come out from behind his screen to get a book so he could take a look at her.[18]

It was surprising that she was a woman, when 'George Egerton' had been on the manuscript's title page, but the stories proved no problem to the publishers. 'Their workmanship was excellent, they were exceedingly well written,' May wrote. *Keynotes* sold 6,000 copies in the first year and (rather importantly for a linguist like Egerton) was translated into seven languages in two years.[19] George Egerton (born Mary Chavelita Dunne and known variously, then at the end of her life as Mrs Golding Bright) became literally the keynote writer of the 1890s. *Keynotes* was so appreciated by John Lane that he not only published it in 1893 but made its title that of his series of new novels and books of stories. The name had been chosen as a musical reference (the elision of barriers between different art forms was an 1890s theme) but also related to the personal expression of the search for a more satisfying life by young women. This was often reduced to a symbol: the right to a latchkey – for a young adult woman to have the same freedom to come and go in her own home as her brothers had, without the accompaniment of a chaperone. Most middle-class homes had experienced these battles, with daughters asserting their rights. Each book had a separate cover design and keynote monogram – a key with a design of the author's initials – by Aubrey Beardsley.

By the end of its run, out of 137 writers who appeared in the *Yellow Book*, 47 were female, making women a third of the total. It is possible there were more women as a handful of contributors have not been identified and they may have been women using male pseudonyms. An analysis of poetry in the *Yellow Book* shows an even larger proportion of women's work: the thirteen volumes had 116 poems of which 44 were by women, making 37 per cent.[20]

The *Yellow Book* was not alone in the field but it came to be at the forefront in engaging women writers. In a search for the women in the *Yellow Book* it is helpful to return to the original idea, which had its genesis in a meeting of writers and visual artists at a holiday home in Sainte-Marguerite, Brittany. Henry and Aline Harland had rented a house in the summer of 1893, along with a number of writers and artists who formed a creative colony. Beardsley was not there, though his sister Mabel and their mother Ellen Beardsley were. Mabel, a little older than her brother and rather similar to him in appearance, had appeared on stage with him from childhood at the behest of their music-teacher mother. She was at this time starting on a successful career as an actress. Another visitor was Netta Syrett, Mabel's friend and already a published writer of short stories. Three sisters of the name Robinson were also part of the gatherings, but no more is known of them. A note saying 'Propriety to Let or Sell' on the side of the house gave an indication of the bohemian atmosphere of humorous digging at the Victorian establishment. Participants, in the local community if not necessarily living in the house, and perhaps visiting only for a short time, included landscape artist and New English Art Club member Alfred Thornton, another artist called Litellus Goold, Charles Loesser (perhaps the art collector of this name), critic and artist Dugald S. MacColl, American novelist and translator Jonathan Sturges, artists Charles Conder and Walter Sickert, and publishers John Lane and T. Fisher Unwin.[21]

Being creative artists by pen or brush, they tended to talk of markets for their work. The illustrators felt the most hard done by, their pictures being used to accompany a story rather than treated on their own merits, and often expected to be given for free by way of advertisement for works which they would sell. All were dissatisfied with the stultifying atmosphere of publishing in the UK, where all but a few publishers submitted to the constraints of late Victorian morality. MacColl reports that he first suggested the idea of a publication comprising literature and art, independent of each other, but it was undoubtedly Harland who took off with it.

Henry Harland was born in New York; he and his wife Aline Merriam had settled in London in 1889 and benefited from introductions to literary men afforded him by his close friend the American poet Edmund Clarence Stedman, who was also his godfather. Harland, in one of the many chameleon-like tricks that characterized people who came to prominence with the *Yellow Book*, had previously succeeded with the pseudonym Sidney Luska as the author of supposedly authentic novels about Jewish life in New York. It was one of Harland's more profitable fantasies, which also included his claim to be the heir to a Russian prince. The young couple left the United States when Harland was revealed to be a gentile and so his recent book *The Yoke of the Thorah*, which urged intermarriage between Jews and gentiles, was considered in bad taste and occasioned criticism from former friends and admirers. He left that persona behind and adopted the new one of having been born in St Petersburg, a place that neither he nor his mother had ever visited.

Aline had French forebears and had family still in France. She was a year older than her husband, whom she married in New York in 1884. She was a pianist and a writer who herself was to contribute stories to the *Yellow Book* under the name Reneé de Coutans. Harland had been told by specialists in both London and Paris that his tuberculosis meant he would have only two years to live unless he moved to a milder climate. These cities were his lifeblood, however, and he took his chances.

Harland's fondness for female company meant the *Yellow Book* had an open door to women contributors, much to the disgust of some of the more staid members of literary society. Albert Parry remarked:

> Harland liked to imagine himself a wild Bohemian and a rakish woman-fancier. He was proud of the premature streak of grey in his black disordered hair. He wore his hair longer than any of his Paris and London friends. He paraded the goatee and the gesticulating habits that made him seem more French than any of his French acquaintances... In his rooms in Cromwell Road he arranged literary dinners, after which he would sit on the floor and mete out your-eyes-remind-me-of-the-moon-rising-over-the-jungle compliments to the women.[22]

Ella D'Arcy gave a similar if much more sympathetic picture of Harland entertaining at home in Cromwell Road:

> I see him standing on the hearthrug or sitting on the floor, waving his eye glasses on the end of their cord, or refixing them on his short-sighted eyes, while assuring some 'dear beautiful Lady!' or other, how much he admired her writing, or her paintings, or her frock, or the colour of her hair. He would rechristen a golden red-haired woman 'Helen of Troy'; he would tell another that her eyes reminded him of the 'moon rising over the jungle'; and thus put each on delightfully cordial terms with herself... and with him.[23]

Whether sympathetic or not, both his detractors and admirers agree on the outlandish nature of his compliments to women. Ethel Colburn Mayne, writing many years later, felt that

> Even by the standards of today he was strikingly ribald, indecent, at times blasphemous; for though my upbringing had left me unsophisticated to a degree which sometimes amused or touched, but quite as often irritated him, I have had my share of experiences

in modern talk since then, and yet can feel his to have been far in advance of it.[24]

The idea for the *Yellow Book* was developed in the Harlands' drawing room; Netta Syrett was present one foggy afternoon in January 1894. She and some others were sitting around the fire in the Cromwell Road apartment on New Year's Day when Harland – 'he was like a boy in his enthusiasms' – was talking about a magazine that should represent the 'new movement'. Aline Harland recalled how 'books from the study, brought into the gay pink drawing-room with its Persian carpets, its pictures and its old furniture, were called in consultation.'[25]

Netta Syrett was now well acquainted with terms such as New Woman, New Morality, New Paganism, 'not to mention the word decadent so frequently on the lips of writers'. She knew exactly what the publication would be with its intended high standard of written work and art; 'Johnny Lane' was to be persuaded to publish it and 'Aubrey' was to be art editor.[26] Aubrey Beardsley, though only 21 at the start of 1894, was already a feted artist who had been encouraged by Pre-Raphaelite master Edward Burne-Jones and Joseph Pennell, Elizabeth's husband and the founder of the Society of Illustrators. It is said that Beardsley had met Harland in the waiting room of a lung doctor they were both seeing for tuberculosis, but this is not true: there is an extant letter from Joseph Pennell which introduces Beardsley to Harland.[27] Harland's account concurs with Syrett's recollection of the day early in 1894 when the *Yellow Book* had been discussed around his fireside, noting it was 'one of the densest and soupiest and yellowest of all of London's infernalist yellow fogs.'[28]

The further development of the journal is an object lesson in how business was conducted in literary London in the 1890s. Much of the commissioning and technical construction of the publication took place amid the smoke, dark suits and carpeted floors of men's clubs in Mayfair and the surrounding area. This was a serious impediment to women's making much of a mark on the *Yellow Book*, which renders their eventual contribution all the more remarkable.

The first key business meeting was at lunch on 2 January 1894 with Lane at the Hogarth Club, around the corner from his Vigo Street offices. Harland said it took five minutes for the publisher to agree to publish the *Yellow Book* and they proceeded, within the hour, to sign up Henry James for the first issue. They were joined by newspaper editor Frank Harris and novelist George Moore in what was clearly a gentlemen's meeting at this gentlemen's club.

Later that week Arthur Waugh was lunching at the National Liberal Club at 1 Whitehall Gardens when Henry Harland and John Lane came to tell Edmund Gosse all about their new project. As a friend of Harland and a cousin of Gosse, Waugh joined them. Harland was voluble as usual, offering in his new journal 'prose and poetry, criticism, fiction, and art, the oldest school and the newest side by side, with no hall-mark except that of excellence, and no prejudice against anything but dullness and incapacity'.[29] Waugh continued:

> Harland was in a great sense of excitement that day, rolling off the list of magnates who would appear in the first number. He would have Henry James and George Saintsbury; of course Gosse must come in; and how about Dr Garnett? That would be a sound bodyguard of the old brigade. Then, of the newer school, Hubert Crackanthorpe was indispensable; and they must have Arthur Symons . . .

Gosse suggested the son of the Archbishop of Canterbury, A. C. Benson, and Waugh agreed to contribute. Waugh said that in terms of editorial tone it was 'an ingenious study in compromise; there was, in point of fact, no real *Yellow Book* atmosphere; the sly newcomer intended to be all things to all men.'[30] 'All men' is appropriate. No women were, it seems, mentioned at this seminal gathering and since it occurred in a gentlemen's club there were no women present. Indeed, women would not be active at 1 Whitehall Gardens for some time; they were not admitted to the National Liberal Club as associate members until 1967 and full members until 1976.

News got around the literary world of the new publication and a number of writers responded. Some sent manuscripts: one came from Ella D'Arcy, who sent a story 'dog-eared from rejections', which Harland immediately recognized as the sort of writing he wanted.[31] He put her forward as a named writer in the prospectus. Beardsley suggested Netta Syrett, a friend of his sister Mabel from the school where they had both worked, and already known to the Harlands. Newspaper advertisements went in on 1 April 1894 inviting people to apply for a prospectus: they named eighteen people of whom three were women, Ella D'Arcy, George Egerton and John Oliver Hobbes (Pearl Craigie).[32] If they applied for a prospectus, members of the public would receive an announcement of an illustrated magazine 'which shall be as beautiful as a piece of bookmaking', which would be read 'and placed upon one's shelves', which would differentiate it from the literally paperback periodicals with which it would be in competition. The prospectus proposed a freer hand for contributors than 'the limitation of the old-fashioned periodical can permit'.

The prospectus listed 44 writers expected to contribute. Only eight were women, or nine if 'Michael Field' is counted as two. Of that number, three (or four) were not, in fact, published in the *Yellow Book* in the end: Lanoe Falconer (Mary Elizabeth Hawker), Michael Field (Katharine Bradley and Edith Cooper) and Elizabeth Robins Pennell, though she was a constant presence in the rooms where the *Yellow Book* was discussed and edited. The other women mentioned in the prospectus, and so clearly in on the enterprise from the start, were George Egerton, Ménie Muriel Dowie, John Oliver Hobbes, Ella D'Arcy and Netta Syrett.

The prospectus offered: 'THE YELLOW BOOK will seek always to pre-serve a delicate, decorous, and reticent mien and conduct, it will at the same time have the courage of its modernness . . . It will be charming, it will be daring, it will be distinguished.' This could easily be a description of a modern woman, notably the sort whom Beardsley drew. The poster for the *Yellow Book* showed a Beardsley drawing of a woman in a summer dress holding a sun hat. The prospectus depicted a woman going through a book bin outside a bookseller's shop that might have been the Bodley Head's Vigo Street premises. In fact women featured on all the *Yellow Book* pro-spectuses: for volume II it was a woman by a bookcase; for volume III a woman at a dressing table; for volume IV a boy offering a woman a flower and for volume V a faun reading to a woman: by its presentation the *Yellow Book* was a very feminine product.

The book was going to be yellow because it seemed right: the Pre-Raphaelites had favoured yellow and French novels with their yellow bind-ings were the exemplar of advanced, 'realist' fiction, carrying the suggestion of decadence. Another source is Wilde's description of a fateful French yellow book in *The Picture of Dorian Gray*. Regardless of the inspiration, it should be noted in the present context that in *The Picture of Dorian Gray* women are present, if at all, as offering an opportunity for men's capacity for vice. It was going to be hard for women to enter this decadent temple in any meaningful way as artists in their own right.

Elizabeth Pennell observed the eager editors approach her husband at their home:

> Beardsley, ever grateful for that *Studio* article [in which Pennell had lauded Beardsley's work], would come to consult him about new

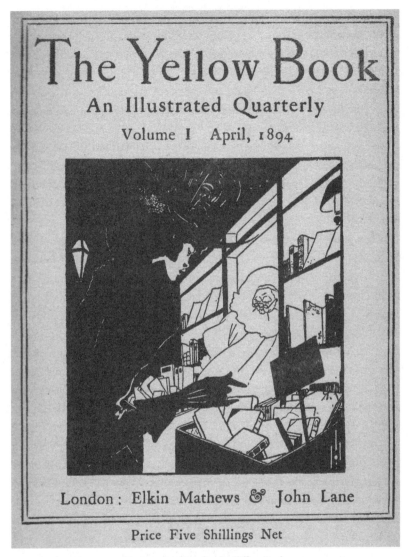

Prospectus cover for the *Yellow Book*.

schemes and when the *Yellow Book* was taking shape, long before any announcement was made, brought Harland to talk it over with him. They begged for ideas, begged for contributions. He rather laughed at the qualifications of these inexperienced art and literary editors, but he made suggestions out of his unfailing supply.[33]

Elizabeth and Joseph Pennell dined with Aline and Henry Harland in February 1894 and passionately discussed the technical side of the operation:

should the *Yellow Book* aim to 'startle . . . the public from the outset by giving them lithographs and coloured wood-engravings'? Printing each picture separately on art paper, they noted with pleasure, should obtain results far better than those of any other periodical. Later the gathering was joined by Leila MacDonald and Hubert Crackanthorpe, the golden couple of the 1890s bohemian set: attractive, rich, talented and married almost exactly a year previously. They urged Harland to publish the *Yellow Book* early so they could attend the launch party. Harland considered the proposition seriously enough to suggest it to John Lane, but the publishing timetable was against them and the Crackanthorpes were on a planned trip to the South of France at the time of the launch dinner in the Hotel d'Italie.[34]

The new publication was a magazine bound like a book to emphasize its permanence: the material in it, its originators were saying, was not ephemeral; the various challenges to the British establishment of the decadent, the realist, the New Woman, were the modern face of the arts, they were here to stay. They were also, by their price, the artefacts of a cultured elite: the *Yellow Book* cost five shillings per copy (a quarter of a pound). Many other journals could be had for a tenth of that. The price was not offset by advertisements, except those for books, so the *Yellow Book* could boast that its artistic contents could be approached 'without being pre-occupied by a consciousness of the merits of Eno's Fruit Salt and Beecham's Pills.'[35]

Male writers could be found in gentlemen's clubs, but social events also often excluded women, who might not even know they were taking place. Evelyn Sharp's book *At the Relton Arms* was accepted for publication by John Lane in 1894. The acceptance letter was 'the most thrilling letter I ever received', she said.[36] Lane was anxious to make the acquaintance of this writer, whom he assumed to be male, though the name is epicene. Lane sent an invitation to, as she explained, 'Mr Evelyn Sharp to a smoking evening at the Bodley Head. I think the occasion was a meeting of the Odd Volumes literary society of which Mr John Lane was at that time president.'[37] She politely explained her female status, which duly disqualified her from the event and whatever bookish networking was taking place at this, which was in fact a launch party to open the full use of his building at G1 the Albany.[38]

Harland's willingness to go the extra mile for women made a difference. He went to see Ella D'Arcy in Kent after having received her manuscript and wrote about the event to the great networker Richard Le Gallienne:

I got home last night from a short trip in the country . . . During my trip out of town I stopped for a day at Hythe and made the acquaintance of Ella D'Arcy in the flesh. She is interesting-looking, very good-natured, and most intelligent, though perhaps a trifle inclined to take things somewhat too seriously in this least serious of possible worlds. We talked much of you, I was made to describe you in uttermost detail; and she looks forward eagerly to meeting you when she moves to town in April. I even promised to ask Lane to send her one of Steer's lithographs. Will he do it?[39]

She was obviously soon to make the acquaintance of Philip Wilson Steer, as he painted her as 'A Lady' in an illustration that appeared in the *Yellow Book* volume II in July 1894. Harland and Steer would have met a woman who was short in stature with ginger hair, small green eyes and a protuberant upper lip that gave her the appearance of a permanent pout.[40] She described the man she met as blue-eyed with longish black hair that had already gone white on top; 'he wore a dark moustache which hid his mouth, and a small pointed beard which supplemented his want of a chin. His face was of the Kalmuck type, high cheek-bones, upturned nostrils, a damp-looking pallid skin.'[41]

Biographical knowledge about D'Arcy is so poor that even her birth-date is not known; it was 1856 or 1857 in Pimlico, London. She was one of nine children of a corn factor and maltster, Anthony Byrne D'Arcy, and his wife, Sophie. Her father died in 1873 when D'Arcy was sixteen or younger and her mother died in 1891, probably thus freeing D'Arcy, at the age of 34 or 35, from family responsibilities. The family had an estate in Ireland from which D'Arcy received a small income – less than £100 a year.[42]

She was partly raised in the Channel Islands, which accounted for her excellent French and her knowledge of the folklore of that area, which was to feature in many of her stories. She studied at the Slade School of Art for two years, making her one of a number of *Yellow Book* writers who also pursued a career as an artist, but poor eyesight made her abandon this career.[43] She became a short story writer, contributing to *Temple Bar* and *Blackwood's* magazines, and also published under the name Gilbert H. Page in *Good Words* and *Argosy*. The story that she sent to Harland for possible inclusion in his new journal was 'Irremediable', which had been rejected by *Blackwood's* as too daring for their readership.

She needed a permanent outlet for her stories, which featured sensitive, humane men dominated by conniving women, and it seemed she had found that in the *Yellow Book*, which printed more of her work than that of anyone except Harland: she appeared in ten out of thirteen volumes. She clearly made an impression on Harland and he on her: she described him as 'the most brilliant, witty and amusing of talkers'.[44] They must have discussed at their first meeting that she was free to do editorial work, with which he was in need of assistance, as after the meeting he helped her to get a flat at 13 Edwardes Square, Kensington, which was close to where he lived. He asked her to help out on the *Yellow Book* and paid her out of his own pocket.

J. Lewis May, who would have been tasked with the transfer of manuscripts and page proofs from Harland in Kensington to Lane in Piccadilly, writes that Harland

> was assisted in his editorial labours by Miss Ella D'Arcy, a lady of brilliant gifts who herself contributed several short stories to the *Yellow Book*, at least one of which, Irremediable in Volume I, is, by the subtlety of its psychological insight and the grace and charm of its style, entitled to take rank among the great short stories in the language.[45]

In later life D'Arcy was to tell a researcher, 'I was around a good bit, and helped as I could. But I was never really an editor.'[46] This remark shows her diffident nature, which was to cause her problems in promoting her work. Harland himself referred to her as 'the Sub-Editor of the *Yellow Book*' in a letter of recommendation when she was looking for a job at the end of the journal's life. Such letters often contain exaggerations to help a friend, but Harland used the same term in a letter to John Lane, which puts the designation beyond question.[47]

They were based in the tiny office in Harland's apartment at 144 Cromwell Road. The official address of the *Yellow Book* was Vigo Street, where Lane's Bodley Head office was, with its telegram address 'Bodleian London'. There was no space for a magazine office in the 'poky little den' there and it was also convenient for Harland to be at a distance so as not to have Lane breathing over his shoulder.[48] Lane saw the magazine as a way of promoting his list of writers and fully expected Harland to include writers who had work published by the Bodley Head. Harland thought that decision should be his. Ethel Colburn Mayne, who was later to work with Harland, described the place, down a short flight of stairs from the rest of the flat, as the most modest office an editor ever had:

The big writing-table nearly filled it; there was a bookcase against the wall, a very small but solid table near the fireplace, which just left room for his revolving-chair. The window looked out on the underground railway (above ground there) but was high enough for the noise to be little noticed. There were mottos stuck up on the wall: 'Glissez n'appuyez pas' [slide don't push], 'Cultivez l'art d'omettre' [cultivate the art of omission] and other literary precepts.[49]

Mayne would have heard Harland's oft-repeated aphorisms such as, 'I learned in sorrow what I teach in jest.'[50]

Harland was budgeting for £250 to pay contributors each quarter. Prices ranged from £5 to £10 for prose pieces and a varying price for poetry depending on the celebrity of the writer and the length of the work. Olive Custance received a guinea (£1 1s) for the sixteen-line 'Twilight'; John Davidson received six guineas (£6 6s) for the 156-line 'Ballad of a Nun'.[51]

THE *Yellow Book* was much awaited, both by supporters and those who were preparing to sneer at it for its pretensions, whatever it contained. The editors had cleverly designed the inaugural issue to forestall such criticism by enlisting the work of the widely admired Henry James. James was welcome at *Yellow Book* gatherings, where younger writers would wait for him to finish his interminable sentences, with lengthy pauses to find exactly the right word, which any of them could have supplied. They were delighted to have been in the company of this literary giant, but breathed a sigh of relief when he left. His contribution to the first *Yellow Book* showed exactly why he was held in such high regard. He knew what the big literary theme was in 1894: it was gender. In 'The Death of the Lion' James plunges his hero into the menagerie of current identity; 'I was bewildered; it sounded somehow as if there were three sexes,' the narrator remarks at one point.[52] In a story about fame and celebrity the male narrator is a first-person witness of the success of a fifty-year-old author, Neil Paraday.

The narrator is writing an article on Paraday ('Parody'), which allows him to survey the literary landscape. One of the current crop of writers, known for daring subjects, is Guy Walsingham, whom *Yellow Book* readers would have identified with George Egerton. He remarks, 'I presently enquired with gloomy irrelevance if Guy Walsingham were a woman. "Oh, yes, a mere pseudonym; but convenient, you know, for a lady who goes in for the larger latitude. '*Obsessions* by Miss So-and So' would look a little odd, but men are more naturally indelicate.'"[53]

At one point the narrator has to ask "'Is this Miss Forbes a gentleman?'" to be told, "'It wouldn't be 'Miss' – there's a wife!'" Dora Forbes, it appears, is a man with a big red moustache, author of *The Other Way Round*. 'He only assumes a feminine personality because the ladies are such popular favourites,' it is explained. The hapless narrator laments, 'in the age we live in, one gets lost amongst the genders and the pronouns.'[54]

The narrator maintains a homoerotic tone throughout, with devoted admiration for the writer, fussy solicitude for his health and attempts at all costs to keep him away from women. These efforts ultimately fail and the narrator must see his lion tamed by the literary ladies. The strain of celebrity being too much for him, he succumbs to illness and dies.

As well as 'The Death of a Lion', the first issue contained such female subjects as Max Beerbohm's 'A Defence of Cosmetics', an explicit and detailed comparison of the decadent phase of the Roman Empire with Victorian Britain, concentrating on make-up. In a deliberate mockery of the earnestness of the Victorian establishment, he hymns Artifice in female form, using several Latin and Greek phrases to emphasize his erudition and his relationship to the classical tradition. He writes, 'If men are to lie among the rouge-pots, inevitably it will tend to promote that amalgamation of the sexes which is one of the chief planks in the decadent platform.'[55] Of the representative 'woman', he notes, 'she cannot rival us in action, but she is our mistress in things of the mind.'[56]

As if to demonstrate this, it was followed after a few pages by 'Irremediable', the work by Ella D'Arcy that had so impressed Henry Harland. In this story bank clerk Mr Willoughby, suspicious of women, is pleased to meet a working-class girl, Esther, because of 'an earlier episode in his career having indissolubly associated in his mind ideas of feminine refinement with those of feminine treachery'.[57] He has 'dabbled a little in Socialism' and so is moved to render fluid the barriers of class and enjoys flirting with Esther, from Whitechapel. The location is synonymous with vice and crime, notably since the Jack the Ripper murders of the late 1880s. She tells him of her life of hardship and beatings and he resolves as a decent man to take her away from all that. They marry on his £130 a year. The story then finds him with a slatternly wife in a house 'repulsive in its disorder'. Esther 'never did one mortal thing efficiently or well' and is scornful of his needs.[58] He pines for his bachelorhood of books and solitude, while she 'evinced all the self-satisfaction of an illiterate mind'. Thus the dangers of inter-class relationships. D'Arcy presents a sour view of women that is rather more complex than that proposed by the feminists such as Mona Caird, who were battling against male domination in marriage. In D'Arcy's world, the greater discourse between men and women that was permitted in the 1890s, as compared to earlier decades, led only to deeper bewilderment and more disappointment on both sides.

Further in this first *Yellow Book* volume Fred M. Simpson offers a play about a woman whose writer fiancé abandons her when fame beckons, though she has inspired his best work. George Egerton in 'A Lost Master-piece' offers the thoughts the writer has towards a 'unique little gem' of literature when a woman with big feet and an umbrella comes on the omnibus and destroys the artistic flow of the writer's mind.

In 'Reticence in Literature' Arthur Waugh complains of modern writing that instead of 'leaving these refinements of lust to the haunts to which they are fitted, it has introduced them into the domestic chamber, and permeated marriage with the ardours of promiscuous intercourse.' He notes that he is told that a lack of modesty regarding the physical 'is a part of the revolt of woman, and certainly our women-writers are chiefly to blame'.[59]

The next page carried a sketch by Walter Sickert of 'A Lady Reading', after which, by way of response to Waugh, was a piece by Hubert Crackan-thorpe, one of the brutally realist writers about whom Waugh is so exercised. 'A Modern Melodrama' is about a woman who has to send her servant to hear what her doctor and her lover are saying about her condition. It turns out she has galloping consumption – aggressive tuberculosis. She thinks, 'Damn it! She wasn't going to be chicken-hearted. She'd face it. She had had a jolly time. She'd be game to the end. Hell-fire – that was all stuff and non-sense – she knew that. It would be just nothing – like a sleep.'[60] For a more considered response to Waugh, Crackanthorpe was allowed a full essay on 'Reticence in Literature' in volume II, where he defended the principle 'Art is non-moral'.[61] The final piece in the first volume was 'The Fool's Hour', the first act of a comedy with a cast of Victorian stage aristocrats swapping epigrams about a failed marriage by co-authors John Oliver Hobbes (Pearl Craigie) and George Moore, the couple who had been getting along so well at the launch dinner.

The first volume, then, offered only three women writers (D'Arcy, Egerton and Craigie), though much of the subject-matter covered by the fifteen men was about women or written with women chiefly in mind. The female incursions into the *Yellow Book* by women's own writing would take time. In terms of the appearance of the *Yellow Book*, the 'Beardsley women'

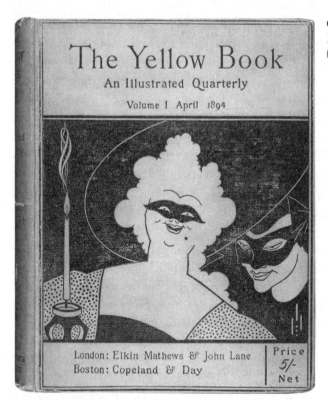

Cover of the
Yellow Book, vol. I
(April 1894).

received the most attention, and they dominated the book, with a woman in a mask at a party on the front and the party or performance continuing with three female figures on the back. The title page had a woman playing a piano. 'Portrait of Mrs Patrick Campbell' attracted criticism in supposedly making the actress unrecognizably skinny in her part as Paula Tanqueray from Pinero's play *The Second Mrs Tanqueray*, about a woman with 'a past'. Besides this, there were three other Beardsley drawings in the volume, all of them of women. 'L'Education Sentimentale' took its title from Flaubert's book about a young man's passion for an older woman, as all readers of the *Yellow Book* would know. In 'Night Piece' he depicted a woman walking alone at night, which by itself would have indicated she was a prostitute, even if the reviewer for the *New Quarterly* had not been able to identify the building behind her (or claim he had) as the Chelsea Barracks.[62] The last was a book plate with a sneering woman of fashion in black looking down at a white-clad supplicant. The *Times* critic noted the *Yellow Book's* 'combination of English rowdyism with French lubricity' and opined that 'it may be intended to attract by its very repulsiveness and insolence, and in that case it is not unlikely to be successful.'[63]

Of the fifteen art pieces (therefore excluding the cover and title page) eleven were of women, including Walter Sickert's painting of a performer centre stage at the Old Oxford Music Hall and Will Rothenstein's picture of a fully dressed woman in a fashionable hat reclining in the pose she might have been asked to adopt had she been painted nude.

BEARDSLEY'S pictures of women were described in terms of their physicality as if they were pictures of actual women who grotesquely failed to measure up to the writer's idea of a woman; they

> resemble nothing on the earth, nor in the firmament that is above the earth, nor in the waters under the earth; with their lips of a more than Hottentot thickness, their bodies of a lath-like flatness, their impossibly pointed toes and fingers, and their small eyes that have the form and comeliness of an unshelled snail.[64]

The comparison of Beardsley women's features and those of Africans feeds into contemporary notions of racial degeneration, according to which 'primitive' people were supposedly closer to animals than those of the colonizing nations, so the more European a person looked, the more civilized they supposedly were. This hit at the *Yellow Book*'s pretension. It was, in this writer's opinion, the opposite of high art; it was akin to the art of savages. The *Westminster Gazette* critic felt in response to Beardsley's women, 'We do not know that anything would meet the case except a short Act of Parliament to make this kind of thing illegal.'[65]

The disgust at the unwomanly slender shape of women depicted in the *Yellow Book* also resonated in cultural concerns. The woman as presented in the *Yellow Book* was a degenerate. An article in the *Nineteenth Century* by the journalist Eliza Lynn Linton characterized new women not in terms of what they thought but how they looked, and how they failed the biological test of procreativity: 'the bass voice, flat chest, and lean hips of a woman who has physically failed in her rightful development'.[66] This focus on the procreative role and contemporary woman's failure to fulfil it was a frequent theme, and not only among those who held the new woman in contempt. It is a theme in Ella Hepworth Dixon's work, for example; she had no children and nor, among her *Yellow Book* contemporaries, had Ella D'Arcy, Ethel Colburn Mayne, Gabriela Cunninghame Graham, Netta Syrett, Evelyn Sharp, Leila Macdonald or Charlotte Mew. Sometimes they addressed this matter head on, as does a character in one of Mayne's stories who says, 'I don't at all like children, you know . . . I never did . . . I haven't got the "maternal instinct" one is forever hearing of. People make such a fetish of it.'[67] Others such as George Egerton, Ménie Muriel Dowie, Olive Custance and Pearl Craigie had one child, far below the contemporary average of five children per married woman.

Once a woman was nulliparous, had abandoned her supposedly pre-ordained destiny, what was the difference between men and women, particularly in relation to writing, which presented no physical challenge to either sex? In Arthur Waugh's 'Reticence in Literature' he noted, 'A new school has arisen which combines the characteristics of effeminacy and brutality.'[68] The supposed divisions between what was male and what was female were being distorted. Waugh's essay was judged 'sane and manly' by the *Academy* critic Frederick Wedmore, which gives an indication of what he perceived its negative opposite to be: mad and womanly.[69]

The very clear counterposing of male and female as opposites was part of the Victorian world view that many of the *Yellow Book*'s contributors, and the periodical as a whole, challenged. Le Gallienne was later to be explicit: in the *Yellow Book* volume VI in July 1895 his 'Four Prose Fancies' included 'The Arbitrary Classification of Sex', which argued that gender was a matter of fashion and personal choice, nothing more: 'surely the essentials of "manliness" and "womanliness" belong to man and woman alike – the externals are purely artistic considerations, and subject to the vagaries of fashion . . . There is no such thing as looking manly or womanly. There is looking beautiful or ugly, distinguished or commonplace.'[70] Le Gallienne makes an obvious nod to his master Oscar Wilde's preface to *The Picture of Dorian Gray* with its epigrams about art.

The *New Quarterly* reviewer criticized 'the more than masculine George Egerton', knowing it was a woman's pseudonym.[71] In its short jokes section *Punch* gave a comic definition: 'The New Man – Woman.'[72] The *Yellow Book* was obliging both literary critics and the public to engage with the concepts of eroticism, gender difference and gender roles that presented them with stark questions about their civilization. As Linda Dowling said, 'the loosening of sexual controls apparently encouraged by literary decadence and New Woman fiction was almost universally believed by late Victorian critics to threaten the vital bonds of state and culture.'[73]

Unnatural or not, with its contingent of women in print and in pictures and literary adventurism, the *Yellow Book* was a roaring success from its publishing sites in London and Boston, selling out the first edition of 5,000 in five days. Within twelve days of that launch dinner in April 1894, Harland was able to put a notice in the press to reassure the public that a fourth edition was already on the press.[74]

2

Gabriela's Deceptions

The old man pulled on the oars across the lake with limbs strengthened by years of horsemanship. He was still tall when standing erect, but his striking mane of hair was now white as he rowed out to a grave he had dug himself to fulfil a vow he had made to a woman. On the anniversary of her death he would, in accordance with a promise, row out to the island and smoke a black Brazilian cigarette by her grave in her memory. One day in 1932 he sat by the grave in the ruins of the priory and wrote a letter:

> An overclouded and windy day here, and I can hardly write owing to a hard pull in the boat. Everything as usual and I stood long and smoked a cigarette at her grave. Rooks flew past cawing and it was very quiet. Now the wind has gone down and the lake is like the back of a looking glass.[1]

The woman in the grave, Gabriela Cunninghame Graham, was one of the literary characters of the 1890s: a friend of Oscar Wilde, W. B. Yeats, William Morris and Keir Hardie. She was known for speaking on international platforms for radical causes, giving lectures on socialism and mysticism, writing a major biography of St Teresa and contributing to the *Yellow Book*.

Her funeral had taken place on 19 September 1906 in the chancel of the ruined church of the Priory of Inchmahome, where the remains of her husband's aristocratic ancestors lay, on the island of the Lake of Menteith, Perthshire. Newspaper reports said:

> It was fitting that the gentle lady should sleep in the historic little island in the placid waters of the Lake of Menteith . . . She was the

Gabriela Cunninghame Graham, *c.* 1890, photograph by Frederick Hollyer.

daughter of Don Francisco José de la Balmondière, Chili [*sic*], and her sympathies were largely Spanish. Nevertheless she showed an abiding interest in all that appertained to the welfare of the district of Menteith, where she was greatly loved, and where she received many spontaneous tokens of admiration and regard.

She was described as 'a woman possessing the highest accomplishments and a keen and penetrating intellect which overcame every difficulty that a language foreign to her could present'.[2]

Robert Bontine Cunninghame Graham, her husband, was a charismatic figure, the first openly socialist Member of Parliament, who opposed racial discrimination and imperialism, campaigned for universal suffrage, free secular education and the eight-hour day, and fought on behalf of exploited workers in the docks and the chain-making industry.

The romantic first meeting of this celebrity couple was well known when they were alive and has been frequently retold in biographies of Cunninghame Graham and in such books about the 1890s as Katherine Lyon Mix's *A Study in Yellow.* There she writes that 'no *Yellow Book* contributor could boast a more romantic history' and describes a riding accident in which Cunninghame Graham nearly knocked over his future wife.[3]

Cunninghame Graham's friend A. F. Tschiffely gives what became the definitive account of this meeting in Paris, taken from Cunninghame Graham himself, who chose Tschiffely as his biographer:

> One day he rode a horse which gave him a certain amount of trouble, and when the animal suddenly began to prance about wildly, it nearly knocked over a young lady who happened to be near. Don Roberto immediately dismounted to apologise, and, being some-what embarrassed, he inadvertently spoke to her in Spanish. To his surprise and delight she answered in the same language, and then, for a while, the two chatted and arranged to meet again next day. As this was a case of love at first sight, things happened quickly.

He notes that she was born in Chile of a French father and a Spanish mother, and had come to Paris at twelve on being orphaned, when her aunt had put her in a convent school.[4] Tschiffely described her as a 'dark-haired and soft grey-blue-eyed young lady'.[5] Will Rothenstein, an artist and *Yellow Book* contributor, later wrote, 'as I saw her the first time, in a white monk's habit, & her black hair over her shoulders, & that fire burning deep in her eyes that seems to us so fitting in those who have Spanish blood.'[6]

Gabriela's literary achievements, her radicalism, her travelling adventures and her friendships with literary greats were genuine; everything else about Gabriela was a fake. In fact she was a doctor's daughter from Yorkshire called Carrie Horsfall, who as a teenager had run away to London to become an actress. In a way she did go on the stage: a public performance of social action was running concurrently in her adult life with a private narrative of deceit. Most obviously this was in everything she said: Gabriela spoke English with a 'foreign accent' of her own construction. It was said to be 'neither French nor Spanish, but most attractive and charming', accounted for supposedly by her early upbringing in Chile followed by schooling in Paris.[7] Her 'natural' accent would have been middle-class English with, presumably, some trace of a regional Yorkshire accent.

Carrie/Gabriela was the second eldest daughter and second child of thirteen of Henry Horsfall, surgeon, and his wife Elizabeth, née Stanfield. She was born on 22 January 1858 in Masham, Yorkshire. A younger sister, Grace Horsfall, became a novelist under the name George Stevenson (the surname was her married name). She wrote a novel, *Benjy*, based on her family, partly telling the story of her sister, giving her the name 'Adelaide

Ainsworth', so she was writing a fictionalized version of her sister's life under an assumed name and gender of her own – truly a process of revealing concealment. Adelaide (Carrie/Gabriela) was expected to take care of the younger children, but 'she didn't like children and hated looking after them and more than once expressed her wish that Herod had been alive when they were born'.[8] Gabriela never seems to have been tempted to have any children of her own, despite the requirement after her marriage that the lord of the manor's wife should produce an heir.

She would put on plays for the family and would frighten her siblings with stories. She is said to have had a 'fantastic aptitude for transferring herself into some favourite heroine of romance or history – Heloise writing to Abelard, perhaps, or Lady Hamilton'.[9] She is described as having 'held herself among her brothers and sisters as a sort of wild swan among more homely fowl'.[10] She 'had the consciousness of a gift; and with it she cherished the determination that [she] should not die unknown and unsung'.[11] Madge, another sister, wrote:

> Still I see her now, holding forth mounted upon a chair behind a funny old book case door in the nursery, where she was supposed to be looking after Muriel who was about six months old then and I was sitting on the floor holding the big baby on my inadequate lap, but both quite content to stay as we were, as long as she would declaim and act for me . . . she was a very fine looking girl, and though at that time she could only have been about fourteen or fifteen years old, she was quite grown up.[12]

Whenever possible she would disappear into her own room and throw herself down with a book to escape from the narrowness of middle-class family life in a provincial town. Her mother expected her to become a governess but she refused even to contemplate it: she would be an actress or nothing. Her niece, Marthe Stevenson, recounted:

> She was crazy to get on the stage and ran away twice from home, the first time she was brought back in disgrace but the second time she did not return . . . One can imagine what a disgrace this must have been at that period. The other children suffered, were not allowed to mix with other young people or to speak about Carrie. Their poor mother was ill for nearly a year.[13]

That is all the recorded information about Carrie Horsfall, until her appearance three years after running away when she emerges in the record as the exotic bride of Robert Bontine Cunninghame Graham.

He was born on 24 May 1852 at 5 Cadogan Place, London, to Anne Elizabeth Bontine and Major William Bontine, a Scottish landowner. He attended Harrow School and spent holidays riding and fishing on the family estate in Menteith. His father had hoped for a military career for his son but he was obviously unsuited to the discipline of army life. In 1866, when Robert was twelve, Major Bontine had gone mad, which left the family estate and business affairs in the hands of court-appointed administrators. Between 1870 and 1877 Robert went on two extended trips to South America, to Uruguay, Paraguay and Argentina, learning the trade of the gaucho and wearing the costume of the skilled horseman.

The custodians of the estate during the time of his father's incapacity granted him an allowance of £400 per annum, which was no fortune but was sufficient to live on and to travel. He went to Spain and France, which is where Gabriela is said to have met him in a park in Paris. The account of the meeting, the place and even the country in which they met may be a complete fiction, but what is verifiable is that they were married at the London Registry Office on 24 October 1878 with no relatives present. His profession was given as 'gentleman'. She was named as Gabrielle Marie de la Balmondière, though in her writing she used the name Gabriela. There were two witnesses, who were said to have been 'hired at half a crown each'.[14]

Herbert Faulkner West, another friend and an earlier biographer, described her as 'a Chilean lady, a Roman Catholic, Gabriela, the daughter of Don Francisco José de la Balmondière'.[15] She gave her age as 19, when in fact she would be 21 on 22 January, almost exactly three months after the wedding. Her father was recorded as Francis de la Balmondière (deceased), and his occupation as 'merchant'. No parental consent was therefore required – if she had been asked about her mother Gabriela would have said she was also dead. She presumably said she did not have a guardian (or their consent would be needed). The only official requirement, apart from making declarations that did not require evidence, was living at an address within the registrar's jurisdiction for at least fifteen days. She lived at Haxell's Hotel on the Strand and Cunninghame Graham stayed at the Devonshire Club in St James's Street.

They travelled north to the Cunninghame Graham home of Gartmore on the Lake of Menteith, an imposing William Adam mansion in 10,000 acres of land. It was a place redolent of the tales of Rob Roy and Robert the Bruce, who had visited the island of Inchmahome on the Lake; the abbey there had also been a refuge for Mary, Queen of Scots. After an approach up the grand drive, on entering Gartmore for the first time Gabriela would have seen the rich, seventeenth-century kingwood furniture and sombre paintings, and rows of dark, unopened volumes in the library. There were Indian artefacts brought back from the subcontinent by a dead uncle, high Adams chimney pieces and 'portraits of the favourite hounds and horses of three generations'.[16]

Gabriela probably had an immediate suspicion that the grand house was not all it appeared to be. She would have smelt the pervasive damp and noticed that, though the pieces that were there were very fine, there were spaces where furniture and pictures had been taken and sold to pay the family's debts. Outside the estate was indeed vast and beautiful, but much of it was waterlogged and unproductive. It was in administration because of the insanity of Major Bontine, and was administered with no great efficiency, but even worse was that it was encumbered with three generations of debt. The 7th Laird of Gartmore, Robert Cunninghame Graham's great-grandfather, had inherited at the age of 22 and by his reckless extravagance, speculation and gambling had set the estate on a downward path. His son, Robert's grandfather, had tried to manage the family fortunes with little success, and his son, Robert's father, was restive and impractical; his mental state deteriorated over the years into violent madness before his incarceration.

It must have seemed to Gabriela as if she had married into a Gothic novel, which was in fact what she wrote. *Genara* is a tale of a Scottish laird who falls in love with his Spanish servant girl. Genara is despised by his mother and the lovers are parted by her machinations. The mother tells her son Genara is married. He therefore despairs of his love for her and marries a woman of his mother's choosing, who later leaves him. When he travels again to Spain he finds Genara has entered a convent; he contacts her and begs her to run away with him. She does, but the church drags her back. Her laird, in anguish and despair, suffers a stroke and is found dead beneath the crucifix in the convent chapel.[17]

Cunninghame Graham's mother, Anne Elizabeth Bontine, the daughter of an admiral, was sharp-tongued and had literary and artistic tastes. Cunninghame Graham presented his marriage to his mother as a fait accompli, which is generally an unwelcome way to introduce a daughter-in-law to a family, and particularly so when the inheritance of land is involved.

There were other difficulties: Mrs Bontine (who was always addressed thus by Gabriela) did not warm to the new wife, finding her sullen. Gabriela could be animated enough with others; her taciturnity with her mother-in-law was presumably because she was not interested in communicating with her. Cunninghame Graham felt compelled to ask her, 'Do try & look mother properly in the face.'[18]

Mrs Bontine would most definitely have asked Gabriela about her 'people' and could not have been put off by the tale of an upbringing in Chile: she herself had been born in Venezuela, she had relatives in Cadíz, she knew the Spanish community in Paris well and could have made enquiries should that have been felt necessary. She would not have been fooled by the fake lineage. With a level of mistrust between them, Mrs Bontine was the obvious person to expose Gabriela. However, even though she disliked Gabriela, it was hardly in her interest to attract scandal to the family. Moreover, she adored her son and would not wish to cause him pain. It may well have been also that, as a descendant of the family noted, 'by disguising the origins of the bride, she was to be saved the embarrassment of the world knowing Robert had married beneath him'.[19] It did not get easier: 'Had lunch with my dreadful M in L' is a diary entry for 16 January 1888, six years after their first meeting.[20] Mrs Bontine was said to have been 'friendly and enormously broadminded for her generation, [but] took several years to learn to love her strange little daughter-in-law'.[21]

The young couple spent the winter at Gartmore, which was lit by oil lamps during the long nights. The house had once had gas lighting but they had done away with it, perhaps because of the expense of maintaining or repairing it when it went wrong. Gabriela and Robert sat in front of the huge fire of half-green logs seething and spluttering in the grate with their dogs around them, while outside the deer bellowed and owls hooted and they talked of business and adventures in far-away lands.[22] They decided to go to Latin America to make their fortune and in April 1879 boarded an emigrant ship to New Orleans from Germany, then crossed the Gulf of Mexico to Brownsville in Texas. They made an unsuccessful land venture and sold the land back, and became disenchanted with the romance of the Texas–Mexico border when they came to realize how dangerous it was.

Scenting an opportunity, they bought bales of cotton to sell in Mexico City, where they had been told cotton was in short supply and would fetch a good price. Though they were both to become literary figures, Gabriela began writing before Cunninghame Graham, with her first story, 'The Wagon-Train', telling of the perilous fifty-day journey on horseback from

San Antonio de Bexar, Texas, to Mexico City; it was later published in her short story collection *The Christ of Toro*.

Each wagon was drawn by a team of ten to twenty mules over country sometimes bare of grass for hundreds of miles. Before the trip the major-domo in charge of the train had to hunt his men through different gambling dens and drinking shops, or bail them out of the lockup. Gabriela shows the excitement of riding with the lumbering oxen as they leave San Antonio: 'coffee is boiled, beans put in a pot to stew, bacon fried, and the cook mixes a rough sort of bread.' They gathered round the frugal fire to smoke and indulge in a glass of hot toddy; it was on this trip that Gabriela took to smoking.[23] At one point they hear of a family who were murdered on a previous night and their hut burnt by Apaches: 'We talked over the dismal occurrence at night over the camp-fire, the coyotes howling dismally in the distance, as we sat round smoking cigarettes and endeavouring to chew hunks of tough dried meat, before wrapping ourselves in blankets and going to sleep.'[24]

Unfortunately the cotton market had fallen flat by the time they reached Mexico City, so they lost money on the venture, and they returned to San Antonio, Texas. Living there for two months, Gabriela sketched churches and abandoned Jesuit missions, developing an interest in the relics of Christianity that would flourish in her later work and could certainly not have been part of her Anglican upbringing. Cunninghame Graham studied fencing at the Académie d'Escrime. He rarely, if ever, mentioned his wife in his letters home, so it is easier to know what he was engaged in than what she was doing.

Gabriela stayed when he travelled to Argentina in an attempt to set up a ranching venture. They may have had some disagreement and it was the first of many times their lives were on separate paths. The only document from this time is a rather formally phrased letter addressed to her as 'My Dear Caroline' (which is an interesting use of her old name) and starting, 'I have long promised to write to you but have been so much occupied I have never done so yet.'[25] The suggestion is of a quarrel between them, as that would explain the separation as well as the chilly tone. It was not unreasonable for him to travel alone on a new business venture, though Gabriela could have joined him and stayed in Buenos Aires. This is what he was asking in the letter: 'I wonder how you can still stay among those odious Yankees in Texas when down here is so much nicer and we might have such horse and ostrich hunts and also deer hunts together.'[26] The reply must have been in the negative as she went to New Orleans, where she stayed for eight months. It is not clear what she was doing, though giving language lessons has been suggested. He was negotiating a complex relationship with her, as he struggled with a ranching venture that failed when it was raided by Indians (in the terms of the time), the ranch-house burned and its livestock stolen.

With funds exhausted and his health poor, Cunninghame Graham's mother sent his brother Charles to America to bring him back. They all returned to Europe in May 1881 with £2,000 worth of debt. Cunninghame Graham was obliged to apply to the Court of Sessions to borrow to pay it back; the court still had control of the family finances while Major Bontine was alive.

When in Britain they lived in Liphook in Hampshire, as Gartmore was let. They often travelled, including a visit to friends in Dorset in October 1881, where some romantic event happened at the village of Chideock: Robert would call Gabriela 'Chid' for the rest of her life, and 25 years later when she made a will she signed it Gabriela Chideock Cunninghame Graham. This adds another name to those the many-faceted woman used (though it is unusual in the will in that she normally used Gabrielle for family matters).[27] Her pet name for him was Lob, presumably a corruption of Rob.

Their main home from 1881 to 1883 was an abandoned convent at Vigo in Galicia, overlooking the bay where they could sit on the terrace while she arranged olive jars and planted them with flowers. In a letter written near the end of her life she reflected, 'Looking back upon my life, with the exception of *some days* – alas! Only days at Gartmore – the time we spent at Vigo was the happiest of my life.'[28]

It was in Vigo that she encountered the woman who was to be her companion on many journeys, Peregrina Collazo, who acted as her maid. She was much given to sulks and obstinacy, acting more like a family member or a disgruntled friend than a servant. She is said to have been quick-witted, with a store of pithy Galician proverbs to apply to every occasion. Frequently while travelling Gabriela would write of her discontent with Peregrina: 'I hope to goodness it will never be my fate to set eyes on her again. She has been in constant sulks the whole time.'[29] She is still complaining about her in 1900, and the servant was with her until Gabriela's death.

The death of Major Bontine on 16 September 1883 brought Robert into his inheritance and Gabriela became lady of the manor. It was at this stage of their lives that they took the name Cunninghame Graham (previously they had been known as Bontine; Cunninghame Graham has been used throughout in this account for simplicity). Tenants called him Laird, Gabriela was Leddy. They inherited both the estate and its debts of £94,000; it brought in £10,000 a year, but the estate and family cost that amount to run. Gabriela's adventures in the next few years were in estate management.

Trying to maximize income from the estate while at the same time attempting to keep their properties and land in sufficient order was a task that fell to Gabriela, as Robert was hopelessly impractical. It was her efforts in selling off parts of the estate in feus (a Scottish form of long leasehold) that paid back most of the accumulated debt, though they decreased the income from the estate.

She wrote to a friend that she was 'busier than I ever was in my life before, seeing servants and buying stores'. She had an exacting time with servants, which was shared by many middle-class householders in Victorian times, though she seemed particularly prone to what she called 'the maid agony', sometimes taking on servants only to dismiss them after days.[30] She called on Peregrina to supervise the household of a cook, two maids and three laundrymaids, despite her lack of English. Peregrina was also able to keep her company while Robert was out visiting farms and supervising the estate.

As a practical manager she was said to have smoked fifty or more cigarettes a day as she wrote or handled the estate accounts. She was described as having become

> a slave to this normally harmless vice. As time went on, she became so heavy a smoker that she could never be without a cigarette in her mouth. She was in the habit of doing her work, sitting on the floor, with the books and papers placed around her in a circle, and after she had sat thus for a while, burnt-out or smouldering cigarette ends lay all round the room. Even during the nights, whenever she woke up, she smoked two or three cigarettes in rapid succession.[31]

Doctors implored her in vain to smoke no more than twenty cigarettes a day.

When not working she read ancient manuscripts relating to the saints, notably St Teresa of Avila. She wrote, played the piano, painted and studied botany, making a particular study of native mosses. Still, it was a struggle to stay in the mists and clouds of Scotland, in the damp house set in waterlogged land, and she was glad to escape as often as possible to Spain: 'Scotland does not seem to suit me very well in the winter,' she wrote.[32] She and Robert did not like to be parted, but one of them had to stay on the estate to take care of business.

At some time she made contact with her family in Yorkshire, as her sister Grace told her daughter, 'when she was growing up her Mama [Mrs Horsfall] used to go on mysterious journeys and . . . marvellous parcels used to arrive in which there was a present for every child.'[33] Her sister Madge remembered how Gabriela 'used to write to Mama and send her little gifts occasionally, but we were not allowed to mention her name, nor let anyone know where she was nor anything.'[34]

Both Gabriela and her husband were widening their contacts in the world of letters and politics, often attending literary gatherings when they were in London. She would be present at William Morris's 'Socialist tea meetings' at his home, Kelmscott House. She spoke there and wrote on such subjects as the fraudulence of the work ethic and the ugliness of industrial society. W. B. Yeats wrote of meeting her at Kelmscott House on 14 March 1888, where he 'talked a long time to Mrs Cunninghame Graham, a little bright American'; he should have said South American, of course, as that was her persona.[35] Yeats certainly does not give the impression that there was any inauthenticity about her.

A daily diary for a brief period has been preserved, showing her life as an active lady of the estate and of the London literary world. The entry for 28 June 1888 reads: 'Arrived [at Gartmore] and took them all by surprise. Counted the silver and sent Jessie off. Had a row with Peregrina and beat her. So ill and tired. My courses came on. Went to bed early.' An expenses list in the back shows her spending in London: a bonnet £1 10s 6d, stockings 3s 7d; shoes 3s 6d, a dress £4 6s 2½d, stays 5s 10d; a cab to Oscar Wilde's 1s 6d; telegram to Hardy 6½d. Fares to Dover (to go to Paris) 12s 5d.[36]

Her personal interests included women's suffrage and she writes approvingly of the Women's Franchise League, which was dedicated to votes for women and the removal of the disabilities of married women.[37] Both Gabriela and her husband became known in socialist circles, with Cunninghame Graham emerging as a key figure working with William Morris and Keir Hardie towards the establishment of a parliamentary voice for the labour movement, which was to see fruition in the creation of the Labour Party in 1900. After an initial failed attempt to enter Parliament, Cunninghame Graham was elected as a Liberal Member of Parliament for North West Lanarkshire in 1886. He was the first avowedly socialist MP, advocating free secular education, the eight-hour working day, the nationalization of industry and votes for women. He criticized imperialism, racial discrimination, corporal and capital punishment, profiteering by landlords and industrialists, child labour and the House of Lords.

Gabriela also wrote and spoke on socialist subjects and attracted attention at her meetings for her elegant, even exotically foreign style of dress. She made no attempt to slink into the shadows for fear her former identity would be exposed. Keir Hardie wrote to her on 24 December 1887, 'I have just read your warm hearted speech delivered last night on behalf of the poor crofters, and wanted to congratulate and thank you for it ... Your words will do more to awaken sympathy with the crofters, than whole torrents of talk of the usual kind.'[38] Walter Crane (later a fellow *Yellow Book* contributor) wrote on 1 July 1889 about her talk on 'The Ideals of Socialism' at a meeting in Bloomsbury, 'Dear Mrs Cunninghame Graham, I should like to hear you on Socialism at the Communist Club very much, and shall hope to be there.' She knew Oscar Wilde well enough for him to send a friendly message: 'I wish so much I could come and hear you on Tuesday. But I am dining out. I think your subject most interesting, but what is to become of an indolent hedonist like myself if socialism and the church join forces against me?' He says he wants to see 'a reconciliation of socialism with science'.[39]

Cunninghame Graham came to national attention as a result of the 'Bloody Sunday' attack on a demonstration of 13 November 1887 in Trafalgar Square. The meeting was held to protest unemployment, with additional protesters enlarging the event to include Irish issues. There was a ban on meetings in Trafalgar Square, which the Cunninghame Grahams considered a basic issue of free speech. The police objective was to prevent the crowd from reaching Trafalgar Square and to disperse them.

Gabriela watched from the overlooking Metropole Hotel as the marchers with their bands, banners and red flags neared the square. Her tall, russet-haired husband was a striking figure among the working-class demonstrators, who were generally smaller than upper-class people, their development having been restricted by poor nutrition in childhood.

Cunninghame Graham was with trade union leader (and later cabinet minister) John Burns in the front ranks, making for the square, which was guarded by police cordons. Sir Edward Reed, a Liberal MP, watching from another upstairs window, reported:

Before they reached the pavement on the opposite side the police, who were ranged several deep in line around the square, pressed forward over the pavement to meet the advancing group. No measurable time had elapsed before Mr Graham's head was split open or at any rate was bleeding, and he was being much struck from the front by the fists and truncheons of the police ... When he was perfectly secured by the police and held powerless two policemen in succession stepped up from behind and struck him repeatedly on the head.[40]

Blood poured from his head amid the melee of fighting and flailing bodies. Gabriela from her window in the Metropole above the square saw him go down in the crowd. She described, 'My husband forced his way through a serried crowd of police, who batoned him the whole time, and stepped, fainting on to Trafalgar Square.'[41] When she saw him fall under the blows, she thought he had been killed or mortally hurt.

Edward Reed spoke of the 'needless violence and brutality' with which Cunninghame Graham was treated: 'Even after this and when some five or six policemen were dragging him on to the Square, another from behind seized him most needlessly by the hair (the abundance of which perhaps tempted him) and dragged his head back and in that condition he was forced forward many yards.'[42] Cunninghame Graham was dragged to the centre of the square where Burns, now also under arrest, brought water from the fountain in his hat to bathe his friend's wounds. The police now deployed troops with a cavalry charge into the square that dispersed the demonstrators.

Cunninghame Graham and Burns were taken to Bow Street police court to face charges along with the three hundred others who had been arrested. Gabriela joined him there, finding he had a bad wound to the head; one eye was almost closed and he had serious bruising. Among the others at Bow Street were William Morris, Oscar Wilde and Walter Crane, who had all gone in support of the demonstrators. Cunninghame Graham was charged with assaulting the police, causing a riot and illegal assembly.

Having friends prepared to stand bail was to no avail, as Gabriela complained in an angry letter to the press: 'He had to wait five hours, ill, feverish and wounded, before the charge was preferred against him. We had bail all ready, but it was refused, and he passed the night in the cells.'[43] The next day she sat in the court from the time his case was scheduled to be heard, 10.30 a.m., until it was heard at 2 p.m. and court was adjourned. She wrote to the press, 'my husband acted nobly and bravely. The first steps to the fearful coercion and tyranny which has embittered Ireland for so long have now been taken in London.'[44]

There were two further appearances at Bow Street, the tedium of which was somewhat relieved by the support of well-wishers, summoned by Gabriela with messages such as 'My husband's trial is postponed until tomorrow, Wednesday – Hoping very much that you will be able to come', which was a message Walter Crane received. He noted her 'spiritedly issued invitation cards: "Mrs Cunninghame Graham At Home Bow Street Police Court".'[45]

Gabriela and Robert stayed in the Metropole Hotel until the following week. Two detectives in plain clothes were said to have observed their movements from the entrance.[46] They returned home to a hero's welcome at Glasgow Central Station with a brass band, cheering crowds and flowers.

When his trial finally took place, at the Old Bailey on 16 January 1888, his defence was conducted by the young Herbert Asquith, a Liberal MP for a Scottish constituency. Gabriela watched, surrounded by friends and well-wishers, as Cunninghame Graham was cleared of all counts excepting unlawful assembly, and received a six-week sentence. He served it picking oakum in Pentonville, where he continued to suffer from his injuries. Gabriela was not permitted visiting rights, even after direct appeals to the home secretary. She wrote in response to a letter from the miners of Kilsyth, 'I neither see nor write to him and I do not know at this moment how he is, or whether he is ill or well.'[47]

The imprisonment led to a friendship with W. T. Stead, whom she visited at the *Pall Mall Gazette* office in an effort to drum up publicity. He was delighted to meet the pretty young wife of a political prisoner and made his pleasure in her company clear; 'I often think of you, my dear widowed heroine,' he wrote at one time. On another occasion he wrote, 'I telegraphed you today in the vain hope that I might see you, for I am in rather low spirits and felt as if it would have been inspiring to see your face.' Stead's pinings aside, meeting him did get Gabriela into writing for publication, which she had long wished to do.[48]

After his release Cunninghame Graham was much in demand; Gabriela tried to rein in the public speaking engagements he was taking after he nearly collapsed with exhaustion. She wrote to John Burns,

> We will come if possible to your meeting but I do not want Mr Graham to speak. Indeed, he must not speak. His voice is anything but right. It sounds to me weak and hollow, so I am very anxious about him ... If the sight of him will do, he will come, but he must not speak. I shall rely upon you to prevent it.[49]

Now that the cause of the right of free assembly had been brought to the fore by the Trafalgar Square riot, the House of Commons debated Public

Meetings in the Metropolis on 1 and 2 March 1888 with Cunninghame Graham speaking and Gabriela watching from the ladies' gallery.

At the end of this busy year, Cunninghame Graham told a well-wisher in December 1888 that Gabriela was unwell: 'I grieve to say so seriously ill that I start tomorrow for Spain. I fear there is little chance of her ultimate recovery.'[50] Some strenuous adventures were still ahead of her and she had eighteen years more to live, so predictions of her imminent demise were premature. She may have had a diagnosis of diabetes, which he referred to after her death. There was a history of diabetes in the Horsfall family: Gabriela's sister Dorothy died from it as a teenager.

Cunninghame Graham's imprisonment had increased his celebrity and this reflected on Gabriela. They went on marches together and attended rallies; both appeared on platforms supporting the match girls' strike; they would both turn up at the gates of the London docks during the dockers' strike to give encouragement to the picket lines. They also became known on the international socialist circuit: Cunninghame Graham was expelled from France in May 1891 after a speech to strikers who had been fired on by the police; he was escorted to the steamer to Dover and sent back to Britain. A commentator for *The Times* noted Gabriela's activism along with his: while he 'is endeavouring to relieve French workmen, his wife is running all over Spain making Socialist speeches which have a great success, rather like that of a Spanish farce'.[51] The *Times* correspondent described 'a meeting of about 4,000 workmen and Socialists' at which Gabriela, speaking in Spanish, 'denounced the middle classes, and declared that the English Socialist party, although opposed to a general strike, was an advocate of the eight hour working day'.[52] Friedrich Engels called her 'la Española' in a letter written after May Day 1892 when she had been speaking on an international platform with speakers from other parts of Europe.[53]

The *Glasgow Evening News* called her 'a Spanish lady' in a profile of Cunninghame Graham, 'a helpmeet as volatile as himself'.[54] No newspaper or even a friend of the couple writing in private gave any impression that she was anything other than Spanish. Presumably in Spain she used the fiction of having been brought up to the age of twelve in Chile and then lived in France, to explain to those with an acute ear for language why she was not obviously a native speaker. Tschiffely commented that she had spent her early youth in Chile and spoke Spanish 'fairly well but not always correctly, nor without some difficulty, for her parents had always conversed in French'.[55] She was often at international meetings that would require some linguistic dexterity. Presumably she would tell the French people her French was not perfect because she had been brought up in a Spanish-speaking country, and tell the Spanish that they had always spoken French at home, and hope they did not compare notes.

In 1892 Cunninghame Graham unsuccessfully contested Camlachie in Glasgow as a Labour, not a Liberal, candidate, at a time when left-wing politics was moving towards the creation of the Labour Party. She threw herself into the fray, the *Glasgow Evening News* describing her as 'adding fuel to the fire which is raging in Camlachie'. In an 'impassioned, denunciatory and eulogistic' speech she railed at her husband's opponents:

> on the one hand they had men of far reaching aspirations, on the other dull, heavy, beery-brained dullards, men of no political convictions, men who would sell their souls if they had any ... miserable, piddling, party hacks who would sell Home Rule, who would sell themselves, if they could, for a mess of party pottage.[56]

The period of intensive involvement in politics ended for Gabriela when Cunninghame Graham failed to win the seat.

By this time Gabriela had already commenced her great work, a life of the mystic St Teresa of Avila. From 1888, when she first started research, her adventures were in Spain. Writers often choose biographical subjects that reflect aspects of their own lives and characters, particularly in the subjects they pursue as a personal mission. Thus biography becomes covert autobiography, as it may have been for Gabriela on the trail of a woman who had as a child been obsessed with reading the lives of the saints and who had run away from home seeking martyrdom. She described St Teresa as 'a dreamer and a schemer in one – she was never entirely the one or the other.' Describing why the Spanish took to Teresa, she wrote:

> She was the type of all that was vigorous and healthy in the Castilian character – a character singularly simple, straightforward, chivalrous and noble. They were touched by that old creaking cart which jolted her over Castilian roads; they were touched by the tenacity which never gave in; they were touched by her hungers and thirsts and her old ragged habit. We talk about ideals; she lived hers.[57]

Gabriela is repeatedly referred to as Catholic, but this seems to be presumed because of her supposed Latin American birth and her fondness for St Teresa. She was brought up in an evangelical Anglican family and there is no record of her being received into the Catholic faith; she was married in a civil ceremony and was buried with an Anglican one. It is probable that, like the rest of her life, she wanted something to be so, said it was and everyone accepted it. She was of her age in her interest in Catholicism: mystical religion was much favoured in the 1890s – decadent life was said to lead to the scaffold or the cross. Many of those in the *Yellow Book* circle became Catholic, including Aline and Henry Harland, Aubrey Beardsley, Ernest Dowson and Pearl Craigie.

Gabriela started the work in 1888 and signed a publishing deal with Adam & Charles Black in 1891, giving her 10 per cent of royalties. Now she would be in Spain for two or three research trips a year. Cunninghame Graham wrote that she

> spent all the summers of six years, wandering about the sweet thyme-scented wastes of Spain, sleeping in rough pasadas, rising at daybreak and jogging on a mule through the hot sun, to find in upland world-forgotten villages a trace of the saint's footsteps, and happy, after a long day's ride, if she came on a house where once the saint had slept.[58]

In her essay 'The Batuecas' she called herself an eccentric 'to whom the past lives more vividly than the present', staying in a venta or wayside inn,

> its floor on the same level, and paved with the same rough cobble stones as the street outside, and the zaguan or great covered porch into which it opens from the inside, around which last night muleteers, shepherds, charcoal-burners laid their blankets, and slept in close proximity to their mules and donkeys.[59]

She never writes with such warmth of her home in Scotland – and certainly not of Yorkshire.

She shared her love of Spain in one of a series of lectures on different nations at the South Place Institute; of the 21 lectures, hers was the only one given by a woman.[60] She and Cunninghame Graham were often parted because she was in Spain or he was in London. He wrote touchingly about one such departure, seeing her off at Glasgow, 'My dearest Chid, your little face looked so sad over the ship's side.' They were often asking when the other would be back or she would be sending instructions as to her next address so he could write to her.[61] She was frequently ill when she travelled, with bronchial complaints, for example: 'My dearest Lob, I have had an awful time. From seven at night the day before yesterday to three yesterday, I thought I was going to die.'[62] She missed him too, when he was away and she was back at Gartmore, writing to him once when he was off in Morocco, which he had taken to visiting, 'My dearest old Lob, Do take care and come back safely, & in future we will go about together, as I have felt lately in Spain how lonely one is without the other ... It is very dull and will be very dull without you.'[63]

Santa Teresa: Being Some Account of Her Life and Times went to press in October 1893 and was published in April 1894 (incidentally the month the *Yellow Book* launched). It was received with uneven reviews. The anonymous *Times* reviewer conceded that 'much patient study and research' had gone into the writing of the book, but 'the author's enthusiasm for her subject and her exuberance of style give her work the air rather of an historical rhapsody than of a critical biography.'[64] A more positive review in the *Morning Post* praised her research and found 'a picturesque warmth of manner which, combined with much discrimination and perspicacity, renders it both instructive and attractive'.[65]

Gabriela's passion for esoteric religion was also apparent in her translation of *The Dark Night of the Soul* by St John of the Cross, accompanied by her preface, which she used to trace the tradition of mysticism through the Kabbala and the alchemists. Her story 'The Christ of Toro', about a Spanish village icon, was published in the *Yellow Book* in April 1897. It is about the transcendent power of art, which was very much a decadent theme. She attended at least one of John Lane's tea parties. The illustrator E. H. New recorded her in his diary as being present at Lane's rooms in G1 the Albany on 25 July 1895 along with poets and the critic Arthur Symons. New's comment on her was, 'very beautiful'.[66]

Her contribution was in the last volume of the *Yellow Book* and she is not recorded as having been to Henry and Aline Harland's 'At homes' at their flat in the Cromwell Road. She was said to have kept her distance from the Harlands' parties because her husband had called Harland and Beardsley 'cretins' and 'liars'.[67] She experienced Lane's notoriously dilatory approach to payment; even after her death Cunninghame Graham was complaining in a letter asking for permission to republish 'The Christ of Toro', noting, 'As the story was never paid for, I cannot conceive but that the rights remain rested in myself.'[68]

Gabriela was exploratory in her attempts to render mysticism accessible to an increasingly materialistic age. A published transcript of a lecture shows her trying to reconcile the unseen forces of ancient mysticism with the infant science of nuclear physics with its radium, Röntgen and Becquerel rays. She wrote:

> We have denied, scouted the possibility of any other plane than that in which we live and breathe and have our being, although these planes press on us from every side, and for all our physical senses can tell us, we may be moving at every step through invisible streets, passing invisible ships – be surrounded by a stream of life as keen, as ardent as our own.[69]

Gabriela struggled as lady of the manor to make the estate yield a profit, an endeavour that softened her mother-in-law's attitude towards her, though they never became friends. Gabriela had some success but finally in 1900 the couple had to sell Gartmore to Glasgow shipping tycoon Sir Charles Cayser for £126,000, allowing them to pay their debts and giving them financial security for the rest of their lives. The tenants said farewell to the couple at a cake and wine banquet in which the laird and his 'worthy lady' were applauded at a ceremony where it was noted that she was 'well known nearly over the world by her writing'.[70]

With the furniture auctioned and the servants discharged, they spent the last night in the empty house with even the beds gone and in their stead mattresses put on the floor in the drawing room. Gabriela wrote to her mother-in-law:

> Dear Mrs Bontine, We are alone in the 'house desolate'. The rooms in all their desolation strangely preserve their old habitableness . . . I ran into the garden this afternoon. The birds were twittering (I never saw so many birds as at Gartmore) . . . Tomorrow night we shall be in London and then comes the awful unpacking. I am glad we have a flat, as servants there seem most difficult to get. I have secured one, but I am never optimistic now, where servants are concerned, it is a sea of troubles . . . This is my last letter from Gartmore, the dear old Gart. It may be better so, but it is ill to bear.[71]

Mrs Bontine would have had a reason to expose Gabriela had she been squandering the family fortune; as the opposite was true, she kept her counsel. The couple moved to a flat in Margaret Street, near Piccadilly Circus.

Cunninghame Graham missed Scotland, so in July 1904 they bought a cottage on the banks of the Clyde, on the estate they used to own, Ardoch.

Gabriela returned to her old love of the theatre. She adapted *Don Juan's Last Wager*, from the Spanish of José Zorrilla, which had a short run at the Prince of Wales's Theatre in 1900. It was cursed by mechanical failure that meant the supernatural aspects of the play failed on the opening night on 27 February 1900; it was also savaged by the critics for being too tame. The character of Don Juan and his eventual fate were softened in the play in a way which 'spoils both moral and dramatic effect', according to the *Reynolds's Newspaper* critic.[72] Fellow *Yellow Book* contributor Max Beerbohm condescendingly described the tone as 'poordearfellowesque'.[73] Gabriela blamed the poor reviews on the 'moralisation' and 'sentimentalisation' of Don Juan that had been imposed on her by Martin Harvey, the actor-manager, and she asked him after the flop to write a letter to some leading newspaper to say the softening of the character of Juan was his doing, not hers. She felt it was 'Not asking very much', but he obviously disagreed and no letter appeared.[74] The play was withdrawn after a month.

Another theatrical venture was a play called *Mariana*, which Gabriela translated from the Spanish and presumed that the translation would give her acting rights (which she later found were owned by Mrs Patrick Campbell). She had entered into an agreement with the drama critic T. J. Grein, who was to receive £200 to have the play produced; it couldn't be done and they argued about how much he would have to pay back, eventually accepting a court-backed compromise. This abortive attempt at another production seems to have been her last, and reflects the difficulties other 1890s women had in breaking into the theatre; her *Yellow Book* colleagues Netta Syrett, George Egerton and Mabel Dearmer were to face similar problems.

Gabriela had a diagnosis of tuberculosis in summer 1903, which was a slow death sentence. Travel to rest in warmer climes was the prescribed treatment in the days before sulfonamides or antibiotics. Travel Gabriela could manage; rest was not in her nature. She travelled again to Avila, accompanied by Peregrina, in June 1906 and left there towards the end of August. Gabriela was taken ill on a train just over the French side of the border, at Hendaye, where she had to leave the train and book into a hotel. Cunninghame Graham was summoned by telegram. Her family was contacted and her brother William also came, though not in time to see her alive. Cunninghame Graham wrote to her sister, 'I was there for nine days but there was no hope from the first. She died brave, resigned and peaceful,

Gabriela Cunninghame
Graham, frontispiece to
*Rhymes from a World
Unknown* (1908).

conscious to within an hour of the end. It has been a dreadful blow to me after 25 years of married life and affection.'[75]

Now, when she was no longer physically present, there still seemed a real fear that the secret would be found out. A sister, Mary Horsfall, wrote at the time of Gabriela/Carrie's death:

> of course her burial is very different to anyone else's – I shall watch
> the papers for I am certain in spite of all the story will come out
> – but we need not mind him – what I want to find out is what
> name he registered her death in for then – if other than Papa's and
> Mama's he can be charged with Perjury.[76]

She was clearly not eager herself to betray Cunninghame Graham, who had, indeed, ensured that almost every single piece of information on the death certificate was false, even down to the dead woman's age. She was described as Gabrielle Marie de la Balmondière, aged 44, born in Chile, the daughter of Joseph [*sic*, the marriage certificate gives his name as Francis] de la Balmondière and of Carmen Suarez de Arecco.[77]

He brought her body back to Britain to be buried in the chancel at Inchmahome on the island of the Lake of Menteith. The night before the funeral, as a last service to her, he dug the grave himself with the help of a tenant, with only a lantern to give a flickering light. They completed their work by lining the grave with heather from Gartmore, as she had requested.

The day of the funeral was one of cold winds and icy showers. The coffin, borne by old servants and tenants from Gartmore, arrived on the shores of the lake with the sun just visible through gaps in the dark, overhanging clouds, and the island, with its stately trees, barely visible through a curtain of mist. The coffin was placed on a boat with a high prow and stern. Cunninghame Graham sat beside it as they rowed towards Inchmahome. Gabriela's brother, the Rev. William Horsfall, Vicar of St Saviour's, Colgate, near Horsham, Sussex, read a brief Anglican funeral service.

Cunninghame Graham later collated her verse, which had not been published in her lifetime, in a volume called *Rhymes from a World Unknown*. It included 'The Promise':

Love, when I am dead, I shall not be very far,
I will peep in at your window, a faint white star;
Or when the wind arises – see the cedar tips –
They'll be my ghost-like fingers seeking for your lips.
I'll wrest the coffin lid and speed me from my lair,
You'll feel the aura of my presence steal softly though your hair.
Forgotten, unforgetting – for you I cannot die,
Nor you for me – We've drunk too deep Love's Immortality.[78]

The Cunninghame Grahams were descended from two ancient families, the Cunninghams, earls of Glencairn, and the Grahams, earls of Menteith, through whom Robert could claim descent from King Robert II. A case could reasonably be made that he was Robert IV of Scotland and Robert I of Great Britain and Ireland.[79] Had the Cunninghame Grahams wished to make something of their claim to aristocracy, Gabriela's secret would have been exposed by people probing the lineage. However, as she was a socialist, she was not mixing with those who wished to question her pedigree, but rather with those who hated the class system and enjoyed being with a couple who might have had aristocratic pretensions but disdained them.

Gabriela's own family feared scandal, and stories about Carrie/Gabriela's whereabouts were only whispered among the children. Gabriela's great-niece Marthe said, 'There were rumours such as her being adopted by a wealthy Spanish don.'[80] Sister Madge wrote, 'Somehow Mama got to know that she had been adopted by a wealthy old Spanish Don and was somewhere in the Americas and later it leaked out that she was married to RBCG.'[81] Gabriela maintained contact with her mother, at least after her marriage, and Marthe explained that her mother, Grace, and her grandmother used to visit Cunninghame Graham when they were in London. She described the lack of secrecy between them:

> He used to call his wife Carrie, and talked freely about her to Grace, but I don't think that even she knew why the couple made up this story about Gabriela de la Balmondière. There is a possibility that she deceived him over the name, and when he knew the truth he may have decided to leave it as it was.[82]

Was Cunninghame Graham himself at any time deceived? The most recent biographer of Cunninghame Graham, his great-niece Jean Cunninghame Graham (Lady Polwarth), used a great deal of family material for her book *Gaucho Laird* and she fictionalized events for which there was no record. She has Robert and Gabriela simply meeting in a park in Paris; she is working as an actress and uses the stage name Gabrielle de la Balmondière. Within their first conversation she tells him her real name and provenance.[83] This is believable, but if there was no reason for the deception, why did he allow it to persist through 28 years of marriage and the following thirty years? He was telling the tale of the runaway horse to his biographer Tschiffely in the last years of his life.

One of his biographers, Alexander Maitland, notes that on two other occasions Cunninghame Graham used a spirited horse as a device to account for sudden meetings.[84] One of these equine stories accounts for his meeting with Gabriela's replacement after her death, a widow called Elizabeth Dummet whose runway horse Cunninghame Graham is said to have stopped in Hyde Park, a tale so close to the Gabriela story that one or both are obviously an invention. 'Spirited horse' can perhaps be taken as a metaphor for 'animal passions'.

The bridling horse and the startled convent girl story brings other questions to mind: what was a young woman doing unchaperoned in a Paris park where she might meet men? Cunninghame Graham supposedly addressed her in Spanish – not the first language of either of them or the language of the country they were in. She was not in a convent – she was not even a Roman Catholic. As Cunninghame Graham was complicit in retelling this story it indicates that the real facts of their meeting had to be concealed.

There is good reason to be suspicious that the secret the Cunninghame Grahams kept was a shocking one. Grace Horsfall was in contact with her sister, who was fifteen years older than her, so she was able to learn the details she was later to use in her novel *Benjy*. Her daughter Marthe said,

> they somehow got together, largely I suppose because of their mutual interest in writing. Grace visited Carrie at Hyères, South of France ... Something happened there to shock the young Grace profoundly – she was so frightened that she ran back to Yorkshire ... Grace never talked about the incident and I foolishly never questioned her.[85]

The shocking fact had to be something that would continue to disturb, and could cause enduring damage to the Cunninghame Grahams in the eyes of society generally. Marthe suspected bigamy but the absence of any supporting evidence (or the first spouse reappearing in the lives of this very public couple) means there is no justification for this suspicion.

What is certain is that a young woman left Masham as Carrie Horsfall in 1875, and is recorded in London in 1878 with a fictitious name and lineage. Her easiest deception was simply to take years off her age; she was in fact born in January 1858, so she was twenty when she met Cunninghame Graham in June 1878 (presuming that is the date of their meeting). She therefore had three years to account for. She was frequently described as a 'convent school girl' who had been brought up in Paris since the age of twelve. She was said to have been living with an aunt about whom no more has been said (certainly not by the family), so she is obviously a fiction. If she was seventeen when she met Cunninghame Graham, she could claim to have been still at school before then and did not have to account for the missing years. There may have been a progressive eliding of age: the couple's marriage certificate says she was nineteen when in fact she was twenty; the two biographies by people who knew Cunninghame Graham, published in 1932 and 1937, have her as eighteen at their meeting.[86] Other descriptions of her as a 'schoolgirl' when he met her suggest she was even younger.[87]

What was actually happening in the period between 1875 when Carrie ran away from Masham and 1878 when Gabriela met Cunninghame Graham in Paris? Some attempt to find acting work is certain, as it had long been a childhood dream, but there is no evidence of any success in this endeavour. In her sister's book, partially based on Gabriela's life, the heroine runs away, as Carrie/Gabriela did, at the age of seventeen, and goes to 'the stage door of almost every theatre in London' asking to be an actress, charming doormen with her aristocratic air.[88] She progressively spends what little money she has gained as a governess in the quest for acting work, and is eventually invited to an actor-manager's house in St John's Wood. This man has an easy way with women, something known to his wife, who listens at the keyhole while he speaks to the aspiring actress. The actor-manager knows his wife is there, so is restrained in his dealings with the young would-be actress, though he gives her the hope of seeing him again at some time when his wife is not around. Before this can happen she is killed in a road accident. Grace therefore makes her fictional character die before succumbing to the seduction of the actor-manager – for the fictional death of the heroine was better than prostitution. Perhaps the secret that Gabriela was trying to contain was teenage prostitution, or having been a rich man's mistress.

She must have been somewhere and it is reasonable to think it was with a Spaniard or Latin American, perhaps in South America, as she emerges from this period speaking fluent Spanish and able convincingly to claim former Chilean residency. The family story that she had been 'adopted' by a rich old Spaniard has the ring of euphemism about it. It is a reasonable assumption that, on the lookout for acting work, she met one of the older men who hung around actresses and he made her an offer which, in her impoverished state, was the best option for her. Her being a 'kept woman' up to the time of meeting Cunninghame Graham is a reasonable assumption. She may well have been using the working name of Gabriela; perhaps she invented the lineage, perhaps Cunninghame Graham and she concocted it together. The invention that she was supposedly orphaned at twelve might have been a Cunninghame Graham contribution; this was his age when his father was incarcerated.

Alternatively, it is perfectly possible that she was working as a prostitute, perhaps in a brothel, when Cunninghame Graham met her. Early biographers are silent about his sexual life, but Watts and Davies's 1979 biography includes a comment made by Herbert Faulkner West in conversation with them in 1963 that Cunninghame Graham 'was probably as knowledgeable a connoisseur of courtesans as of horses'.[89] He certainly knew brothels, writing of them 'with revealing affection', as Watts and Davies remark.[90] One of his editors, Paul Bloomfield, notes, 'He wrote a good deal, on the whole too sentimentally, about prostitutes.'[91] His work shows a genuine affection and practical concern for prostitutes, including 'Signalled' in *His People* (1906), 'Dutch Smith' in *Faith* (1909), 'Buta' and 'Un Monsieur' in *Hope* (1910), and

'Preface', 'Un Autre Monsieur' and 'Christie Christison' in *Charity* (1912). While it is otiose to analyse every detail of a creative artist's work in terms of his life, it is clear from his stories that Cunninghame Graham lived in a milieu in which marriage between clients and prostitutes could take place, and one in which as a narrator he is entirely sympathetic. He described marriage as 'often a clerical absolved prostitution'.[92]

With no further information, the question of whether Gabriela's missing three years were spent in prostitution or as a mistress has to be open, but it remains the most probable explanation for the couple's dissimulation. Cunninghame Graham was not a hypocrite, and if it was through such work that he met his future wife, he would not have thought less of her. However, he had made his name as a man of the highest integrity in public life, and he did not want his wife to be shown up as a liar and imposter, so he kept up the pretence even after her death.

Gabriela's secret thus stayed as such so long because everyone who had the means to expose her hidden narrative had a vested interest in keeping it quiet: her husband, her family and his family; and their friends enjoyed the story of the deception so much they were not inclined to look further. Gabriela was the prototype of the adventurous 1890s woman whose ambition was to go to London, change her name, become famous, promote outrageous beliefs, find a soulmate, consort with celebrities and die loved by all. It was this cohort of women who first came to public notice in the pages of the *Yellow Book*.

Cunninghame Graham outlived Gabriela by thirty years of political engagement, horsemanship and romance, in a career in which he wrote more than thirty books and was one of the founders of the Labour Party and a leading figure in the Scottish independence movement. He died in 1936 and was buried beside Gabriela. The inscription on the plaque on her grave is 'Los muertos abren los ojos a los que viven': the dead open the eyes of the living.

3

The Forerunner

When George Egerton burst into the Bodley Head offices in summer 1893 in that 'flood of sunlight', as the office assistant later recalled, her life had taken her on a long journey from Australia to Chile, Ireland, the USA and Scandinavia.[1] Her interior journey was as great.

She was born Mary Chavelita Dunne in Australia on 14 December 1859, the eldest of six children of an Irish and Welsh family; she always called herself Chavelita or Chav. The maiden name of her mother, who came from Wales, was Isobel George and Chavelita later used this name as part of her pseudonym. She would emphasize the Irish part of her heritage from her father, Captain John Joseph Dunne, whose military title came from having served in the British army in New Zealand. He was descended from a noble Irish family and had all the airs and graces associated with wealth, but no actual money. He had many talents – drawing, singing and acting – but did not make any of them a career and failed to find any job that he could stick at. The family relied on the generosity of friends and relatives, and at least once their goods were sold at auction to cover their debts.

The family was on restless wanderings between Chavelita's birth in 1859 and 1870, from Australia to New Zealand and Chile (where they had relatives), finally settling in Ireland. It was Dublin that gave Chavelita the earliest memories to be found in her *The Wheel of God*, one of the unjustly neglected biographical works of the century. This book starts with her early memories of visiting her father in the Marshalsea debtors' prison where he is drinking with the prisoners, and she has to ask him for money for her unhappy mother.

It describes how as a child the pressure of caring for her siblings and her feckless father kept her spirit down. 'The big dark chambers in her inner self troubled her, and made life less nice to live,' she wrote, referring to herself in the third person as Mary, her birth name.[2] As they are taken from one lodging to another Mary has to look after the family, begging credit from shopkeepers: 'shiftless poverty had many stratagems; but how they made her cringe.'[3] Her father drew well, but did not deign to draw what might sell; even when he had commissions he would labour at work he enjoyed rather than what paid. He was forever talking about his acquaintance with Cecil Rhodes and other celebrities, but none of this led to any kind of advancement.

She looked after her consumptive mother, 'Mumsie', who was no kind of housekeeper and who died in 1875 when Chavelita was fifteen. The young writer recalled of her relatives, 'When she lay in her coffin dead, not one came near – when she was taken to Rearey [near Montmellick] and we six of us, I the eldest, were left in the house alone – they confessed and communicated and were good Catholics but did not come near.'[4] Her death was soon followed by that of a sister who lost the will to live without her mother. Chavelita was freed from family responsibility when Dunne split up the remaining family, keeping the two boys with him to sponge on whatever relatives would have them, while the two younger girls were sent to a boarding school outside Dublin. Chavelita's grand-uncle (on her mother's side) in Chile had sent money for the funeral, and with some of the remainder she was sent to school in Germany in September 1875.

This was fifteen-year-old Chavelita's first opportunity to prove her worth. She was a brilliant linguist who within months had learned German well enough to teach in the language. This stood her in good stead when the money ran out for the school fees after the first quarter and she had to teach art to other girls in return for her board. Though she could survive, she had no money of her own, and no clothes except things left by former pupils. Her poverty rankled, leading her to a lifelong resentment of Catholicism and priests and nuns, whom she contemptuously called 'celibates'.[5]

She returned to Ireland in 1877 to take care of her siblings and her father, who was increasingly indebted and no more capable than he had been when his wife had been alive. He did have artistic friends, however, some of whom encouraged her in writing. She did sporadic work and published some reviews in *Vanity Fair*, but it would be a long time before she was a fully formed writer.

Like many others seeking a better life, in 1884 she joined the flocks of largely destitute emigrants on a boat to New York. There she stayed in miserable lodgings with bad food and inadequate clothing for the climate. In

George Egerton
(Mary Chavelita
Dunne), *c.* 1894.

The Wheel of God she describes her search for any work, however tedious or ill paid, protecting herself from the 'vulgarity and coarseness' of everyday life.[6] She records working as a clerk in an insurance office filled with other girls from Brooklyn and New Jersey, and she took on work as a German tutor. She later described herself as 'a little girl who fagged out policies on her office stool' on Park Place and Church Street. She lived on 14th Street and 7th Avenue, a 'very lovely little maid who lived lonely and clean and thought high and read much'.[7] It was during the New York phase of this 'vagabond, hard up life' that Chavelita first began reading Scandinavian writers – in translation at this stage, starting with the stories of Bjørnstjerne Bjørnson.

Her father moved to London to try his luck there in 1885. Chavelita was homesick and, failing to live at anything but a subsistence level in the USA, re-crossed the Atlantic to join him. Now she was back, the pressure was again on her to earn for the family. She obtained work though employment agencies including the Society for Promoting the Employment of Women, which is, incidentally, the only time Chavelita is recorded to have engaged with an overtly feminist organization. She is most reflective of the weight of cultural (which she calls 'racial') difference, between the openness of the Irish and the reticence of the English.[8] She did work copying manuscripts by hand. For a time she worked as a nurse, including assisting at operations in St Bartholomew's Hospital. 'One thing had always been the same,' she wrote, 'the need to work and the sense of loneliness.'[9]

As a young woman she was distant and superior; her mother had been genteel, despite the wretched poverty of the family's existence. Chavelita remained proud and cold to others. She had probably never had a sweetheart; she certainly has not recounted any romances, and since she was seemingly incapable of living an experience without writing about it, that probably means she did not have any. She battled her reluctance to talk to men. At the rare dances she had gone to while staying with relatives in Ireland she had come across as shy or aloof. 'She was not amusing,' she reflected of herself, 'life pressed too heavily upon her.'[10]

Margaret Stetz describes her at this time, at the age of 27, as a 'caricature of a spinster' with an erect bearing, fine hair worn in a bun, thin lips and round spectacles.[11] She was said to be sarcastic rather than witty, her small talk dull. She was, however, on the track of a discovery. She wrote of her character in *The Wheel of God* that she

> was realising, for the first time, one of the tragedies of her sex, her affectability; the primitive element in her, untouched by its passage through all the centuries, keeping her sib to the earth and the things of it; closer to the forces of nature than man – genetic woman, answering to the call of the generative season.[12]

One night in her room in New York she recalls that she undressed and danced in the moonlight thinking of 'the pity of it' that the 'white wonder' of her body might not be taken up by someone 'whose very step would be a keynote of music' and that instead she might became 'shrivelled and grow brown and hard as a last year's lemon'.[13]

In London she 'worked all day, came home faint in body from insufficient nourishment and clothes'.[14] She was going 'home' to a women's lodging house in Gower Street, where 'a puff of hot, close air, the smell of overcrowded women, struck her as she opened the door of the sitting-room'.[15] She describes a Saturday night in which the sitting room was full; a long table down one side of the room was crowded with girls mending garments and trimming hats who gossiped and laughed, whispered and giggled. Some talked near the piano; a quieter circle sat near the fire. A girl played a waltz on the piano while another was sewing beads and bows on satin to pieces of buck-ram while she read words from a German phrase-book propped on her work box.

In the big room upstairs lit by gas, 'the four jets without globes gave a poor light and hissed as they burned. The room was divided into squares by iron uprights and cross rods, with hanging curtains – four shillings a week for each cubicle. There were seven in this room.' Chavelita/Mary described how she received a half sovereign (ten shillings: half a pound) for a week's work as a hand in a stationer's. She paid four shillings for the room, a penny for insurance; she would clean her own boots and save the twopence charge for bringing in dirty boots; she had seven breakfasts at threepence each and seven suppers of bread and cheese or bread and sausage at twopence halfpenny, but she was obliged to have a cup of cocoa at another penny in order to be able to eat them. Her washing was a shilling, which left her with fourpence for lunch during the coming week and all her wants. She regretted she could not afford to pay sixpence towards the tea fund, which made her look mean before the other girls, and she had to budget for soap and darning cotton.

Like the girl doing embroidery for sale while studying German grammar, Chavelita knew that self-education was the key to advancement. *The Wheel of God* notes that Mary 'had learnt two fresh languages, sought forgetful-ness in many a book'.[16] The boarding house was far from being the lowest type: the women there included an art student, a clergyman's daughter and a sea captain's daughter, and Chavelita herself was an army captain's daugh-ter. Likewise the employment agency Mary attended was not for unskilled labour but for genteel women who needed employment.

In the boarding house common room Mary hears stories of boyfriends, short-term work for low pay and the ruses of the newly poor. Miss Evans, a girl who does casual but well-paid work as a 'buyer' for a warehouse (earn-ing around fifteen shillings a week), comes in after a night out to talk about how she got taken out by an old man, with dinner and a box at the Alhambra to watch the ballet. She speaks openly to the whole common room about her adventure, describing her seduction techniques. She pretended to be an innocent country girl,

> up from Devonshire, you know, fresh as cream! . . . drooped my eyes and turned my dimple to him, old galoot! Ugh! Well, we came out, and he kept close, tucked his old claw under my arm; I began to get frightened, didn't know what to do; awful crush; bit of a

fog. I told him he must hurry with a cab, or I'd get most frightful toothache; always did in a draught.

He was intending to take her to supper – it is unstated in the story but presumably this would be to a 'supper club', an establishment where rooms were available to hire by the hour where a gentleman could order food and wine and continue his seduction in private. Once Miss Evans has sent the old man off for a cab, she darts across the street and around some railings, and grabs a hansom cab herself. When she tells this story the women laugh at the thought of his face when he finds his prize is gone. 'I love doing an old beast like that,' she says, 'thinks he's only got to look at a woman.'[17]

After decades of struggle in different countries and at different jobs, still earning nothing but the bare minimum to keep alive, Chavelita realized she must take her chances where she could. One of her father's rakish friends was a colourful character called Henry Higginson who had been a bank clerk, fishmonger's agent, travelling salesman, missionary and finally titled himself 'Reverend', though he had no right to do so. He assumed the clerical title in order to become domestic chaplain to Charlotte Whyte-Melville, an aristocratic widow, who paid for his divorce from his wife, who was in Michigan, USA. Charlotte then paid for his marriage to her in Switzerland, a union that horrified her family. Her brother Lord Bateman and her daughter Lady Massereene declared Higginson was a bigamist and took out a newspaper advertisement to that effect. Higginson retaliated and the newspaper, the *Morning Post*, was obliged to print a retraction.

Theirs was not the happiest of marriages, Higginson and Charlotte were said to have quarrelled incessantly. They spoke to Captain Dunne about their marital differences and Chavelita's genial father came up with a novel solution: they were going on a trip to Ireland, so why not have Chavelita travel with Higginson and Whyte-Melville as a companion to Charlotte?[18] Dunne presumably thought it would help to have a third party come between them, and it would also give his daughter a refined employment, more suited to her temperament than addressing envelopes and copying.

At the age of 27 in 1887 she therefore embarked on an adventure that soon gave her the excitement she craved. Higginson was middle-aged and, if the character based on him in *The Wheel of God* is a reliable picture, had known her since she was a child when, he says, 'you were a rum little shaver, all eyes and legs.' He seduces her with words such as 'You are erotic, even if you don't know it,' and 'You have a great capacity for love going to waste in you; why not turn a little of it over to me?'[19]

He was doubtless the original of the man who speaks to the Chavelita-like woman in her *Keynotes* story 'A Shadow's Slant':

You queer little thing. You are no beauty; but you creep in, and I, I love every inch of you. I'd kiss the ground under your feet. I know every turn of your little body, the slope of your shoulders, – I that always liked women to have square shoulders – the swing of your hips when you walk. Hips! Ha, ha! you haven't got any, you scrap! And yet, by the Lord, I'd lick you like a dog.[20]

No critics commented on this phrase with its scarcely veiled reference to cunnilingus.

When the Irish trip was over, Chavelita returned to her father, who also received an indignant letter from Charlotte about her travelling companion's behaviour, claiming Chavelita was 'carrying on' with her husband.[21] Captain Dunne realized the situation at once and instead of blaming Chavelita, as conventional propriety would have him do, he threatened Higginson with 'a thrashing' if he communicated with her again.[22] This unlikely moralist's threat was not to be carried out: Higginson communicated daily with Chavelita via a mutual friend, Lord Belfast, who took letters between them as well as working to pacify Charlotte.

On Chavelita's 28th birthday, or near to it in mid-December 1887, Chavelita disappeared with Higginson. Some £800 disappeared from Charlotte Whyte-Melville's account at the same time. Captain Dunne was soon in pursuit, with Charlotte urging him on and threatening imprisonment for Higginson because of bigamy, which since she had paid for his divorce is curious, unless the divorce was a fake. She contented herself with calling on her lawyers to declare the marriage null, which does imply that it was bigamous and that she knew it. Captain Dunne proceeded to sue her for the expenses he had incurred in his unsuccessful quest for her husband.

Chavelita and Higginson got clean away, dodging from one country to another using ruses that Higginson had developed in a lifetime of shady adventures. *The Wheel of God* describes her feelings: 'There was a feeling of security in being with him. Curious, it was possible to feel secure and insecure at the same time; one might feel safer on a lonely road beset by tramps, in the company of a dog, even if one were not sure of the brute's temper.'[23]

Mary's character in *The Wheel of God* describes her husband as a bully and jealous. Whether this is an accurate description of Higginson is uncertain, but he was definitely an alcoholic and not in good health. He had promised her, when courting, that he would control his drinking, which went the usual way of such promises. Regardless of his deficiencies, it did her no harm to be having her first sexual encounters with an experienced man who 'had rather a genius for erotic nomenclature'.[24]

Evading apprehension, they styled themselves Mr and Mrs Melville (so appropriating Charlotte's name). Finally they arrived in Norway, not a place of frequent excursion of Victorians who were more likely to travel to France, Italy or Germany, and know the languages of those countries. They bought an estate, Slottnaes Park, at Langesund, around 100 miles south of the capital, Christiania. Life was passionate with what Chavelita called 'an untamed, natural man'.[25] She described in one story a drunken 'storm' lasting two days in which a man, recognizably Higginson, is raving at her. 'What a man I would have been . . . if it hadn't been for women!' She is represented as the 'pale little mistress' of the house who tells herself, 'he abuses her most when he loves her most'.[26]

Higginson's personality aside, as Margaret Stetz says, the real beginning of Chavelita's intellectual development can be dated from her arrival in Norway. For all that can be said against Higginson, he provided her with 'the leisure and the means to continue her self-education. With the elopement, she had cut herself loose, at least temporarily, from her ties to Ireland and the Catholic Church, the moorings of her youth . . . she now immersed herself with a passion in the culture and the literature of her new homeland.'[27] In the northern countries, she found an intellectual and artistic liberty unknown for women in Dublin or in London. She read Ibsen, Bjørnson, Strindberg, Hamsun and Hansson.

Like other women who emerged at the time and other *Yellow Book* contributors, she had assembled a quiver of women's weapons. The professions were still largely forbidden to them (at least without the most strenuous efforts); university education required money, but women could learn languages at little cost. Many people spoke French; a large number spoke Italian and German. Almost no one spoke Scandinavian languages, so that was a clean field for women where they would not be competing with men. Travelling was difficult for a single woman but if she chose a man who travelled, she could escape the drawing-room expectations of Victorian society.

Within two years, in June 1889, Higginson died. Chavelita wrote of his character in *The Wheel of God*, 'He had been good to her in his own way, but it was life at a tension, almost a tobogganing downhill. It was only when he lay dead that she realised that she had, as it were, been holding her breath and sitting tight all the time in fear of the unexpected.'[28] In another of her barely disguised autobiographical pieces she wrote, 'the strongest feeling I had when he was dying or dead, though I was sorry in a way, and dreaded the loneliness, was a fierce inward whisper of exultant joy that I belonged to myself again.'[29] Higginson left Chavelita with an income of £220 a year, which would have been enough to get by on comfortably had she not felt the need to give so much of it to her family. She used her new-found freedom for literary and sexual exploits, living between Christiania (later Oslo) and London. She was restless and undecided, living on her nerves, as she put it. She had a relationship with her Norwegian lawyer, Arndt Schiander, who proved too steady and normal for her. She learned Russian in a few months, intending to travel there to write folk tales, but the project did not take off.

She was in London to witness the flowering of Scandinavian literature, remarking of Ibsen's *Ghosts* that the English were 'going into virtuous fits' over it, which she felt, 'is all humbug, part of the most positive British doctrine, of commit adultery, seduce any woman you can, in fact sin as you please but don't be found out. It's all right so long as you don't shock us by letting us know.'[30] She was adept enough at Norwegian to be able to criticize the translation of the play that was on at the Independent Theatre.

In reading modern Scandinavian literature, she was most impressed by the work of Knut Hamsun, whose novel *Hunger* was published in 1890. Hamsun, born in 1859, the same year as Chavelita, was the most important early modernist, who later had the recognition of the Nobel prize for literature for his literary innovation. *Hunger* describes the author's impoverished struggle for survival, driven by a bizarre psychology which is described in his internal monologue. *Hunger* has all the innovations of style associated with modernism: his work was an intensely personal stream of consciousness, without plot and indifferent to narrative; Chavelita felt on reading it that she had finally found a home. In 'Now Spring Has Come', a short story closely based on her experiences with Hamsun, she wrote, 'let the telling words, the passionate pain, the hungry yearning, all the tragedy of a man's soul-strife with evil and destiny, sorrow and sin, bite into my sentient being.'[31]

'I was consumed with a desire to see and know the author,' she continued. 'I never reasoned that the whole struggle might only be an extraordinarily clever intuitive analysis of a possible experience. I accepted it as real, and I wanted to help this man. I longed to tell him in his loneliness, that one human being, and that one a woman, had courage to help him.'[32]

In the story, she tracked him down and they corresponded until her desire to see him became overpowering, and they arranged to meet at a town on the Norwegian coast in autumn 1890. Waiting in a hotel to see him, she observes herself, 'I can see the very childishness of my figure, the too slight hips and bust, the flash of rings on my fingers; they are pressed against my heart.' As a grown woman she was still describing herself as a girl. She recounts, 'I told him all about myself, turned myself inside out, good and bad alike, as one might the pocket of an old gown, laughed at my own expense, hid nothing.'[33]

Inevitably they had an affair, this very real event being reflected in her fictionalized version: 'I was nearly thirty when I found him and . . . life is short!' as she wrote. She had to leave on a steamer and they corresponded: 'I was insanely happy, then I was intensely miserable. I sent him my portrait and a letter, and counted the days and the hours to a reply.' He wrote that she 'came as a strangely lovely dream into [my] life.'[34]

When they met again, when spring 1891 had come, they saw each other in a different light: 'I felt a curious stiffening in my face, and the touch of his hand did not thaw me.' He comments on her thinness and she feels ashamed of her inferior bosom: 'I felt as if I were being totted up. Item, so much colour, item, so much flesh.' They kiss (presumably a euphemism for having sex) but 'they were merely lip kisses; his spirit did not come to mine, and I was simply analysing them all the time.'[35]

She wrote, 'He thought of me as a dream lady with dainty hands, idealised me – and wrote to the dream creature. When I came back in the flesh, he realised that I was a prosaic fact, with less charming hands, a tendency to lean-ness, and coming crow's feet.' She described their conversation as they talked about 'Tolstoi and his doctrine of celibacy. Ibsen's Hedda. Strindberg's view of the female animal. And we agreed that Friedrich Nietzche [*sic*] appealed to us immensely.' The talk is not passionate, however. They parted without rancour, though he said he would burn her letters, which caused her pain: 'I felt as if I had a sponge with a lot of holes in it, instead of a heart, and that all the feeling had oozed away through them.' She remarked in the story, 'If one has made an idiot of one's-self, it is at least self-consoling to have done so for a genius.'[36] He was the first major writer Egerton had known and her first literary work was translating *Hunger* into English, which she started in 1891. She dedicated her book *Keynotes*, containing 'Now Spring Has Come', 'To Knut Hamsun In memory of a day when the west wind and the rainbow met.'

Before the literary endeavours, however, Chavelita was to have another marital adventure. While recovering from the emotional trauma of the affair with Hamsun, she fell for the attentions of Egerton Clairmonte, one of the feckless wastrels to whom she was so attracted. Her family was surprised to find her marrying him, in autumn 1891, but he was one of a type. 'Egie' was a Canadian with a colourful past, having worked in a South African gold field, a diamond mine and an ostrich farm. He shared her father's love of sports, and his tendency to live off Chavelita; he soon found ways of spending his way through her money.

They rented a cottage in Ireland called Ardrath, near Millstreet, County Cork, with a neglected garden and access to 'a river with trout to whip, and pike to be speared with a carving fork whipped to a pea-stake'.[37] Her finances had been strained by her decision to take responsibility for the keep of her father, her brother Jack and her sister Nan. Her workshy husband was another drain on her limited resources and soon she was unable to afford books and magazines. She became bored sick with rural life. She wrote to her father, 'I would rather die from overwork than vegetate here. I detest it – I wonder where the notion first arose that women liked quiet lives.'[38]

She began to write with the intention of selling her work to make money and wrote six stories in school notebooks on the back of an upturned tea tray. She recollected, 'I never remember the time I had not a story to tell, but I never remember wanting to write them down. I would have liked to go in a caravan from hamlet to village, stopping to tell a story with a can for pennies.' The editor T. P. O'Connor had a feature in his publication the *Weekly Sun* for new writers. Chavelita noted it and said:

> all at once I saw my way clear. I would write some stories and send them in. I realised that in literature everything had been better done by man than woman could hope to emulate. There was one small plot left for her to till: the terra incognita of herself, as she knew herself to be, not as a man liked to imagine her – in a word to give herself away, as man had given himself in his writings.[39]

'If I did not know the technical jargon current today of Freud and the psycho-analysts, I did know something of complexes and inhibitions, repressions and the subconscious impulses that determine actions and reactions. I used them in my stories.'[40] She sent the stories in and O'Connor's literary editor Thomas Gill saw merit in them, though they were not right for his publication, and he advised her on further submissions. He replied taking

'George Egerton' at face value and was full of confusion and apology when he was informed by her of his error, saying it

> shocked me when I learned that you were a woman and thought of what I had written under the full belief that I was addressing a man. It never once dawned on me that the author of those virile sketches was not one of my own sex or I would never for a moment have written as I did,

indicating how the drawing room niceties of Victorian Britain were a serious constraint on frank discussion in the literary world, and how much was concealed from women writers even in direct discourse.[41]

Ultimately the stories came to the office of the Bodley Head. She signed a contract with Lane on 26 August 1893 to publish *Keynotes* at 3/6d, for which Chavelita would receive 6d per copy for the first 5,000 sold, 8d thereafter, and an advance on the first 1,000 (which would have given her an advance of £25).[42] This was a key moment for Chavelita and not only because it was the start of her writing life. She had parted from Ireland for good, never to live there again, and she had evolved into George Egerton, adding her husband's first name to her mother's second.[43] She had also established herself as an expert in Scandinavian literature at a time when it was in vogue and few others had her language skills. Most importantly, in the desperation of poverty in 1893, she had written one of the most important books of the decade in English.

It was not only the subject-matter that was innovative, but the style. Camilla Prince has written about Egerton's 'literary impressionism', which was nurtured in her study of Scandinavian writers, particularly Hamsun. She developed an internalized style similar to his, with similar disregard for narrative conventions. Prince describes Egerton's style as having distinctively modernist characteristics: subjective impressions, fragmented structures, plotlessness, capturing an impression of a floating time or place, engaging dreams and reveries, focusing on minute details, employing a fragmented chronology and showing an interest in psychology. All these characteristics distinguish her work and justify her description as a modernist before modernism existed. All would be further developed by the likes of Virginia Woolf and James Joyce.[44]

Stylistic innovation aside, Egerton plumbed uncomfortable questions of sexual attraction, contemplating

Title page of George Egerton, *Keynotes* (1894).

why a refined, physically fragile woman will mate with a brute, a mere male animal with primitive passions – and love him – the why strength and beauty appeal more often than the more subtly fine qualities of mind or heart – the why women (and not the innocent ones) will condone sins that men find hard to forgive in their fellows. They have all overlooked the eternal wildness, the untamed primitive savage temperament that lurks in the mildest, best woman. Deep in through ages of convention this primeval trait burns, an untameable quantity that may be concealed but is never eradicated by culture – the keynote of woman's witchcraft and woman's strength.[45]

There was no doubt that the scent of sex about her work unnerved the critics. Barrister and sportsman Hugh E. M. Stutfield, who was born in 1858 and so was almost the same age as Chavelita, still delivered his judgement 'The Psychology of Feminism' from a lofty height. He put women writers in the same category as decadents and aesthetes: 'Mrs George Egerton is to my mind the ablest of our women writers of the neurotic school.' She was

> essentially a womanly writer. Her gifts are intuitive rather than intellectual, and she owes nothing whatever to the reason or the research of man. Her perceptions are of the nerves, for, like some of her favourite Swedish and Norwegian authors, she personifies our modern nervousness, and her best characters are quivering bundles of nerves. The reader can hardly fail to recognise the auto-biographical character of her writings, redolent, as they are, of the spirit of discontent and disillusionment.[46]

He was correct about the autobiographical core of her work. It is usually naive to ascribe exact biographical meaning to a fiction writer's work but in Chavelita's case we have her sanction. She presented a copy of *Keynotes* with a green satin cover she had embroidered to John Lane and annotated some of the stories. In the case of a scene of passionate embracing in 'A Cross Line', for example, she noted: 'All this scene may have been suggested by incidents of our life together touched up fancifully, the woman is me at least in her caressing deviltry.'[47] Further passages are linked in written side-notes to lived scenes and even to addresses.

The most effective way for the establishment to respond was not outrage, but by satire. The 10 March 1894 edition of *Punch* carried a piece titled 'She-notes', of course mocking *Keynotes* but also underlining its distinctively feminine character. The *nom de plume* Borgia Smudgiton parodied George Egerton's name while Beardsley, who had drawn the title page and cover design for *Keynotes*, was mocked as Mortarthurio Whiskersly (up to this point Beardsley had been best known as the illustrator of Malory's *Morte d'Arthur*). The illustration was of a skinny woman smoking a cigarette with a fishing rod beside her. This was a reference to 'A Cross Line', the first story in *Keynotes*, in which a woman meets a strange man by a trout stream and they discuss fly fishing (one of the skills Captain Dunne passed on to Chavelita and, of course, a very masculine pursuit). They have an affair until she dismisses him, having tired of him, though there are no consequences and she still loves her husband, with whom she is still having sex, as a scene between them shows: 'His eyes dilate and his colour deepens as he crushes her soft little body to him and carries her off to her room.'[48]

In the *Punch* parody version her solicitous husband says to the female character, 'Off your pipe, old chappie? Feel a bit cheap?' to which she says, 'Yes, beastly, thanks, old man.' He offers her a whisky without soda, which is 'for boys'. After a discussion about riding, 'With a supple bound she is on his shoulders curling her lithe fishing boots into one of his waistcoat pockets. Surely gipsy blood runs in her veins!'[49]

These parodies may have been offensive (and Chavelita never showed much of a sense of humour) but they brought the ideas of new women into the middle-class drawing room. The following month *Punch* expanded the theme with a poem titled 'Donna Quixote' comparing New Woman ideas to the fantasies of Cervantes's hero. A woman looking rather like Chavelita with her pince-nez sits holding a latchkey aloft, while women warriors around her assail such demons as the marriage laws, decorum and Cerberus, whose three heads are 'Mamma', 'chaperone' and 'Mrs Grundy' (the embodiment of conventional propriety). Books lie around her, including an open copy of Ibsen, who is also referenced, as is George Egerton, in an accompanying verse that calls on Donna to 'be not stupid/ Fight not with Hymen, and war not with Cupid.'[50]

The *Punch* writer thus picks up on Scandinavian influence on the new woman, something more than evident in *Keynotes*, half of whose stories are set in Norway. This sets her apart from male writers such as Henry Harland and Crackanthorpe, who published volumes of naturalistic stories the same year, 1893, and whose works referenced France as Egerton's did not. Egerton makes allusions to people such as Strindberg, Bjørnson and Nietszche. This is the earliest reference in fiction in English to Nietzsche, who was German but was influential in Scandinavia, initially owing to the championing of him by the Danish critic Georg Brandes.[51] Brandes was enthusiastic about *Keynotes*, which helped Chavelita's acceptance in a Scandinavian circle of writers; the book was translated into Norwegian (as were her later books *Discords* and *Symphonies*). The Swedish writer Ola Hansson introduced himself to George Egerton by letter in summer 1894. She was hard up and so suggested to John Lane that she translate Hansson's short stories *Little Ofeg's Ditties*. This fact alone, that she needed money and so did a translation, is telling that Scandinavian writing found a market in Britain.

If we reverse the gaze from Egerton's self-examination to ask what she was looking at when she wasn't looking into herself, the answer is: at men who were self-consciously examining themselves, Hamsun and Strindberg and Hansson. She was relating to a Scandinavian rather than the more buttoned-up British Victorian masculinity. She also met and corresponded with

DONNA QUIXOTE.

["A world of disorderly notions *picked out of books*, crowded into his (her) imagination."—*Don Quixote.*]

Donna Quixote, by Linley Sambourne, in *Punch*, 28 April 1894.

literary women including Laura Marholm (born Laura Mohr), Ola Hansson's partner who was of Danish-Norwegian ancestry. Marholm took Swedish nationality with her marriage to Hansson but she wrote in German. Egerton, of course, fitted well into this multilingual literary community. Marholm described Chavelita, 'She had a small, delicate face, with a pained and rather tired expression, and a curious, questioning look in the eyes; it was an attractive face, very gentle, very gentle and womanly, and yet there was something disillusioned and unsatisfied about it.'[52] Chavelita began translating into

English Marholm's play *Karla Bührung*, which is a veiled treatment of literary life: it is about the relationship of Georg Brandes with Swedish realist writer Victoria Benedictsson, which culminated in her suicide.

Laura Marholm was so impressed with Egerton that she wrote about her in *Das Buch der Frauen*, which was translated as *Six Modern Women* and published by John Lane at the Bodley Head in 1896. The title of her Egerton chapter is 'Neurotic Keynotes', and there she writes about the book:

> 'Keynotes' is not addressed to men, and it will not please them. It is not written in the style adopted by other women Georges – George Sand and George Eliot – who wrote from a man's point of view, with the solemnity of a clergymen or the libertinism of a drawing room hero. There is nothing of the man in this book, and no attempt is made to imitate him, even in the style, which springs backwards and forwards as relentlessly as a nervous little woman at her toilet when her hair will not curl and her staylace breaks. Neither is it a book which favours men; it is a book written against them, a book for our private use.[53]

Keynotes was also successful in America, where it was said to have the largest sales of any short story collection excepting Kipling's.[54] Doubtless partly on the strength of it, Lane opened a branch of the firm in New York in 1896. The book was also notably successful in Germany. According to Chavelita, it went into seven languages in two years, which was very gratifying for a linguist.[55] After the great success of *Keynotes*, Chavelita faced two major problems, both relating to her own nature rather than the obstacles put before her. The first major difficulty of her life was entanglement with selfish men whom she loved and who used her, starting with her father and continuing in a series up to her death. The second problem was more of a professional curse: she was not an enthusiastic writer and was not prepared to put herself out to sell books. In later life she recognized this, writing, 'I never, alas, experienced the marvellous thrill, the walking on winged feet, or shouting to the dawn, which I had read so many men have felt on seeing their first book in print.' She disliked the press publicity on which the book industry thrived. 'I was a bad incense-swinger,' she said, 'I was intransigent, a bad seller of myself.'[56]

She was diffident even to friends. When Clement Shorter wrote to her asking to feature her in his magazine the *Sphere*, she replied:

Mr Lane told me some weeks ago that you would like to have a
portrait and if possible an interview. I have a very strong dislike to
interviews, in fact I have refused many applications. I do not desire
to be anything but 'George Egerton' to the public; personally I
resent all details of writers and painters, because I find that they
crop up in an [irritable?] way to the prejudice of my enjoyment of
them and they seem to me to savour of vulgarity. At the same time
knowing that I am considerably indebted to you for much nice
appreciation and much active kindness, I shall be pleased, if you
will kindly waive the interview, to let you arrange for a photograph,
if you wish to have it.[57]

Shorter persisted and intended to publish some remarks that Chavelita
had made. She heard of the plan and insisted on seeing them: 'Dear Mr
Shorter, You put me under an obligation. If you do not really mind I will
take it as a favour if you do not insert "copy" enclosed … it is all wrong; all
misrepresented perhaps not intentionally – but I don't want it in, particularly as "Discords" is coming.'[58] The notion of a writer turning down publicity from a favourable source, particularly when she has a new book out,
is the sort of thing that ruins a publishing relationship.

Most egregiously, she failed to make a friend of her publisher, often
treating him with disdain. She had always been proud and sensitive about
her relationship with Lane, seeing a publisher as a tradesman who should
not interfere in the relationship between a writer and her audience. Even
when *Keynotes* was being edited she was too aloof to go to see him. He said
he could see her at any time on Monday except between one and three
o'clock. She said it was inconvenient for her to go into town, she would
prefer to do business by letter, and, as she wrote to her father, 'I object to
1–3, his lunch time – I will not dance attendance on anyone from the Pope
to the Tzar of Russia.'[59] She seemed unable to realize she was on to a good
thing with Lane, and that by daring to publish her work he was taking a
risk. Moreover, she was in a prime position as the leading female author of
someone who conspicuously liked women as much as Lane did, but she
failed to take advantage of it.

She was later to touch on this to Shorter, correcting a misunderstanding between them: she had promised her next story to him, which in fact
came out in the *Yellow Book*, but she protested it had been written prior.
She wrote:

You touched me on my most sensitive point by saying that I have treated you badly – I never willingly treat anyone badly – not even in retaliation – life is too short – and besides you are the last man in London whom I would intentionally offend . . . Now I hope I have made my peace with you – a woman is always handicapped, if I were a man I should have run across you long ago and have had the opportunity of saying this.[60]

A woman's lack of presence in the traditionally male places of business was a curse for women writers; it was a deficiency that had to be made up in personal friendships. She developed a flirtatious relationship with Richard Le Gallienne, who called her 'Dear Little Witch-Woman' and signed himself 'Narcissus'.[61] He wrote to her, 'Is it so unclean, so evil a thing for a woman to be drawn to a man – just a little bit – because he is a man?'[62] If they failed to have an affair, it was not for a lack of effort on Le Gallienne's part. He had already, before knowing her, done her the great service of praising the manuscript of *Keynotes* to John Lane. He was also the perspicacious reader who recommended that 'A Cross Line' should go at the front of the book, as the best presentation of Chavelita's unique style.[63] Through him she met his sister, Sissie Welch, and her husband, Jimmy Welch, Le Gallienne's best friend from back home in Liverpool, now a successful comic actor. On Friday afternoons they would host gatherings in their flat in Gray's Inn overlooking the lawns and trees of its garden; people from the world of the stage and of literature would meet there. The actor Harold Child said Chavelita was a regular attender, describing her as 'a very slender, grave-faced Celt'. There Chavelita met fellow *Yellow Book* writers Evelyn Sharp and Netta Syrett.[64] It was at these gatherings, or perhaps at the Harlands, that she met Ella D'Arcy, who was to become a lasting friend. John Davidson and his wife Margaret were also close enough to Chavelita to exchange letters and visit each other's homes.[65] She knew W. B. Yeats well enough for him to write in relaxed style in 1896, 'If you have no engagement on Monday evening will you come here (I am but a few minutes from Gower Street) and meet some friends of mine? Havelock Ellis and Arthur Symons will come if you can and both are very anxious to meet you. Come any time after eight.'[66]

Her *Yellow Book* contribution in April 1894 was 'A Lost Masterpiece' about a writer struggling to write but being waylaid by the minutiae of life. It is not a strong piece but it accurately conveys the struggles of a writer attempting to focus. Her fame was at its height in 1894–5 with the publication of the Keynotes series inspired by her first book, and her portrait painted at John Lane's request, a reproduction of which was featured in the *Yellow Book* volume v in April 1895 (he hung the original in his office). However, she struggled with the business of writing, habitually blaming her health. She wrote, 'my illness and other things have made me disinclined to write this year.'[67]

Discords was published in December 1894 and dealt with alcoholism, violence and suicide in stories such as 'Wedlock' and 'Gone Under'. It was criticized from the usual quarters for portrayals of female drunkenness and frank depictions of sexuality such as seventeen-year-old Flo in 'Virgin Soil', angry because of her mother's refusal to tell her the facts of life. 'What is it that I do not know, mother?' she implores but her mother only cries. Later the daughter visits when her husband 'has gone to Paris with a girl from the Alhambra [music hall]'. The young woman confides to her mother that she finds his infidelities 'lovely oases in the desert of matrimony'.[68] She describes marriage for many as 'a legal prostitution, a nightly degradation'.[69] The virgin soil of the title is of course a reference to her virgin state at marriage, but also to the soil of marriage being ripe for the seeds of resentment. She has left her husband, and at the end of the story she walks out of her mother's house into a ripe autumn, a 'delicate season of decadence'.[70]

This all put Chavelita clearly in the camp of the New Woman who questioned her assigned role as daughter, wife and mother, with particular emphasis on the unsatisfactory nature of the marriage deal given to women. Chavelita was not an active feminist and played no part in women's campaigns for higher education, entry into the professions or the vote. For Chavelita it was not political freedom she desired for women but sexual freedom – at least the same freedom as was given to men, to follow their desires without moral stricture. This put her clearly on the fringes of the feminist camp, which was dominated by women who spoke with the propriety of drawing room ladies, aiming for a world in which men were expected to observe the same rigid sexual standards as women of the Victorian middle class. Chavelita's distance from them was ideological but it was also one of class – she had been poor, had worked for a living, and knew of factories and boarding houses where life was raw.

Discords was moderately successful, going into four printings in the first months of 1895, but it could not compare to the runaway success of *Keynotes*. Egerton continued to receive critical notice: a commentator in 1896 noted that she was 'certainly the best and the cleverest of the "sex" or "problem" school, and it would be impossible for her to avoid being a great writer if she tried'.[71]

Life with Egerton Clairmonte had not gone well; he was as feckless and careless of her feelings as her father or Higginson, but he was less exciting to her than either of those. She had dramatized the relationship she experienced in one of her *Keynotes* stories, 'An Empty Frame', in which the central character in another one of these frankly autobiographical stories looks at the frame where her former lover's picture used to be. She compares his passionate love for her with the equivocal affection of the man with whom she now lives. 'There, it's all right, boy!' she says. 'Don't mind me, I have a bit of a complex nature; you couldn't understand me if you tried to; you'd better not try!'[72]

She reanalysed this relationship in *The Wheel of God*, where Clairmonte appears as Cecil, who was

> bound to drift, bound to sink, bound to be a wastrel of life and its chances through physique, temperament and inclination . . . She had tried every way: tenderness bored him; appeals to his honour or principles were fruitless; his conception of either was elementary. Once she had tried sharp, incisive speech, he had rolled a cigarette and listened in silence; and when her quick passion had exhausted itself he asked, 'Finished? Then I'm off.'[73]

The relationship was more complex, however; despite his reckless spending and ordering from tradesmen, his urge to bet on race meetings (and his proverbial lack of luck), she still loved him with feelings she struggled to fathom:

> It was difficult for Mary, with her great tenderness for all weak, erring and helpless things, her tendency to trace back to the seed and root of everything, to keep her resentment. After all, his very weakness, the very poverty of his nature, gave him a mortgage on her strength. She laid her hand on one of his and patted it, as she might have done to a little child.[74]

She wrote to John Lane about her travails with Clairmonte, such as one day in October 1894 when he had been out all day with friends and, presumably, came back to ask her for more money:

> You know pretty well my financial affairs and you know Johnnie how little I spend on myself. Last night unstrung me. I am not

disloyal as you know and I have made the best of things but the game is a little unequal. This last year has told and is telling on me and if I tell you that I broke down tonight … you will read between the lines, I have cried myself sick and as I write this my tears will get in between my words.[75]

With this wayward boy of a husband to care for, it was no joy to her to find early in 1895 at the age of 35 that she was pregnant. She had been told by doctors she was sterile and later said, 'I was always glad when they told me I could not have children, I desired none.'[76] She succumbed to self-pity, 'hysteria' and wishing she were dead.[77] Her husband, brother, sister and father were still reliant on her, and she was borrowing from her lawyer against future income from the Norwegian property left her by Higginson.[78]

Her son George was born on 24 November 1895. Her *Yellow Book* friend Ella D'Arcy wrote to her, 'I was so pleased to hear from John Lane that you have a boy, and are doing well. Please accept my warm congratulations. And I should be so delighted – I wonder if you are? – that it is a boy and not a girl. Boys, to my mind, are so much jollier and so much more interesting.'[79] She later reflected on the cost to her work of childbirth, saying it was 'a snag for women. Art is a jealous and arbitrary mistress and brooks no rival … I still believe that Marriage, Motherhood and Writing are each whole time jobs.'[80] All of these became part of her relationship with John Lane in negotiations over her third volume of stories, *Symphonies*. Lane had clearly told her to tone down the sex, for she protested in a letter of 10 November 1896, 'You did not say you wanted a "milk and water" book on entirely different lines to that which made the success of *Keynotes* when we made our autumn arrangements, and now on the eve of completing my book it comes as a backhander.' Having made a petulant stand, she now backed down and conceded that she would make the requested changes:

> If I had only my husband and self to consider, I would not bowdlerise my poor Symphonies, because I would fall back on bread and tea and waiting, as I have been forced to do before now when sticking to an ideal. As I have the unfortunate little child to consider, and not a shilling in my purse, I must make a sacrifice, however resentfully I do it.[81]

She was still entirely the keeper for Clairmonte, who exhausted the strategy of looking for a job in London and borrowed the money from one of Chavelita's sisters to go to South Africa, where he lived off another sister, Kit, and her husband. Chavelita moved again, in a repetition of her parents' treks to cheaper and cheaper lodgings. Clairmonte did not prosper in South Africa and the plan of his building up a business there and then sending for her and their child was not viable. She had anyway decided in her period of estrangement from him that she did not want to go to South Africa, and called him back. As she wrote of his character in *The Wheel of God*,

> she always felt when she was away from him as if a great wet sponge soaked in ether was lifted off her face, as if the very soul of her was stretching its arms in exultant relief as if freshly loosed from bondage. She was conscious of a sensation of actual physical weariness when with him. Her dear, curly-haired, warm-eyed boy . . .[82]

He took his time, refusing her direct order to return, but eventually came back at the end of 1896.

Symphonies fared poorly in the market, and she wrote to Lane blaming him, 'I am sorry your sales are bad. You must go back to your days of advertising and push, as it is for your own sake now you ought to sell *Symphonies*, I having no hand in the game.'[83] He had tired of her by now. She was complaining in summer 1897 that she could not get a reply from Lane; she was writing to Frederic Chapman, the Bodley Head business manager: 'I am really ill – nerve collapse – can't do anything, can't rest, reaction after the months of worry.'[84] She wrote again to Chapman on 20 August to complain that the *Daily Chronicle* announcement of her book as *Fantasies* when it should be *Fantasias*. 'I am still wretchedly ill – can't get up again, can't work, life presses a bit heavily.'[85] Her difficulties with writing, her finances and her family usually manifested themselves as illness, as a form of coping strategy when things got too much for her, though she had no underlying medical problem. Margaret Stetz remarks of her treatment with concoctions of arsenic, strychnine and morphine that 'her ability to survive such cures only testified to her basic strength and good health.'[86]

She was at work on this fourth collection of stories when her brother Jack died in July 1897. She had kept him financially and he was of no more use than the other men in her life, but she had loved him and took his death badly. Just as devastating was a new pregnancy: Clairmonte had impregnated their housemaid, Florence. Chavelita was able to rise above these challenges to her life and, against the usual Victorian moral code, she did not blame the girl for her loss of virtue, but gave Florence some money and the baby clothes George had grown out of. She then had to deal with her husband, and in February 1898 somehow found money to send him to Nova Scotia in Canada, where he had relatives, and thought herself well rid of him. Chavelita had hoped she would never see Clairmonte again, but two years after his departure she learned he was intending to return to Britain. She immediately filed for divorce, which was granted on 10 August 1900; she was informed of his death in May 1901, marking the end of another unhappy chapter in her life.

In professional terms she had not relished and embraced success, treating it as just her due, and was surprised when it slipped away from her, not realizing her failure to cultivate it was at least partly at fault. There was also the question of her material. Her sales figures had been dwindling before the Oscar Wilde debacle of spring 1895. A resistance to anything to do with the new woman or decadence did not help, but an important factor must be the techniques she had in part instigated and the subjects she had covered were no longer new – she was no longer ahead of the game. She had also been told bluntly, 'There is no market for short stories.'[87] More than half the *Keynotes* series had been short stories, yet just five years later the vogue was gone.

After *Fantasias* she parted company with Lane, who had declined to publish her translation of Hamsun's *Hunger* – and had irritated her by keeping it for a year before the rejection. Leonard Smithers eventually published it, confirming her position in the sphere of the morally questionable as he was 'publisher to the decadents', prepared to publish work by Wilde, Beardsley and Dowson even after 1895.[88]

The Bodley Head advertised her next book as in preparation but they did not publish it. Egerton went with Grant Richards, a young publisher whom she thought was more likely to take a chance with racy material. Richards, a nephew of Grant Allen, after whom he was named, was well known to the *Yellow Book* crowd and was a particular friend of Richard Le Gallienne. She therefore wrote to him in August 1897 about the book she was working on: 'scenes of working woman's life in one part and many studies of women in various callings'.[89] Recognizing that short stories were no longer to the taste of the public or publishers, she had looked to what material she had and begun on her longest work, *The Wheel of God*, a 322-page bildungsroman about the life of a character known as Mary. The manuscript was finished by winter 1897; Richards published it in May 1898 at six shillings.

The book is in three sections, showing Mary in her childhood, as a young woman and a mature woman. It closely follows the contours of Chavelita's own life: Mary endures a Dickensian childhood in section one, then travels to New York and works in a variety of jobs in section two. Finally, at the age of 28 at the beginning of the third section, she runs off with a man she does not love but who offers her adventure. He dies as had Higginson, and she marries 'Cess', a character like Clairmonte who proceeds to spend his way through her money. The novel diverges from life (as it had been up to that date, at any rate) when 'Cess' dies in an accident, and Mary does not have a child, as Chavelita did. Now free, the last image is of a vision she has of 'myriads of women' calling to her: 'And her heart seemed to grow hot within her, and to burn out the last atom of self; and she hastened down the slope with eager steps to where the women were calling in the gloom.'[90]

The Wheel of God is among the earliest examples of novels in which a woman character interacts with the world, not necessarily in relation to men. Great women novelists had written *Jane Eyre*, *Wuthering Heights* and *Middlemarch*, but the essential plots had been marriage-based and the motivating characters men. *The Wheel of God*, fellow *Yellow Book* writers Ella Hepworth Dixon's *The Story of a Modern Woman* (1894) and Netta Syrett's *The Victorians* (1915) foregrounded women's education, work and personal development, with male encounters as one of a series of events, not the culmination of life's journey.

A long review in the *Morning Post* remarked that there is 'much that is well observed and admirably expressed' in the book, but the reviewer was perplexed by what he saw as the absence of the features of a nineteenth-century novel (something that later critics would see as evidence of its modernity). He wrote that there is a heroine,

> and so far the book follows the ordinary course. Of a plot or hero, however, not a sight is to be seen. The absence of the hero may be explained by the alleged fact . . . that there are no men now alive who are fit for the best women to associate with on such terms as a heroine would desire. The absence of plot is less easily explained, and is all the more inconvenient on account of the want of definite chronological indications throughout the book.[91]

The reviewer therefore conflates the literary originality of the text with the social originality of women going their own way.

Grant Richards, musing over the records of his career in publishing, remarked, 'On George Egerton's *The Wheel of God* I made sixty pounds.'[92] The book had not sold well, however, and Grant Richards asked for £1 14s of his advance back.[93] The uneven distribution of wealth and power in publishing finally took their toll on Chavelita. She struggled desperately with money issues and finally took the step that should have always been obvious: writing hack work in order to pay the rent and put food on the table for her and her son.

As she put it in a letter to Bram Stoker, 'Have been forced to go in to journalism and to chase away all the little fanciful moths that come fluttering out of the darkness and are sometimes pretty enough to pin on paper.'[94] She wrote anonymously for magazines such as *Vanity Fair* but was usually shy of using her own name, which would have been of bankable benefit, except for an article she wrote for *Outlook* on the Norwegian writer and social reformer Arne Garborg. She was now doing the celebrity author interviews she had so disdained when she was the subject of them. She wrote to Stoker, 'I am doing a series of small portraits of Irish men and women of letters in London, with a review of their books embodied in the sketch. May I ask you to be kind enough to allow me to meet you for a short interview as a representative Irishman?'[95]

In 1899, free of the financial burdens of her husband and brother, and earning something from her own pen, Chavelita eventually felt financially secure enough to travel. As the century ended, she went back to Norway, where she still had property, to seek renewal.

4

Yellow Book Types

'I think no literary youth of any epoch ever passed through a more entrancing nursery than the one whose door Henry Harland and John Lane threw open when the younger generation of the nineties came knocking,' wrote Evelyn Sharp on later reflection.[1]

She was not alone in her enthusiasm; the novelist William Locke remembered, 'For years the Saturday evenings in the Harlands' flat in the Cromwell Road were symposia in the most delightful sense of the word. Nobody dressed unless they wanted to, or had to for some previous function. The simplest material entertainment was provided; just drinks, sandwiches and tobacco.' Harland himself was clearly the centre of attention. 'Who thought of wanting more from a host of such gentle courtesy and delightfully vehement polemics?' continued Locke:

> I see him now, standing in the middle of the room, his shoulders and arms working in aid of his denunciation of something abominable in the world of Art, which he held sacred. And few bothered to disagree with him, for all loved him, and loved to hear him talk. When he made a joke, which was often – for he had a flashing, fanciful wit – he was childishly eager for appreciation. Anybody else's quip he would seize and go round and retail generously to the company.[2]

Another attender writes of 'Harland's wild rushes from one guest to another, talking to each rapidly, huskily, and intermittently drinking gallons of milk.'[3] Ella D'Arcy felt Aline and Harland were 'both the most cordial of hosts, praising good work royally, and he knowing precisely how to put each guest on the best possible terms with himself... Harland was the most

Henry Harland in his London home, from *Booklovers Magazine* (March 1904).

brilliant, witty and amusing of talkers. The sweetest of companions. Never were there such evenings.'[4]

Netta Syrett described 'the gay pink drawing room with its Persian carpets, its pictures and old furniture' at 144 Cromwell Road, West London.[5] On a Saturday night a few people would have dined with Aline and Henry Harland, such as Mabel and Percy Dearmer, Aubrey Beardsley and Stanley Makower. The room began to fill up by nine o'clock when Aline and Henry would receive personalities of the 1890s, from struggling poets and critics like Arthur Symons to established authors such as Edmund Gosse, Henry

James and George Moore. Ella D'Arcy remarked, 'Any young writer showing artistic promise was sure of his help, for he was a fanatic for Art with an immense A.'[6]

Among the women, Ella D'Arcy, Netta Syrett and Evelyn Sharp were regulars; it was probably here that they first met and became friends. Charlotte Mew attended over the summer of 1894 and became friends with these three (and was to fall hopelessly in love with Ella D'Arcy).[7] These evenings were central to the success of the *Yellow Book* as a forum for women's creative work, since women could take part in them on an equal footing as they could not in gentlemen's clubs and public houses. Sharp mentions other women who were present at least on some occasions: Mabel Dearmer, Olive Custance, Dollie Radford, Ménie Muriel Dowie and Rosamund Marriott Watson.[8] Ella D'Arcy additionally mentions Ethel Colburne Mayne (whom she was to treat with cruelty), Victoria Cross (Vivian Cory) and Charlotte Mew. William Locke recorded Violet Hunt and Mabel Beardsley, 'a sweet symphony of a woman', as being there.[9] Mabel Kitcat (who continued to write under the name Mrs Murray Hickson) also said she was a regular attender, which was confirmed by Netta Syrett.[10]

Hubert Crackanthorpe is noted as one of the male attenders and, as he and his wife Leila Macdonald were recorded to have been at the Harland apartment at other times, it is reasonable to consider she would have been present at the Harlands' 'at homes'. Frederick Rolfe wrote of 'a very handsome, large young woman, bright-haired, azure-eyed', which certainly describes Leila Macdonald.[11] Ethel Colburne Mayne mentions 'the unforgettable' younger brother of Hubert, Dayrell Crackanthorpe, as often being with them. He was a civil servant but very welcome among the artists: Mayne describes Crackanthorpe's and Harland's 'contagiously – not to say outrageously – high spirits' when he passed his civil service exams in 1896.[12] He was to play a key part in the disaster of Leila Macdonald's life.

Sissie Welch is a rarely mentioned *Yellow Book* figure, though she was a frequent presence and was pictured in volume v in April 1895. She had been, since January 1893, the wife of James Welch, an actor and best friend of her brother Richard Le Gallienne. Evelyn Sharp mocked their boyish camaraderie: 'Richard Le Gallienne, living on the last shilling he had borrowed from James Welch, the actor (unless at the moment Jim happened to be living on the last shilling he had borrowed from Dick).'[13]

In later years Syrett directed an enquirer about the *Yellow Book* to her description of one of her characters' entrance into the world of 'The Puce Quarterly' in *The Victorians* so, though fiction, it can be taken as drawing directly on her own experience as a young woman. She writes that as soon as she met them,

> she could even now hold her own in conversation, and in her turn amuse them. The new atmosphere in which she found herself pleased, excited her, and stirred her curiosity. It was as though she had exchanged flat beer in pewter mugs, for champagne served in sparkling, slender glasses, and that there was something besides the foam and froth on the surface of the goblets she was dimly aware. Beneath the affectations, the rather studied levity, and the straining after effect evinced by these people, she realised a keenness, an enthusiasm, a real love for the art whose varied aspects they glibly discussed in terms often to her unintelligible.[14]

So many of her books are about girls who do not fit in that it is reasonable to assume Syrett knew something of that feeling; with the *Yellow Book* crowd, she fitted in. As one of her characters reflects, she found her way 'into that inner circle whose eroticism was well known, acknowledged, flaunted even'.[15]

Evelyn Sharp also noted: 'The personal and often unconventional relationships of acquaintances were discussed sometimes with a frankness that at first embarrassed a country-bred person like myself'.[16] She favoured the company of Kenneth Grahame, another frequent attender, of whom she said, 'He answered my idea of a *man* and I suppose half consciously (I was young for my age and much of what I heard and saw at the Harlands was uncomprehended) I was comparing him to the more or less effeminate young men I met there.' She found 'affectations which so puzzled me in other men of the set. I remember sometimes enjoying these evenings and sometimes not at all. Everything depended on the moods of the host and hostess, both of whom were erratic and, when bored, made little effort to disguise their feelings.'[17]

Netta Syrett was not embarrassed by the ambience, but later felt a need to comment on the presence of 'those young gentlemen who revelled in a reputation for exotic tastes and perverted instincts'.[18] Occasionally, Netta would take her sister Nell to these gatherings. The art student, though she was seventeen, looked younger and Harland would pretend he was afraid to speak to anyone so young and used Netta as an interpreter: 'Ask her why they take babies at the Slade?' 'Tell her she has very pretty hair.'[19]

Doubtless reflecting the author's own feelings, one of Syrett's heroines felt like a daisy that has strayed into 'a conservatory full of orchids', but

Syrett overstates the wallflower motif as it relates to her own life.[20] She was fortunate enough to have Grant Allen as a relative and Mabel Beardsley as a work colleague, which gave her access to creative people, but, having had the access, she then had to be interesting enough for them to continue to want to see her.

Evelyn Sharp remembered how Harland used to call her 'Darling of my heart! Child of my editing.'[21] She said the conversation was largely about their own work or that of French authors: 'Most of the time we talked, about ourselves and those few outsiders, generally French, who were our masters in the short story the *Yellow Book* tried so hard to graft on to the literature of this country.'[22] Sharp remembered the entertainment, as when Aline Harland might sing such arrangements as Stanley Makower's setting of the French lyric 'Gardez vous d'être sévère' – 'Don't be too harsh' (when someone speaks to you of love), which Sharp thought 'peculiarly appropriate to her audience' – or when 'we all adjourned to the kitchen to see a poet and a painter settle a dispute as to the right way to make an omelette.'[23]

The 'at homes' preceded the launch of the *Yellow Book* but became all the more lively after the periodical was in circulation. Amid his recollection of 'talk. Brilliant talk', William Locke recollected that Harland's parties attracted 'many strange oddments, jetsam on the shores of literary London, interesting and exciting; among them one Baron Corvo [Frederick Rolfe], author of "Stories that Toto Told Me" whose life, the outlines of which I know, would make a grotesque romance'.[24] In his novel *Nicholas Crabbe* Rolfe presented the *Yellow Book* in thin disguise as the *Blue Volume* with Sidney Thorah as its editor (taking words from Harland's novel *The Yoke of the Thorah* and his pseudonym Sidney Luska). He describes one of the Harlands' evenings with D'Arcy 'the sub-editor', described as 'an intellectual, mouse-mannered piece of sex, inhabiting a neighbouring flat'. 'What was the relation between him [Harland] and the mouse-mannered sub-editor?' he asks.[25] This shows Rolfe's poor judgement where women were concerned, for D'Arcy was more cat than mouse (Rolfe was a better judge of boys). It may have been that D'Arcy, who was markedly territorial, simply declined to engage with him, which gave him a false impression of timidity. D'Arcy got her own back by recounting that he left fleas on the armchair. This is perfectly possible, though it is as well to remember that D'Arcy used her longevity and access to later chroniclers of the *Yellow Book*, notably Katherine Lyon Mix, to 'set the record straight' in her favour. It may have been a calculated insult from both of these '*Yellow Book* celebrities': she called him flea-ridden, knowing he was proud, and he called her mild-mannered,

Aline Harland, *c.* 1906, when she had taken to calling herself by the assumed title of Lady Harland.

knowing she was caustic. H. G. Wells records that Rolfe was among the people present at Edith Nesbit and Hubert Bland's parties at Well Hall, Eltham, which would not have been the case if he were hosting fleas.[26] He was also invited to parties more than once at Rev. Percy and Mabel Dearmer's home. He described the Dearmers at the Harlands' as 'a curate, obese, olive-skinned, curatical, with a dazzling soft, red-haired wife, who answered to the name of Helen of Troy' (which was indeed what Harland called Mabel Dearmer). Rolfe may be describing George Egerton when he speaks of 'a rather pretty worn Irish woman, excruciatingly and incessantly witty'. Evelyn Sharp is described as 'a thin, wide-mouthed suffragist of thirty, coy and silent, whose huge black eyes yearned for the secretary of a bank': this was Kenneth Grahame, with whom Sharp did, indeed, spend time, as mentioned in her recollections, and who worked at the Bank of England.[27] Rolfe gives a sympathetic picture of Aline Harland trying to put her awkward guest at ease but 'his desperate fear of women restrained him' from responding warmly.[28]

Recollections give a picture of harmonious charm but it could be unpleasant when Aline and Henry had fallen out. Syrett wrote:

The Harlands were more like spoilt children who can be charming when they are good, than any grown-up people I have ever met before or since . . . It never seemed to occur to them to disguise the mood of the moment, however uncomfortable the result to their guests, and really devoted to one another, they bickered in public with as little concern as a couple of quarrelsome children.[29]

She recollected, 'When he was in a "good mood" I enjoyed nonsensical talk with Mr Harland, who could be delightful, but was sometimes "difficult". He struck me as being a terribly moody man. Sometimes in the wildest spirits and full of wit and almost schoolboy nonsense and at others, gloomy and irritable.'[30]

Contemporary records show a darker side to these evenings. D'Arcy wrote to John Lane after one night, scolding him:

I wish you had shown a little more warmth in consenting to see me home last night. Though I was dying with sleep, the Harlands kept me until a quarter to one, and then, of course, I was spoken to on the way back. It's most unpleasant, because when you're walking about alone at that hour, you almost feel people have a right, a reason anyhow, for speaking to you.[31]

D'Arcy was not being hysterical, as a woman out at night on her own was assumed to be a prostitute and a man might ask her terms. Netta Syrett wrote of a time, returning from a different house but also in West London, near the Kings Road, when she was taken to be a working girl by a policeman who 'gave me the glad eye and tenderly observed, "Ullo Ducky! Out alone? Is that right?"' Rather than feeling this was an infringement on her right to walk as she chose, she reflected, 'I didn't blame him. I had no business to be walking at midnight in a gaily-flowered frock and a lace hat as big as a cart-wheel!'[32] It was another one of the impediments a woman in literary life faced, which she must learn to rise above or take lightly.

There may be more to D'Arcy's complaint about Lane's reluctance to take her home, particularly as the distance was short (only half a mile, down the Cromwell Road with a right turn down Earl's Court Road and left to Edwardes Square). Her letters to him show much greater enthusiasm for a relationship on her side than is apparent on his. The very familiar tone she takes with him implies they already had a relationship of some kind; it may have been that Lane did not want to see her home to rekindle it.

Frederick Rolfe described John Lane, with whom he had one of his innumerable editorial disputes, as 'a carroty dwarf, with a magenta face and pendulous lips and a vermilion necktie'.[33] A more sympathetic picture of 'Little Johnnie Lane' describes him as having parted, sandy hair and a pointed beard.[34] Lane, one of the key figures in the lives of literary women in the *Yellow Book* set, probably enjoyed his literary cenacle all the more because of his experience of a very different kind of life. He was born in Devon in 1854 and went as a teenager to London to work as a clerk in the Railway Clearing House at Euston Station from 1868 until 1892. That year he set up shop at 6B Vigo Street with his partner, bookseller Elkin Mathews, announcing that they were 'Publishers and Vendors of Choice and Rare Editions in Belles Lettres'.[35] *Belles lettres* implies art, not run-of-the-mill publishing, and they made self-conscious efforts to cultivate an arty image using such ruses as buying end rolls (which were therefore cheap) of very fine quality paper on which they would print short runs of beautifully designed books, thus manipulating the market by constructing a scarcity value.

The shop displayed polished mahogany bookcases, set up with the private book collections of Lane and his partner. Mathews had nothing to do with the *Yellow Book* and the men parted company in October 1894, 'heartily glad to be rid of one another' and dissolving the partnership.[36] Lewis May explained, 'Lane was full of energy; Lane had ambitions; Lane intended to "arrive" and arrive he did. But Mathews could not stay the course.'[37] A less partisan view is that Lane was increasingly going his own way, and the final, insulting demonstration of this was Lane's failure to invite Mathews to the *Yellow Book* launch party where, as Mathews complained, Lane 'with the boldest affrontery said that he deeply regretted the unavoidable absence of his partner', when in fact he was free and would gladly have attended.[38]

In January 1894 Lane had taken a place at G1 in the Albany, the fashionable bachelor apartment block between Regent Street and Piccadilly that backed on to Vigo Street. There were posts across Vigo Street to debar hansom cabs and carriages from going past the entrance of the Albany, so exclusive was the address.[39] By agreement, when the partners split, Lane kept the Bodley Head sign that had stood over the shop at 6B Vigo Street, while Mathews kept the shop. Lane leased offices opposite but Mathews did not realize that his former partner had obtained permission from the Albany authorities to change one of the windows from what had been his dining room, looking out upon Vigo Street, into a doorway. Lane's rival establishment, opposite that of Mathews, was then, in summer 1894, crowned with the Bodley Head sign. Mathews soon moved to larger premises, and

Lane's palace was complete with his shop, publishing house and home where he could entertain all in one place. The office assistant J. Lewis May said Lane's kingdom was bounded on the east by the Café Royal and on the west by the Hogarth Club.

Lane's passions were for poetry, beautifully crafted books and women, which last gave him the soubriquet 'Petticoat Lane'. Lewis May commented, 'Lane was unquestionably fond of women's society . . . and women liked him.'[40] He was also keen to make a profit from a contemporary trend and the New Woman was one such. There was another reason why women and the more daring male writers featured so much in the *Yellow Book*: they were cheap. The Bodley Head had been set up with the profits from Elkin Mathews's antiquarian bookshop and the small investments John Lane had been able to attract. Harland gave Lane an itemized account of costs for each individual author: payment for established prose writers was at the magazine rate of three guineas (three pounds three shillings) per thousand words; lesser-known writers had to be satisfied with less than a guinea per thousand.[41] The journal simply did not have the money to attract big literary names. Instead, as Margaret Stetz observes, 'it deliberately went after unknowns and

John Lane in the 1890s.

rebels, authors who could not count on any publisher to be interested in their work or who had manuscripts that had already been rejected on the grounds of risqué or unpopular subject matter and who, therefore, were unlikely to argue over financial terms.'[42] This made him a haven for New Woman fiction, stories of contemporary realism and decadent poetry.

Grant Richards described Lane's methods:

> To some of the least sophisticated of his ladies he would endear himself by taking them round the corner from Vigo Street and giving them lunch at a restaurant a few doors down Sackville Street, and they would come away and praise him and his lunch and, musing on the excellence of his champagne, would say they had paid little attention to the details of the agreements they had signed.

Richards, a publisher himself and in a position to know, felt (probably as did the young women) that the opportunity of publication was more important than the financial reward. 'Lane gave these young people chances for which they would otherwise have searched in vain; nor did he impose unjust terms considering the risks he was taking in a market that he had himself so largely created.' The 'champagne', however, was Asti Spumante; he had a trick of keeping the bottle turned so that his guest could not read the label.[43]

The would-be author would enter Lane's beautiful room in Vigo Street 'with its leaded panes and its disordered profusion of books and prints and pictures encumbering the tables and chairs and overflowing on to the floor'.[44] There were so many pictures it was said to resemble an art gallery. One of the paintings, by Gertrude Hammond, was called the *Yellow Book*, in which a young man on a sofa reads from a copy of the *Yellow Book* to a stylish woman who looks at it sidelong with interest while at the same time attempting to stand aside from it, as if it is immodest yet compellingly attractive, titillating and not quite decent. The picture appeared in the *Yellow Book* volume vi; John Lane bought the original.

Thus Lane blossomed in his role as an advanced publisher, enjoying the celebrity, the notoriety, the *Yellow Book* gave him – and the female attention. This persona was celebrated by J. M. Bulloch, whose publication of mocking verses about Lane in the *Sketch* illustrated weekly indicates a wide knowledge among the reading public of the extent to which Lane was meeting women writers, and quite how noteworthy this was.

Yellow Book by Gertrude Hammond, in *Yellow Book*, vol. VI (July 1895).

And now the Maiden Muse has fled
For shelter to the Bodley Head,
And there, with Mr Lane's *elite*
Our Sappho sings in Vigo Street

They sing, the modern Muses Nine,
On hand-made paper, gorgeous print,
With Aubrey Beardsley's weird design
Of satyrs, leering-eyed and squint;
Nor pipe they for a vulgar set –
Their price, you know, is always net.
The hearts of women throb and beat
For Mr Lane in Vigo Street.[45]

It was clearly a matter of comment that a publisher should have so many women authors on his list. The widening of gender barriers necessitated the creation of new spaces, because if women were to be major contributors to a journal, there had to be places in which they could meet. Lane could not take women to his club, but he could certainly entertain them at tea parties at his home, just as women entertained each other. Lane's tea parties became famous, as Lewis May said: 'his rooms at G1 Albany were thronged with literary and artistic notabilities, among whom the little man with the trim pointed beard and smiling face would move about saying a tactful word to everyone.'[46] Ella D'Arcy, with a suggestion of jealousy, mocked Lane with, 'I expect you are having a good old time, with tea parties every day, and Evelyn Sharp, and Netta Syrett, and the weirdly beautiful V.C. [Vivian Cory, who wrote as Victoria Cross] for ever popping in upon you? What it is to be a popular publisher!'[47]

In an indication of the public knowledge of a new phenomenon, the *Westminster Gazette* mocked this emergence of women into professional places:

There's a room in Number G1
Where this publisher can see one;
Femininity invades it
Scent of many flowers pervades it:
Here are violets – and a sonnet
(Writer wears a witching bonnet);
Here's a novel and a lily

(One is pure – the other silly);
Here's a drawing wrapped in roses
(Its creator yonder poses):
'Tis a matter most astounding –
All these geniuses abounding;
Over tea and bread and butter
Many compliments they utter.[48]

The suggestion is that feminine coquetry rather than literary talent has brought them to this place. To be fair to the professional standards of those involved, the primary quality required was talent, and submissions were usually sent by post, so personal charm was limited to what could be conveyed on paper. Poet Olive Custance was twenty in February 1894 and had a body of work she had written as a teenager. A young heiress living on the family estate in Norfolk, she was eager for the experiences of life and love. She had sent some verses for publication after the emergence of the *Yellow Book* and was overjoyed to have them accepted, and to have an invitation to meet Lane, which she did in the company of 'Tanie' (presumably Constance) Davidson. Tanie was officially her maid, but they became friends and Tanie served as her chaperone. Olive wrote in her diary:

> I shall never forget our quiet 'tea' at G1 The Albany, our first meeting with John Lane and Richard Le Gallienne . . . We were both very shy, Tanie and I, as we stood in John Lane's little sitting room waiting for him to come in . . . I was in pale pink, with a large black [indistinct] hat trimmed with tulle and carnations; and I carried a sheaf of white summer lilies on my arm . . . John Lane was shy too, I think, when he shook hands . . .[49]

The ellipses are Custance's own and do not indicate omissions; she wrote using them, presumably to replicate her own breathless delivery.

She used to travel to London with her father from Norfolk to their town house in Curzon Street. The location of Lane's office in the West End was significant – it was a respectable area, with one side of the Albany bordered by the vast exclusive shopping aisle of the Burlington Arcade with its liveried doormen, and with the shops of Bond Street, Piccadilly and Savile Row nearby. This was not just a place where a woman of Custance's class *could* be, it was a place where she was *expected* to be.

Olive Custance
in the 1890s.

Custance's verse was first published in the third volume in October 1894. Later that year Custance wrote in her diary after a sojourn in the capital:

> I had tea at 'Johnnies' Ye Bodley Head several times and met there some interesting people such as Sir Frederick Leighton, Barry Pain, John Davidson (who was most kind about my poem in the *Yellow Book* which he said he much admired), Mrs Pennell and Walter Sickert. I liked Walter Sickert very much – he looks clever and that is so nice. I am going to have another poem – 'The Waking of Spring' in the next *Yellow Book* [January 1895]. I did not see Dick [Le Gallienne] in London. He was too busy to come to tea one day when I went to 'Ye Bodley Head', he is doing 'great things' they say – I am very glad.[50]

Lane's tea parties were a place where Custance could meet other poets in a way in which she simply could not attend, for example, the Rhymers' Club, which met in an upstairs room of the Cheshire Cheese public house, just off Fleet Street.

The personal contact that such literary men enjoyed was made up for in Custance's case by letter-writing. She began a passionate correspondence with Harland, who took up his pen to respond enthusiastically:

> I read yours three times through, every word and line three times, before I even noticed that there were other letters . . . the beautiful poet-girl who signs herself my little friend! My little friend – with the wonderful burning soul, the deep burning heart, the great yearning eyes looking at the Norfolk landscape, away, away, towards the horizon where she divines the world, looking, and wondering, and longing. Oh, sometimes it seems her heart must break with that desperate unsatisfied longing – as if she could not endure such hunger and more. I know, I know, I know how she hungers, how she suffers.[51]

She wrote in her diary, 'Henry Harland, the clever editor of the *Yellow Book* wrote me a most charming letter the other day – and only because I sent "A Mood" – collected direct to him and told him how much I liked some of his work.' Harland was not the only recipient of her missives; she wrote, 'I had sent John Gray some of my poems, and the new year brought a beautiful letter from him.'[52] It is apparent that her first contact with the *Yellow Book* was in writing to the Bodley Head (doubtless trying to get her poems published in a volume, which Lane did in 1897) and Lane responded. Harland and Lane were often at odds over the writers to feature in the *Yellow Book*. To Lane the periodical should be a showcase for writers on his list, while Harland was committed to printing what he saw as the best in contemporary literature; these were not necessarily identical.

Custance must have sent a picture of herself to Lane as Harland writes, 'I have seen a picture of Miss Custance, at the Bodley Head. I do devoutly wish she would send me a duplicate of it.' She promises to send a picture of her room, at which he responds, 'Why can't I come and take tea there with you and Tanie?' In a further letter she has obviously shared information about her forays into adult sophistication as he writes, 'Oh, to think of you and "Tanie" smoking cigarettes together, after luncheon!' He goes on to write about growing up as a child in Russian Poland near Norevicz – which is a complete fiction.[53] When he receives the picture he is enraptured:

I think it is the portrait of the loveliest girl, the most interesting-looking, the most poetic-looking, the most appealing that I have ever seen … I never saw such a lovely mouth, such lovely hair, such lovely hands, such lovely eyes – dreamy, mysterious eyes. Oh, what wouldn't I give to be looking into the real eyes.[54]

Custance was to become the poet who featured most frequently in the *Yellow Book*, with eight contributions over the thirteen volumes, so her charming of the men in charge of it did her career no harm. She failed to melt Beardsley's heart, however, in 1897 when he was designing a book-plate for her. He was writing of 'Silly little O' and lamenting he had received 'Eleven pages from Olive this morning plus two pages of verse. Ye gods!'[55] Beardsley's waspish remarks should not be taken to mean he did not respond to Olive: his comment in March 1897 that 'I have written at great length to Mdlle Custance' is presumably sarcastic – he had written the briefest of letters.[56] Two days later, however, there was 'a huge letter this morning from Olive Custance'.[57]

Custance's first appearance was with the poem 'Twilight', which was a hymn to the 'Spirit of Twilight'. It was one of four poems by women in volume III: the others were a French translation by Ellen M. Clerke, who as well as a translator was an astronomer and a novelist, and verses by Nora Hopper and Annie Macdonell. Macdonell was the London correspondent for the New York *Bookman* and had recently finished a book on Thomas Hardy.

This third volume started with an unequivocal piece of women's writing as it was clearly labelled as being written by 'A Woman' and was on the feminist topic 'Women – Wives or Mothers?' It was, of course, by a man: the 64-year-old journalist and former editor of the *Queen* magazine Frederick Greenwood. The gender misappropriation was partly from devilment, partly to give authenticity from one who knew his readership. Greenwood had not only written about women novelists, he had *been* a woman novelist; it was he who finished Mrs Gaskell's book *Wives and Daughters* when she died with the final chapters unwritten in 1865, while it was being published in serial form in the *Cornhill Magazine*, of which he was editor.

Greenwood's essay in the *Yellow Book* volume III addressed 'the leaping, bounding new womanhood', but the phenomenon was presented as a social problem because of 'the too rapid growth of the female population … the redundant female birth-rate which threatens more revolution than all the forces of the Anarchists in active combination'.[58] The jocular portent

Olive Custance's bookplate by Aubrey Beardsley, 1897.

referred to a genuine social phenomenon of the preponderance of women over men in the UK, disclosed in the 1891 census for England and Wales as in the proportion of 1,064 females to 1,000 males.[59]

Ella D'Arcy, Leila Macdonald and Nora Hopper also contributed to this volume. Beardsley's drawings were as before primarily female in subject-matter, showing an old woman escorted by men at a ball, women opera-goers and a woman at her toilette. Other pictures were Walter Sickert's of a female music hall performer, and 'Charley's Aunt', a portrait of the cross-dressing character in Brandon Thomas's West End farce of 1892. Philip Wilson Steer contributed two pictures of his young women models. Other portraits of women meant that of fifteen pictures, ten were of women, giving the volume a decidedly feminine flavour, though there were no women illustrators.

The month previous to the 16 April 1894 launch party for the *Yellow Book* the cabinet had met at 10 Downing Street and received the resignation of the stern prime minister Gladstone, a man whose earnestness, rigidity and self-righteousness epitomized the most sanctimonious aspects of Victorianism. In his place came Rosebery, effortlessly superior, flippant, a passionate bibliophile who was utterly distrusted by the conservative establishment as an effete intellectual – and worse, in their eyes. Lord Queensberry had already pursued him with a horsewhip before he had turned his attention to Oscar Wilde. Queensberry condemned the playwright as 'a damned cur and coward of the Rosebery type'.[60] In disgust at the hypocrisy of the Oscar Wilde case, George Egerton listed the prime minister among other prominent society men who could genuinely have formed a jury of the playwright's peers.[61] Rosebery's urbane pose and relationships with handsome young men supposedly gave justification to the popular conception that the ruling class was irredeemably decadent. Scandals touching them involved Lord Henry Somerset and telegraph messenger boys, the suggestion of Prince Albert in a brothel and any number of remarks about the Prince of Wales's dissolute lifestyle. The *Yellow Book* gave little quarter to politics (high art was above such things), but the journal emerged into a changing political climate where the pre-eminence of the British Empire was to be challenged before the century was out, and any suggestion of decadence was suspect.

Volume III of the *Yellow Book* included John Davidson's 'Ballad of a Nun', which stimulated outrage and delight. Netta Syrett was at Harland's apartment when the submission arrived in the post:

> Mr Harland was in a particularly capricious mood and he read the
> poem aloud with mocking comments though I was then young

Cover of the
Yellow Book, vol. II
(July 1894).

Cover of the
Yellow Book, vol. III
(October 1894).

enough to regard all literary people with awe, and the *Yellow Book* people in particular as the last word in wisdom and culture. I plucked up courage enough to say I liked the poem and was instantly 'jumped upon' by Mr Harland, who continued to jeer at it with increased vehemence.[62]

Syrett was clearly a good and swift critic. Arthur Waugh commented that Harland did not have taste, but he surrounded himself with people who did, who gave him good advice; Syrett was obviously one of them.[63] Harland must have relented as the poem was published in October 1894. It told the story of a nun who leaves the convent to become a prostitute. It therefore focused on two specific areas of women's activity, religious devotion and sex work, and was one of those pieces for which the *Yellow Book* was singled out as immoral and mocked by satirists. Owen Seaman wrote a parody for *The World* called 'A Ballad of a Bun':

'I am in Eve's predicament,
I sha'n't be happy till I've sinned;

Away!' She lightly rose, and sent
Her scruples sailing down the wind . . .

A Decadent was dribbling by,
'Lady' he said 'you seem undone;
You need a panacea; try
This sample of the Bodley Bun.'[64]

In the eyes of their critics, the Decadent and the New Woman meet over this confection of the Bodley Head. Decadence was 'either hurled as a reproach or hurled back as defiance', said Arthur Symons, who lived through the whole period and helped to define English decadence.[65] His book *The Decadent Movement in Literature*, advertised as such, was eventually published as *The Symbolist Movement in Literature* because by the time of its publication, in 1899, decadence was no longer an acceptable subject to place before the public. 'Decadence' had such negative connotations that Evelyn Sharp later felt it necessary to defend her contemporaries, saying she wondered if there was anywhere in the world 'a literary artistic circle so full of vitality and promise as the one, absurdly labelled decadent'.[66]

Critics saw dangers in the foreign import of decadence: Hugh Stutfield asserted, 'Decadentism is an exotic growth unsuited to British soil, and it may be hoped that it will never take permanent root here. Still, the popularity of debased and morbid literature, especially among women, is not an agreeable or healthy feature.'[67] Hubert Crackanthorpe in the *Yellow Book* volume II mocked the cry 'Decadence, decadence: you are all decadent nowadays.'[68] However, his mother, Blanche, saw the seeds of dissolution when she secretly wrote to Harland:

> one thing I am certain of is this: that if the *YB* is to prosper – to have the future which we all hope for it – true wisdom on the part of its owner lies in avoiding – for some time to come, any contributors who, men, or women, who belong markedly to the avowedly decadent school . . . this letter is for no one else please.[69]

Thus the patrician tones of the author of 'The Revolt of the Daughters', an 1894 paper that attempted to reconcile middle-class mothers' versions of what a daughter should be with the aspirations of modern young women.[70]

Decadence is easy to recognize but surprisingly hard to define. Few men referred to themselves as decadents but there were some for whom the title was certainly appropriate, such as Oscar Wilde, Ernest Dowson, Richard Le Gallienne, Arthur Symons, Lord Alfred Douglas and John Davidson. Their common characteristics as an artistic movement were an acute awareness of living at the end of the century at the height of the British Empire, when the hard work of previous generations had produced luxury that was now being enjoyed, and a dedication to art and artificiality but also to realism in writing, often with influences from French prose writers. They looked to classical civilization for the eternal truths of art, which must be judged by its own standards, not any external values. Some were actively homosexual, but all were tolerant of sexual difference and foibles of personal behaviour, without concerns for conventional morality. They were very different individually. Some such as John Gray were dandies, others like Ernest Dowson were wretched; Arthur Symons was a bon viveur, Lionel Johnson was a reclusive alcoholic. The pose of cultural superiority was a common theme, as was the importance of art in life, with a frequent blurring of distinctions between one and the other.

Most women writers for the *Yellow Book* would nod towards the principle of art for art's sake (and not that of conventional morality), but women had come from a separate sphere to enter the public realm of literature; they had less reference to the classical world with its decadent precedents. Classical civilization had less to offer women, who tended to look to the future, not the past, for a vision of a better world. The 'Michael Fields', with their devotional poems to Sappho of Lesbos in *Long Ago* of 1889, are an exception in this regard.

Despite this, women engaged with decadent themes in sensual, transgressive lyrics like those of Olive Custance and Rosamund Marriott Watson; in the aesthetic revelry over art by Vernon Lee; in futility and ennui in the work of Ella Hepworth Dixon and Ethel Colburn Mayne, and realism in the work of Ella D'Arcy and George Egerton. Volume IV, for example, had the poem 'Vespertilia' by Graham R. Tomson [Rosamund Marriott Watson], a work of supernatural love where a young man meets a woman, perhaps a vampire, while out in the country, and refuses her offer of love. Sexual licence was more difficult for women than men, but once they had broken the bonds of propriety, women such as 'Graham R. Tomson' lived life much as they pleased. She was born Rosamund Ball in Hackney, London, on 6 October 1860. Family opposition prevented her early aspiration to attend art school, but she was to develop in literature and was to complete six sensual volumes of poetry. Her erotically charged work was full of decadent images of love and death; her themes were frequently 'death, disillusionment and the failure of love'.[71] Her life was 'modern' in her numerous marriages and affairs. After an early marriage to a wealthy man, George Armytage, from whom she was separated in 1885, she wrote verses criticizing marriage. She paired up with a painter, Arthur Graham Thomson, in 1886. In 1894 she became the lover of H. B. Marriott Watson, a writer from the circle of W. E. Henley; they never married, but she adopted his surname. Edmund Clarence Stedman included her work in his *Victorian Anthology* in 1895, in which year he wrote in a letter, 'The Armytage-Tomson-Watson sequence is interesting. Well, a woman who can write such ballads has a right to be her own mistress – to touch Life, one might say, at as many points as she cares for?'[72] So whatever criticism might be levelled against her because of her relationships with men was expunged by the quality of her writing; she had poems in eight volumes of the *Yellow Book*. The high literary standing she attained as an individual was compromised not by her private life but by her name changes – she published under three names in all, as R. Armytage, Graham R. Tomson and Rosamund Marriott Watson (using both the last two in the *Yellow Book*), which made name recognition difficult for those who admired her. The expectation of women to change their names on marriage was another problem for literary success, and is another reason why so many adopted pseudonyms.

The same volume IV carried Dolf Wyllarde's 'Rondeaux d'Amour', which was also of a decadent hue, being about a night of passion, and Edith Nesbit's 'Day and Night', about a woman having sex with her husband but thinking of her lover in the conceit of enjoying the sun but longing for the night. These works fitted into the literary definition of 'decadence', but a definition of 'decadent women' by their context is also significant. The 1890s scholar Linda Dowling has argued that to most late Victorians, 'the decadent was new and the New Woman decadent' – both inspired emotions ranging from hilarity to disgust and outrage.[73] Both the New Woman and the decadent were considered to have a revolutionary potential. Another scholar who has addressed this matter, Lyn Pykett, talks of the types that made their emergence in the *fin-de-siècle* period: 'the decadent, the homosexual, and the New Woman were not formed *by* each other, but were produced *in relation to* each other, from the same complex of social anxieties and within the same network of discourses, or ways of thinking about and representing masculinity and femininity.'[74] Jerusha McCormack, in her study *John Gray: Poet, Dandy and Priest*, says decadence was indicative of 'a kind of counterculture, generally employed as a gesture toward anything that appeared to threaten the then quite monolithic conventions, moral and social, of the Victorian middle classes; "decadence", quite simply, applied to that which was deemed unhealthy, uncouth and emphatically un-English.'[75] Elaine Showalter in *Daughters of Decadence: Women Writers of the Fin-de-Siècle* notes how 'outraged male reviewers . . . saw connections between New Women and decadent men, as members of an avant garde attacking marriage and reproduction.'[76] She observes that they were different but complementary: 'New women and decadent artists were linked together as twin monsters of a degenerate age, sexual anarchists who blurred the boundaries of gender. Thus decadent art was unmanly and effeminate, while New Woman's writing was unwomanly and perverse.'[77]

These connections were not a discovery of later scholarship, they were evident to observers at the time. In a rather laboured parody of Lewis Carroll's 'The Walrus and the Carpenter', published in *The World* in 1895, the New Woman (here a diminutive New Girl) and the Decadent are seen together, taking the ten commandments for a walk:

> The New Girl and the Decadent
> Had on a stroll agreed
> They wept like one o' clock to think
> What rubbish people read;
> 'If this could all be cleared away,'
> They said 'T'were grand indeed.'
> [. . .]
> 'The time has come' the New Girl said,
> 'To talk of many themes:
> Of soul – and sex – and scarlet sins –
> Of discords – and of dreams –
> And why they cut off Bodley's head –
> And why life's sides have seams.'[78]

Discords was, of course, a book by George Egerton, *Dreams* one by the New Woman writer Olive Schreiner. Evelyn Sharp supported the contention of a joint artistic enterprise, writing on reflection:

> It was part of the *Yellow Book* pose to have experienced everything, though most of us were so young in actual fact that we had some difficulty in maintaining even the necessary appearance of depravity popularly attributed to us. But this was only the superficial part of the pose. Our real objectives were the sentimentalities and

hypocrisies of a dying age, and in attacking these and seeking to set up a new standard of beauty and sincerity in art we perhaps justified our other gay absurdities, even our occasional tragedies.[79]

It is the curious relationship of decadence to modernism that gives the best clue as to how women fit into the culture of literary decadence. Decadence implies the end of an empire or a civilization, but endings are often new beginnings. If the 1890s was an age of decadence for the British Empire, a decline of patriarchal attitudes and the certainties of the old ruling class, it was also a time of an emerging confidence for women and for socialism, for Irish nationalism and for freedom of sexual expression. All of these were felt by the old guard to threaten the fabric of British society, but also in themselves offered renewal and vibrant models of future social development. Women writers formed part of a forward movement of literature that emerged along with decadence in a way described by comparative literature scholar David Weir as one in which 'historical decline and renewal, social decay and regeneration, artistic decadence and avant-gardism appear increasingly interrelated.'[80] No woman actively adopted the term 'decadent' to describe herself in the 1890s. Their very behaviour, however, as 'new' or 'modern' women was considered by the critical public to be evidence of a decline in the proper restraining structures of civilization: the hallmark of the decadence of empire.

By the time of volume IV, the publication was riding high with a distinctive voice in the crowded world of literary journals. Olive Custance and Leila Macdonald made a second appearance in this volume. Other women contributors were Victoria Cross, Marion Hepworth Dixon (Ella's sister) and Evelyn Sharp, and the travel writer and novelist Ménie Muriel Dowie. There were nine female contributors out of 22 written pieces.

The volume ended with a poem mocking *fin de siècle* pretensions by John Davidson. It accompanied his novel *Earl Lavender*, featuring supposed flagellation brothels under Piccadilly, which, since the interaction was all beatings with no sex, were an acceptable subject to write about and did not attract prosecution. Davidson's verse poked fun at the older generation that had failed to understand the change in sentiments and made a pretence of being aghast at women writers coping with social issues, before rounding off with a challenge:

Oh! our age-end style perplexes
All our elders time has tamed;

On our sleeves we wear our sexes,
Our diseases, unashamed.

Have we lost the mood romantic
That was once our right by birth?
Lo! the greenest girl is frantic
With the woe of all the earth.
[...]
Though our thoughts turn ever Doomwards,
Though our sun is well-nigh set,
Though our Century totters tombwards,
We may laugh a little yet.

By the beginning of 1895, with five years yet to run to the end of the century, the independent New Woman was inextricably linked with the morally dubious and sexually ambiguous Decadent. The next year would show that the establishment had had enough of being mocked.

5

'Hast thou slain the Yallerbock?'

The life cycle of a quarterly publication is laid down in a series of certainties like a genetic code. By volume V of the *Yellow Book* the pattern was well established: there were yellow board covers with the imprint of a Beardsley drawing on the front, with additional drawings from him on the back and spine. There were 250 to 325 pages, just over twenty pieces of literature, just under twenty illustrations. The graphic art was not connected to the literature that surrounded it, and it was protected by tissue guards. The literature would have catch-words (the first word of the following page) throughout. At the end were advertisements for books, mainly featuring those of the Bodley Head. There were no other ads or the serial fiction that was usual in magazines.

For the editorial staff the new volume began its gestation before the old one was off the presses. Harland and Beardsley would have material held over from the last number and a stock of new submissions, and were always seeking new talent. D'Arcy was fierce in whipping Harland into literary decisiveness. She would turn out bulging drawers of manuscripts and force him to make a decision on each until the backlog was cleared away. She said it was a Sisyphean task: 'Too many people wanted to write for the *Yellow Book*.'[1]

As the weeks passed from the previous volume, the literary pieces were selected from copy submitted and set in Caslon-old type; proofs made and corrected; plates made for the artwork and an order chosen for the poetry, fiction and prose that made up the book. The life cycle of a volume sped up in the weeks towards the publication date in the tiny 'editorial office' in Harland's flat in Cromwell Street as page pulls would be worked and returned for correction. Messengers were incessantly running between the printer Ballantyne in Tavistock Street, Covent Garden, and the office.

Harland and Ella D'Arcy would be chasing late submissions and Beardsley would be examining reproductions for their quality.

Perhaps under pressure from his health, and at Aline's urging, Harland went to Paris in March 1895, leaving the final publishing details to Ella D'Arcy. As soon as the final, fully corrected proofs were approved, they would be submitted to the printer, who would lock the type and the presses would get to work. D'Arcy described Thursday 11 April 1895: 'I'd proof-corrected, paginated, arranged the pictures, indexed, interviewed everybody, and, like the fly on the wheel, congratulated myself on having driven the Y.B. coach most successfully to its goal.' She said she 'left the Bodley Head in the best of spirits'.[2]

In entirely unconnected proceedings, and not mentioned by D'Arcy when she wrote a letter about the events of April 1895, Oscar Wilde was arrested on the evening of 5 April. This followed the collapse of his libel suit against the Marquess of Queensberry, who had accused him of being a 'posing somdomite' [sic]. When Wilde's charge was withdrawn in the light of the evidence Queensberry had compiled against him, law officers felt compelled to use that evidence to charge Wilde with offences under the Criminal Law Amendment Act of 1885, which had hardened laws against same-sex behaviour to cover any 'unnatural relations' between men in public or in private, regardless of consent.

Wilde had nothing to do with the *Yellow Book* and was no friend of it, but it was connected in the public mind with all things decadent and therefore with him. There was also a considerable overlap between his circle and that of the *Yellow Book*. Ella D'Arcy could not have been unaware of the arrest but it did not interfere with her editorial labours or her expectation of seeing the fifth issue of the *Yellow Book* in print just after Easter on 16 April (the publication date was in fact 15 April, but that was a bank holiday). According to the editorial timetable, Ella D'Arcy completed her work, delivered the corrected proofs ready for the press to the Bodley Head on Thursday 11 April, and went off for the Easter holidays, 'which I lived through with a light heart'.[3]

At the time of Wilde's arrest John Lane was crossing the Atlantic on his way to New York where he was setting up an American branch of the Bodley Head, which made him particularly sensitive to changes in the temperature towards the authors who were his capital. Lane left the company in London in the hands of his general manager Frederic Chapman.

Two of Lane's most prestigious authors, Alice Meynell and William Watson, were horrified to see the accusations against Wilde. Meynell was a leading poet of a markedly respectable hue, and not a contributor to the *Yellow Book*. William Watson was Lane's favourite contemporary poet and was a significant contributor to the journal; his long poem 'Hymn to the Sea' was set in type for publication in the current *Yellow Book*, volume v. According to the *Dictionary of National Biography* entry on Watson, as a public figure he was preoccupied with 'the decline of traditional modes and values in literature and the political and social shortcomings of his own times' and the 'misbegotten strange new gods of song'.[4]

Alice Meynell and William Watson leaned on Chapman and he sent a telegram to Lane on 6 April setting out their demands: 'Propose delete last name [Wilde's] from catalogue and announce decision to supply no more books failing this Watson and Meynell withdraw.' It was not the threat to withdraw their books alone that convinced Lane: he too wanted to distance himself from Wilde. The reports of Wilde's arrest (and of the details that came out in the Queensberry trial) had been sent by wire to New York newspapers and preceded his arrival there.

It is valuable to know the information on which Lane based his subsequent decisions about the *Yellow Book*. The arrest of Wilde occurred at 6.30 p.m. London time on Friday 5 April; the evening editions of the New York newspapers were able to cover it because of the time difference across the Atlantic.[5] There was then ample time for the New York daily papers on

Ella D'Arcy, *c.* 1895, photograph by Alexander Bassano.

Saturday 6 April to expand on the event, including such details as what Wilde was wearing and what kind of vehicle conveyed him to Scotland Yard. The evening papers on Saturday covered Wilde's arraignment that morning and the Sunday morning papers did the same the following day.

When John Lane's ship docked on Sunday 7 April the Wilde affair was therefore well known. He was some 27 years later to record that 'I was greeted on the landing stage by the posters of Sunday papers, bearing in large letters "ARREST OF OSCAR WILDE. Yellow Book under his arm."'[6] This is not credible; Wilde's arrest was three-day-old news by Sunday, and the news for Sunday papers was of Wilde's appearance in the police court with its portent of salacious evidence to come, the refusal of bail for Wilde and the arrest of his co-accused Alfred Taylor.[7] The *Yellow Book* did not feature in the coverage of the New York newspapers it has been possible to examine, but it was certainly mentioned in some agency copy about the Wilde case. The *Daily Inter-Ocean* in Chicago on Saturday 6 April had a down-page crosshead, 'Took the *Yellow Book* to Jail With Him', which continued, 'When accompanying the detective who made the arrest he had under his arm a copy of the *Yellow Book*.'[8] Whether that is true or not is widely open to question: it has not been possible to reference it in contemporary British newspapers, though the *Illustrated Police Budget* of 13 April (so almost a week after Lane's disembarkation in New York) carried a suspiciously detailed account of the scene in the hotel room, which included: 'He grasped his suede gloves in one hand and seized his stick with the other. Then he picked up from the table a copy of the *Yellow Book* which he placed in security under his left arm.'[9] Some later sources have said Wilde picked up 'a yellow book' (presumably a French novel, which were traditionally bound in yellow), but even that does not occur in contemporary accounts that give no mention of what he was carrying, despite their detail on other aspects of the scene. Whenever he learned of the alleged juxtaposition of Wilde and the *Yellow Book*, the important fact is that John Lane was prepared to believe there was a connection, however slight.

The connection between Wilde and the Bodley Head was very close: Lane was his publisher and Wilde had met one of his lovers, who was named as a witness, in the Bodley Head offices where the young man was employed. Lane was happy to accede to Meynell and Watson's request and distance his business from Wilde, who had become a contaminated brand. He not only accepted Meynell and Watson's ultimatum and withdrew Wilde's books from his catalogue, but issued a cable to the press to declare it had been his own idea: 'After seeing the papers here on my arrival last Sunday I immediately called to my manager to withdraw all of Wilde's books.'[10]

Alice Meynell and William Watson's response to the charges against Wilde (his trial would not begin until 26 April) was sanctimonious but understandable. They did not wish to be associated with Wilde when his life, like the stained hotel bedsheets that were to feature so prominently in the trial, was about to be revealed in court. The next stage, their moving against the *Yellow Book*, was merely vindictive. Watson was in contact with the noted novelist Mrs Humphry Ward (née Mary Arnold), an earnest, didactic social reformer. She became part of the story of women and the *Yellow Book*, not from the point of view of radicalism and artistic independence, but its opposite. She had already taken sides in public as an opponent of women's suffrage (and was later to found the Anti-Suffrage Association). She was ever eager to promote the principle of 'respectability' and, as her biographer noted, 'She bullied Wilde's publisher, John Lane, into further hounding Aubrey Beardsley, so as to purge English culture of the infection of yellow-bookery and sodomy.'[11] Despite the lack of direct connection between the *Yellow Book* and Wilde, the association of decadence with Wilde's lifestyle and Beardsley's drawings made it a dangerous time for the journal.

Mrs Humphrey Ward was not one of John Lane's writers, so in order to put pressure on the publisher she had to work via her friend William Watson as an important Bodley Head author. The poet was highly regarded by Lane, who was so concerned about his happiness that when Watson showed an interest in Evelyn Sharp, Lane played Pandarus. She wrote:

> I do not know what he told William Watson about me, but to me he used continually to enumerate the many charms of his favourite poet, ending up with the assurance that he had never seen him so much attracted by any other girl, to which my answer, if it had not been tactfully left unspoken, would have been that I knew more, in that case, of William Watson's susceptibility than he did.[12]

Watson was so close to Lane that the poet would correspond with his publisher about, among other things, his need for regular sex. As Watson's biographer remarked, he was 'unable to form a permanent or regular relationship with women of his own class, and the shop-assistants, land-ladies and barmaids he could contact had to be paid for in one way or another', so he asked Lane for an increase in fees to meet the costs.[13] Mrs Humphry

Ward may not have known where her money was going, but she knew that Watson needed it, and she bribed him to go beyond the assault on Wilde to attack the *Yellow Book*. She told Lane she had offered Watson 'private help', which he was unwilling but eventually tempted to accept. He was already hostile to some contributors and complained about the editorial policy of the *Yellow Book* that 'Harland will print such rubbish & such filth as disgraces its every number.'[14] His disgust cannot have been quite so extreme, as he appeared in five volumes of the *Yellow Book* (four of them while Beardsley was in post). Haldane Macfall, a friend and biographer of Beardsley, cited information from Joseph Pennell that 'William Watson was a far from willing actor in the drama and was forced into it by Mrs Humphry Ward, a very powerful and outstanding figure in the nineties.'[15]

Whatever machinations went on in the drawing rooms of literary influence, and from participants willing or not, two days after the first telegram to Lane in New York, another one was sent upping the stakes. On 8 April the message came from Chapman: 'Watson demands exclusion from five and future all designs art editor with whose name he refuses connect.'[16] For good measure Watson sent a message direct to Lane: 'Withdraw all Beardsley's designs or I withdraw all my books.' His insistence that Beardsley's designs were to be removed from the *Yellow Book*, and there should be no more in future volumes, was effectively an order to sack Beardsley, an amazing demand from an author to his publisher.

Lane acceded, which therefore left Chapman in the office with the brief of removing Beardsley's material, which he was not competent to carry out, short of stopping the presses on the *Yellow Book*. He did that by not sending the printer the final, press-ready proof Ella D'Arcy had delivered to him. It followed that when Ella D'Arcy went into the Bodley Head on Thursday 16 April after the Easter holiday (ten days after Wilde's first appearance in court), she arrived confidently expecting to see the first copies of the *Yellow Book* volume v. 'Well,' she asked Chapman, 'is the Y.B. out?' Chapman was not a jolly man so his air of gloom did not perturb her. 'Oh, will it be out tomorrow?' she asked, not in the least alarmed. Chapman, 'in the most mysterious tones', begged her to step through the shop and into the back office. She stood for some seconds opposite Chapman, who was speechless with emotion. 'But what is it? What is it?' she implored him. In a broken voice he announced that the *Yellow Book* would not be out that day, nor yet that week, nor for many a long day yet. He told her of the telegram from Lane, which he dishonestly told her had arrived after she had delivered the final proofs, accepting Watson's order to suppress the Beardsley drawings.[17]

The previous week Chapman had accepted the *Yellow Book* proofs without telling D'Arcy of the need to alter volume V or about the intended sacking of Beardsley. As she said, 'Mr Chapman tells me as little as he possibly can; I'm afraid he doesn't recognise my status on the Y.B. at all, or else maybe it's excessive modesty?' She was excluded from the debate as a woman, and also doubtless because of her low status. However, as the only member of the editorial team on site, Chapman would have done well to have confided in her.

Now she was his only chance of saving the *Yellow Book*, whose current volume still languished in the Bodley Head offices, having never gone to the printer. D'Arcy was astonished:

> for Chapman would give me no reasons, would shed no light at all upon the meaning of such a course; and I, who for the last year, have been struggling heroically to acquire a taste for Beardsley's work – incited thereunto mostly by you, isn't it true? For how have you not praised Beardsley's drawings when I, poor ignorant, Philistine that I am, have seen nothing in them but repellency?[18]

Whatever the reason for the expurgation, aside from a suggestion of mysterious and nameless indecency that was never made clear to her, D'Arcy took it upon herself to save that volume of the *Yellow Book* by substituting other material for the Beardsley drawings. Time was of the essence, as volume V should already have been on sale. It was not a matter of simply finding new drawings; they had to be made into blocks in an engraving process that was done for the *Yellow Book* by the Swan Electric Engraving Company. Ella D'Arcy went down to their offices at Northumbria House, 116 Charing Cross Road, and hunted down blocks already made of pictures planned for future volumes.

The next day, Wednesday 17 April, she arrived at Vigo Street with the new plates for the replacement of the four Beardsley drawings arranged. It was only now, she said, that 'Chapman launched at me the stupefying news the cover design too was condemned! Then I gave up everything in despair, sat down and mingled my tears with Chapman's, and the junior clerks gaily floated a fleet of paper boats upon the seas that we shed.'[19] D'Arcy simply did not have the skills and contacts to commission a fresh cover and get the blocks made for it. The despair was short-lived. D'Arcy was not prepared to let the *Yellow Book* fail, when she had invested so much in it. She sent a telegram to Henry Harland in Paris, telling him to come urgently. Chapman

Telegrams
BODLEIAN
LONDON.

JOHN LANE PUB
LISHER OF BELLES
LETTRES · ✤ ✤ ✤
The BODLEY HEAD
VIGO St LONDON W

OFFICE OF
THE
YELLOW
BOOK.

But I'm wandering from the story. On this Tuesday,
and at this interview, it never occurred to me the
cover and title-page were also to be suppressed:
I understood your orders to refer only to the four
Beardsley drawings. So I set to work to hunt
up blocks to replace these, and still, was confident, we'd get the book out without much delay.
It was not until the next day, Wednesday, that,
when all this affair of the new blocks had ~~been~~
arranged, as I thought satisfactorily) that
Chapman launched at me the stupefying news
the cover-design too, was condemned! Then I
gave up everything in despair, sat down &
mingled my tears with Chapman's, and
the junior clerks gaily floated a fleet of
paper boats upon the seas that we shed.

Then, I wired to the Editor, and on Thurs-
-day morning at 9.30., I met him at the
Bodley Head.

After that, as you can imagine, some en-
-ergy ~~harbes~~ was infused into things;
weeping was strictly prohibited, and strenu-
-uous action became the order of the day.

Page from Ella D'Arcy's letter to John Lane, 20 April 1895.

Cover of the
Yellow Book,
vol. v
(April 1895).

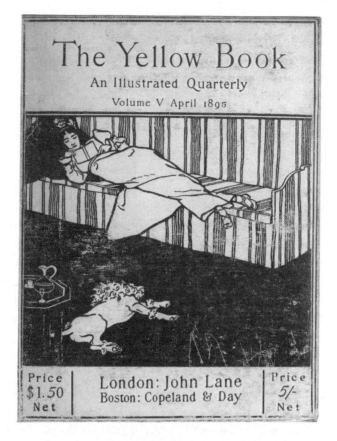

could, of course, have done this himself but he presumably had resisted calling the editor, knowing that Harland had the authority to challenge the peremptory dismissal of Beardsley on spurious grounds. D'Arcy met Harland at the Bodley Head office at 9.30 the following morning, Thursday 19 April (coincidentally on the morning Wilde was committed for trial). Harland had Patten Wilson design a new cover of a woman lying on a couch reading a book with a dog on the floor beside her. By noon on Friday 19 April the *Yellow Book* was again on track, minus most of the Beardsley (the designs for the back cover and spine were retained), and Harland went back to Aline in Paris the following morning.

Harland was concerned to save his publication, not his art editor, and by D'Arcy's account seems to have had a hilarious time with his assistant editor over the crisis. D'Arcy explained to Lane Harland's comic presentation of her encounter with the general manager: 'when he tells you I thought that Chapman, in his emotion on the Tuesday, was endeavouring to make me an offer of marriage, and that I took him by the hand, and promised to

The

be a sister to him, you may accept this with a very large saltcellar full of salt.'[20] The comic aside, the fact is, as Anne M. Windholz has commented, 'that a female sub editor should be represented interpreting a professional crisis as a romantic crisis necessarily diminishes her credibility.'[21] D'Arcy later said, 'If Harland had only been at the Bodley Head, everything would have been different. He would have made Chapman wait until Lane got back. But Chapman was a little man and he didn't like Beardsley. He took this opportunity to be important.'[22]

Though there was no direct connection between Wilde and the *Yellow Book*, Lane accepted that there was an association in people's minds. He wrote to George Egerton, 'I have been terribly worried re Oscar-Beardsley-*Yellow Book*. I have had no peace since my arrival, nothing but cables (Oh! The expense of them!)'[23] From his position in New York, Lane endeavoured to take the sting out of an imagined connection between Wilde, the *Yellow Book* and Beardsley by condemning the first and praising the latter two (irrespective of the fact that he had just sacked or was about to sack Beardsley). In an interview with the *New York Times* published on 12 April, a week after Wilde's arrest, he commented:

> The *Yellow Book* is doing well, and will continue to be issued as long as I have a penny to do it with. I consider Mr Aubrey Beardsley to be the modern Hogarth. His fierce satire on the absurdities and morbid fantasies of Oscar Wilde and his adherents has done more in my opinion to discredit them and to minimise their influence than any other factor previous to Wilde's appearance in a police court.

From the point of view of the women on his list, he introduced them with reference to their education, saying the best of the new writers did not attend the universities of Oxford or Cambridge, calling them 'non-college men' who

> are reinforced by many bright women, who certainly cannot be credited to the universities. There is the woman who writes under the name of George Egerton, the author of Keynotes. Iota, the authoress of The Yellow Aster; Evelyn Sharp, who writes a good deal for the *Yellow Book*; Mrs Marriott Watson, Mrs Wilfred Meynell, sister of Lady Butler, the painter, and Beatrice Harraden.

Lane therefore exonerated Beardsley and deflected criticism away from 'decadence' by indicating the contribution of women and of men who did not have the stain of that classical education which would leave them hankering after Greek relationships and Roman decadence. 'The cause of the success on the part of the non-university men and women is not far to seek. They have not been hampered by tradition, and have shown originality in their work before all other qualities.'[24]

Lane's attitude to Beardsley may have been shame that he had acted against him so rapidly and with so little cause. Removal from the *Yellow Book* did not mean removal from the Bodley Head; Beardsley was designing the cover for Ella D'Arcy's story collection *Monochromes* when he was dropped as art editor, and he continued to work for John Lane afterwards, to the irritation of William Watson, who had shot his bolt as far as threats were concerned.

The Wilde-Beardsley debacle was over what a man did sexually with other men, and the loss of an unconnected man's job because of guilt by association; women featured hardly at all. Wilde may have been the most talented playwright of the era and the best-known wit, but he did not contribute to the *Yellow Book* and had little to do with the *Yellow Book* women. He was rarely, if ever, seen at Aline and Henry Harland's Saturday soirées. Evelyn Sharp remembered seeing Wilde only twice in her life, both at John Lane's offices at the Bodley Head.[25] Wilde made his contribution in encouraging women writers during his early career as editor of *Women's World* (which title he changed from *Lady's World*, marking his understanding that a woman was a physical entity, a lady a social construct), but thereafter he was a male surrounded by young men. *Yellow Book* writer Ella Hepworth Dixon wrote a waspish satire of Wilde, whose acolytes 'copied his neckties and buttonholes, and whom one sometimes saw giggling together in corners, and calling each other by pet names . . . were heard addressing each other as "my dear".'[26] Very witty women such as Ada Leverson and Julia Frankau (who wrote as Frank Danby) were welcomed, but Wilde did not bestow his literary favours equally. Wendell V. Harris remarks that Wilde's influence, with which Lane's Bodley Head premises were presumed to be so infected, 'is discoverable only in Florence Farr's *The Dancing Faun*, and here the imitation of Wildean situation and dialogue is so close that one suspects parody rather than discipleship.'[27]

Women had little part to play in the drama of Wilde's trials, excepting *Yellow Book* writer Ada Leverson, who gave a home to Wilde when others rejected him in the period between trials. Those *Yellow Book* women who recorded comments on the Wilde affair were not judgemental; George Egerton wrote, 'I am very sorry for Oscar – he was the finest literary artist we had and I don't care a bit for an artist's private life.'[28]

She explicitly told Lane, in a letter of 5 May:

> I think Oscar has been very unfairly treated and that the English are the biggest hypocrites in the world. Everyone knew of it for years, and no one cut Oscar, yet when he is down they all hold briefs for virtue, pretended astonished indignation, howled like old women and kicked the man like cads when he was down. I disliked him all through, as you know, but if I continued to know him whilst I knew the unacknowledged fact, I wouldn't cut him when it became a known one … All genius is more or less abnormal and from my point of view – the seduction of a girl leaving her with a child of no social standing is a much bigger crime.[29]

Egerton's short story 'The Mandrake Venus' in her *Fantasias* of 1898 has been suggested as a response to Wilde with its Salome-like dance of seduction and attack on the sexual double standards of English moralists.[30] Later, in 'The Well of Truth' in *Fantasias*, she wrote of 'a sacrifice to the Moloch of morals. The choice of victims was . . . out of the ranks of art or literature.'[31]

Gabriela Cunninghame Graham interpreted Wilde's downfall in terms of personal preference rather than higher morality. She wrote to a Spanish correspondent, 'What do the affections of Oscar Wilde matter? Less than nothing for the progress of society. If he likes such ugliness . . . the worse for him.' Rather than ponder personal morality, she saw the case in terms of the wider social failure to tackle important issues: 'they give more importance to a sexual aberration, which in my opinion should not be a matter for the state, but at the most of the doctor, than to grave and serious social questions.'[32]

Ella D'Arcy's story 'The Death Mask' has been seen as a plea for a more tolerant, less morally censorious way for the public to regard the Wilde case.[33] The observer sees, in the making of the death mask of a French artist, 'A fat, loose throat … a vile mouth, lustful, flaccid, the lower lip disproportionately great.' But when the mask is lit from above, 'You saw a splendid dome-like head, Shakespearean in contour; a broad, smooth, finely-modelled brow.'[34] D'Arcy invites her audience to note the feet of clay, but not ignore the head of gold: 'this man with the lofty brain, the perverted tastes, the weak, irresolute, indulgent heart, will never again be met with to the end of time.'[35]

In the same July 1896 issue Vernon Lee (Violet Paget) writes in 'Prince Alberic and the Snake Lady' a Wildean fairy story set in a ducal palace with a lonely child, his only love a tapestry of a figure half-woman, half-snake. His obsession with a forbidden love object and his imprisonment echo the recent tale of Wilde's life (and his contemporary incarceration) without making direct reference to it; the author's sympathy is entirely with the boy.

Linda K. Hughes considers that some of the women poets featured in the *Yellow Book* after the Wilde trial, such as Rosamund Marriott Watson and Dollie Radford, were writing signs of sympathetic response to the imprisoned poet. 'Women were,' she notes, 'from an editorial perspective, a surer conduit than men for material associated with him. The trial was a reminder of the high stakes of masculinity in securing bourgeois regimes of gender and morality; women, already marginal, could more easily articulate thoughts that had become dangerous for men.'[36]

In some ways the tragedy of the Wilde case for women was not what happened, but what did not: the avenues that were now barred by respectability. Charlotte Mew saw the first issue of the *Yellow Book* and immediately wrote and sent off her story 'Passed'. The narrator on an aimless wander meets a girl in a church who begs her to go back to her wretched home where her sister is dying in images of Gothic horror in a room where 'her doll-like lips hissed out the same half-meaningless but pregnant words.' The tale is full of the despair of regret, of missed opportunities and guilt. Mew's startling originality of diction led Henry Harland to accept it immediately and invite Mew to visit him at 144 Cromwell Road to discuss some 'very trifling' changes and to encourage her work.

The diminutive, high-voiced author attended as requested at 3 p.m. on 30 April 1894. Harland was unperturbed by her peculiar manner and masculine dress. He gave her his usual advice for the very talented, that if she gave up her family and friends, and shut herself away to write, she could do wonders.[37] She set to work on a 15,000-word manuscript, 'The China Bowl', which Harland received in January 1895. He intended to meet her, though he did note the manuscript was too long for the *Yellow Book*. Perhaps it could be part of a collection of stories he was eager to put together. She was hurt at the lack of so swift an acceptance as she had for the first submission, and did not rush a meeting.

Soon the Wilde scandal had broken and Mew withdrew. As Penelope Fitzgerald commented, 'The curious and pathetic side of Charlotte which felt even the faintest breath of scandal as a threat told her that she must have nothing more to do with the *Yellow Book*.'[38] Mew was petrified that her tormented inner life would reveal itself to the world. For a lesbian with a cripplingly respectable family that had its own secrets of madness and poverty, any taint of decadence was too much. She never wrote again for the *Yellow Book* or even for the Bodley Head; it would be twenty years before she again received the encouragement she had found there.

For some women the events of April 1895 represented an opportunity. If some established writers eschewed the *Yellow Book* after the Wilde trial for fear of guilt by association, women writers hungry for publication showed no such disdain. Volume V (the last in which Beardsley was involved) had seven women writers from 27 contributors: Ella D'Arcy, Rosamund Marriott Watson, Mrs Murray Hickson (Mabel Kitcat), Leila Macdonald, Nora Hopper, Evelyn Sharp and Ada Leverson. Leverson (whose picture by Walter Sickert was also to appear in this volume) was to publish another story in volume VIII, 'The Quest of Sorrow', in which a cynical aesthete seeking new sensations tries to make himself unhappy with a love affair. It is clear therefore that a close association with Wilde did not damage her standing. The next *Yellow Book* after the Wilde trial, volume VI, had 7 women among 24 contributors; volume VII 10 from 23; and volume VIII 11 from 23 contributors, more than had ever appeared before.

After the Wilde trials, which finished with his conviction on 25 May 1895, writers associated with decadence continued to find a place in the *Yellow Book*. The first post-Beardsley volume of the *Yellow Book*, VI in July 1895, contained Richard Le Gallienne's 'The Arbitrary Classification of Sex', in which he scoffed at the Victorian convention that 'To be truly womanly you must be shrinking and clinging in manner and trivial in conversation, you must have no ideas and rejoice that you wish for none; you must thank Heaven that you have never ridden a bicycle or smoked a cigarette.'[39] Thus he defined by its opposite what the *Yellow Book* woman was: commanding, opinionated, bicycle-riding and smoking a cigarette.

Volume VI had to show a confident face to the world, so Harland again led with a story from Henry James. George Egerton continued to contribute a story in volume VI, despite her being the writer most closely associated with the outrageous New Woman. Other women who contributed to volume VI, well after the Wilde conviction, were Rosamund Marriott Watson, Dollie Radford, Evelyn Sharp and Olive Custance; Ethel Colburn Mayne made her first appearance as 'Frances E. Huntley'.

Lane and Harland's combined seductive powers were sometimes insufficient. Susan Christian attended a tea at Lane's and recalled, 'It was not a very successful party, for Mr Lane was socially shy . . . and Mr Harland overexuberant. I thought from both looks and speech he must be a Slav of some sort.'[40] Christian nevertheless contributed a story to volume VII and was later, as Susan Hicks-Beach, to continue a writing career up to the 1940s.

Linda Hughes suggests that a period of 'gender equity' settled on the *Yellow Book*, at least as far as poetry was concerned, from volumes VII to XII.[41] Katherine Lyon Mix believes Lane let himself be 'got at', in D'Arcy's (and Harland's) terms, and promoted contributions because he found the women who wrote them attractive. There were thus many women poets who had one or two appearances in the *Yellow Book*, none of whom, as Mix put it, 'grew wealthy from such undertakings in metre and rhyme'.[42] These were Elsie Higginbotham, Frances Nicholson, Lily Thicknesse, Rose Haig Thomas, Mary Howarth and Constance Finch. There are also male names in the list of single or double appearances of writers in the *Yellow Book*, however: Lane simply had a weakness for poets, his fondness for women aside.

The *Yellow Book* continued to be challenging to some, as noted by another Henry Harland protégée, Mrs Murray Hickson (who used this, her widowed name, for writing, though she married again in 1896 and became Mabel Kitcat). She remarked that, 'Even the humblest of contributors came in for a share of execration and – "Don't have anything to do with the *Yellow Book*. We hear it isn't quite – *nice*" – was the mildest commentary.'[43] Nevertheless, she, along with Hubert Crackanthorpe and Richard Le Gallienne, two writers closely associated with decadence, found a place in volume VII, as did Crackanthorpe's wife Leila Macdonald and Olive Custance. The *Bookman*'s reviewer declared that the new issue 'lays more serious claim than any of its previous numbers, perhaps, to our studious attention'. The reviewer singled out Ella D'Arcy's 'Web of Maya' for special commendation, stating that this work placed her 'among the masters of the short story'.[44] This is about a wife led astray from a life of domestic obedience by a sophisticated mentor, the Professor, who has encouraged her independent tendencies with books and vegetarianism. The break-up of his marriage under these circumstances leads the husband to unhinged fantasies of violence after he confronts the Professor: 'You've persuaded her to leave her husband, to give up her position, her duties; you've persuaded her to go and live in London, to be near you, to complete her education, to develop her individuality, and a lot of damned rot of that sort.'[45] It is an experiment in perspective where the reader's sympathies are with the wife, but the tale is told from the point of view of the husband in the manner of a Browning dramatic monologue.

Volume VIII, coming out in January 1896, showed no withering in the face of the journal's critics; at 406 pages it was the longest *Yellow Book*. It contained work by familiar names: Evelyn Sharp, Ella D'Arcy, Olive Custance and Rosamund Marriott Watson. Bodley Head author Nora Hopper made her third appearance, while Ethel Colburn Mayne (as Frances E. Huntley) made her second. Two men who made their only appearance in the *Yellow Book* in this number also wrote stories in which women featured prominently: H. G. Wells's 'A Slip under the Microscope', which has young women studying science beside young men, and George Gissing's 'The Foolish Virgin', about an older woman living in a genteel boarding house. She is a sour spinster who has to find a way of earning a living when her relatives refuse to support her further.

A frequent *Yellow Book* theme was the limited opportunities for women, particularly clever women. Evelyn Sharp's 'In Dull Brown' ponders the difficulties for the intelligent, when 'a woman is only to be tolerated as long as she is cheerful.'[46] There was always the option of being a muse, or servant, of an artist, that staple of bohemian fiction. Volume VIII's 'P'tit-Bleu' by Henry Harland is an affectionate picture of a music hall performer who cares for an opium-addicted artist, giving Harland every opportunity for descriptions of French scenes, a signal that Continental influence was still welcome in the journal's pages.

Despite the continuing suspicion of Gallic excesses, there was no apparent critical reaction against the *Yellow Book* following the Wilde trial specifically relating to Wilde or homosexuality. For example, during the case the *Pall Mall Gazette* (whose sensationalist campaign had promoted the 1885 Act, a clause of which had formed the charge against Oscar Wilde) reviewed volume v of the *Yellow Book* in less than fulsome but not morally damning terms. The poetry in the volume was praised but the prose condemned as 'seventh-rate fiction', said to be pretentious and worthless in literary terms. This was indeed a negative criticism but there was no mention of moral shortcomings.[47]

Nor did the provincial press show outrage. The *Leeds Mercury* critic lauded William Watson's poetry but condemned the volume's moral tone, not for the unnameable sin of Oscar Wilde but because the 'atmosphere of the book is heavy with the fumes of conjugal infidelity, and often of infidelity of a very vulgar description.' Mrs Murray Hickson was exonerated from this charge, but the book was said to be 'disagreeably contaminated by the shadow of one low passion'.[48] This shows moral superiority, but hardly outrage. In the *Glasgow Herald* in May 1895 the *Yellow Book* was regarded as an example to be followed. 'The *Yellow Book* is not to have all its own way,' it declared on the publication of a *Yellow Book*-like journal called the *Evergreen*, which included in its four volumes some *Yellow Book* contributors including Nora Hopper; Bodley Head author Fiona Macleod contributed under that name and as William Sharp.[49]

The assault on the *Yellow Book* was satirized in May 1895 in Mostyn Pigott's parody of Lewis Carroll's 'Jabberwocky', which concluded:

One, two! One, two! And through and through
Excalibur went snicker-snack!
He took its dead and bodless head
And went jucunding back.

And hast thou slain the Yallerbock?
Come to my arms, my squeamish boy!
Oh, brighteous peace! Purlieu! Purlice!
He jawbled in his joy.

'Twas rollog, and the minim potes
Did mime and mimble in the cafe;
All footly were the Philerotes,
And Daycadongs outstrafe.[50]

In fact, the *Yellow Book* was in good health, and was to continue for more than twice the number of volumes that had been overseen by Beardsley as art editor. Not only had the Yallerbock not been slain, but the disappearance of Beardsley from editorial control had made the *Yellow Book* altogether a more woman-friendly publication. In the five issues under Beardsley's direction 84 works of art were commissioned, but only one was by a woman: *Plein Air* by 'Miss Sumner' (Margaret L. Sumner) in volume IV. Stetz and Lasner talk of 'the sudden opening of opportunities to women artists and illustrators' consequent on his departure.[51]

Ella D'Arcy shed no tears at the art editor's departure. She had long been jealous of Beardsley, sniping at Lane in late 1894 for his supposed favouritism: 'Do, like a dear Sir Thomas, advance me another £15 on my immortal forthcoming works. Or better still, imagine I'm Aubrey Beardsley and make it £20, for I know you hand him out £20 notes, just exactly as you hand me biscuits.'[52] She harboured ambitions for Beardsley's post herself, writing a year later to Lane in her teasing style:

> Why didn't you make me Art Editor? Then all the Celia Levetuses, the Mary Holdens, the Mildred Gaskins, the Kitties, the Carries, the Annies, the Fannies; all the young Persons, in short, who send you their portraits and write you sonnets unfit for publication; would be kept outside of the *Yellow Book* (and certainly outside of GI!) with a firm hand. Ah, why didn't you make me Art Editor?[53]

Their relationship had developed since she arrived in London as Harland's assistant editor and rented rooms at 13 Edwardes Square in 1894. Her main claim to literary merit before publication in the *Yellow Book* was her story 'Elegie' in *Blackwood's Magazine*, a story of emotional longing, betrayal and artistic achievement that showed a mature appreciation of relationships. D'Arcy was flattered that George Egerton praised it. D'Arcy loaned her copy of *Blackwood's* to Lane and wrote to him on 25 April 1894 (shortly after the first *Yellow Book* had been produced when everyone was riding high on its success) that she would like it sent back, 'Or better still, if you happen to be in the neighbourhood any evening, and would bring it with you, I should be so very glad to see you.'[54] This was a daringly open invitation – a visit by a single man to a single woman was not completely forbidden, but would certainly have been a matter of comment in rural areas. In west London, it was tolerated.

D'Arcy seemed unable to write without conveying an undertone of personal neediness such as: 'Your T party was jolly yesterday. I enjoyed it *so* much. I so enjoyed all the pretty women you had.'[55] That sort of remark, made in winter 1894, implies a jealousy that she expresses as if she had a right to it, as if they were already intimate. If that is the case, their relationship started in the first half year of the *Yellow Book* (the second half of 1894). Another, undated, letter is more pleading: 'Do you think you could tear yourself away from the charms of the Misses Cross [Vivien Cory] and [Evelyn] Sharp, and come here to tea with me tomorrow? Do forsake them for *once* and come!'[56]

She never seems to have passed up an opportunity to comment on other women in whom Lane was interested. In riffling through Harland's correspondence she had turned up Olive Custance's romantic letters to him and wrote to Lane (of course, also a correspondent of Custance), 'What an appalling imbecile your Wild Olive seems to be. Such letters of hers as I have found in the Y.B. room, oh, such letters!'[57] Her imprecations went far beyond a working relationship, but normally also included a specifically pecuniary requirement, interspersing personal messages with requests for money, so she writes in January 1895, '*Why* don't you write to me? Why, why don't you make me your Secretary at a high salary and then I could answer myself?'[58] The tone does not imply a relationship that engaged mutual rapture. It was usual for D'Arcy to be importunate because she was ambitious and had no money, but she surrounded her requests with mockery, which allowed them to be disowned. Her cattiness about other women claiming Lane's attention also suggests a romantic possessiveness that would not be improper in contemporary terms if they had an arrangement, as both were unmarried, but no formal relationship was declared to others.

D'Arcy was no typical Victorian spinster; she had a relationship with short story writer M. P. Shiel in the 1880s and stayed in touch with him: an inventory of his books after his death shows a copy of her first book, *Monochromes*, of 1895 with a letter from her.[59] There may be something in Frederick Rolfe's observation that there was some 'relation' between D'Arcy and Harland, though this would have been limited by the presence in the apartment of Aline, who was ever vigilant of Harland's behaviour.[60] Nevertheless, D'Arcy and Harland were alone in the small *Yellow Book* office for a good deal of time and there were ample opportunities for physical affection, which may have (as Victorian intimacies often did, because of the danger of pregnancy) stopped short of actual intercourse.

Whatever their affections, Harland did not have the post of art editor in his gift: that was down to Lane. D'Arcy obviously had an expectation that she would take Beardsley's place, and from the letter where she asks why he did not appoint her, it is clear this had been mentioned between them. Apart from her practical experience on the *Yellow Book*, she was qualified from her early training at the Slade; she was an obvious choice.

In the event, she did not get the post that Lane left vacant, making the decisions himself guided by his connoisseur's appreciation of art with advice from Patten Wilson. She wrote to Lane:

> The *YB* progresses – slowly – because up to now, impossible to get the pictures, or their names. I could not, therefore, pass revise for press. Today, Chapman sent me pulls of some of the pictures; and dear, dear John Lane, they are simply atrocious. Yes, you are much too soft-hearted, you let yourself be 'got at'.[61]

Some letters show evidence of an emotional misunderstanding between them; when he went off to the United States he wrote to her, and she replied she was glad to get the letter, 'but what meant those reproaches? How was I "stiff" or "unkind"? . . . I did think *you* were a bit unkind not to invite me to come and see you off, but I suppose you had any amount of more important people, and so I should only have been in the way.'[62]

Something happened at the end of December 1895: probably she realized she would never get the job as art editor; maybe she realized Lane would not marry her. Perhaps she resisted his advances with an ultimatum – rarely a good negotiating position. However it happened, she referred somewhat apologetically to it in a letter of 30 December 1896, which she signed 'Your submissive Keynote', but with a postscript, 'Who was the unsubmissive Keynote who came to a bad end last New Year's Eve?'[63]

Her stories appeared in ten of the thirteen volumes, and there were other editorial contributions such as working with Harland to translate Dauphin Meunier's article on Madame Réjane for volume II. Early in her career reviewers suggested Ella D'Arcy might be a man, doubting whether a woman could write in such realistic terms of human relationships. *The Spectator* suggested, 'The signature of Ella D'Arcy may or may not veil a masculine personality,' and went on to remark that 'in "Irremediable" it is a perverse feminine taste that has chosen a heroine from the slums of White-chapel,' so if the story were written by a woman, it was not a very nice one.[64] Her first book, *Monochromes*, appeared in June 1895 in the Keynotes series with a Beardsley-designed cover and the key motif made from her initials. It contained six stories, four of which had previously appeared in the *Yellow Book*. She dedicated it to 'The Chief', which was her affectionate name for Harland.

The first review D'Arcy would have seen was in the *Morning Post* under 'Books of the Day', which described *Monochromes* as 'far above the average in its own class of literature'.[65] Another good review came from the *Pall Mall Magazine*, where the novelist Israel Zangwill called it 'the cleverest volume of stories that the year has given us.'[66] *The Graphic*'s writer particularly praised 'The Elegie': 'this study of the ideally artistic temperament, to which a broken heart means nothing but raw material for working upon' is executed with 'severe simplicity of style and method'. The writer criticizes a 'too uniformly tragic close' to the pieces, but finishes, 'it is rare indeed to meet, in English, with a number of short stories of such distinction.'[67] The most clearly gender-specific remark was the *Saturday Review*'s 'We doubt if any other living woman-writer could have written quite so well.'[68] D'Arcy

Title page of Ella D'Arcy,
Monochromes (1895).

MONOCHROMES

BY ELLA D'ARCY

LONDON: JOHN LANE, VIGO ST.

BOSTON: ROBERTS BROS., 1895

kept a close eye on the reviews, writing to Lane, 'Did you see a review of "Monochromes" in the *Queen*? What did the writer (Douglas Sladen I presume?) mean by saying that "The Pleasure Pilgrim" lacked certain touches that a man could have supplied? Do tell me.'[69] Another negative review came from the *Pall Mall Gazette*, calling *Monochromes* an 'immature' treating of subjects with 'unfailing inappropriateness of method'.[70] It may have been the same writer who mocked the notion of an English Academy of Letters along the same lines as the French by proposing an Academy of unknowns who 'have never yet struck home to the great heart of the people'.[71] This ponderous Victorian humour showed its weakness when the writer had to name his proposed academicians because without name recognition there would be no joke. Ella D'Arcy was on the list, along with a number of other *Yellow Book* writers including Victoria Cross, Ménie Muriel Dowie, Nora Hopper and Evelyn Sharp.

D'Arcy did not find writing easy. She was so given to procrastination that Harland once locked her in a room, refusing to let her out until she had finished a *Yellow Book* story. This event was mythologized, so Evelyn Sharp remarked in reminiscences on

Ella D'Arcy, a writer of real genius, and Irish ancestry, who never produced anything but brilliant and caustic conversation, unless – so tradition ran – the editor shut her up with a day's food, a treatment that would have reduced a mere Saxon to idiocy, but in her case invariably resulted in a wonderful short story.[72]

Netta Syrett noted:

> though her prose was indeed distinguished, and she herself very clever and amusing, she was the laziest woman I ever met! She once came for a fortnight to the little flat in Paris which had been lent to me, and every morning during my own hours of work I used to lock her into her room, with strict orders to write. Instead, she read French novels on the balcony and when I released her, merely laughed and owned she hadn't even taken up her pen.[73]

Though clearly a friend, Syrett continued:

> In spite of her erratic behaviour and lack of dependability in word and deed, she could be a delightful, amusing and often witty companion. We called her 'Goblin Ella' and pretended that when she disappeared for months, even years, at a time, and then one day walked into our London flat as though she had been absent half an hour, she had flown to a Witches' Sabbath on her broomstick and returned by the same means.[74]

Thus it was that Ella D'Arcy at the end of 1895, tired of being taken for granted, the game played out with Lane, short of money and with no more permanent post in prospect, just left London, with no word to her friends or to Harland or Lane. This would show them how much they needed her.

6

Office Wars

Ethel Colburn Mayne, a 'plain, gawky and sallow girl', led a quiet life seething with unspoken passions in the southwest of Ireland.[1] She was born on 7 January 1865, the eldest child of Emily and Charles Mayne; they lived in Johnstown, County Kilkenny, but by the early 1890s the family had moved to Cork where her father was a resident magistrate. Ethel Mayne had two siblings, her sister Violet and brother John, who was an army officer. She may have experienced 'the torturing *espionage* of family life' as a character in one of her stories does, and wished, 'If only she could be quite alone!'[2]

Charles Mayne's position meant he was a powerful representative of the Anglo-Irish Ascendancy, which limited the amount of social contact the family could have to a small circle. If there was resentment and suspicion of a Protestant family in the garrison town with a largely Catholic population, it did not manifest itself in any political content in Mayne's writing.

She had studied in Irish private schools, excelling at French, German and history, all of which were to serve her well in her literary career. She already conceived of herself as a writer and avidly read magazines of literary life in London. How long she had written is not known, but her reluctance to draw attention to herself and disdain for self-advertising led her to adopt the 'very stupid nom de guerre' of Frances E. Huntley. It is typical of her reticence on personal questions that she elucidated no further except to say, 'My reasons for that folly were as uninteresting as the pseudonym itself.'[3]

In her literary explorations she came upon the *Yellow Book* prospectus with its declared intention to print complete stories and not serials and to aim for literary quality – it could have been directed at Mayne herself. She had been submitting stories to the London magazines and had at least one accepted for publication, by *Chapman's Magazine*, when she received a letter from Henry Harland. The *Yellow Book* was one of a number of publications to which she submitted work but, as she later wrote, Harland replied: 'Almost before I had realised my own temerity in thinking to begin my literary life at such an altitude, there came a letter in his exquisite script, not only accepting this story but praising it in words which even now it thrills me to recall.'[4]

This story was 'A Pen-and-Ink Effect', published in volume VI, a story of uncertainty, disappointment in love and the cruelty of convention. Mayne and Harland began a correspondence on literary subjects that showed they were of like mind; she later recalled 'the many letters I received from him'.[5]

By winter 1895 she was approaching her 31st birthday. At the end of the year in Cork she could count on rain and grey skies overhead, sometimes with fog and occasional snow, family life continuing unchanged. Social life, such as it was for a spinster in rural Ireland, was without excitement. Mayne's writing reflected her upbringing; her stories are set in domestic interiors filled with menace, the children in her stories are often ugly, the women plain and lonely, the mothers unsympathetic. Her writing shows an intensity of emotion about the perverse and petty tyrannies of everyday life; they tell of impossible yearnings and unspoken sentiments with the course of whole lives changed by a few words misunderstood or unsaid. Her fiction shows a dark and brooding vision of Victorian domestic life, particularly the lives of women. As she wrote in one of her *Yellow Book* stories, 'She tasted in that moment something of the weakness of womanhood – its pitiful groping artificiality, its keen passionate realness.'[6]

In December 1895 a letter came from Harland with a way out. It was, as she wrote, 'offering me what he called the "derisory" post of his sub-editor, Miss Ella D'Arcy, who had hitherto acted in that capacity, having left England for a stay in France.' She recollected, 'I need not enlarge on how little derisory it seemed to a girl who had lived all her life until this in Ireland, and was entirely unknown to the literary world. Nor will I say with what ardour the invitation was accepted.'[7]

She left Cork on New Year's Day, taking a ferry to Swansea, from where the Irish boat-train took her to London on Thursday 2 January. Harland 'reassured' her he would not be meeting her off the train, for their mutual ease, he said, for he knew she would not like their first meeting to be at Euston on a January morning at 6 a.m. Mayne later remarked, 'even then I was able to divine that the decision was not entirely self-sacrificing,' but she had a porter take her bags and took a four-wheeler 'growler' to Marloes Road, off the Cromwell Road, where Harland had arranged rooms for her close to the *Yellow Book* office at his home.[8] It was also close to where he had arranged rooms for Ella D'Arcy, doubtless through the same letting agent who found his own flat for him.

When he arrived he met a rather angular woman, slender with alert, intelligent eyes but none of the attributes that contemporary men, or women, found attractive. She encountered

> a tall man, slender, a little stooping, very pale with a thick white 'Russian looking' skin; grey eyes behind the pince-nez, broad black eyebrows and his 'snub' nose he had prepared me for by a caricature of himself in a letter. The most attractive of noses I thought it then, and think it now.

She noticed a scent about him and remarked on it, saying how pleasant it was. He said, 'Oh, I am relieved – what a mercy! I was afraid you would dislike it. It is eucalyptus. I must use it as I am supposed to be consumptive.' The knowledge of Harland's fatal illness was thus with them from the first. Mayne invested it with a world of possibilities: 'I never smell it that that

Ethel Colburn Mayne, portrait from *Georgian Stories* (1922).

moment does not come back to me. Unromantic in itself, romantic to me, for whom so many things began that morning.'[9]

Mayne was besotted with Harland and always wrote fondly of him; she recollected, 'On how many mornings, afternoons and evenings did I listen to him – privately in the small "office", more publicly in the big drawing room at Cromwell Road.'[10] She recalled being '"off my head" with pride and gratitude at being so included'.[11]

She described the *Yellow Book* regimen: 'We spent the working hours in reading reviews, MSS for the new volume, and in his teaching me my job. He was a ruthless teacher – there were no indulgences.' She was thirty when she met him and he 34, so there was no natural reason for him to behave in such a paternal way, but she expected and appreciated it. Every day she would arrive eagerly in the office for a day of opening mail, correcting proofs and making an initial judgement on the pages that were sent in. 'I knew pretty well what he was looking out for in the hundreds of MSS that we considered,' she said.[12]

In 'the countless offered manuscripts' for the *Yellow Book* she remarked on what they were seeking: 'a perception that penetrated beyond the surface of things and people, a shaft sunk in our common consciousness, a theme that reached further than the experience it transcribed; and then, of course, the manner of the telling . . . coming of itself to the "clearer vision" of a consciousness humbly alive to its waiting presence'.[13] She so naturally grasped such notions of literature that it is unsurprising that she and Harland found themselves in accord.

She wrote of the atmosphere in the *Yellow Book* office that 'A hundred Browning verses sing themselves around my memories of the flat in Cromwell Road.' She gave a flavour of his conversation with its constant literary allusions: if she asked Harland what he was thinking of, he would reply:

> 'And thinking too – oh, thinking, if you like, How utterly dissociated was I . . .' Browning's phrases (how alert we were for the 'phrase' in those days) would fall grave and vibrant from the voice with its subtle foreign colouring; you would always infuriate 'H.H.' by telling him he had a foreign accent.[14]

She showed a provincial astonishment at their joy on the few occasions when they went out, such as when they celebrated Dalyrell Crackanthorpe's passing the exams for the diplomatic corps by 'dining at one restaurant, going to another for coffee, and to yet another for beer and sauerkraut'.[15] The conversation was often broad but she was so taken by the charm of Harland's 'wilful and spirited' appearance when he was making risqué comments that 'Nothing he said could offend you when he looked like that!'[16]

For three months she laboured with him to produce volume IX of the *Yellow Book*, which would contain a story of hers, 'The Only Way', and an editorial congratulation from Harland, who, writing about the journal as a fictitious critic, the Yellow Dwarf, advised the editor to 'cultivate' Mayne as a writer.

One day in early April, near the end of the preparation period of the new volume, Ella D'Arcy again appeared in the *Yellow Book* office. She was nine years older than Mayne, much more worldly wise and, crucially, had almost two years of editorial experience. She had left the *Yellow Book* in the hope she would prove to Harland and Lane how essential she was, that they could not get along without her. In fact her absence proved entirely the opposite. She was not the sort of person to hide her disapproval at this turn of events.

Mayne was later to draw a veil over the disruption caused by D'Arcy's return. She wrote of 'many little stabs that had been inflicted on me', but with what extremes of her famed caustic wit D'Arcy castigated Mayne is not known.[17] A first novel by Mayne based on her experiences at the *Yellow Book* was not published and the manuscript has been lost. It cannot have helped the situation that both of them were women of Irish extraction and writers of closely observed short stories not much admired by the masses; both invested Harland with romantic appeal, and neither were to have long-term partners or children. It is tempting to see the conflict as an example of what Freud called the narcissism of small differences.

Harland witnessed some of the unpleasantness in the office, but it showed an aspect of his personality that he had described whimsically: 'I am like a cat, I make for the door when there's any trouble.' Mayne confirmed, 'he did make for the door, both literally and metaphorically, when things went wrong. But once safely out of the way, he was sympathetic; from his distance, he could be sorry for you!'[18] She suggests therefore that he sympathized, in private, with Mayne because D'Arcy was cruel to her in a workplace that he theoretically controlled.

It is clear that Harland had not sacked D'Arcy for leaving the job without agreement and she fully expected the position of subeditor to still be there for her. She had, indeed, defended herself by letter from France, 'I told you all I meant to come; there was nothing underhand about it that

I can see.'[19] She doubtless at some time said she would go to France; she just did not give a specific time when she was leaving or returning. With no leave agreed, she could reasonably be said to have quit the job. Harland's neglecting to make this clear to her was one of the failures of management that became more apparent as the story progressed.

He did not seem able to tell D'Arcy to leave; he simply lacked the managerial expertise to deal with a difficult member of staff. It may have been, too, that Mayne was technically deficient while D'Arcy was competent at that side of literary business, so she may genuinely have been more usc to the *Yellow Book* project than Mayne as press day approached. At any rate, D'Arcy 'banished' her from the *Yellow Book* room, doubtless under the pretext that there were too many people in the small office. Mayne retreated to her small flat, keeping in contact with Harland by mail until, as she wrote, 'one day, after wondering why I had not seen him or heard from him ... I was told that he had left for Paris several days before.'[20] Mayne was alone with her position uncertain.

Mayne had no friends in the *Yellow Book* office – the stalwarts Netta Syrett and Evelyn Sharp were friends of D'Arcy's; they did not even mention the engagement and expulsion of Mayne in their memoirs. Harland was her only friend at court, and he was a broken reed, simply going off to Paris as he usually did at this time, but with no word to Mayne and not establishing her situation. Nor had she, as D'Arcy had, endeared herself to Lane, either because she failed to understand the power dynamics of publishing, or because she disdained to make herself agreeable to a man because of them. Perhaps she simply disliked Lane; he is not present in her writing about the period, and she is absent from his letters files in the archives. He did not publish any of her work (except in the *Yellow Book*).[21] She was not, anyway, his kind of woman. D'Arcy did not fear Lane's disapproval of her behaviour; she remarked: 'I know you don't hold to Miss Mayne.'[22]

D'Arcy explained to Lane in a letter of 11 April 1896 from the 'Office of the *Yellow Book*' what she had done while left in charge of finalizing the proofs after Harland's departure: 'I'm proving such a Guardian Angel to the Chief – though he doesn't know it. I'm completely revising his Contents-list, just according to my fancy! I found "The Only Way" with that idiot Frances E. Huntley [Mayne] was to leave her out altogether.'[23] So she had deleted a story of Mayne's with that title in the *Yellow Book* volume that Harland had left almost ready for the press. Even more egregiously, she rewrote her editor's words of praise for Mayne or, as she put it:

I've also, kindly, expunged her name from the Yellow Dwarf's mistaken eulogies. He will, certainly, murder me when he discovers it; he is already very angry because I don't send him any revise; but of course, I shan't send him any until I've passed it for press, and so my changes have become 'Irremediable'.

She told Lane (who was in New York) on the assumption that, because Lane did not sympathize with Mayne, the publisher would therefore support her undermining of her editor. Of course, her behaviour to Mayne, usurping Harland's authority, was not something to inspire confidence in her in Lane's mind, and it was the crudest of office politics to approach the boss over the head of her manager. She cheekily remarked that 'you, too, won't get the news until it is too late to do anything but gracefully submit.'[24] She failed to realize how disloyal, untrustworthy – downright unemployable – her actions made her seem.

Towards the end of April the news was out. She wrote to Lane on 23 April:

There's been the most unholy row! The Chief somehow got wind of my proceedings, and but that the Channel mercifully flows between him & me, I should not now be alive to write you this tale. How he heard I can't imagine. At first I thought you must have cabled to him; but then I saw that was impossible. Why should you? You're not such an admirer of Miss Mayne's rubbish, as to waste money, cablegramming about her. No: I suppose he wrote to Chapman or the printers, to know why he didn't get Revise, and so the secret came out. But it came out too late for him to change anything! The book could not be remade, so he has taken comfort in sending me abusive wires. Poor dear Chief! He must have spent a small fortune over them.[25]

She explained Harland's anger:

Now, he won't write a letter at all to me; but has informed me on a peremptory post-card that I 'may consider myself relieved of the duties of a Sub-Editor, & he will seek for a less untrustworthy person'! Ah, I can see the Cromwell Road blocked with the crowd of needy females all struggling for that high salaried post![26]

The sarcasm aside, there was someone else ready to take the post, close to the Cromwell Road office, who was waiting for the call, but it did not come. It may have been that Harland did not want Mayne back because she was not actually very good at the job. Middle-class women from a traditional family like hers had not been brought up to work for a living, and while fitting in well with the editor's literary talk, she may have struggled with the practical work environment.

Harland wrote to Mayne saying he was 'FURIOUS' about what had happened but not offering to reinstate her (not that he had actually sacked her).[27] There was then silence from Harland, as Mayne said, 'I never heard from him or saw him again.' This was curious. Mayne was able and willing to retake her post as subeditor; Harland could have had the story that D'Arcy had pulled, 'The Only Way', published in a later volume; he could have reinstated his praise of her in a new Yellow Dwarf letter; he could have published further stories of hers. In fact he did nothing. She eventually despaired of hearing from him and returned to Ireland, chastened, to the family she was to live with for the rest of her life. Two years later, in 1898, she sent Harland her first collection of stories, which she had titled *The Clearer Vision*, one of Harland's pet phrases for what he wanted from fine literature. He did not even acknowledge receipt. She later considered:

> I think it was meant kindly; he wanted me to forget him, or at any rate remember an oft-quoted saying of his 'A door must be open or shut.' Shut it was, and for me remained shut to the end. But as to forgetting him, no one who ever knew him has done that.[28]

Back in Cork she wrote a first novel, *The Gate of Life*, which she submitted to T. Fisher Unwin in November 1897. The report from the reader, Edward Garnett, was not encouraging. He remarked, 'There are no such circles as Miss Mayne describes – *none*. The art-talk – the Oscar Wildeian posing people – Are all *idealised*, imagined by a clever girl.' He thought her 'analysis of a woman's feelings is very good' but 'the sketches of social celebrities, artists, famous critics etc. etc., all the *art atmosphere* & art *gossip* is – well humbug.' Mayne had clearly omitted to say in her covering letter that the book was drawn from her actual experiences at the *Yellow Book* (to which Garnett's father contributed). This would have been a major selling point; the fact that she did not use it indicates her innocence of the marketplace of literature. Garnett felt, 'In the future she must place her heroine in a social milieu she herself has lived in, & *knows*. She must write of the people she knows, & *then* she may do good work.'[29] Mayne cannot have been anything but infuriated at this but she must have taken the criticism to heart, for she embarked on another novel that has the heroine, Jessie Vandeleur, leaving a small town in Ireland for literary life in London. She probably used some of the material from *The Gate of Life* for *Jessie Vandeleur*, but as the earlier manuscript is lost, it is impossible to say.

Mayne set *Jessie Vandeleur* in the Campden Hill district of London, where her friend Violet Hunt lived. Her relationship with this literary celebrity was one friendship that endured from her time in London. Mayne had met Hunt, who was three years older than her, at an Authors' Club tea early in 1896, when Hunt was already advanced on a literary career.

Towards the end of the century Mayne was writing *Jessie Vandeleur* and preparing *The Clearer Vision* for publication by Fisher Unwin. This was seven stories of which two had previously appeared in the *Yellow Book*. They were set in domestic interiors filled with menace, with barely understood, casual conversations that change lives. In 'One Near One' the narrator says, 'I know myself cosily opaque.'[30] Mayne is indeed opaque here, writing as a male narrator called Frank observing a married couple who understand each other too much, so as to be 'two souls, at war with one another for a little peace'. Typical of Mayne's men, the central character here is unimaginative but sensitive; he has an affair in order to be with a woman who does not understand him, as his wife does. He enjoys being with this stupid woman for 'just the pleasure of not being understood'.[31]

Mayne's closely observed complexity and concentrated power of expression is apparent in 'The Lost Leader', set in the febrile atmosphere of a school where schoolgirls hate the fact that the most popular of them was to marry but, with an intensity of pettiness,

> we had still one golden robe of glamour left with which to invest our Lost Leader. We talked it over, we burned our very souls to tinder with ardent eager curiosity, we made, finally, a holocaust of our dreams, our romance, our love-lore – and offered it, humbly, upon Mary's altar. 'She was not in love with Page [her fiancé].'[32]

Mayne excelled at the immensities of passion focused on tiny spiteful thoughts, the sheer waste of women's lives in pettiness.

Violet Hunt's review in the *Daily Telegraph* must have pleased her:

There is no doubt about the striking cleverness of these fictional studies, the wealth of refined cynical observation that has been brought to bear upon these types of feminine – 'depravity' we were going to say, for it is as it were, the 'cranks' among women whom Miss Mayne elects to portray in that curiously insistent, passionately analytical style of hers.[33]

Like Ella D'Arcy and other writers of short stories for the *Yellow Book*, Mayne set her sights on a novel that would be the breakthrough into literary success: this would be *Jessie Vandeleur*. The eponymous heroine, perhaps the most dislikeable leading female character in fiction since Jane Austen's Emma, is due to marry her school playmate Hugo Grantley, now secretary to Lord Ruttledge, with whom he goes off to West Africa when Ruttledge receives an appointment there. This leaves Jessie free to pursue the novelist Deyncourt, but the usual feminine wiles will not work with him, for 'Deyncourt worships brains.'[34]

She stealthily scouts the terrain, for 'she was brought up short before that enduring puzzle for women – the tradition of men's silence; the experience, ever-repeated, of men's small, significant betrayals.'[35] Her rival Miss Leader is a writer who has dedicated a book to Deyncourt. The novelist's fascination with this writer tempts Jessie, for she is feeling a sense of freedom while her fiancé is away: 'his absence had made more change than she had dreamed of; a hundred little liberties were hers, of which she had not known herself deprived, till she enjoyed them in their flowing ease.'[36]

She plagiarizes her fiancé Hugo's nearly finished novel, passing it off as her own work, even before the inevitable plot device of his dying while on his posting abroad. Jessie almost gets away with it, but Hugo's sister knows of the novel and intends to expose her. It is evidence of the murky waters in which Jessie Vandeleur swims that when he learns of the plagiarism, far from being appalled at her dishonesty, Deyncourt is flattered that she has done this thing for him, and they are united. Deception rewarded is what counts as a happy ending in an Ethel Colburn Mayne book.

As the century's end approached, Mayne was working on *Jessie Vandeleur*, which was published by George Allen in 1902, the year her mother died at the age of 62, leaving to Ethel the entire burden of caring for her ageing father and her sister. Despite her foray into the light of the *Yellow Book*, at the end of the century she was back where she started under the dull skies of Cork, but she was working on plans to return to literary life in London.

HER RIVAL Ella D'Arcy did not fare particularly well out of what she called her 'exquisite little joke' of sabotaging Mayne's work.[37] Susan Winslow Waterman thinks D'Arcy embodied the 'queen bee syndrome', where being the single woman in a group of men has its benefits, and rewards come in solidarity with men and denigrating other women.[38] It was a dangerous game and D'Arcy may well have regretted it. She did not tell the story of her ousting of Mayne to Katherine Lyon Mix, who spoke to her about the *Yellow Book* when she was doing research in the 1930s, so it seems she may have realized how poorly the tale reflected on her.

D'Arcy's sabotage of the *Yellow Book* reduced the length of volume IX to 256 pages, the shortest it ever was (the longest was VIII at 406). This came at a particularly difficult time for the journal. Beardsley had gone, but not into obscurity. He was preparing a new journal, along with Arthur Symons, that was to be published by Leonard Smithers, who had a reputation for printing what would later be termed pornography. Mabel Beardsley suggested the new journal should be called the *Savoy*, which associated it with the elegant hotel in the Strand that was the site of some of Oscar Wilde's indiscretions, as reported at his trial. This was going to be a work that jumped neatly into the decadent niche that the *Yellow Book* had been skirting.

Volume IX of the *Yellow Book*, appearing in April 1896, was the only volume in which there is only one story by a woman: Ella Hepworth Dixon's 'The Sweet o' the Year'. The quota of short stories by women in the *Yellow Book* went up after volume IX: there had been a previous average of 3.5 stories by women, compared with five per volume in the final four.[39] D'Arcy was to continue to publish in the *Yellow Book* – there is a piece by her in each of the next four volumes, X to XIII.

D'Arcy did not have anything to do with editing after being sacked by Harland, but as a contributor she was sent the volumes as published. She took the trouble to make her criticism known to Lane about volume XIII:

> Many thanks for the YB. I'm truly sorry to find it such a poor number. These snippety stories, fit only for the sixpenny weeklies, are not worth reading, much less paying five bob for. If you are going on with it you must screw it up for the Jubilee number.[40]

D'Arcy had not mastered discretion in her criticism of fellow women authors, telling Lane that Ménie Muriel Dowie's 'The Idyll of Millinery' (in volume X) was 'a silly, poorly written tale'.[41]

D'Arcy's complaint – linked to a criticism of the amount of money that Lane had paid Dowie for the work – concealed a bitter, class-based antagonism. Ménie Muriel Dowie and Olive Custance (a frequent target of D'Arcy's contempt) were upper class, as was Leila Macdonald, whom D'Arcy sneered was only published because her husband was the important realist writer Hubert Crackanthorpe.[42] Class-conscious men like Lane knew they had to treat rich women well, while they could keep poorer writers waiting because they would still come back. This was not a trait of the Bodley Head alone, as novelist Constance Smedley writes in her memoirs:

> The difference of the treatment accorded in newspaper offices to women who looked shabby and wretched and those who looked prosperous and insouciant was so great that it infuriated me. I never had any difficulty in getting payment but friends of mine had to call and wait to be sent away, to return again and again when the money was direly needed.[43]

Even people who frequently socialized with Lane such as Netta Syrett had to beg him repeatedly for payment, as she wrote: 'Dear Mr Lane, I am sorry to trouble you again about the cheque for my *Yellow Book* story but I shall feel obliged if you can let me have it as soon as possible.'[44] As Smedley said: 'Women were only just entering the professions and payment was very small and the hope of financial success exceedingly shadowy.'[45] One thing the miserable story of D'Arcy's attack on Mayne shows is how precarious literary work was for women in the 1890s that they should be squabbling over scraps of preferment. In a world in which starvation and suicide were not unknown, women soldiered on, economizing on food and repairing threadbare clothes.

For Ella D'Arcy, mere financial stability was a dream. She wrote to Lane, 'Oh *do* dear Publisher, get me some work, I'm *so* low! And to think that all, all my dear little £15 has to go to old debts ... it's heartbreaking.'[46] In another place she lamented the gulf between what she needed to live on and what she earned. 'I do so want to earn £500 a year. I *can't* live on less, and you know my income is not a tenth of that amount.'[47] She was therefore bringing in less than £50 from her writing in spring 1896 (though she had an unknown but not great amount from property in Ireland). A domestic servant of D'Arcy's age in the 1890s could receive £28. At this time a clerk might receive a guinea a week (a pound and a shilling, so £54 12s annually), though women's rates of pay were lower. A shopkeeper or bank clerk would be doing well to bring in £1 a week (so £52 a year).[48] Payment for a story was £15 and even that could be a hard-fought prize. She wrote to Lane on 13 April 1897: 'that debt of £10 from me to you [presumably a loan in the form of an advance] is wiped off by the story I have just given you for the April *Yellow Book*, and on which you owe *me* £5 on publication.'[49]

Her next book was *Modern Instances*, whose very title suggests both the fleetingness of a short story with an up-to-date outlook. All the stories in this 1898 volume first appeared in the *Yellow Book*. It was not widely reviewed though the *Pall Mall Gazette* critic remarked it was 'distinguished by the light and graceful satire of the author's style'.[50] One of its stories, characteristic of both D'Arcy and *Yellow Book* writers in general, 'A Marriage', asked why 'the gentlest, the sweetest, the most docile girl in the world' should be so changed by matrimony: 'Marriage is the metamorphosis of women – the Circe wand which changes all these smiling, gentle, tractable little girls into their true forms.'[51] A wedding was not a happy ending but a miserable beginning for *Yellow Book* writers. Their publisher had other ideas.

Whether or not D'Arcy herself wanted to marry Lane, by the time the *Yellow Book* was nearing its end, he was embarking on a matrimonial adventure. John Lane told Evelyn Sharp he was engaged on 3 August 1897.[52] As this was at a business lunch to discuss the publication of a book, this was no disclosure of a secret. George Egerton heard casually from Chapman about it later that month; D'Arcy would soon have known.[53] His intended was Anna Eichberg King, a widow and author whom he had met at a reception in Connaught Square, but had subsequently visited in the USA. As a young woman 'Annie' King was the author of the patriotic hymn 'To Thee O Country', which she wrote to accompany her composer father's music. She was a year older than Lane, having been born in Geneva in 1853, but was brought up in Boston. Lewis May remarked on her that, 'She was accustomed to dress in light-grey silk, which, shining like steel, gave her a warlike appearance.'[54]

There were a variety of reasons for the marriage, as well as the undoubted affection between the happy couple. The 'confirmed bachelor' label was raising a whiff of suspicion in the post-Oscar Wilde atmosphere; it was now best not to be a single gentleman in artistic business circles. The marriage also 'notably increased his financial stability', according to Lewis May.[55] Annie Lane borrowed money on her own security to invest in the firm, and the couple lived on her income with the company's profits being reinvested.[56] The couple settled at 8 Lancaster Gate Terrace; tea parties with ladies at the bachelor apartments at GI the Albany were curtailed now the Lanes were society entertainers at their lavish home.

Lane's engagement and marriage, which took place on 13 August 1898, coincided with a weakening of his commitment to daring fiction. Annie Lane had considerable literary skills and Lane placed great reliance on her judgement. She wrote her own books and translated from French and German. She was not, however, a woman given to challenges to the social order or gender representation. In Annie, John Lane had gained a literary advisor who looked towards conservative readers and prized domesticity. As if in evidence of this, her volume about Dutch provincial life, *Kitwyk Stories*, which had come out in 1895 under the name Anna Eichberg King, was republished by Lane in 1903 as *Kitwyk* under the authorship of 'Mrs John Lane'. This was despite the fact that women were abandoning the convention of taking their husbands' full names; creative artists such as authors were at the forefront of this move. Katherine Lyon Mix remarked: 'Soon after the new century began, the title "Mrs" vanished from authors' lists.'[57] Annie Lane was one of a number of women who saw where the avant-garde was leading and politely declined to follow. She wrote wittily about British and American social life in a book called *The Champagne Standard*, in which she compared experiences of servants, dinner parties and other details of bourgeois life.

There were other challenges for the women of the *Yellow Book*, which weighed particularly heavily on Ella D'Arcy. One of her problems also affected other *Yellow Book* women including George Egerton, Charlotte Mew, Victoria Cross and Edith Nesbit: their reliance on the short story. Others, such as Ella Hepworth Dixon, produced novels but their main output was short stories. Many Keynotes series authors originally appeared as short story writers at a time when the short story had a brief vogue. This was a major bar to the entry of 1890s women into the canon because of the disdain of the literary establishment for the short story. Lena Milman complained in volume VI that 'the contempt for the short story prevalent in England, but unknown elsewhere, is surely . . . traceable to Puritan influence.'[58] It was rare for anyone to make their name by short stories: Kipling was an exception, though he did feel it necessary to struggle to write novels such as *The Light that Failed*, his 1891 comment on the New Woman and the dilemmas she posed for men. To be taken seriously a writer was expected to produce a novel.

It was also a declining market. The naturalistic short story flourished in England for only a few years, remarks William C. Frierson, who dates it narrowly from 1893 to 1898. He comments, 'Various reasons for its decline might be indicated, but it seems probable that the authors found the financial returns disproportionate to the earnestness of their endeavours.'[59] It was possible to keep supplying magazines with stories, but the business of grinding out market-appropriate stories and then selling them was a struggle and not particularly lucrative unless an author was very prolific.

Recognizing this problem, Ella D'Arcy reassured Lane, 'I'm going to work too. I'm going to give you a book. Yes, really! I'm going to begin it next Monday as ever comes!'[60] D'Arcy wrote a piece that was halfway between a short story and a novel, *The Bishop's Dilemma*, about a Catholic priest who falls in love. She had high hopes for it, writing to Lane from what was presumably a family home at Nelson Villa, Hythe, in Kent:

> I gave it to the young Irish priest here, to read. He was intensely interested in it, and speaks of it with great enthusiasm. He says it ought to be an immense success in Ireland. And this makes me see, that the wise course would be, frankly to advertise it as a book about Roman Catholics, 'A book about Roman Catholics by a Roman Catholic', if you liked, and not my name at all.[61]

She thought the quality of *The Bishop's Dilemma* was so high it would restore the *Yellow Book*'s fortunes with the sort of 'sensation' the publication needed.[62] In fact it was too late for the *Yellow Book*, which was soon to cease publication, but it was published as a stand-alone novella by the Bodley Head under her name and 'author of *Monochromes*'. The *Belfast News-Letter* gave it a good if unenthusiastic review, concluding:

> There are veins of rich humour and poignant satire in many of its pages and not a little very excellent character drawing... The story however is one that one wishes to forget almost as soon as one has read it. There is nothing of lasting or lovable quality in the theme. When our author chooses a more rational subject she should accomplish great things[63]

The themes that interested D'Arcy were no longer those which inspired the reading public, it seems.

A novel by her titled *Poor Human Nature* was listed by Lane in advertisements for forthcoming books as 'in preparation' as late as 1897; in October of that year an American edition was advertised at 75 cents.[64] The novel

ran aground on D'Arcy's irascible temperament and Lane's parsimony. She
wrote to him:

> It occurs to me that nothing has been said as to payment for Poor
> Human Nature. I want fifty pounds for it, and I want to know if
> you are prepared to give this sum. Otherwise, please stop setting
> it up and let me have the manuscript back. I cannot go on in this
> condition of pauperdom.[65]

The answer must have been negative as she wrote three days later:

> As there is no money in the book I decide not to publish it, as I
> cannot help being influenced by Henry Harland's strenuously
> expressed opinion that it is a rotten book the publication of which
> can only damage my literary reputation. Will you please order its
> return to me as soon as convenient.[66]

She was torn between her request for money, which gave the book a high
value, and Harland's opinion, which gave it a low one. Lane was unmoved
by her threats and would rather lose the book than pay more than he
thought it was worth; it never appeared.

D'Arcy lived with Evelyn Sharp for a time in the mid-1890s; then Sharp
moved to a flat further from Cromwell Road than was acceptable for
D'Arcy. Sharp wrote to Lane about D'Arcy, 'I am afraid she is very hard up,'
but things must have looked up as she took on the tenancy of a new place
at 150 Cromwell Road, close to the Harlands, in summer 1898.[67] Sharp
wrote to Lane on 12 June:

> Ella D'Arcy has moved into a new flat in Cromwell Road, a most
> sumptuous abode, I went to see her and found her in a glorious
> muddle, with one knife for everything, no blankets, and a bad
> cold. Her Irish nonchalance supported her through everything,
> however, and I sent her round some blankets and a match-box in
> the shape of a pig – I felt a pig was certainly wanting in that
> household![68]

All was not well, since D'Arcy was to write to Arthur Stedman the
following year that she was subletting the flat, which she probably had on
an annual lease:

I've just let this flat, because I'm so hard up. I've sold nothing for the last 2½ years [presumably since *The Bishop's Dilemma*] and consequently am at my last crust. Letters here, however, will always find me and I'll write and let you know what becomes of me. I'm so glad I saw you here again, and that you came this week instead of next. This was such a bit of luck for me, that possibly my luck is going to turn at last.[69]

She went to live with her family in Hythe, Kent; her mail was sent on and she continued to use the Cromwell Road address, so it is not obvious where she was at any one time.

At the end of the century she was again attempting to assail the heights of the novel, this time with a 60,000-word piece based on the life of Shelley. The book had been some time under way, as in January 1895 she had written to Lane, 'I have begun the Shelley story today.'[70] She had set it aside to do other work and completed it only in 1898. Around March that year she sent the manuscript on which she had laboured to the Bodley Head. She was less than delighted to receive a reader's report from Frederic Chapman, of whose judgement she had no high opinion. His less than fulsome praise gave her an opportunity for her acid comments:

> Thank you so much for reading the ms and for your criticisms. I am relieved to know that it will not please the average reader, or the average critic. I do not write for such dull elves, and I had serious fears that I must be degenerating into popularity as my typist praised the first portions so enormously. However, the third part left her speechless, which restored my self-respect. A novel about Shelley which did not alienate the man in the street, which did not evoke the obloquy of the mutton headed, would be a failure per se. The man in the street is no more fit to comprehend Shelley than he was eighty years ago.[71]

She then wrote to Lane on 31 May, 'I am anxious to know whether you want my 60,000 word story, which Mr Chapman has read, and can report on, or not. I'm badly in want of funds, so please let me hear soon.'[72]

A letter without a date but presumably in June shows that Lane called on D'Arcy at home but she was out and says she could not see him the following day. He must have given her manuscript to another, outside reader, who must have been negative; he offered her sight of the report but she responded, 'I don't think I care to hear the reader's opinion, at any rate not now. I am so tired of the book, I want to withdraw it and forget it.'[73] By 11 September she was writing, 'Will you please give orders that my MS be returned to me? . . . it has been in your hands nearly six months, and that you should not have been able to accept it in that time, I take to be equivalent to a refusal.'[74] She offered another volume of short stories the same length as *Modern Instances*, to which the reply was probably negative, as no such volume appeared.

The following year she was still trying to find a publisher. She wrote on 15 April 1899 from Cromwell Road to Arthur Stedman, whom she knew via Harland but with whom she had just become reacquainted. She knew him well enough to address him by a pet name, 'Sampson', while she was 'Delilah': 'Would you be prepared to consider my novel of 60,000 words for Lippincott's?' Lippincott's had published both Kipling's *The Light that Failed* and Wilde's *The Picture of Dorian Gray*, so she was aiming for the big league. She wrote:

> The novel ought to be a success, as it is the story of Shelley and Harriet Westbrook. For outsiders it would read as a vivid and dramatic novel; for good Shelleyans it is a picture of Shelley and his circle, which I flatter myself is, in all essentials, an accurate picture . . . I really think I do not flatter myself in believing the heart of Shelley to be well portrayed.[75]

The response cannot have been positive, as July 1899 found her writing to the editor of the *Century Magazine* in New York, Richard Watson Gilder, offering the still unnamed novel on Shelley, which concerns 'the unhappy girl who was his first wife and who, had she married a commonplace man, would have been the ordinary, happy commonplace woman without a history'.[76] It was not until 8 September 1899 that she was finally invited to submit, but she had lost confidence by this time and her tone has none of the airy certainty of earlier messages; she undermines the credibility of her own work:

> I send the ms today by book-post, and I send it with many misgivings, for while I still think the two first portions of the story fairly good, I am beginning to fear that the third portion is violent and crude, and I know how particularly obnoxious crudity and violence are to you. Probably the subject – a difficult one – is altogether

beyond my capacity, and I have rushed in like the fool where wiser men have forborne to tread.

The letter continued that she didn't think of it for the magazine, but should have been pleased if the company wanted to publish it in book form: 'If it is no good, I wish to offer you a volume of short stories similar to "Modern Instances" which I have ready, and the best of which have not been published before.'[77] She expects sympathy for her insecurity, as she expected sympathy from Lane for her neediness. The answer was no in both cases and her last recorded letter to Gilder asks for the return of a manuscript.[78]

The freelance market was no place for someone so disdainful of low art with such a high opinion of her own abilities, coupled with a denigration of those of others, and a diffidence about pushing her own cause. These were contradictions that battled for control of her creative personality. Harland's biographer Karl Beckson said of D'Arcy that the demise of the *Yellow Book* in 1897 'substantially ended the brilliant promise of her literary career'.[79] It was the loss of an outlet that gave her companions and a focus (inasmuch as someone with such poor work ethic had a focus). 'But for her incurable idleness she should have made if not a great, at least a very distinguished writer of elegant and witty prose,' wrote Netta Syrett.[80] There is always a hint of jealousy in other women's comments about D'Arcy, however, as when Syrett remarks, 'the praise she received as a writer was astonishing.' Syrett's career was successful, but such literary praise eluded her.[81] William Locke called D'Arcy 'one of the great short story writers of her time', but added, 'because she couldn't at once live in the Sun despised a seat on a Planet'. Thus he considered her overambitious, which is not a criticism one frequently hears of men.[82]

There was nothing to keep her in London; the lease was up on the flat at 150 Cromwell Road (probably on the quarter day, 24 December 1899) and it was cheaper to live in Paris. At the end of the century she left London's hissing gas lamps and acrid fogs for a new lease of life in the French capital.

7

A Paris Mystery

Late in 1896 the story began to be voiced in *Yellow Book* circles that something had gone disastrously wrong: Crackanthorpe had disappeared in suspicious circumstances in Paris. 'I hear tragic things of Hubert Crackanthorpe,' Aubrey Beardsley wrote to the *Savoy* publisher Leonard Smithers around 3 December 1896.[1] Just as mysterious was that his glamorous wife, Leila Macdonald, was in London in an emotional state, visiting Aline and Henry Harland, John Lane and other mutual friends including James Welch, the husband of Sissie Welch, with whom, gossip had it, 'Crackie' had been having an affair.

The grim whispers were reported first in the *Daily Chronicle* under the headline 'A Mystery of Paris: Disappearance of Mr Hubert Crackanthorpe' on 12 December. It was explained: 'On the evening before the morning fixed for his return to England he went out for a walk, and from that walk, he never returned. His clothes and money supplies were left at the hotel, and no arrangements whatever had been made by him for any journey or departure of any sort.'[2]

The Crackanthorpes were the golden couple that everyone wanted to be: they were both good looking, wealthy, upper class, well connected, well travelled and talented. If any of the *Yellow Book* writers could have been predicted to have a great future, it was them. Leila was a tall, commanding figure with blonde hair and prominent blue eyes. She was born at 2 Chapel Street, Westminster, to wealthy parents on 7 February 1871. She was of the Scottish family known as the Lords of the Isles and was the great-great-granddaughter of the Jacobite heroine Flora Macdonald, who assisted Bonnie Prince Charlie. Her father, Reginald Somerled Macdonald, was a barrister (as was Crackanthorpe's father) and an old Etonian (as was Crackanthorpe). Her mother, Emma, was the daughter of Sir William Grove, a judge. She

Missing notice for
Hubert Crackanthorpe
from *The Graphic*,
19 December 1896.

MR. HUBERT CRACKANTHORPE
Photo by Bassano, Old Bond Street

The disappearance of Mr. Hubert Crackanthorpe, the son of Mr. Montague Crackanthorpe,
Q.C., will cause great concern among a large
circle of London society. Mr. Hubert
Crackanthorpe was a clever and promising
young novelist, his story, "Wreckage,"
attracting considerable attention. He disappeared from his hotel in Paris about a
fortnight ago, and, though diligent search has
been made for him, no trace has yet been
discovered

died of tuberculosis at the age of 24 on 5 May 1875 when Leila was four.
Leila's father, a clerk at the Colonial Office, was diagnosed as a 'dipsomaniac'
(alcoholic) from 1874, with heavy drinking coinciding with his wife's decline
and death. He died fifteen months after Emma, also at the family home, on
26 August 1876 aged 35, of alcohol poisoning leading to cardiac arrest.

Thereafter Leila moved to her maternal grandfather's home at 115
Harley Street. She was brought up by her old nurse, Mary Anne Gibbs, who
became housekeeper to Leila's maternal grandfather, Sir William Grove,
who combined being a jurist with scientific investigations. A fellow of the
Royal Society, he made important contributions to the development of
batteries and to the theory of energy. Characteristically of many women of
the *Yellow Book*, records of Leila's early life are scant and no information is
available about her education. She obviously had literary and artistic tastes,
which was an area of alignment between herself and Crackanthorpe.

Leila Macdonald was close to Hubert Crackanthorpe in age and background; both were from well-to-do families with connections to the north. Their families may have been known to each other: Hubert witnessed a codicil to Leila's paternal grandmother's will in August 1892. Among other things Leila was bequeathed an 'inlaid marqueterie meuble' to be found in the 'Watteau bedroom', which gives an indication of the wealth of her upbringing.[3]

Crackanthorpe was born Hubert Montague Cookson in London on 12 May 1870, the eldest of three sons of Blanche, a writer and social commentator who, at their home in Rutland Gate, Knightsbridge, hosted literary receptions where guests included George Meredith, Thomas Hardy and Henry James. His father was Montague Hughes Cookson QC, sometime counsel to the University of Oxford and a writer on eugenics.

In 1888 the Crackanthorpes succeeded to the 6,000-acre Newbiggin Estates in Westmorland and Cumberland on the death of Montague Cookson's first cousin William Crackanthorpe; the family took the name Crackanthorpe on 28 July 1888 as a condition of inheritance. The pride of the estates and the ancestral home of the Crackanthorpes was the manor house Newbiggin Hall, the oldest remaining part of which was built in the fourteenth century.

Crackanthorpe was at Eton for five years, between 1883 and 1888, but for the next four years of his life there is no record. He was said to have spent a year in Orthez in southern France and, back in England, to have studied with the poet, painter and designer Selwyn Image. His mother was later to write that his friends 'saw in the unfolding flower of his manhood a renewal of the bright promise of his early youth'.[4] The suggestion given by the word 'renewal' is of an interruption between his youth and manhood. This can be conjectured as mental illness, probably depression, which would explain the missing years when he did not go to university, the usual destination for a young man of his background and talents. Not having gone to university was, at any rate, another facet of life that Leila had in common with Crackanthorpe. They certainly both loved books; his library has survived and she is known to have given him a copy of De Quincey's *Confessions of an English Opium Eater* for Christmas 1892.

Crackanthorpe next appears in the record making a name for himself at the age of 21, editing a literary magazine named the *Albemarle*, financed by his father, and featuring work by advanced authors showing politically liberal views. He edited it between January and September 1892 and included in it his first published stories and essays, two of them an interview with

Emile Zola and an article on Henry James as a playwright. Leila did not contribute to the *Albemarle*, which suggests her writing was at an inchoate stage at this time (when she was twenty and twenty-one) or that the magazine was already in terminal decline when she became close to Crackanthorpe. Leila has been described as 'a handsome young woman of literary tastes', but also as 'unbalanced'.[5] Whether this is a reasonable description it is difficult to say, but she definitely showed the need for constant reassurance, which is characteristic of people who have had a disturbed childhood.

Hubert received a stipend from his father, Leila had received her parental inheritance, but neither was rich in terms of the world in which they lived, a fact slyly remarked upon by Blanche Crackanthorpe: 'When our sons and daughters come to tell us that they desire to "make their own experiment" in the shape of marriage upon what to our world would appear a minute income, let us be aiders and abettors of their midsummer madness.'[6] She suggests concerned parents 'cannot shut our eyes to what goes on in our midst, and to the daily and nightly dangers to which our sons are exposed'.[7] This was a reference to the possibility of a son catching a venereal disease or making a girl from an unsuitable background pregnant.

Their marriage took place on St Valentine's Day 1893, in St Paul's Church in Knightsbridge; both were aged 22. Crackanthorpe's profession was given as 'author', presumably on the basis of *Wreckage*, his book of stories that was to be published the following month; Leila's was left blank. They first lived in a flat of eight rooms at 36 Chelsea Gardens. After the wedding they honeymooned in France, in the neighbourhood of Orthez, where Crackanthorpe's friend Francis Jammes, the poet and novelist, rented a place for them, the Villa Baron near Sallespisse. Jammes recounted their life with their English tobacco, richly bound books and the horses in the barn on which they would ride gracefully in the countryside.[8] Some of Crackanthorpe's sketches of rural life later collected in *Vignettes* were written on this trip. Jammes does not seem to have got on well with Leila, whom he describes as 'une sorte d'amazone a l'oeil dur' (a kind of hard-eyed Amazon); he later blamed her for the tragedy of the Crackanthorpes' marriage.[9]

During this stay near Orthez, Jammes recounts that Leila was burned on a picnic by fuel from a spirit stove being used to make the obligatory afternoon cup of tea. Spirit lamps are notorious for accidents because their flame is not visible in sunlight, so people can think the flame has gone out and begin to replenish the fuel reservoir with a new container of volatile liquid, and the rising fumes explode. This may well have been the cause of the accident Leila suffered.

As Jammes described it, he and Crackanthorpe were some few hundred metres away. Leila was preparing tea in the company of their friend the artist Charles Lacoste on the bank of the Gave river. Crackanthorpe and Jammes were alarmed to see Leila rolling on the ground and crying out while Lacoste went to her aid. The alcohol lamp had exploded in Leila's face, burning her eyes. Jammes described her eyes as being like two bloody blisters; her hair had also been burned. The men quickly hired a passing carriage, offering a high price, and took Leila to a doctor in Orthez. The doctor burst the blisters over her eyes and she was condemned to a dark room for a month, but eventually made a partial recovery. She was seeing specialists for at least the next two years.

It was probably because of the lingering effects of her injury that their travels were cut short. They returned to rented rooms at 36 Chelsea Gardens while preparing what was intended to be their permanent home at 96 Cheyne Walk on the Chelsea Embankment, formerly the home of Whistler, which the couple had decorated by the artist Roger Fry with white walls, black dados and various decorative features.[10] Such attentions were not cheap; in the bitter words of Crackanthorpe's brother Dayrell to Leila, Hubert 'spent large sums in getting up the Cheyne Walk house to suit you'.[11] Dayrell also charged Leila with a failure to take on household duties:

> you persistently declined to perform, in any sense, those domestic duties which every husband, and especially a husband whose work requires concentration of thought and repose of mind, has a right to expect from his wife. You appeared to imagine that he could alike perform the duties of a housekeeper and pursue the career of a writer.[12]

Dayrell did not consider that she might be faced with the same double choice.

A will Leila drafted in December 1893 makes bequests of a generous amount of jewellery and a large sum that was expected to come to her on the death of her paternal grandmother. The old lady did not in fact die until February 1896 (and Leila's portion was rather less than had been anticipated) but the social commitment the draft will conveyed is revealing. Should Leila die suddenly the draft left her money to Crackanthorpe until he came into his own estate, and to the social reformer Josephine Butler thereafter 'to be used as she thinks fit in her work of female rescue from the streets'.[13] Butler was famed for her campaigning work for the repeal of the Contagious Diseases Acts (accomplished in 1886), which had, by making medical examination of prostitutes obligatory, given effective state sanction to prostitution. Leila was clearly not a shrinking violet who knew nothing of the realities of sexual life. The Crackanthorpes' commitment to social causes is not directly apparent from their literary work but occurs in letters such as one Hubert sent from Siena: 'Have you been taking in the *Daily Chronicle*? The coal-strike has been interesting us keenly: we have been longing for some spare pounds to send to the miners. I see that Cobden-Sanderson [the artist and bookbinder], who is a poor man, has given £100. It's splendid of him.'[14]

In the period after their marriage Leila wrote four pieces that appeared in the *Yellow Book*: a story of French provincial life called 'Jeanne-Marie' in October 1894; a short poem, 'Red Rose', in January 1895; some lyrical 'Refrains' in April 1895; and a poem called 'To the Bust of the Pompeian Coelia' in October 1895. Ella D'Arcy considered that Leila owed her inclusion in the *Yellow Book* to 'the intercession of her husband and the affability of Harland', though D'Arcy was notoriously catty.[15] Leila Macdonald as a poet has in the twenty-first century attracted positive critical attention from Linda Hughes and Sally Ledger.[16] She was the only one of the *Yellow Book* women writers whose work was also published in the *Savoy*.

Leila wrote to John Lane in October 1895 from Wiesbaden, Germany:

Dear Mr Lane, Would you be so kind as to send me my copy of the *Yellow Book* to the above address? I hear it is going to be a splendid number, and shall count the days till its arrival! I have been here for five weeks under Pagenstecher, for my eyes. They are much better and I hope to get away in another ten days.[17]

Crackanthorpe wrote to Selwyn Image that the specialist had explained 'she is suffering from a sort of congestion of the eye-nerves, & that no spectacles could ever have helped her.' She went every morning to Pagenstecher, who massaged her eyes: 'today for the first time she is able to do a little reading.'[18] They were travelling again in the autumn but returned to London in December 1895, Leila now pregnant. They moved into the now fully decorated Lindsay House, their old premises of 36 Chelsea Gardens being taken by Julie Norregard, who was in a relationship with Richard Le Gallienne.

At this time Crackanthorpe was writing of communication difficulties in relationships in his 1895 book *Sentimental Studies*, sometimes to a grotesque degree, for example 'In Cumberland', where a country vicar ruins his life for the love of a woman who cares little for him. All of them involve not just misunderstanding and dissimulation (one of the major themes of *Wreckage*) but parting. In 'In Cumberland' the vicar goes off to Australia without his beloved; in 'Battledore and Shuttlecock' a young man in love with a prostitute is deserted by her and goes to India; in 'Yew-Trees and Peacocks' a colonel who has been in love with his friend's wife says goodbye to her as he has a posting abroad; and the good-time girl of 'Modern Melodrama' contemplates her own death from galloping consumption. Hubert wrote in hand in the copy of the book he gave to Leila, 'A petite âme, this wretched book which one evening she wanted to take seriously'.[19] Presumably they had a heated discussion about how much of the book was based on life.

He dedicated this second book not to his wife but to Henry Harland: 'To Harry, in remembrance of much encouragement.' A flavour of the fun he and Harland had is given in *The Light Sovereign*, a farce they wrote together. 'We'll go to Paris, sirrah, and amuse ourselves incog,' says one character. 'We'll go to the Chat Noir and the Moulin Rouge and the Bois de Boulogne . . . and we'll live in the Latin Quarter under an assumed name; and we'll drink absinthe; and we'll get acquainted with all the decadent poets; and we'll have a ripping old time.'[20]

Despite their love of travel, shared social background and literary interests, Leila and Crackanthorpe did not appear to be having a ripping time. The marriage ran into problems almost from the start; it is probably not a coincidence that Crackanthorpe was contemplating an unhappy marriage in his long story 'A Commonplace Chapter', a part of which was printed in the *Yellow Book* volume V in April 1895. It concerns the Hasletons, a successful literary man and his wife, whose admiration for him has declined in matrimony while he finds it difficult to live up to the image she had of him. Sometimes the husband would 'openly betray how little she had come to mean to him', while she felt 'sometimes she hated all this success of his, because it seemed to emphasise the gulf between them.'[21] The husband finds relief for the pressure of his circumstances in infidelity with a woman who 'belonged to the higher walks of the demi-monde'.[22]

As if in response, after the end of Crackanthorpe's story in the *Yellow Book* Harland and Beardsley had placed a picture of Sissie Welch by Philip Wilson Steer. She is shown as a good-looking woman in a hat staring slightly away from the viewer. The actor Harold Child described her as

Sissie Welch, drawing by P. Wilson Steer from the *Yellow Book*, vol. v (April 1895).

a largely moulded, handsome woman with hair of a beautiful shade of dull gold. The drawing of her by Steer in the *Yellow Book* under an enormous hat gives the facts, the broad brow, the large eyes, the right eye turned ever so little outward with almost alluring touch of oddness, the full lips; but the whole is lifeless and conveys no idea of her voluptuous beauty.[23]

A friend of the Welchs and Le Galliennes, the novelist Constance Smedley, wrote:

Sissie was entirely English and there was something Spenserian about her freshness and her dignity . . . [Her] clothes were a revelation of beauty. Sissie Welch collected old lace and had a wonderful collection of collars. In their early married life when she joined Jim in London and they found themselves invited everywhere, they managed on an income of a hundred and fifty pounds a year. She had one black evening gown and rang the changes on the beautiful old collars . . . Her aesthetic tendencies were tempered with a cosmopolitanism which was new to me, and at the same time she radiated a sweet and wholesome sanity.[24]

Unlike Hubert and Leila, therefore, Sissie was not independently wealthy. Another difference is that it is obvious from the extant memoirs that Sissie endeared herself to people where Leila did not.

Sissie Welch, born Mary Elizabeth Gallienne on 7 December 1868, was 'confidante, listener and counsellor' to her large family of which she was the eldest girl, hence the name Sissie by which she was known all her life.[25] The publisher Grant Richards ungallantly calls her 'an almost beautiful woman'.[26] Sissie and Richard Gallienne were brought up in Liverpool as allies against their tyrannical father, a severe Baptist who restricted every attempt at independence or flirtation. Richard (who added 'Le' to his name) left for London at 21 in 1887 and later lived in rooms with the aspiring actor Jimmy Welch, who had also come to London to seek his fortune. Sissie and Jimmy had been childhood sweethearts and married without her father's blessing in January 1893 (weeks before Crackanthorpe and Leila's marriage). Richard Le Gallienne had introduced Hubert Crackanthorpe to the Welchs, and had been Hubert's chief promoter in a world where critics reviled him.

Leila and Crackanthorpe attended the Welches' Friday-afternoon 'at homes' at their flat on a top floor in Verulam Buildings in Gray's Inn, overlooking the gardens. Constance Smedley remembered:

> I appreciated the simple niceties of the ménage at Gray's Inn whose square green room, with its windows looking out into the tree-tops, always seemed a haven of peace and a heaven of literature and art: not professional art but art-lovers' art . . . we all sympathised and delighted in one another's first steps on the ladder of fame.[27]

Along with the Crackanthorpes and Richard Le Gallienne, the actor Harold Child records, 'Other pretty regular visitors at the Welches' were George Egerton, now Mrs Golding Bright, then a very slender, grave-faced Celt . . . Evelyn Sharp . . . Netta Syrett, and the eminent Henry Harland.'[28] Child wrote:

> Sissie's demands on life, I fear, took a good deal of satisfying. It was the time of the craze for bicycling; and daily she would take a hansom, with her bicycle on the roof, from Gray's Inn to Battersea Park, bicycle there for an hour or two and take a hansom all the

way back again. Jim was always ready to work himself to death; but that sort of thing was too much for any actor's salary.[29]

Roads were dangerous for cyclists and bicycles were banned in open spaces under the Parks Regulation Act, but Battersea was exempt, so cyclists, predominantly women, gravitated there and cycled en masse. Child's reference to this habit of Sissie's suggests she was something of a free spirit and not under strict spousal control, which is his intention in mentioning it because he no doubt knew (but was too fastidious to mention) that Sissie Welch and Hubert Crackanthorpe were having an affair. There is no information as to when it began, but it was certainly under way in spring or summer 1896.

Leila miscarried early in 1896 and it is hardly pushing the boundary between art and life to see this event represented in her verse play 'The Love of the Poor', which appeared in *The Savoy* in April, in which the characters are an old man, an old woman and the soul of their dead child, who brings them comfort in their misery. The miscarriage had disturbed her and upset the marriage. In words reported by Hubert to his mother, Leila had 'conceived a physical repulsion to him'.[30]

Leila's later accusation was that she had contracted a venereal disease from Crackanthorpe, presumably syphilis. It may be that the miscarriage was caused by syphilis, but until there were other signs of the disease, Leila would not have known this was the cause. Often women did not know they had syphilis because the first sign of it, the primary chancre, was internal, perhaps on the cervix. The second stage – rashes, feverishness and headaches – could be confused with other minor conditions or might have been concealed by the immunological side effects of pregnancy in the case of Leila. This was a well-known conundrum; the birth of a child with the obvious signs of congenital syphilis to an apparently completely healthy woman led to speculation by doctors that the disease might be communicated directly to the foetus by the diseased father.

After this second stage syphilis would characteristically go into a latent form and slowly attack the nervous and cardiovascular systems. This tendency to go into latency convinced people they had been cured, particularly after they had sought treatment that suppressed the symptoms, but there was no cure in the nineteenth century. An important question for the time was whether Crackanthorpe contracted syphilis before marriage or after: if before the marriage, then a woman had a right only to a separation – if after, she had a right to a divorce because adultery was therefore obviously implicated.[31]

THE LOVE OF THE POOR

PERSONAGES.

THE OLD MAN.
THE OLD WOMAN.
THE SOUL OF THEIR DEAD CHILD.

SCENE.—*The interior of a small cottage, almost devoid of furniture. Two chairs drawn up to a fireless grate. Time : twilight.*

THE OLD WOMAN *enters, walking feebly, carrying a few twigs.*

The Old Woman.

AR, far have I wandered in my search for wood.
My arms are stiff, my eyes are dim
From cold and want of food.
But soon dear God will give us help,
I know that God is good.
       The Soul of the Dead Child. Yes, God is good.
The Old Woman. My foolish brain seems all to reel,

'The Love of the Poor' by Leila MacDonald, with illustration by William T. Horton, in *The Savoy* (April 1896).

Leila later knew she had contracted syphilis and probably believed it was responsible for her miscarriage, but she most likely did not know it in spring 1896. Doctors habitually concealed from women that they had syphilis – and concealed from married women medical diagnoses that were instead reported to their husbands. This is the theme of Crackanthorpe's story 'Modern Melodrama', in which a woman has to send a servant to eavesdrop on a doctor's conversation with the man of the house about the woman's illness. In Leila's case, though only 'venereal disease' was mentioned, if the presumption that the miscarriage was caused by it is accepted, it had to be syphilis because of its abortifacient qualities – gonorrhoea may cause sterility or ectopic pregnancy long-term, but not miscarriage.

Not a few Crackanthorpe stories turn on a guilty secret harboured before marriage: in 'Dissolving View' a rich hedonist about to marry finds he has had a child by a chorus girl, goes to see her, and is delighted to find that both girl and child are dead. Anthony Garstin in 'Anthony Garstin's Courtship' has to deceive his mother that the child his intended is carrying is his; Lilly in 'Profiles' has sex with an acquaintance of her intended husband while waiting for him to come to marry her. Despite his preoccupation with the seamy side of relationships, it is noticeable that Crackanthorpe does not feature venereal disease in his stories, as he certainly could have – Sarah Grand (incidentally, the mother of Haldane Macfall, who was to play a part in the Crackanthorpe story) famously did. Crackanthorpe's choice not to do so, except by allusion, suggests a suspicious reluctance to confront the issue of venereal disease contaminating a relationship.

It is quite possible Crackanthorpe had been infected before marriage – his first stories, mainly written during the *Albemarle* period, show adequate familiarity with prostitution and with *demi-mondaines* to suggest genuine experience. Or he might have contracted syphilis after marriage; the story in Richard Le Gallienne's family was that Sissie Welch gave Crackanthorpe the disease.[32] If this were so, and the miscarriage was syphilis-related, it would be necessary for Crackanthorpe's affair with Sissie Welch to have begun prior to Leila's pregnancy. Haldane Macfall was on the scene as a friend of the Welches and of Hubert Crackanthorpe and his family (excluding Leila). He remarked:

> Now it so happened that soon after the marriage [February 1893], other intimate friends of mine became intimates of Hubert's – James Welch the actor and his charming wife, Cissie Le [*sic*] Gallienne, sister of the poet ... Hubert seems to have been fascinated by Cissie Welch, or she by him, at any rate, whether any harm came of it or not, they became very intimate and Hubert, Cissie and Jimmy Welch were much together.[33]

Macfall is a very questionable source, but it seems reasonable to accept as accurate this version of people and events in which he was actually involved, and which is merely scene-setting to dubious allegations he made later in the letter.

Ella D'Arcy wrote to John Lane in April 1896, 'the Cracks and Cissie [*sic*] Welch are back in Paris.'[34] The three were, therefore, known to associate and travel together. Though Leila literally left the marital home in spring 1896, this does not mean she had renounced her husband – she had previously been abroad alone after her marriage, and it was not of itself evidence of desertion. She was on her way to Italy, and may well have travelled the first part of the journey with her husband and their friend Sissie.

On another occasion, on 11 August 1896 Le Gallienne crossed the Channel to France on his way to deliver a lecture in Switzerland and met his sister Sissie and Hubert Crackanthorpe travelling to Paris together. His letter to his future wife Julie Norregard expresses surprise at the encounter but Le Gallienne was a past master of dissimulation (particularly where his wives and girlfriends were concerned), so it is not possible to judge whether the meeting was pre-planned, or how much he knew about the affair. It was a jolly meeting nevertheless; 'Crackie stood us lunch with champagne!!' Le Gallienne wrote, and Crackanthorpe helped his friend on his way: 'Crackie was a perfect dear – got my luggage through the customs, changed my small fortune at the bureau, and generally did everything for me – for which I was the most grateful, as my asthma rendered me rather helpless.'[35]

Meanwhile, at Viareggio on the Tuscan coast, while travelling alone Leila met a man referred to by others as a 'French adventurer', a sometime artist called the Comte d'Artaux. Later testimony said she was 'infatuated' with him and he was after her money.[36] Leila's grandfather Sir William Grove died that summer, making her even wealthier. Leila did not attend the funeral in London on 4 August, though we cannot know the circumstances (it may be that had she travelled from Italy she would not have had time to get to London for the funeral). Hubert and his father did attend.

Hubert and Sissie stayed in hotels in Paris, then Leila and d'Artaux arrived in the city at the beginning of September and the Crackanthorpes took an apartment at 18 Avenue Kléber between the Place de l'Etoile and Place du Trocadero, where they lived with d'Artaux. At first Sissie remained at a hotel, but at Leila's invitation Sissie joined them and for two months they lived together.

Literary life and future plans continued. On 6 October 1896 Crackanthorpe wrote to the publisher Grant Richards, who was in Paris:

I have just heard from Symons that the *Savoy* is to cease in December. Would you be disposed to consider the idea of taking it over then with me as editor? . . . I believe, without vanity, that my name (for reasons which I need not specify) would be more valuable than Symons', and certainly yours would be an improvement on that of Smithers.

There was no secrecy at his being with Sissie; twelve days later he wrote from 18 Avenue Kléber, 'Sissie and I will be at the Café de la Paix after dinner (about 9) tonight: would you care to come round to meet us there and have another chat about things?'[37] That meeting did not in fact take place and Crackanthorpe wrote an embarrassed note at the Café de la Paix at 10 p.m.:

I'm so sorry: we delayed in starting, and didn't get here till twenty to ten. I do hope you didn't come and go away at last in disgust. If you did, please forgive me. However the loss is mine, for I have been thinking over the idea we talked of last night; I've reduced it to some sort of shape which I should have liked to have expounded to you.[38]

They did manage to meet and discuss the project, and arranged to meet a few weeks thence.

A few details of life at 18 Avenue Kléber are known: Hubert went everywhere with Sissie; they had adjoining rooms; d'Artaux painted a portrait of Leila in bed; the four of them played cards together. The atmosphere at Avenue Kléber was strained; Hubert's brother Dayrell Crackanthorpe later wrote that Leila was angry and offensive to her husband.[39] At the beginning of November Leila sent to London for her solicitor, John Hills, who arrived on 4 November. On the afternoon of that day she entered Sissie's room where Sissie was dressing and saw Hubert there. The precise reason for Leila's entering (for there can be no doubt that she knew Sissie and Hubert were in a sexual relationship) was to provide grounds for divorce proceedings, for which not merely general knowledge of a relationship but a precise place and date would be necessary. The testimony of the chambermaid was also sought to substantiate the charge. Leila and d'Artaux left the Avenue Kléber.

That day Hubert and Sissie went to tea and then to the opera, but on their return found Leila gone, having left a 'curt note' saying she wanted a divorce. Hubert rushed out to try to trace her but failed. He was in a desperate state and was said to have had an argument with a cabman that had to be settled by the police.[40] The following morning, on 5 November, he sent Sissie back to London because 'her name and her husband's must not be besmirched,' according to Dayrell; Crackanthorpe traced Leila to the Hotel Mirabeau where they argued and she threatened to call the police.[41] She was never to see him again.

Crackanthorpe had contacted his parents; his father was unable to come but Blanche Crackanthorpe arrived on 5 November to find her son in a wretched state, and was presumably able to gather all or most of the story from him. They took rooms at the Hôtel de France where Hubert and Blanche had an interview with Hills the solicitor. Adultery was not the most serious charge. Leila accused Hubert of communicating venereal disease to her, a charge known as 'legal cruelty' (because it was not legally possible for a married woman to refuse sex with her husband).

Dayrell wrote an account of the meeting in an angry letter to Leila. He called her accusation of legal cruelty 'a dastardly outrage on the sanctity of married life', and remarked high-handedly, 'I can only say that there are many women on the street who would recoil in horror from making such an accusation.'[42] Dayrell's familiarity with the women of the street aside, he is clearly telling Leila that a decent woman would accept venereal infection without complaint. It is revealing that Dayrell Crackanthorpe charges Leila with making the accusation against her husband, not challenging its verity. Did this notice of Hubert's medical condition perhaps come as no surprise to Dayrell, who is only appalled that a woman should complain about it? It may be that Leila innocently infected d'Artaux and he then charged her with it (the signs of syphilis being generally more obvious in a man than a woman) and it was this that stimulated her fury at Hubert at the beginning of November. She was certainly seeing a doctor while in Paris; Dayrell Crackanthorpe referred to it in his letter to her.

Hubert's response to the crisis does not suggest innocence of a charge easily disproved by a medical examination. After the conference with his mother and the solicitor Hills, on the evening of 5 November Hubert left the hotel. He was last seen walking along the Quai Voltaire by the Seine. He had arranged to return to London with his mother by the night train, but he did not arrive at the station to join her and she travelled alone. He was not seen alive again. The Seine was in full flood when Hubert disappeared, and his brother had no doubt that he was dead (though there was as yet no evidence that he was). Dayrell harangued Leila that it was entirely down to the soon-to-be public accusation of venereal infection that Hubert had disappeared and probably killed himself:

> whatever step he took that evening is entirely attributable to that hideous charge. If my brother should be dead, it is this that has killed him. For my own part, I would sooner my brother was at the bottom of the Seine than again under the influence of a woman such as you.[43]

Under such an onslaught, Leila left Paris, returned to London and spent at least some time with Henry and Aline Harland. She wrote from three different addresses, none of them the marital home. From the Harlands' home at 144 Cromwell Road, dated 'Sunday evening', she wrote to John Lane: 'Dear Mr Lane, I am in very great trouble. I think perhaps you could help me. Could you possibly come to see me here tonight, at any hour up to 12.30? Or, if that is impossible, early tomorrow morning. Please forgive my bothering you. Yours very sincerely, Leila Crackanthorpe.'[44] Lane had obviously been friendly with her in the past and she needed someone known and trusted by Welch to act as an intermediary with him; the tubercular Harland could not be sent out into a damp London night on such an errand. Aline Harland was prepared to accompany Leila, but it would not be proper for a lady to be seeing an actor at the stage door at night.

She was keen to contact James Welch, perhaps to tell him Sissie was infected with VD. She had already confronted Sissie – Dayrell referred to 'the explanation of your ailment afforded by you yourself to Mrs Welch'.[45] However, it would be surprising if Lane was involved in delivering a letter on such a matter. More likely she was simply asking if Jimmy or Sissie had any knowledge of the whereabouts of Hubert; she writes, 'this suspense is getting almost unbearable,' so a reply was expected.[46]

Welch was performing one of the comic character parts that had made him famous, in this case as the elderly post boy in Murray Carson and Louis N. Parker's play *Rosemary* at the Criterion on Piccadilly Circus. Lane said he was prepared to deliver a letter to Welch at the stage door, but told her to see a solicitor first. She consulted Hills and then went to see Lane in his office in Vigo Street and found him absent, so wrote a note that she left (the letter to him was on his own business notepaper):

> Dear Mr Lane, I had a consultation with my solicitors this morning, and they see no harm whatever in the letter being given to Mr

Welch – so I should be very grateful to you if today you would do it after the theatre. Mrs Harland and I will wait in the carriage close to the theatre. Where shall we meet to settle the time of our rendezvous? Or could you send me down a line or wire to 24 Lowndes Square before 4 o'clock and I will communicate with Mrs Harland. Yours very sincerely, Leila Crackanthorpe.[47]

The address in Belgravia may well have been the home of her uncle Richard Fort or a close relative; her maternal grand-aunt was called Fort. In 1897 a Mrs Fort was listed as the occupant.[48] On Tuesday 17 November 1896 on paper headed 24 Lowndes Square she wrote:

Dear Mr Lane, Thank you so much for saying you will take the letter to Mr Welch tomorrow night. I shall be extremely grateful to you if you will. It appears he is not in the last act of *Rosemary*, nor in the last part of the preceding act, so I suppose he will be out between 10 and 10.30. In that case I think it will be better for me to wait for you at the Harlands, if you will kindly come on there to let us know the result . . . Thanking you again for your great kindness.[49]

James Welch was performing at a top West End theatre; his career could have been seriously harmed by the scandal. He seems to have received Sissie back with remarkable equanimity. With the memory of the Oscar Wilde debacle fresh in the collective theatreland mind, Welch must have known he would be tainted by association, however innocent he might be. The only record of his response to the events has him expressing concern for the fate of Crackanthorpe, which was very decent of him, considering the circumstances. Le Gallienne wrote to Julie Norregard:

Siss and I have been talking and talking all evening. Dear girl, she is of course very upset, but wonderfully brave too – the more I think of it, the more I think it may not be the worst, but that he has simply gone right away from some wild notion of honour. Jim and I both think this and we can only hope it may be true. There is no further news, and it is now midnight.[50]

There was no news of Crackanthorpe for Leila or anyone else, but from mid-December there was frantic newspaper speculation. As *The Times* recorded, 'it was firmly believed that Mr Crackanthorpe was purposely keeping out of sight. This belief was strengthened by reports stating that he had been seen at Rouen, Havre, and Rheims, and finally in London some days ago.'[51] Gossip spread of how Crackanthorpe and a young lady who 'appeared to be on very affectionate terms with Mr Crackanthorpe', and who was described as 'slim, petite, exceedingly pretty, and dressed somewhat loudly', called on Grant Allen, who was staying in Paris. After that visit, neither Crackanthorpe nor his companion were seen again, the report read.[52]

The family was able to crush this, putting it out that the woman seen with Crackanthorpe was 'on a visit to Mr Crackanthorpe and his wife'; soon after seeing Grant Allen 'she left Paris to re-join her husband in London.' Thus Sissie was diplomatically removed from the scene.[53] David Crackanthorpe remarked that his grandfather seems to have taken on the role of protector of Sissie, 'assuming a tenderness for his brother's mistress that perhaps augmented his dislike of the widow'.[54]

Dayrell and his mother, Blanche Crackanthorpe, and her youngest son Oliver rushed to Paris on 23 December on being informed by the French police that a body, almost certainly that of Hubert Crackanthorpe, had been recovered from the Seine. Before the Crackanthorpe family arrived that December day in 1896 the body, decomposed beyond recognition, had been identified at the morgue from the clothes, linen marks and articles upon it such as a single cuff link, a silver cigarette case and matchbox and a ring bearing the family crest. The police found no evidence of robbery or foul play; they judged from the appearance of the corpse that it must have been in the water for fully six weeks. That being the case, the death on 5 November 1896 was either suicide or accident. Dayrell, an official at the Foreign Office, was at pains to ensure his brother's death was not subject to an inquest. The police concurred, one presumes with a shrug; there was nothing in it for them to hold an inquest on a foreign national where there were no suspicious circumstances. The body was released to the family to be shipped back to England.

Some deft diplomatic work was being done on Anglo-French relations. The correspondent of the *Northern Echo* remarked:

> The police refuse to give any information whatever, and refer all inquirers to the British Embassy. The same extraordinary reserve is maintained there, the officials when applied to declining to make any statement. All requests to view the body are also met with a courteous but firm refusal on the part of the Morgue officials.[55]

That secured, Dayrell set to ensuring the family's view of events was the public one. On 27 December 1896 Dayrell Crackanthorpe sat down in the Hôtel Metropolitain, rue Caraban, Paris, to explain to John Lane exactly how the death of his brother should be interpreted. He wrote, 'I was so closely linked to him in point of years as well as by natural sympathies that I feel it my duty to get rid of any wrong impression that may have been produced as to the cause of his death.' Dayrell, who was soon to take up his first overseas post in the British embassy in Madrid, was described by his grandson David Crackanthorpe, who knew him well, as a man who 'held discretion to be almost the first of virtues, and he developed, to a high degree, manipulative skills in dealing with those around him, particularly within his own family.'[56] Dayrell explained to Lane:

> My brother's death was self-inflicted: on his body was found a letter written to him by his wife, to whom he was devotedly attached, on the 4th of November last. They had been living in the Avenue Kléber during the two previous months, and in this letter she announced to him her intention of leaving him. This she did the same evening. Having traced her to a Paris hotel, my brother went to her early on the 5th of November and implored her to give him an explanation. She refused to see him and that same night my brother disappeared.

'I beg you will make all possible use of this letter,' he wrote, in this small gem of what would in later diplomatic terms be called not lies but being 'economical with the truth.'[57] His death was received with the reverence due to youth cut short in his own literary circles. Richard Le Gallienne wrote, 'I venture to believe that posterity will deem the youth who could write *Wreckage* at the age of twenty-two something like the Chatterton of the English novel.'[58] Le Gallienne's obituary and later homage to Crackanthorpe missed any mention of the women in the story, Leila and Sissie, though he was in a position to know a good deal about the background to the disappearance of Crackanthorpe.

The Crackanthorpes issued a statement to the London newspapers:

> according to the medical evidence, there is no doubt that Mr Hubert Crackanthorpe met with his death on the evening of Thursday the 5th November. He had been with his mother until 11.30 that evening when he went for a walk, and was last seen at

11.50pm on the Quai Voltaire, within 300 yards of which place his body was found seven weeks later. For the last two months of his life he was living in Paris; during that period he never left it for a single day, and the circumstances of every day of his life there are said to be perfectly well known to his family. Mrs and Mrs Crackanthorpe having been much pained by numerous statements in the press, for which there is no foundation, earnestly request that this statement may be accepted as fact.[59]

Hubert Crackanthorpe's body was taken in a lead-lined coffin back to Britain and a funeral service was held on 1 January at All Saints', Knightsbridge; Leila was not present. Such 1890s luminaries as Max Beerbohm and Henry and Aline Harland were recorded as attending, but not Sissie or James Welch.[60] He was cremated at Woking that evening; Ella D'Arcy wrote to John Lane, 'Dayrell writes to me they particularly wish all Hubert's friends to go to the final ceremony at Woking.'[61]

The extent of the Crackanthorpe family's duplicity is shown in a letter from Haldane Macfall to the American journalist and writer Vincent Starrett:

His suicide was a hideous thing – far more hideous than for the love of a woman … Now for the confidential truth. Young Hubert Crackanthorpe was heir to Newbiggin – a castle of King Stephen's time in the north country. The woman who married him was making a very brilliant match socially. I won't put it stronger than that. Soon after the marriage she began to show pretty openly her preference for a certain French count – we need not go into names … She wrote to Hubert an appalling letter (which was found on his dead body) in which she told him that she had taken legal proceedings to divorce him, intended to make Cissie Welch the co-respondent, and threatening him that if he contested the case she would produce evidence that whilst at Eton and afterwards Hubert had been in the habit of committing unnatural vice with boys! Well, it was a hellish position. And Hubert after cudgelling his wits as to how to save Cissie Le Gallienne from this hideous business decided that there was no way out but death. He sent for his mother to whom he was devoted, of course never mentioned his intention but spent a lingering day or two with her in Paris, and on her returning to her social duties in London, he walked out from his hotel in the night, filled his pockets with stones and slipped into the Seine.[62]

This was wrong in almost all its particulars. Leila was Hubert's social equal and was independently wealthy; she did not meet d'Artaux until after she had miscarried and left Hubert (we have no certainty this was a permanent split, but her taking up with d'Artaux and his doing so openly with Sissie made it so). There is no suggestion of homosexuality in Hubert's life unless we include that which he wrote himself: his character Hillier in 'A Commonplace Chapter' had, 'of course, erotic adventures, purely physical; for he had lived, during his early years, in the unwholesome atmosphere of an expensive public school'. It is a factual statement lacking in irony; homosexuality among boys at Eton was a given.[63] There were no stones in Crackanthorpe's pockets – the stones detail comes from the intended suicide of the character in his story 'Egoists'; no letter was written by Leila excepting a brief note saying she was seeking a divorce. As David Crackanthorpe, the biographer of his grand-uncle, commented, 'no such letter as that claimed by Haldane Macfall existed. Leila's accusation of adultery and venereal infection were made by her solicitor on her behalf and in her absence, to Hubert and his mother on the night of his disappearance.'[64] However, the story of the letter that put the blame on Leila for 'deserting' him had been widely spread on the best authority.

The story of Leila's desertion as being the main reason for Hubert's suicide was maintained in the memoirs of such men of the 1890s as William Rothenstein, who wrote, 'Forty years ago a man felt it more of a disgrace when his wife took the reins into her own hands and drove away with another man on the box seat, than he would do today.'[65]

Haldane Macfall now had a part to play in the affair. He wrote:

I shall never forget the anguish of his people. If I had only been in Paris as I was a week or two later, and Hubert had consulted me, which was unlikely as I was not in such intimate terms with him as with his people or as with Welch and his wife, I believe I could have prevented the hideous thing; but thank God it was granted to me in the years afterwards to thwart the woman of the money for which she had done this hellish thing.[66]

This is a curious claim. Leila was not in need of money (though she might have felt she deserved some for the lasting injury she had sustained).

However, looking at the amount she might have any right to as a widow, it was not great. Hubert Crackanthorpe may have been the eldest son and in line to inherit Newbiggin Hall, but he and Leila had no children and both his parents were alive, as were two brothers; all these close members of his family stood in the way of Hubert's widow and a sizeable inheritance. Crackanthorpe's wealth at death was £1,131, not a paltry sum but no great fortune by the standards of this society. He died intestate and the Letters of Administration were granted to his father, Montague Crackanthorpe QC. Why not to his widow? The probate document specifically states, 'Leila Crackanthorpe the lawful widow . . . having renounced the letters of administration of his personal estate', so a likely explanation is that Macfall, acting as an intermediary, persuaded Leila to abandon any claims she might have against Crackanthorpe's estate.

More benignly, care was taken to preserve his literary legacy. Blanche had three of Crackanthorpe's final stories published as *Last Studies*, with an appreciation by Henry James and an introductory verse by literary curate and family friend Stopford A. Brooke continuing the theme of injured innocence:

Pity he could not stay for he was true,
Tender and chivalrous, and without spot;
Loving things great and good, and love like dew
Fell from his heart on those that loved him not.

There is a suggestion that Blanche wished to manage Crackanthorpe's legacy in her choice of stories and distance her son's image from the *Yellow Book*. She could easily have included his October 1895 *Yellow Book* sketch 'Bread and Circuses', but did not do so.[67]

Meanwhile, Leila was trying to put her life together. For some time she must have stayed in a relationship with the Comte d'Artaux as on census night 1901, at the age of thirty, she was calling herself Mrs Leila d'Artaux and living at a boarding house kept by a German woman in Victoria Square (which was in a good part of London: her neighbours included a knight and a baronet). She was said to be living on her own account at home from journalistic work, though no examples of this work have come to light.

She had a single selection of poems published: *The Wanderer and Other Poems* came out in 1904 from T. Fisher Unwin, in a white cover with gold lettering. It is a testament to the importance she placed on motherhood that this book was dedicated 'to the memory of Mary Anne Gibbs', her old nurse and substitute mother. D'Artaux is not mentioned so presumably that relationship was over. Leila was now without children, husband, parents or grandparents (her sister, married to an army officer, is never mentioned; perhaps they did not get on).

She was developing as a poet, and the experience of miscarriage, her broken relationship with Crackanthorpe and his death seem to have invigorated her verse. She dedicated individual poems to named people (it was a very 1890s practice; Ernest Dowson and John Gray also did so). The verse play after which the book was titled is dedicated 'for George Moore'; in it a lonely wanderer meets death in the form of a radiant woman. French names feature strongly in the dedicatees; Leila seems to have had quite an affection for members of the French nobility (one remembers the relationship between the Scottish aristocracy and the French, and she had French relatives as her grand-aunt had married a Frenchman). Among the dedicatees of the twelve short poems that follow the three verse plays are two counts and a baron. Desolation and loneliness feature strongly, as in 'Farewell':

> Now that we stand at parting ways
> How lovely lies the road behind!
> The gracious path to tender days
> When you were true and I was kind,
> Our spirits should remember yet
> Though Time bring change and we forget!

In 1907 she was writing to Aline Harland, who had contacted her about her intention to publish the play Crackanthorpe and Harland had written, *A Light Sovereign*:

> It was very kind of you to write to me about the play – there is no need for me to employ a solicitor – I know you will do what is right and fair. If you would like to see me let me know and I will see you here, or come to see you – but if you prefer to treat the matter by correspondence it is as you like. There is only one thing I do ask you – for pity's sake do not let the Crackanthorpes know I am in London. You see I give you my address – but I do beg you to treat it as confidential – and not even to give it to the Gosses – as I am terrified lest they, inadvertently, would give it to the Crackanthorpes. Please, in writing, or if you call upon me, ask for

Mrs Macdonald. I have gone back to my maiden name the past 6 years. Yours sincerely, Leila Macdonald.[68]

As the next eldest son Dayrell inherited the estate. Now he alone had the right to the coat of arms, the armorial bearing that was on the ring by which Hubert's body was identified. Its motto is an adaptation of Horace, 'Misi res subjungere conor' – I subject circumstances to myself.

Leila's life afterwards is uncertain; probably she was treated for her condition. Salvarsan, the first effective treatment for syphilis, was developed in 1908. Leila Ellen Macdonald, described as a widow without issue or close relative, died intestate at 52 rue de Théâtre, Paris, on 29 December 1944 at the age of 73; her estate as administered netted £726, which, she having no closer relatives, went to two cousins. A suggestion of her life is given in her poem 'Unwoven':

Give me not life, I have no joy of it;
Nor pleasure with its odour of dead flowers;

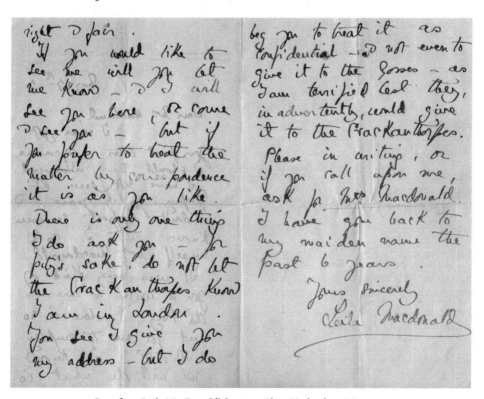

Page from Leila MacDonald's letter to Aline Harland, 27 May 1907.

Nor pale desire, with eyes of sad disgust;
Nor love that spurns its own satiety.
White death alone, unweaves the strands of pain.

The fang of cunning stings beyond repair

Sissie and Jimmy Welch stayed together until she took off with another lover; they divorced in 1906. She died on 18 July 1907 at the age of 39 of complications following a hysterectomy.

8

Mabel's Urge for Fame

Beardsley's departure as illustrator of the *Yellow Book* was a gift for women who were now able to fill the space left by him and his almost all-male commissioning process. The primary illustrator was the unsettled and ultimately tragic figure Mabel Dearmer, who in April 1896 was the first woman to design a *Yellow Book* cover. The illustration for the cover of volume IX was a child riding a butterfly, or perhaps a moth as it is a night-time scene. Dearmer, the most widely talented of the women of the *Yellow Book*, was to be an artist, novelist, playwright, performer and theatre producer in her search for the task that would bring her fame.

Jessie Mabel Prichard White, always called Mabel, was born on 22 March 1872, daughter of Selina White, née Prichard, and William White. Her father was described as a 'gentleman' on her birth certificate but he has also been described as a surgeon-major, so his life of military medicine foreshadowed his daughter's tragic end.[1] They were living in the town of Llanbeblig in Wales, and Mabel's father may have been the William White who died in Carnarvon in 1875, when she was three, at the age of 58.[2] Her mother certainly felt free to have a church wedding to another man in 1878, when she described herself as a spinster (not a widow) on the marriage certificate and as Prichard (not White), so it is possible she was not married to Mabel's father. Mabel Dearmer's novel of 1908 *The Alien Sisters* deals with illegitimacy, showing Mabel's anger at visiting the sins of parents on their children, which may have been informed by her own background.

Mabel was described as having had 'a lonely childhood' that 'fed her imagination'.[3] It was to some extent reflected in her 1909 novel *Gervase*, in which the central character's mother dies when he is a small child, perhaps drawing on emotions felt by Mabel at having an absent father. It seems she had a physically unsettled early life: she was born in Carnarvon in 1872, but her mother married in Hastings, Sussex, on 28 October 1878 and at fifteen in 1887 Mabel was living in Richmond, Surrey. Her stepfather was Alfred Beamish, a barrister. Mabel's friend Stephen Gwynn, who wrote a memoir of Dearmer, described her stepfather as 'a steady, orthodox conservative'.[4]

The painter, playwright, poet and novelist W. G. Wills was a great influence on Mabel in her teenage years. They met when she was fifteen; it is not known how they became acquainted, but he 'made a companion of the clever girl', according to Stephen Gwynn.[5] She later told an interviewer enquiring about her that she 'first began to study under Mr Wills', who, though best known as a playwright, 'took himself very seriously as an artist'.[6]

She was first moved to go on the stage but later reported, 'They thought I was not pretty enough,' without reference to who was making this judgement.[7] Gwynn said she had 'a precocious and uneasy girlhood, fevered with ambition'.[8] She was described as headstrong and impetuous. A comment after her death said, 'At fifteen she held views that startled her friends, and led them to have strange fears. She was so bold in her opinions, so daring.'[9] Gwynn said she was 'eager not only for fame, but the rewards of fame,

Mabel Dearmer's cover of the *Yellow Book*, vol. IX (April 1896).

wealth and luxury, costly dresses, all the beautiful things in which she always found delight'.[10]

Still influenced by Wills, she decided to become famous by painting. At eighteen she enrolled as an art student at Hubert Herkomer's art school at Bushey, Hertfordshire, which had been set up in 1883. He was taken by the ideas of William Morris and the art of the Pre-Raphaelites, which chimed with Mabel's artistic interests. To apply for the school Mabel sent in a head drawn in charcoal from nature; after that was deemed of acceptable standard she went into the preliminary class, which was under the supervision of advanced students. Their work consisted of 'painting from the living head, drawing from the life-cast and drawing from a partially nude figure'. The preliminary classes were mixed, allowing for what was described as a 'safe camaraderie between the sexes'.[11] Herkomer had more women than men students on a campus comprising the school and his magnificent house and grounds. The earnestness of the endeavour is indicated by Herkomer's statement, 'There are no prizes given. The prize they work for is individual progress.'[12] Students in the preliminary class could present work to qualify for admission to the life class, which was taught directly by Herkomer. The Bushey site became an artistic centre of 150 students, who supplemented painting with music, acting and dancing. Dearmer's novel *The Difficult Way* presents the art school the central character goes to before marriage as a kind of Eden. It was the best training for a girl who was 'full of life and ambition', as she was described.[13]

Mabel had met Percy Dearmer at the age of sixteen in 1888 at the home of mutual friends when she was living at Richmond with her mother and stepfather. She was described as 'a slender girl with a crown of red-gold hair' and said to be 'mature for her age' (meaning physically developed).[14] They bonded over her wish to become an artist and his socialist vision of future society, which she came to share. They met frequently, attended meetings and exchanged books.

Percy was five years older than Mabel. He had been born on 27 February 1867, the son of Caroline, who ran a girls' school, and Thomas Dearmer, an artist who died when Percy was ten. Percy was educated at Westminster School, at a private school at Vevey on Lake Geneva, and then at Christ Church, Oxford, in 1886 where he read history. Mabel corresponded with him frequently during term time and they met in the vacations. Both volunteered in the East End during the dock strike of 1889 for the 'dockers' tanner', a sixpence an hour wage, where Mabel joined Percy in serving six hundred meals a day to dockers' families at the Christ Church Mission,

Mabel Dearmer aged sixteen, 1888.

Poplar. Being artistic, socialist and Christian was a far from unusual combination in those times. Stephen Gwynn spoke of her 'extreme socialist views', which were 'crudely thought out and crudely uttered' at that time, but her principles were not to be altered with the passage of time: 'here as in other matters, she knew her own mind from the first.'[15]

The young people' lives now moved fast. In autumn 1891 Percy took up work as a curate (assistant to the priest) at St Anne's, South Lambeth;

he was to be ordained on 21 December 1892. Mabel and Percy declared their love for each other in 1891. Percy wrote to his friend Lord Beauchamp, 'the great thing has happened to me which I had hardly ever hoped for. I am in love. And I am loved almost more than I love . . . Oh it is infinitely more strange and strong and sacred than I had ever dreamt.' He and Mabel had become engaged on 5 November. He reported, 'you know we were always great friends – only all that is gone, utterly gone.' He described their falling for each other after being friends as something swooping down on them and filling them with love. He ended with foreboding, however: 'Our respective parents hate us, and we are in a cloud of difficulties.'[16]

Their parents argued that they were too young (Mabel was 19 in 1891, Percy 24) and that Percy had not the financial means to support a wife and, one had to assume, a family. They were forbidden to meet; Percy's mother and Mabel's stepfather withheld the financial assistance they needed for marriage. Mabel showed the defiance and organizing ability that was later to distinguish her: she applied to be made a ward in chancery as a minor whose affairs were under the guardianship of the Court of Chancery and not, therefore, of her stepfather. The court seems to have sympathized with the parents' misgivings, however, as the couple were bound over neither to see nor to communicate with one another. Percy had already been threatened by his mother with being cut off financially if he insisted on studying for holy orders. He looked up the terms of his father's will to discover that he was entitled to a small yearly income and in fact had been for the past few years, since he came of age, but no one had informed him of it.

Finally the young couple prevailed, as they were so obviously determined. None of the usual arguments against early marriage applied: neither of them was of 'bad character'; they were not marrying for money. Mabel reached twenty in March 1892; now it would be only months before she came of age and needed no parental (or court) permission to marry. Marriage at that time and in those circumstances would cause lasting family resentment with no benefit to anyone, so the parents succumbed. Mabel was allowed to receive her small income, presumably from her father's will, before she reached her majority, and his mother gave Percy some money. With these sums, plus his clerical salary, they married on 26 May 1892 at St John's Church, Richmond.

Mabel had to leave Herkomer's school as, despite the gender balance of his intake, he did not allow women students to continue if they were married. They set up home at 59 South Lambeth Road, decorating the old house in William Morris style with chintzes, wallpapers and tapestries in

Arts and Crafts patterns, with engravings of Burne-Jones's paintings on the walls and exoticism guaranteed by a Turkish rug on the floor. They both worked in the downstairs sitting room, she on her drawings, he on articles for newspapers and sermons. Gas had not yet arrived for domestic premises in this poor area of London and the house was lit at night by oil lamps. One visitor to a reception at the house said they had spent all their money on decoration and had little furniture: 'my recollection is that some of the company sat on packing cases; I did!'[17]

The streets around smelled of meat extract from a neighbouring factory and malt from a brewery. The butchers connected to the meat essence works attracted flies that settled in the Dearmers' sitting room on pictures and ornaments. Traffic links were poor: they could take a halfpenny omnibus to Vauxhall Station, but when they went to see friends it often meant a long walk, particularly at night after the omnibus had stopped running. Visitors to them would, of course, face the same difficulties and Percy's work commitments further limited Mabel's opportunities for entertaining.

She was described (admittedly by her successor as Percy's wife and therefore not perhaps the most impartial of witnesses) as 'impetuous and wayward, an artist in all her being, she found herself in South London, faced with the problem of learning to keep house on a tiny income. The management of money was always a difficulty to her even in later years when there was more to spare. Pretty things were so important and necessities often so dull.'[18] Nan Dearmer continued:

> It can be imagined that her looks and her unconventional ways called down considerable criticism from parish workers . . . In appearance she was striking, never pretty, but giving somehow the impression of a gay spring morning, with her tresses of red-gold hair, slender figure, and original clothes. She was very short-sighted, which caused her to wear pince-nez always. She had one great asset to help her in her work and that was her unfailing interest in people, no matter who they might be. She could find people unpleasant or 'appalling' (a favourite word) but she rarely found them dull.[19]

Mabel was to write in her novel *The Difficult Way* in 1905 about the transition between a location like leafy Bushey and grimy Lambeth, describing the challenge of living as the wife of a young vicar in a poor parish in an old house on an income of £200 a year: 'Expenses seemed to increase daily until it had become almost impossible to meet them. Tradesmen's accounts were allowed to stand over. Small bills were stuffed unopened into chance handy drawers to await some windfall – some wedding or funeral fee – that might unexpectedly arrive.'[20] The young wife has no great sympathy with her husband's religious calling and has 'extreme dislike of parish organisations, parish workers, and of the poor generally'.[21] The novel recounts arguments with tradesmen whom the lady of the house cannot pay and the pettiness of parish life. The novel's heroine takes to posing for an artist she knew before her wedding to make money, which imperils her marriage.

By the time she was 22 Mabel had two sons, Geoffrey and Christopher, born 21 March 1893 and 21 March 1894, and presumably they used contraception after that. The Dearmers certainly fell into the category of a family that would be plunged into poverty if they had any more children, which was a main argument of birth control pioneers such as Annie Besant, about whose work they would definitely have known. They were in 'genteel poverty' where the 'poverty' was relative to that of their neighbours in Lambeth; they had three servants after the children were born, presumably a nanny, a cook (Mabel did not cook) and a maid of all work.[22]

Mabel wrote her affectionate novel *The Noisy Years* in 1902 about two little boys. It shows a close observation of the boys with their military interests and admiration for Lord Roberts of Kandahar, hero of the Boer War, which was the great event of their childhood. Nan Knowles (later Nan Dearmer), who knew Mabel when she was a child, wrote of children hanging on Mabel's every word and her son begging for repeated stories with 'Tell it again Mother; tell it again.'[23] Mabel later wrote *Roundabout Rhymes*, in which she said, 'I simply try to put into the simplest possible rhyme whatever strikes me in the sayings and doings of my own little boys.'[24]

The family moved from Lambeth when Percy was offered the curacy of St John's, Great Marlborough Street, settling at 9 Devonport Street, near Paddington, in autumn 1895. It was now possible to entertain artistic friends and visit people like the Harlands, whose Cromwell Road flat was on the same side of London, though some distance away, across Hyde Park. They hosted what were called 'Mabel's lurid Mondays' at Devonport Street, entertaining members of the *Yellow Book* set including Aline and Henry Harland, Netta Syrett, Evelyn Sharp and the artist and writer Laurence Housman.

Percy was also a friend of Richard Le Gallienne, presumably through contacts in the artistic community that he had made from an interest in improving the standard of church decoration. It was Le Gallienne who introduced the Dearmers to the *Yellow Book* set and the Harlands' Saturday evening soirées. Henry Harland in particular took a liking to Mabel; it was she whom he called Helen of Troy for her bearing and her flaming hair. It was said that 'All the leading ladies of his tales have a family likeness, and in a sense Mabel Dearmer sat for all of them.'[25] Frederick Rolfe in his fictional autobiography clearly draws from life with his description of such a woman: 'The red-haired Helen of Troy glowed in apple-green. An excessively beautiful girl, with a face like a fifteenth-century Florentine child, strong, delicate, hardy, voluptuous, dark and mysterious as night, wore black with old amethysts.'[26] The Dearmers were kind to him, including inviting him to their home, which is perhaps why he was not his usual acerbic self in describing her.

It was at this time that she became friendly with Stephen Gwynn, who was a schoolmaster but in 1896 became a journalist. He wrote:

> In those first years when I knew her she was the most vivid creature that imagination could conceive. If one does not call her beautiful, it is because the word is accepted in a conventional significance and the photographs are there with their record. But no photograph was ever like her; what they omit is precisely her beauty – for beauty it was – the colour, the movement, the poise of her figure, crowned with its mass of brilliant hair, the living quality of her voice, all the radiation of her personality. She was tall and slender in those days, as a young tree; but in those days also wild with the sheer desire of living – grasping at life with both hands.[27]

Gwynn was clearly in love with her but whether this was consummated cannot be known from existing material; the manner of her death would have drawn a veil over gossip, even if there had been any substance to it.

She may have offered her work to Beardsley, but there is no record of it and nothing appeared until her *Yellow Book* cover design of 1896, after his departure. To move from no representation in the journal to the cover seems a considerable leap: it is likely that Mabel's pictures had been seen for some time in the *Yellow Book* office, as she was certainly on affectionate terms with Harland. Beardsley did use her work in *The Savoy*, making her one of the few people who contributed to both the *Yellow Book* and *The Savoy*; she drew the very *fin de siècle* subjects of a wood nymph and a piping faun in the September and November 1896 issues. She also contributed to *The Commonwealth*, 'A Christian Social Magazine', published from 1896. Other contributors were her friend Evelyn Sharp and significant Labour figures such as Ramsay MacDonald and Beatrice Webb. Sharp's friendship with Mabel Dearmer led to a successful partnership when she illustrated Sharp's early fairy books with coloured plates. Sharp said, 'Mabel was a brilliant creature, with flaming red-gold hair and so many talents that one never knew in which direction she would branch out in her restless search for expression.'[28]

Mabel had wished to set up as a portrait painter but, as she said, 'No one would come to have their portraits painted.'[29] She earned a little money by giving dramatic recitals and, when she was going to do so, 'it seemed to me only natural to design my own poster for it'. Her poster art was successful and lucrative, but it is an ephemeral form and little has survived. One that has is 'The Reading Lady': to the left a woman reads from a script that covers her face; from the arm of her dress hang two masks, of comedy and tragedy. The right-hand side advertises Mabel's recital where she performed sections of Ibsen's *Brand* and Sheridan's *School for Scandal* to an audience at the Prince's Hall, Piccadilly, on 12 December, probably in 1895, for an audience paying between two and sixpence and ten shillings (so between an eighth and half of a pound).[30] The poster was independently successful and was exhibited in London, Chicago and Paris and at minor exhibitions.[31] She later made a poster for Sissie Welch's husband James, who was playing in a revival of Louis N. Parker's one-act comedy *The Man in the Street* at the Strand Theatre.

She progressed from these poster and journal illustrations to finding a rich vein in children's publications, publishing in the *Girl's Own* and *Parade* annuals in 1897. In the last, as in *The Savoy*, her work was included alongside (indeed, opposite) that of Beardsley. Mabel Dearmer also contributed a story to this book, as did *Yellow Book* colleagues Pearl Craigie and Richard Le Gallienne.

Mabel Dearmer illustrated Evelyn Sharp's earliest fairy stories, *Wymps and Other Fairy Tales* (1897) and *All the Way to Fairyland* (1898), for John Lane. A reviewer commented:

It is worth going 'All the Way to Fairyland' with Miss Evelyn Sharp, to hear about those tricksters, the Wymps, and other amusing characters, described with a touch of poetry. The illustrations are rather wonderful and fearful, Mrs Percy Dearmer having evidently studied in the Aubrey Beardsley school, and being addicted to harmonies – or discords – in the brightest yellow.[32]

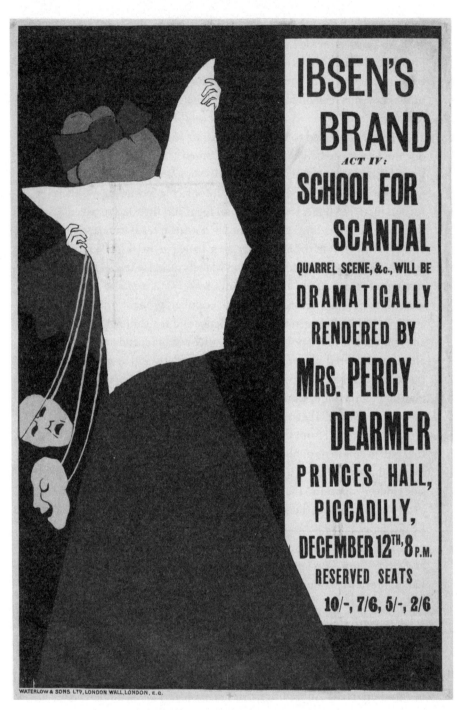

Mabel Dearmer's poster for her readings from
Ibsen's *Brand* and Sheridan's *School for Scandal*, 1895.

She described her illustrations with their bold lines and blocks of colour in an interview in the trade publication *The Poster* as 'posters in miniature' and remarked that the poster seemed 'admirably adapted for children. My two tiny boys unconsciously gave me the hint, and I determined to try.'[33]

She was not only favoured by the convivial Lane as an illustrator; Blackie and Sons had her do the pictures for Laurence Housman's *The Story of the Seven Young Goslings*. It gave her the idea for a book of her own and she wrote and illustrated *Round-About Rhymes* for Blackie and drew pictures for her own *Book of Penny Toys* for Macmillan in 1899. Macmillan also published her *Noah's Ark Geography* of 1900, which was dedicated to Evelyn Sharp. This was the first book she wrote that was structured as a novel with child characters, a storyline and locations such as a cannibal island and the north pole of children's fancy, and exotic places such as Nagasaki in Japan. The development of storytelling techniques was to bear fruit in her adult novels in the new century.

The Dearmers took simple holidays; in August 1895 the family went with Evelyn Sharp to Hedsor. They walked the countryside in sandals made by Edward Carpenter; Percy Dearmer and Evelyn Sharp searched the neighbourhood churches for monuments and brass rubbings showing the traditional vestments worn by the English clergy in the Middle Ages. They were close to Sharp, bicycling with her as a family to Wells, where on the uphill road Mabel complained that 'Percy should not make her do this detestable ride; never again would she allow herself to be persuaded to do it, it was "appalling"'; then when the easy downward stretch came, 'Mabel became radiant again, deciding that they must do this every day, and not to waste their time at home in the garden when they might be on their bicycles.'[34] Mabel went with the children back to London by train, while Percy and Evelyn Sharp determined to bicycle back, though in fact they went only 99 miles and then took a train. Their adventure is indicative of the freedom an unmarried young woman and a man could have without scandal. Bicycling gave licence to the adventurous, even if they had few financial resources.

By the end of the century Mabel had become a widely published illustrator and writer for children, but still relied for stability of income on her husband's job. At last he was given his own church and on 15 February 1901 Mabel was able to celebrate Percy's being inducted as vicar of the church of St Mary on Primrose Hill, the first they had of their own. They now also had a large house in England's Lane and a prosperous parish to look after.

Mabel's evenings of fun with the *Yellow Book* set were behind her; she was now a vicar's wife with parish responsibilities. Work on novels and in the theatre was in the future. Old friends like Laurence Housman resented this new maturity in her:

> all at once she began to take herself seriously; ceasing to write funny books for children, she turned to sombre novel-writing; and then to things of a mildly mystical character; and as her writing changed, she changed also; she became 'good'; and it did not improve her, for it diminished her sense of humour, and still more the unconscious comedy of her behaviour.[35]

In future Mabel Dearmer was to take her own direction.

9

Netta Syrett and the
Flat of Girls

Mabel Dearmer had been the first woman cover designer; later Mabel Syrett designed the front and back covers of *Yellow Book* volume XIII, with a startling art nouveau image for the front cover. Dennis Denisoff and Lorraine Janzen Kooistra remarked, 'Syrett's bold graphic design of two decorative fighting cocks is one of the most striking covers among all thirteen volumes.'[1] Mabel Syrett was the sister of *Yellow Book* writer Netta Syrett. Another sister, Nellie Syrett, who had been a fellow student of Beardsley's at Fred Brown's night classes at the Westminster School of Art in 1892, produced the cover on volume XI.[2]

Three of the Syrett sisters contributed to the *Yellow Book*, therefore. Their career-driven independence and their choice to live together in an apartment in Victoria made them exemplars of progressive young women in the 1890s. In later life Netta Syrett derided the notion of the repressed female that had gained vogue in the twentieth-century reaction against Victorianism. She read novels in which the descriptions of the times she had lived through were unrecognizable. She wrote acidly:

> In writing of the Victorian era the younger novelists seem to have forgotten that what is known as the 'woman's movement' was in the 'eighties already well recognised, and in the 'nineties in full swing. Except for that section of society which spells itself with a capital letter, educated girls of any character, all over the country, were asserting their right to independence if they could prove themselves capable of earning their own living. Or for that matter, even if they couldn't or didn't.[3]

Syrett herself was one of the most successful *Yellow Book* women writers and one who was present throughout the journal's life. She was always called Netta, a contraction of Janet. She was born in Ramsgate, Kent, at 23 Harbour Street on 17 March 1865 and was the eldest of the large family of Mary Ann Syrett and her husband Ernest, who was a linen draper. They were financially comfortable and well connected – the writer Grant Allen was a relative (he is often referred to as Netta Syrett's uncle).[4] Even comfortably off families like the Syretts, however, were without what would later be thought of as essential requirements: there were 'no bedroom gas or coal fires in my youth', and it was not until she was in her twenties and living away from home that she went to bed warm in winter.[5] She was educated at home until 1877 when her parents, giving evidence of their credentials as advanced thinkers, sent her and her sister Dora as boarders to Frances Buss's North London Collegiate School for Girls. Frances Buss had founded her college for 'daughters of limited means, clerks and private offices and persons engaged in trade and other pursuits'. Buss insisted that a sound education was as essential for the daughters from such families as it was for their sons.[6]

Boarding school was a dreadful experience for Syrett, who described the school with scant attempt at disguise in her novel *The Victorians* in which the Myra Lodge where she stayed was represented as Minerva House. Frances Buss, the first woman to use the term 'headmistress', is described in unconcealed form (though with a fictitious name) as 'a pioneer, a breaker of traditions, a woman of indomitable will, inexhaustible energy and ungovernable temper'. Her liberal and advanced 'theoretical views' did not curb her 'outbursts of wrath over trifles'. The institution 'bristled with vexatious rules' where days were filled with calisthenics and prayers. Older girls wore tight-laced corsets and any infraction led to a confession and signature in the punishment book.[7] Buss boasted that she had no need for corporal punishment since she could reduce a girl to tears in minutes.[8] Syrett recalled her 'violent temper, her restless energy, her inability to listen to an explanation before judging a case'.[9]

The petty tyranny of the school, which she endured from the ages of eleven or twelve to sixteen, was not the ideal environment for one of Netta Syrett's liberated temperament. Syrett received a good basic education, however, although she had a persistent difficulty with mathematics, which characteristic is shared by many of her fictional characters. One theme of *The Victorians* is the heroine's developing sexuality, which it is realistic to assume Syrett drew from life. 'Curiosities she had never felt before beset her,' she wrote, 'there were mysteries which she longed to solve, over which she brooded for weeks, furtively seeking for their elucidation in books, or from hints let fall by wiser school-fellows.' She feels anguished at her '"horrid mind" of which at intervals, when the subject of sex recurred to her, she was desperately ashamed'. She resolves not to think of sex any more but to live 'for books and pictures and talking'.[10]

The heroine of *The Victorians* develops a crush on a more sophisticated girl who befriends her and for the first time in her life is 'in a state of blissful infatuation which made every hour of the day a romance'.[11] One night she stands naked looking at herself in a mirror, 'a slim, white figure, erect in the midst of the crimson dress which had fallen round her feet', imagining that this is how a lover would see her.[12] Syrett's description of female sexual development is comparable to George Meredith's *The Ordeal of Richard Feverel*, dealing with the male equivalent. Syrett visited Meredith in the company of Grant Allen, and later read most of his works including *Richard Feverel* (two characters in her novel *Nobody's Fault* have a discussion about it).[13] Jill Tedford Jones compared *The Victorians* to James Joyce's *A Portrait of the Artist as a Young Man* and Somerset Maugham's *Of Human Bondage*, both published within a year of *The Victorians*, which came out in 1915. Syrett dedicated *The Victorians* to Maugham, a friend who used to invite her to his first nights.[14]

One reason for Syrett's enduring animosity towards Frances Buss was that her sister Dora died of tuberculosis while a boarder. Syrett has the headmistress in *The Victorians* admonishing a dying girl for coughing in assembly. It was based on a real memory of Buss 'whose very voice in the distance inspired fear in my delicate sister, whom she once peremptorily forbade to cough'.[15] It is not possible to know Buss's level of culpability for Dora's death, but there were no warm feelings for the North London Collegiate School when Syrett left in 1881. As an adult she was still referring to Buss, by now remembered as a venerable pioneer of girls' education, through gritted teeth: 'the evil that she did . . . shall be interred with her bones. It is the good that will live after her, and of that there is enough to make her name long remembered.'[16]

The trauma of school and the death of her sister led to a period of three years when she stayed at home. There is no evidence to show that she suffered a breakdown, though it has to be suspected when such an otherwise active person becomes quiescent, in what she described as 'two or three years of unsatisfactory drifting'.[17] She brought an end to this period of seclusion when she determined to become a teacher, perhaps surprisingly after her experience of formal schooling had been so negative. Syrett records that she learned German at home and studied at a school in Leipzig for three months, noting there the dirtiness, bad food, wretched bedroom accommodation and lack of bathing facilities except for public baths.

Whether or not she was thinking of a career in writing at this stage, she was certainly influenced by her relationship with Grant Allen. A few months before her college training course, at the age of twenty, she went to stay with Grant and Nellie Allen in Dorking, Surrey. Allen had started writing novels in 1884 after an early career as a science writer; he found fiction more lucrative than his previous popularizing of socialism and evolution. He described himself as an 'impecunious naturalist' who 'dropped into romance . . . by pure force of circumstances'.[18] He was to write more than thirty novels, thus becoming a role model for his niece in the skill of turning storytelling ability into a trade.

Syrett remarked how the conversation in Grant Allen's home 'did much to accelerate me, while I was still young, in the process of growing up'.[19]

Netta Syrett in the 1890s.

Allen was 'the first very clever man I had met', she says.[20] She found the frankness of his views on sexual subjects to be disconcerting:

> much of the talk was strong meat for a country girl whose life had run on very simple lines in a family where the very word sex was never so much as mentioned – not, I think, from prudery, but because in ordinary society it was not a topic for discussion in public.

She does not specifically recount his views but they can be taken as those expressed in his article on 'The New Hedonism' in which he declares, 'everything high and ennobling in our nature springs directly out of the sexual instinct . . . To it we owe the entire existence of the aesthetic sense, which is, in the last resort, a secondary sexual attribute.'[21] She could sympathize with his mechanistic atheism because she had no strong religious feelings herself.

Allen was able to help her further her career by advising her on the stories she had begun to write and by introducing her to other writers, including Swinburne.[22] Like her character in *Strange Marriage*, she was being drawn into 'the world of brilliant, interesting men and women who knew all about books and pictures and music'.[23]

Syrett could have gone to university but felt an academic life was not for her. Instead she took the Cambridge Higher Local Certificate, which normally took three years but she did it in one, then went to the Training College for Women Teachers at Cambridge with students who had already taken a degree at Girton or Newnham and now needed a teaching certificate. She found they were 'talking learnedly on matters beyond my comprehension'.[24] She loved the tiny bedsit where she went to bed warm in winter and she was delighted at having a little bureau on which to work.[25] She writes of teaching fellow students to dance in the 'Tin Tabernacle' of the college, a hall built of corrugated iron, and of students attending cocoa parties in dressing gowns in one another's rooms.

Her first teaching post was at Swansea High School where she taught English for two years from 1886. She commented, 'No one who has not endured it knows what it means to be a young creature full of life and at the same time a teacher living alone in lodgings.'[26] She probably resembled her character Bridget in her first novel, *Nobody's Fault*, who goes to teach in a school in a poor area. As a high school teacher Brigid was earning £80 a year and living in a room of 'sordid ugliness' with a slatternly maid who brings her unappetizing food. 'There's nothing to be done but to go on living

– till I die!' she says; she passes all her time between school and lodgings.[27] This theme of women waiting, working in tedious routines and living in dreary lodgings, is a frequent one in Syrett's work and that of other New Woman writers. Brigid lunches frugally on a scone and a cup of coffee and goes to two churches, not that she is religious, but church is one place a respectable woman can go on her own; her usual bedtime is ten o'clock and the ordeal begins again the next day.

Syrett says she has a schoolteacher character in one of her books living alone, 'so that she could occupy her free time as she pleased without fear of some busybody connected with the school discovering that her friends were of both sexes'; she repeats the remark in her memoirs, suggesting an origin in her own life.[28] Syrett's concern was obviously to evade the eye of propriety, but the object was probably more to have men as friends than as romantic partners, which does not seem to have been a great temptation in her life. She felt, 'I wanted to find my way into the world of new ideas; to meet writers, artists of all kinds.'[29]

The rules of propriety for respectable young women in that locality were such that even to be seen speaking to a man was suspect; Syrett went for two years literally without doing so beyond mere pleasantries with the father of a child. Other aspects of women's lives that were to be opened up in the following decade were still very constrained in the 1880s. A science teacher had arrived on Saturday to begin work on Monday but had brought her bicycle: 'a report that she had been seen riding it was carried to the headmistress. We never saw that girl!'[30] Syrett says that a year or two later women everywhere were riding bicycles.

The expansion of the school brought new friends for Syrett, who writes, 'we were young and light headed enough to get enjoyment out of the undoubtedly dull and monotonous life forced upon teachers.'[31] While she was in Swansea she made her first practical steps to becoming a professional writer. She sent one of her stories to Grant Allen and he passed it on to Longmans, who published the piece in *Longman's Magazine*. This was 'That Dance at the Robsons'', a well-written but slight tale of romance and misunderstanding. The heroine, a graduate of Newnham College, Cambridge, says she had 'lived so long among girls I'm afraid I don't know how to talk to men', though she meets one who is described as 'a universal genius' and falls in love with him.[32] The plot, which revolves around a manuscript which may or may not have been written by the romantic hero, is notable because it shows the young Syrett's fascination with the adventure of literature. It was certainly an attribute that would endear her to men of the *Yellow Book* group. Syrett and her three teacher friends in Swansea shared the excitement of her first publication with a supper party in her rooms: 'we drank a bottle of execrable claret, ate jam tarts, and felt ourselves the gayest of dogs!'[33]

She was to suffer a health breakdown, perhaps because of the industrial smoke of Swansea, or perhaps illness was just a means of getting away, but whatever the cause, the result was that she left Wales. Relief from a monotonous single existence came courtesy of her family. With several of the Syrett girls either working or studying in London, it was convenient for them to be living together and looking after each other. At the beginning of the 1890s five Syrett girls, all under 25, lived in a flat together first in Ashley Gardens, then at 3 Morpeth Terrace in Victoria, both locations overlooking the site of Westminster Cathedral, which was just then being built. Netta taught at the London Polytechnic School for Girls; Kate attended Bedford College; Mabel and Nell studied art, Nell at the Slade. Nell had her own exhibition in a gallery near Oxford Circus before she was 21; her pictures were to feature in the *Yellow Book* volume x in July 1896, where she depicts five young women in a garden under the title 'The Five Sweet Symphonies', doubtless inspired by the fact that she lived with four other young women. For at least some of the time Georgie, the next sister down in age to Netta, kept house for them so they had the equivalent of a wife at home to look after their domestic needs; they also had a maid – or a succession of them – and engaged in the usual middle-class quibbling about the maid's character and behaviour.

Syrett's references to the generosity of her father show he supported his daughters financially, and it is most likely that young women, three of whom were students, would not have been able to obtain a tenancy without the backing of a relative who could stand surety for them. *Kelly's London Trade Directory* for 1896 records the householder as 'Miss Syrett', which could have been any of them. The Syrett seniors were ahead of social thinking but were entirely in line with the economic inevitability that there was the need for many women to work in order to keep themselves due to a national preponderance of women over men. Syrett does not bother mentioning that working-class women had always worked (like the slatternly maid that she mentions) and gives scant attention to rich society women. Her concern is the middle class, daughters of professionals of the law, medicine and the church, and people in trade. The characters in her novels are all girls of this class, usually educated, like her, and uncertain what to do in the world, but willing to give it a try.

For young women to live together was also in advance of the times. The flat was, she notes, 'regarded by some of our older friends as an amusing and perhaps slightly dangerous innovation'.[34] It was sufficiently modern to be the stuff of novels: Ethel F. Heddle's 1896 book *Three Girls in a Flat* is about three young Scottish women who go to London determined to make their way independently.

Syrett and her sisters were pioneers in that they 'made our own friends, gave our own parties, went to those at other people's houses . . . without any of the chaperonage then considered by most parents necessary for their daughters'.[35] Syrett does not think her parents had any theories about young women's freedom – or anything else, it seems – they were just generous people who could not consider that their daughters might not 'behave properly'. She described her father as 'too easy going and lenient perhaps, to be altogether good for his turbulent family . . . I am sure there was much in his nature that we never understood.'[36]

Syrett was to publish one story a year for the next two years, in *Macmillan's* and *Longman's* magazines. She had two rooms in the Ashley Gardens flat; one she used as a study. She used to teach all morning and write all evening, 'when I wasn't going to a party'. She remarks, 'Even in the 'eighties, so long as a girl was working at some art, profession, or business, she was perfectly free, and could go about her lawful occasions without censure – even from the censorious.'[37] Her relationship with her sisters was not always placid, suggesting that the calm demeanour she expresses in her authorial voice is a literary persona. She does not even mention by name Georgie (Georgina), who did the housekeeping for them, and she notes that several times she left the flat for rooms of her own, spending nearly a year at the Victorian (the New Victorian Club in Sackville Street). During this time four women – the youngest of the club's members – had tiny bedrooms at the top of the house. The rooms were reached by one twisting staircase; they were narrow cubicles divided by matchboard partitions, and candles were the only means of illumination. Fellow *Yellow Book* contributor Evelyn Sharp lived next door to her; the rooms were so close together that she and Syrett used to put their heads out of the window to talk to each other.

After looking for a post in a London school, Syrett settled on the Polytechnic School for Girls in Langham Place. It was part of the complex of educational and philanthropic organizations set up around the London Polytechnic by Quentin Hogg and catered for girls of the small shop-keeping class in the streets off Oxford Street. Syrett winced at the 'squalid ugliness' and 'the whole lower middle-class atmosphere of the place', particularly the dining room deep in the basement with no natural light other than thick glass bricks set in the pavement above. One good thing about the school was another young teacher, Mabel Beardsley, whom Syrett described as 'rather a big girl, with a good, erect figure. She held herself well, but she could scarcely be called pretty. Her hair was red, the kind of red usually described as "ginger," and she had a nice pink-and-white, slightly freckled complexion.' They lived in the same direction and so would often meet on the horse-drawn omnibus called the Royal Blue, which lumbered up and down Bond Street. She admired Mabel, who was six years younger than she was, for the courtesy of her manner. She felt they differed greatly as teachers: Mabel Beardsley was conscientious and thorough, but did not like teaching; Syrett did like it and was fond of her charges. Both had other ambitions: while Syrett wanted to write for a living, Mabel Beardsley wanted to be an actress. It was one of Syrett's tasks to lead prayers, which she hated, but Mabel would say, 'Let me take prayers, dear. It gives me a chance to practise my stage walk and diction.' Syrett would struggle to keep a straight face while Mabel moved majestically among the rows of standing girls and up to the platform, where she would read the lesson for the day in a clear, histrionic voice.[38]

Syrett had felt that her younger sisters were more popular and better connected than her, with their art student classmates, but soon after meeting Mabel, who arrived at the school in September 1890, she introduced Syrett to her family. The Beardsleys had been struggling financially, but by the end of 1890 Mabel was working with Syrett at the school and her brother Aubrey, one year younger at eighteen, was working at the Guardian Fire and Life Insurance Company as a junior clerk; Mrs Ellen Beardsley taught music. Their father, Vincent, was a shadowy figure; it was suggested he was a drunkard or had some other problem, and he was never seen by the Beardsleys' guests.[39]

Mabel said, 'I want you to see my brother's drawings, I think they will interest you,' so she went to tea with them in their impoverished rooms one Saturday in 1892. After tea a door opened and a slight, thin youth 'with the most curious face I have ever seen' came in with a portfolio under his arm.[40] This was Aubrey, who said very little, mentioned some appointment he had and went, leaving the portfolio on the table. They were Beardsley's drawings illustrating Malory's *Morte d'Arthur*. In April 1893 several of the drawings were reproduced in a new magazine called *The Studio*, with an appreciation by Joseph Pennell heralding the new illustrator, who was at that time just twenty.

Over the following few years Netta Syrett, by virtue of her own abilities and the fortuitous relationship with the Beardsleys, was at the centre of the most exciting developments in art and literature. She writes of going to see Mabel and finding Aubrey working on a drawing 'at a table pushed up against one wall of the darkened room' by the light of two tall candles. All at once he got up abruptly, a bloodied handkerchief at his lips, and left the room. Aubrey's earnings from art sales and a legacy from an elderly relative allowed the family to move and for Mabel to leave the Polytechnic. Syrett asked her what she was going to do. 'Go on the stage and become a society beauty, dear,' she said.[41] Syrett stayed in contact with the family through their move to 114 Cambridge Street, Pimlico, in early summer 1893; it was a four-storey house, the lease for which was taken in Mabel's name as she was, unlike her parents, both employed and unencumbered by debts. Aubrey decorated the first-floor drawing room with the walls in orange with the woodwork, floors and furniture painted black, upholstery in blue-and-white stripes, and green rugs on the floor.[42] It was in this room where Netta Syrett made some of the most exciting introductions of her life, at the 'at homes' every Thursday evening. She described in one of her novels incense smouldering in a 'strangely decorated drawing-room . . . its glowing orange walls, its black pillars, its effect of dim richness.'[43]

It was doubtless this atmosphere she was describing in the autobiographical novel *The Victorians* where the heroine stays at the aesthetic home of a fellow schoolgirl and encounters earnest arty types discussing socialism, William Morris and related subjects during 'at homes'. She was 'drinking in the conversation with an eagerness like that of a physical thirst.'[44] She describes the scene in *Strange Marriage*, one of the many books in which she mined her own life for scenes and describes their conversation. They talk of Ibsenism, and of primitive art that looked for inspiration to the art of colonized people, such as the work Gauguin was doing in Tahiti from 1891.[45] If the conversation was sometimes perplexing, Syrett still felt, 'I was enjoying more gaiety than I had ever known before.'[46] She describes them as 'men wearing velveteen coats and slouch hats, and women who wore mustard-coloured or sage-green gowns with angel sleeves.'[47] The clothes suggest that these people, influenced by the Pre-Raphaelites, were more aesthetes than the *Yellow Book* crowd of which she was later to become a part. In a similar description from *The Victorians* the guests discuss the Kelmscott Press, which was just being launched (the actual date was 1891), and they pass around specimens of printed or decorated pages.

She went to every one of the Beardsleys' 'at homes', 'sometimes enjoying them, sometimes feeling completely out of my depth and extremely shy with a type of sophisticated men and women hitherto unknown to me'. One of her contacts, the art dealer and friend of Oscar Wilde Robert Ross, later said to her: 'You were shy, and I wonder if you know how many of us found the shyness delightfully refreshing?'[48] The person she found easiest to speak to was Max Beerbohm, who was the same age as Aubrey Beardsley, five years younger than she was. She gives some indication of her uncertainty as a young woman when, even in her memoirs, she recalls, 'He was kind; he always took the trouble to be pleasant, and to seem interested when he talked to me.' It is demonstrative of the power dynamic that, even with a younger man and as a mature woman, she writes that he was the one taking trouble and that he talked 'to' and not with her.[49]

Wilde attended the Beardsleys' at least once, but Syrett does not note having met him there, as she was leaving as he entered. Other notables were Frank Harris, William Rothenstein and Walter Sickert. Mabel would be welcoming attenders in a dress that made her look like a lady from the Italian Renaissance, rising from a carved, high-backed chair to greet her guests. Mabel had grown quickly from the tall, freckled girl Syrett had first met to one who was described as 'beautiful, really lovely, like an orchid, pale with red hair and a tall, graceful figure. She was as brilliant as Aubrey, as deeply read and full of knowledge.'[50] Syrett was plain but, if shy, was certainly able to hold her own in conversation and increasingly also in literary achievement. On the basis of her three published short stories Mabel introduced her to Aline and Henry Harland as a 'brilliant young writer'.[51] It was through the Harlands that Syrett met Sissie and Jim Welch at their flat in Gray's Inn, overlooking the lawns and trees of its garden. Sissie was to be a lifelong friend. It was in the Welches' flat that Syrett first met Julie Norregard, not yet married to Richard Le Gallienne. Norregard had arrived in London in the early 1890s with her sister Ellen to develop her writing career and to sell samples of Danish embroidery at the Danish Art School in Bayswater. She contributed an essay on the leading Danish intellectual Georg Brandes to *Yellow Book* volume VIII.

Syrett was often in the company of Harland, so much that when asked in later life if she had any letters from him, she said she did not as 'I saw him very frequently, anything he had to say about the stories of mine he accepted was said verbally, and I was never sufficiently an intimate of his for him to write to me on other subjects.' Her suggestion that she was an outsider is in contradiction to the many anecdotes she was able to tell about Harland, and the very personal feelings he was revealing to a woman only five years younger than himself. She recalls, 'I remember that he told me once he was often so overcome with the boredom of life that he didn't know how to drag through the days.'[52] Syrett was close enough to the Harlands to go on holiday with them to Paris. She told an anecdote about a young French-man who spoke no English coming to see the Harlands, where they discussed the difference between English and French humour. Syrett knew the Mad Hatter's tea party scene from *Alice's Adventures in Wonderland* by heart, and in order to illustrate English humour, Harland asked her to recite it while he translated sentence by sentence for the benefit of their French visitor. The Frenchman was completely mystified but smiled politely. These anecdotes of intimate scenes show Syrett was no outsider and no literary lightweight. She was a good house guest who could contribute to the literary entertainment.

Syrett's first *Yellow Book* story was published in volume II in July 1894. 'Thy Heart's Desire' is about a woman who, while accompanying her hus-band with a survey team in India, speaks to him with 'a touch of exasperated contempt'. She falls in love with a man but won't give herself to him out of guilt after her husband's death, for which she blames herself. Syrett was soon to eschew such exotic locations in her work for places she knew and the life she had experienced herself.

In some cases the self-directed 'new' and 'modern' woman is as up to date as Greek tragedy or Bible stories. In Syrett's tale 'Far Above Rubies', in *Yellow Book* volume XII in January 1897, Mrs Gilman attempts to seduce her young physician, who resists her. In retaliation she falsely accuses him of assault, after which he loses his reputation and practice; his fiancé leaves him and his father dies after a heart attack on hearing of his adored son's disgrace. This is not new but eternal, a story reflected in those of Medea or Potiphar's wife.

Syrett was soon moving in fashionable literary circles. The 'Wives and Daughters' gossip column of the *Nottinghamshire Guardian* noted that Netta Syrett had been present with nearly ninety other 'ladies' at the Criterion Restaurant for the Women Writers' Dinner, at which the lively conversation, the gossip columnist wrote, put paid to the notion 'that woman alone could never keep up a dinner, and that without the aid of men they would inevitably be bored to death'.[53] Syrett was also welcome at John Lane's exclusive teas; E. H. New, who was staying with Lane, wrote in his diary on Friday 26 July 1895: 'Miss Netta Syrett (Grant Allen's niece) in to tea.'[54] In 1896 John Lane published her first novel, *Nobody's Fault*, in the Keynotes series with a floral and foliage pattern on the binding by Aubrey Beardsley and a keynotes key personalized to Syrett's initials.

Title page of Netta Syrett,
Nobody's Fault (1896).

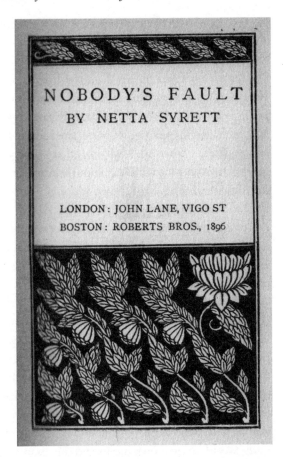

It is a book about a woman's place, but also about class and the obstacle course of social mobility. Bridget Ruan is the daughter of a publican but has received an expensive education so she speaks and acts as a lady. A schoolfriend's father introduces her to the world of the intellect but says, 'She's one of the curious developments for which this very remarkable end of the century is responsible . . . Did it ever occur to you . . . what a girl like that must suffer? Our class barriers are but imperfectly broken down after all.'[55]

Bridget goes to teach in the impoverished Hackney area of London, from which she is rescued by literary life and marriage, only to feel she has tied herself to a cynic who is disdainful of her writing. As a character says of this literary set:

> they'll hurl paradoxes and epigrams at you till you'll begin to doubt your own sanity . . . it's not difficult. Merely remember what a normal man says when he's asked a plain question – invert it; season

it to taste with a few passion-coloured adjectives and serve up as languidly as possible.

She leaves her cruel husband, to the horror of her mother, who says, 'Suppose everyone was to leave their husbands just because they didn't love them, as you call it.'[56] It was a sentiment shared by the *Times* reviewer, who remarked, 'having married in haste, she cannot during her repentance at leisure, shake off her husband altogether and try another. Novelists who get their heroines into such situations seldom seem to realise that, after all, the difficulty is of the wife's own making.'[57] It was positively reviewed in the *Pall Mall Gazette* and *The Graphic*.

By the end of 1896 she had eight pieces published in mainstream journals (three of them in the *Yellow Book*), one book already published and another on the way. Lane's reader (perhaps Le Gallienne) had recommended publication of her second novel, *The Tree of Life*, as 'a careful well written piece of work, full of many fine touches and with a good deal of psychological insight', 'a genuinely clever book' about a girl 'brought up by a learned stick of a father, and in time becomes very learned herself and marries a learned stick of a lover'. Their child dies when it is insufficiently cared for by her husband while she is on a lecture tour that he has urged her to go on. This breaks the hold her father and husband have over her and she goes off with a man who will give her the love she deserves.[58] Thus Syrett was continuing with New Woman themes of women struggling to make their way in the world on their own merits and the disappointments of marriage.

Arthur Waugh, not a flag-bearer for women writers, gave a welcome to this second novel:

> In the early spring Mr John Lane will publish a new novel, the most ambitious piece of work hitherto put forth by Miss Netta Syrett, whose clever story, 'Nobody's Fault' proved her to be possessed of observation and humour. Miss Syrett, who is very young, is practically a product of the *Yellow Book*, only a few of her stories having appeared outside the pages of that entertaining quarterly.

She was 31 when Waugh wrote this, one year older than he was. Presumably she gave a youthful impression; the association of age with women writers in particular was an effortless way to assume superiority for a would-be literary grandee like Waugh. He showed personal knowledge of her: 'She is by no means of the ordinary, depressing type of blue-stocking, but has a merry laugh, a contempt for Ibsen, and a busy bicycle. She can talk on an infinity of subjects, and gathers the materials for her fiction largely from the observation which accompanies her own conversation.'[59]

By the end of the 1890s Netta Syrett was an independent, confident woman with three books to her name and acceptance in the world of letters. Her career was to go off the rails in the new century, not because she failed but because she succeeded in the male sphere of the theatre.

10

Ménie Muriel Dowie's Celebrity

The literary princess who was at the centre of the table at the *Yellow Book* launch in 1894 had come a long way since she was sleeping wrapped in a tartan cloak in the Carpathian Mountains. Ménie Muriel Dowie had led a busy life; by the time her story 'An Idyll in Millinery' appeared in volume x in July 1896 she had already written two of the key works of the 1890s, *A Girl in the Karpathians* and *Gallia*. She was far from the *Punch* image of the New Woman as an ugly harridan; Dowie was an object of fascination to newspaper readers for her beauty and confidence.

She was born in Liverpool on 15 July 1867 to Annie and James Muir Dowie, who was a corn merchant. Her maternal grandfather was Robert Chambers, author of *Vestiges of the Natural History of Creation* (1844), which, with its proposal that the universe evolved and was not created in a single act by God, was to be influential in preparing the intellectual ground for Darwin. Her grandfather Robert and his brother William made Chambers a household name for the Victorians, having founded *Chambers's Edinburgh Journal* in 1832. Robert Chambers died when she was in her infancy but he knew his granddaughter and said, 'he never knew a child with such a wonderful vocabulary.' She was described as 'a little fair-haired blue-eyed girl, with . . . perhaps a half-humorous confidence, and a frank outlook on the world'.[1]

She described her childhood in an interview: 'I was brought up in the country, and to that I consider I owe everything. It led me to observe things accurately, especially things out of doors . . . I had no toys as a child and never played with a doll; but I always had as many animals as I could take care of.'[2]

Dowie was educated at home by a schoolmistress who lived nearby, by the St George's correspondence classes, at a private school in Liverpool and then at schools in Stuttgart and Bordeaux.[3] She therefore travelled young and gained the experience with languages that stood her in good stead for her future adventures. She said she did not attend school after the age of fourteen and was dismissive of what schools had to offer, commenting in an interview: 'The development at the schools is not wide enough. Girls ... live in too narrow a world at school.'[4] On her return to Britain the family lived in Kinross-shire where, she said, 'It was a life like a settler's, and I learned to skin beasts, and sometimes used to fetch home wood from the hills.'[5] An eighteen-year-old character in one of her novellas may well be an image of herself: 'she was as open as the day, and as fearless of anyone and anything as the wind that played among the tree-tops. She was mentally strong, and self-reliant; she had no false pride and no false shame, and she was free too of speech and thought, and original as might be.'[6]

Her father encouraged her to become proficient in the active outdoor pursuits of a country gentleman, notably hunting, shooting and fishing. Annie Dowie, her mother, was interested in science and often went to meetings where current research was discussed. She 'had many scientific friends and interests', according to her daughter, who in later life pursued an interest in eugenics when she bred rare cattle.[7]

Dowie is said to have had a wish to become a surgeon, which would have been a challenge for a woman at the time, but not an insurmountable one; Elizabeth Garrett Anderson and others had been sitting medical exams since before she was born. Perhaps more tellingly, she did not go to university. In this case there was certainly no lack of opportunity for a wealthy and intelligent young woman. Girton College was set up, in its earliest incarnation, in 1869, two years after Dowie was born. This decision not to pursue academic higher education was not evidence of excessive parental control as she did leave home at eighteen to train as an actress and dramatic reciter in London. Dowie gave poetry recitals in which she was said to have been successful, but no written records of her solo performances have come to light. She is recorded as having assisted her cousin, the lyric soprano Liza Lehmann, in a 'vocal recital' on the afternoon of Friday 10 July 1891 at the Prince's Hall in London.[8] Her literary endeavours began when she was a teenager and she wrote stories, one of the earliest of which was published in the *People's Journal*, for which she was awarded the prize of a sewing machine.[9]

A picture said to be of Dowie was drawn by Ethel Heddle in *Three Girls in a Flat*, which tells of three young women who live in a flat in Chelsea, London, based on Ménie Muriel Dowie, Alice Werner and Lilias Campbell

Davidson.[10] Dowie's character 'had received payment for some novelettes in a little-known London periodical', which fits with the known facts.[11] Her character was said to have 'loved blissfully and ignorantly'.[12] Dowie's connection with Heddle was that their mothers had been close friends. Heddle described her first meeting with Dowie as a young woman in the Berkeley Square dining room of Dowie's aunt, 'Mrs Frederick Lehmann'. Heddle wrote, 'I remember the very black gown she wore, and the picture hat on the masses of brown-gold hair. I remember the vivacious and dramatic anecdote, the power that transported one to the scene described.'[13]

On 11 January 1889 Dowie's father died at the age of 53 at their home, Golland House, near Loch Leven; the *Dundee Courier* recorded it was 'after a short illness'.[14] He died from septicaemia caused by an infection of necrotizing tissue in the bones of the face. The necrosis could have continued for a long time without sepsis, but septicaemia in pre-antibiotic days meant a swift death.

That summer she took off on her own to Devonshire, enjoying an experience she later recounted as the happiest time of her life. She described her experience of writing at this time: 'I was writing [for] Family Herald Monthly Magazine of Fiction for which one got £25. It had to be about twice the length of a "Supplement," 27,000 words.'[15] It may be that Dowie is conflating two titles here as the *Family Herald Library of Fiction*, offering three 'complete novels' quarterly at one shilling and sixpence, ceased its quarterly publication in 1885 when Dowie was seventeen or eighteen. It changed title to the *Monthly Magazine of Fiction*, which at threepence offered a 'new and complete novel' in each edition, and it was to this that she contributed. The cover for Dowie's novella 'For Dear Love's Sake', which was published in January 1892, when she was 24, shows she had been prolific in learning her trade as it was noted to be 'by the author of "Beyond the Pale", "Mrs Warburton's Companion," "The Silver Link" &c &c.'[16] She continued:

> I worked all morning and then got up on a lively mare I had hired from the old man at Barnstable [a well-known character who hired horses to the local hunt]. Her I rode all over the place . . . across country or narrow lanes and in the water meadows of sleepy Taw. I spoke to none, save charming landlady of the little cottage I'd hired 2 rooms at Newbridge. Not even a village! And when I wrote Finis after some five or six weeks' work I went off on riding tour to source of Taw and then down Taw to the double estuary where

Taw and Torridge pass outward to the sea. My comb and toothbrush were bought off a card at the village shop of anywhere. Stockings and some skin of underwear were bought when one reached a town and those worn posted home to be washed. My stock shirt and white waistcoat – it was summer and I rode in a piqué one – were 'got up' at night in the village inn where I would sleep by 'the girl' which time I huddled in my buttoned coat and drank cider with the landlord. I dropped into places like Ilfracombe, Lynmouth and Lynton but stayed in none. I slept naked – and very well – in clean sheets. I don't think I was ever happier or ever had a better time but as you know, my best times never come through people, always through commerce with nature, animals. I am most successful in very casual relations with people. When I was young (and of course I was very young then) incredibly so; best always that I do not come too close to people nor they too close to me![17]

Dowie spent the winter of 1889–90 in Paris. Ethel Heddle paints a picture of meals in Dowie's room high up in a house in the Latin quarter with her mother, Annie ('the youngest in heart, and the wittiest of that little group'), and her sister Lucy, five years older than Ménie and an artist who may well have been studying in Paris. Heddle said, 'Lucy Dowie's clever canvases and sketches hung everywhere ... we supped amongst a gay litter of Algerian embroidery and March daffodils, Parisian pottery, and Bon Marché *occasions* [second-hand goods] with here and there a pile of MS.' She describes how Annie

> has introduced a clean table cloth, and sundry extra spoons and forks, and Ménie, in a blue velvet tea-jacket, made by herself, is regarding it aggressively. 'Mother has reduced things to horrid middle-class order!' she says. And we sit down to the yard-long loaf, and the cold chicken, and the vin ordinaire, and we laugh a great deal.[18]

The impression given in her public talks and in the book she later wrote, *A Girl in the Karpathians*, is that Dowie simply struck out adventuring in a foreign country on her own. In fact she clearly ventured out in stages: first the southwest of England, as far from her family home as she could without leaving the country; then the next country, France; and only then further afield, via Germany (where she had been to school) to Poland.

Ménie Muriel Dowie in her travelling costume, illustration by Margaret Fletcher from *A Girl in the Karpathians* (1891). Note the cigarette in her left hand.

Dowie's decision to travel may have been a personal reaction to the tragedy of her father's death. The event also gave her financial independence: she speaks of 'having been left a little money', presumably from her father, which was sufficient to pay for her travel to Poland.[19] She certainly considered herself a free agent at the age of 22, showing the freedom possible to a confident and solvent young woman in the late nineteenth century. In 1890 she travelled alone to the Carpathian Mountains (in her spelling Karpathian), which were then in a region of Poland under Austrian control. She covered the country to Ruthenia riding bareback on Hutzel horses with a peasant guide over a period of ten weeks. She often slept in the open in her tartan cloak. She knew that lynxes, bears and wolves lived in the Carpathians but she was disappointed to be spared the sight of them, so she was not obliged to use her revolver. She later said, 'I know that everybody will think that there are other obstacles for a girl travelling alone; but that is not the case.' She delighted in telling the details of her experiences, giving a vivid image of her appearance: 'The one gown I wore had a short skirt that unhooked in a second, and left me all the freedom of knickerbockers.'

> Unless riding or travelling, I hardly ever wore my socks and sandals ... I went barefoot everywhere and I have found myself, when about to climb a hill, taking off my sandals and slinging them by a cord about my neck, because the way was rough, and I did not want them to get cut to pieces.[20]

She described 'a fair share of accidents' including almost drowning twice while bathing in unknown rivers, dislocating her shoulder in a fall and damaging a rib by falling in a river and hitting a sunken tree.

Her writing gives an indication of the wit of her conversation, as when she introduces the Kolomyja flea:

> large and well built, of a finer growth altogether than its western brother, it betrays little of his athleticism and baffling agility; it moves heavily and deliberately about its work with a due sense of what may be expected of it, and a fine consciousness of what a healthy flea can do, given time, opportunity, and the faculty of organisation. One of them discovered a piece of waste land, so to speak, upon my person, and laid me out in plots and spots, and sort of landscape gardened me with exceptional taste.[21]

She described her journey as a series of incidents: she washed in streams; she lost her watch; she bandaged a servant girl's severed finger with bread, cobwebs and a torn-up pinafore; she spent her 23rd birthday practising shooting a revolver so she would be prepared if she were to encounter a bear. It would be difficult to imagine a greater contrast with the domestic sphere than that which Dowie strove to create for herself. She appears as healthy and robust, an image of active womanhood, but also of the self-directed individual.

On her return to Britain, Dowie's first opportunity to present her material before the public was on 9 September 1890 when she gave a paper at the British Association for the Advancement of Science meeting in Leeds in the Geography section. A clue to why a young woman with no scientific background was invited to address such an august body is given by the chairman's introduction of her as the granddaughter of Robert Chambers. Her mother's relationship with the British Association was doubtless also a factor.[22]

It was this event (rather than the publication of her book on her travels the following year) that launched her celebrity. She was being described in the press as 'the heroine of the hour in scientific and social circles'. 'The fossil geographers have fallen at her feet, and ancient philologists and biologists have bowed before her throne,' the *Liverpool Mercury* wrote, looking forward to a visit to the town from her.[23] The *Birmingham Post* was similarly effusive, saying she was

> evidently bracing herself up to represent the femme forte of literary life in the London drawing rooms of next winter. This young lady may be taken as the representative of the fearless girl of the period – conscious in her own strength and purity of purpose, reliant on her own intelligence and therefore defiant of all danger.[24]

The occurrence of these 'puff pieces' before even a book had been produced is evidence of some deft work with the gossip columnists who relied on titbits of information from those in Society. More evidence that she had found favour with opinion makers was her receipt of the Victoria Wreath in October 1890. This was a gold olive wreath in the form of a bracelet bestowed by the proprietors of *The Gentlewoman* on ladies 'who distinguish themselves in the arts, sciences, literature or by some act of womanly devotion or daring'.[25]

Dowie is not known for her contribution to social causes, but she made a success of speaking to the recently formed Shop Assistants' Union in Liverpool in October 1890, which argued for shorter hours of labour for shop assistants, who were sometimes expected to work until late in the evening or even into the following morning. Dowie is said to have spoken fluently with few notes, mainly addressing women workers whom the organizers were eager to bring into the union. She said she 'wanted to see women have much greater confidence in the value of their labour and refuse to be ground down because they were women'. Not every woman could marry and have children, for there were more women than men, but they would follow trades and professions to keep themselves in their own homes: 'she thought the profession of wife and mother the best profession, certainly for the best women, if not for the cleverest, but there were other women, and something must be done for them.'[26] On the same theme, she spoke at the Early Closing Association's meeting in Chelsea against excessive hours in shop labour.[27] She specifically distanced herself from feminist positions: 'I am not a woman's rights woman, in the aggressive sense; that I do not rejoice in ugly clothes and that I am not desirous of reforming the world, or doing anything subversive of the present agreeable muddle, which is so well suited to lazy women like myself.'[28]

More often she was speaking on such subjects as 'All by Myself in Poland', which was her theme when she addressed the Darlington Sunday Society in January 1891 with tickets at a shilling, sixpence or threepence.[29] The long-expected account of her travels, *A Girl in the Karpathians*, was published by G. Philip & Son in May 1891 to great success, going into four editions in a year; a second edition was being advertised within a month.[30] Dowie responded to descriptions of herself by saying, 'Masculine, by reason of my knickerbockers . . . no more a matter of sex to me than my boots are. Dashing, forsooth! Because I smoke cigarettes and say so.'[31]

Her style was effortlessly superior: 'I stepped out into the dark of the platform, where a crowd of Jews and peasants jostled and shoved one other and yelled in common. I was oppressed by a strong smell of sheep and garlic, and was sensible of being in a crowd of extremely dirty persons.'[32] Her descriptions are notable for the distinction she always makes between Jews and peasants, as if Jews are a different category of humanity. She was so kind as to distribute cigarettes to the curious children who gathered round her. Her smoking was very much an 1890s lifestyle statement – in the picture that accompanied her book she is seen with cigarette in hand. She dressed in a shirt and knickerbockers with a detachable skirt and boots; it would be hard to construct a dress style more at variance with the drawing-room clothing of Victorian women of Dowie's class.

The Era gushed that 'her boy's dress, her prettiness, her "cheek" and her astonishing adventures with beasts of prey, from the domestic flea upwards, should make [such] a character for the centre of, say, a light musical comedy.'[33] Dowie was very much the public lady, being mentioned in society gossip columns as 'the now celebrated lady traveller', which attention she courted by her glamorous appearance. 'A Lady Correspondent' commented on 'one of the most remarkable dresses' to be seen at a reception given by the Salon, an artistic and literary society, 'It was a trained dress of tawny gold satin, with a front made of a leopard's skin. It attracted a good deal of attention for the wearer, who is fair, with bright colours, and an animated expression.'[34] On another occasion the *Dundee Courier and Argus* was calling her 'a graceful, willowy girl in a green gown'.[35]

The habits of literary women were a source of fascination for the press, where they were often seen not as independent agents, but as would-be men. The *Northern Echo* thus reported on a gathering including Dowie and Mona Caird, 'literary ladies who, copying a masculine custom, dined together at the Criterion ... A well-known publisher had sent a box of cigarettes, which were duly smoked by several of the ladies. Decidedly the gentler sex is getting on!'[36]

Not everyone had words of congratulation. Eliza Lynn Linton was scornful of the smoking woman: 'She smokes after dinner with the men; in railway carriages; in public rooms – where she is allowed. She thinks she is thereby vindicating her independence and honoring her emancipated womanhood.'[37] Linton returned to the subject the following year with a scarcely veiled attack on Dowie:

> A woman who smokes in public and where she is forbidden, who dresses in knickerbockers or a boy's suit, who trails about in tiger skins, who flouts conventional decencies and offends against all the canons of good taste, that woman is pronounced 'charming' and the able editor turns on one of his young lions to write her eulogium and celebrate her extravagance.[38]

It is not recorded how Dowie met the journalist and traveller Henry Norman, but they married, perhaps in some haste, at a registry office in Hanover Square on 28 August 1891. The witnesses were Walad Dewlab, Henry Norman's manservant, 'whom Mr Norman brought back with him from his travels', and Lily Garland, Dowie's maid.[39] Henry Norman was working for the *Pall Mall Gazette*; from 1895 he became assistant editor of the *Daily Chronicle*. Nine years older than Dowie, Norman was politically radical and allied to the Liberal Party. He was an expert on the Far East; when he met Dowie he was doubtless writing his first travel book, *The Real Japan*, which was published in 1892.[40]

They went on honeymoon fishing and shooting in Scotland, where Dowie was described as 'electrifying the simple and sober Scot by that unconventional costume which surprised the gentle herdsmen of the Karpathians'.[41] They travelled together to Egypt and the Sudan. As she put it, she 'spent the winter going up the Nile, and as far as our then outpost, Saras, which was fifty miles beyond Wady [*sic*] Halfa'.[42] This was seven years before Kitchener's reconquest of the Sudan, so they had holidayed fifty miles into enemy-held territory; Wadi Halfa was the border town where Dowie

Ménie Muriel Dowie (also named as Mrs Henry Norman) photographed for 'Celebrated Lady Travellers' in *Good Words* (January 1901).

and Norman stayed for a fortnight as guests of the army. On their return Dowie toured the north of England lecturing on her experiences. She used both her maiden and married names: she was pictured in *The Queen, the Lady's Newspaper and Court Chronicle* as Miss Ménie Muriel Dowie with her married name, Mrs Henry Norman, underneath.[43]

They visited the Balkans in 1895. Politically Norman sided with the subject peoples of the Ottoman Empire, whom he felt should be free to determine their own futures. She described Norman, whom she called 'Harry', as 'a veritable prince of travellers' and felt she had made a valid sacrifice of her habit of haphazard travelling to now make planned trips to places where her husband knew 'the interesting people'.[44]

They settled to live in 21 Grosvenor Road, Pimlico, with a view of Chelsea Bridge. Visitors were met by a large stuffed Malayan monkey holding a tray for visitors' cards. It had been shot for food by Norman in Kelantan. Dowie remarked to a reporter who came: 'It is only out of gratitude for that that I keep him, for I have a horror of all stuffed animals and think stuffed human beings would be just as reasonable and pleasant about a house.'[45] The house was filled with travel memorabilia including a boa constrictor, which had crawled into Norman's bed and he had shot, and a spear thrown at him by a native. Dowie had her collection of Balkan pottery, examples of peasant embroidery and books of modern poetry given her by the authors. Over her desk in what was referred to as her cosy 'study-boudoir' was a written sign, do it now, given to her by her husband, who had used it as his motto since he was a student. 'When I see it, it produces an acute sense of discomfort if I have neglected anything,' she said.[46] Marie Belloc Lowndes, who knew the couple, perhaps via her husband, the *Times* staff journalist Frederick Lowndes, recalled that Dowie 'often gave amusing dinner parties' and described her: 'She was tall and slight, with a mass of blond cendré hair, which she dressed in a fantastic way which recalled a fine portrait by Sir Joshua Reynolds.'[47]

When she attended the launch dinner for the *Yellow Book* in April 1894 she had been mentioned in the prospectus, but it was not until 1895 and 1896 that her stories appeared.[48] The first was 'Wladislaw's Advent' in volume IV about a Jewish/Polish artist in Paris who is used as a model for the Temptation of Christ. Dressed as Jesus, he enters the artist's orgiastic supper.

John Lane published a collection of Dowie's stories in 1897, two of which had appeared in the *Yellow Book*. *Some Whims of Fate* maintained Dowie's image as a traveller with stories set in Vienna, Cracow, Paris and Scotland. In the January 1897 *Yellow Book* she contributed 'My Note-Book in the Weald', a series of country sketches; she recounts tales of characters she met on her travels on foot, sometimes driving but mainly on horseback, in the wealds of Surrey and Sussex. Doubtless inspired by her new surroundings, she describes a world of dog breeds, brewers, country cooking, game animals, ostlers, blacksmiths, village weddings and country inns.[49] She continued to use her own name, unless there was an obvious reason to mention her married status, such as when she wrote of household management in the *Daily Chronicle* in 1896.

Dowie's first novel, *Gallia*, appeared in 1895, published by Methuen. It is most noted for its preoccupation with eugenics and its general explicitness. The *Saturday Review* said, 'The author has gone further in sheer audacity of treatment of the sexual relations and sexual feelings of men and women than any woman before. *Gallia* is remarkable for extraordinary plainness of speech on subjects which it has been customary to touch lightly or to avoid.'[50] The *Morning Post* described the eponymous heroine as

> one of those young women who are very often heard about in fiction but very seldom seen in real life – a girl, we mean, who knows everything, and has absolutely no respect for authority in any shape or form when it clashes with her conclusion as to what ought or ought not to be done.[51]

The critic in *The Times* disagreed with the intention they discerned, that 'Miss Dowie regards it as the novelist's function to air strange theories of the sexual relation.'[52]

Gallia makes a Spencerian suggestion that the 'evolution' of an emancipated woman is not a metaphor but an actual part of the natural cycle: 'You cannot make yourself the old style of woman; you cannot interfere with the clock of evolution that is wound up and goes on in each one of us.'[53] That is, Gallia was representing a view that social progress follows the same rules as biological evolution – a fashionable notion at the time which contributed to the acceptance of Marxism as an economic philosophy that offered an interpretation of the development of society.

The book is drenched in ideas of evolution and eugenics. Dark Essex, the love interest, is writing a tract on emotion in animals in response to one of Darwin's. Essex offers 'an unprejudiced consideration of the emotional capacity in women'.[54] Gallia suggests:

> a man may love a woman and marry her; they may be devoted to each other, and long for a child to bring up and to love; but the women may be too delicate to run the risk. What are they to do . . . Sacrifice the poor woman for the sake of a weakly baby? No, of course not, but get in a mother . . . lifting a burden from the shoulders of the weak and placing it on the strong.[55]

This is 'treating the world as a sort of farm and men and women merely as animals', one woman says. In response, Gallia offers: 'if the increase of the lower classes could be taken out of their own hands and supervised on scientific lines, crime as well as a number of diseases would be stamped out.'[56] These ideas were common currency where eugenics was discussed, responding to a widespread fear over the second half of the nineteenth century that the middle class were having fewer children, the poor were having too many, and those with hereditary diseases were passing them to offspring. The logical corollary was that the poor and the diseased would eventually predominate, and empire and nation would fall.

Dowie takes this further than the common concern about the reproductive rates among the poor and applies her thinking to the couplings of the middle class. Gallia wants to marry Dark Essex in order to have his children, but he falls out of favour because his tiny hands and feet 'gave her a feeling of discomfort'.[57] Later her fears are realized as it is revealed that he has hereditary weakness. 'A man with pronounced heart-disease ought not to marry. Nothing is more inevitably hereditary,' he says.[58]

Gallia does marry the other love interest, Guerdon, despite his seducing a teenage girl, keeping her as his mistress and impregnating her, which is given as evidence of his virility and suitability for marriage. She says to Guerdon that she does not love him,

> But I admire you; you fill out my idea of what a man should be, not only in looks, but in qualities . . . I have wanted the father of my child to be a fine, strong, manly man, full of health and strength. A man who is a man, whose faults are manly; who has never been better than a mere man in all his life.[59]

As Gail Cunningham has noted, Dowie has constructed a New Woman masculinity in which the male body becomes the 'object of female scrutiny and evaluation, and manliness is comically reduced to the functional ability to breed'.[60]

Dowie was a frequent feature at women's clubs such as the Pioneer, which had been opened in London in 1892 by Emily Langton with a brooch of an axe as its badge, intended to indicate that members would hew a path through the jungle of outdated and prejudiced ideas about women. Dowie debated on modern fiction there with Annie S. Swan, who wrote romantic novels and was also a temperance and suffrage campaigner.[61]

Dowie was very much the literary society woman, appearing at first nights and mentioned in gossip columns. She was reported as being at the New Vagabonds' Club in June 1895 at a dinner with Frances Hodgson Burnett, Pearl Craigie, Sarah Grand and Marie Corelli.[62] The *Morning Post* reported her attendance at an 'at home' of Pearl Craigie's in the company of Henry James, Edmund Gosse, Violet Hunt, Max Beerbohm, Arthur Wing Pinero, Will Rothenstein, Ella Hepworth Dixon and Henry Harland.[63]

In her next novel, *The Crook of the Bough* of 1898, set in the context of the Turkish defence of the Balkans, again there is a comparison of women and animals. A dinner guest offers the parable of the monkeys – they could talk but won't in case they are obliged to work. Women's position was similar:

> One day some of them broke the long silence: some of them talked
> ... in public places, on platforms, and in newspapers. But for a
> time no harm came of it. The harm is beginning to come now ...
> women are having to work. In time, in response to this female
> clamour for economic independence, equalisations of opportunity
> and the rest ... a half share of the work of the world will be handed
> over to them. Handed over – will be thrust upon them.

Then women will yearn for 'the lazy comfort of the crook of the bough'.[64] Dowie takes this phrase as the title of the book; clearly it is significant. The heroine says that women have always worked; the man says it is the dirty work of running the world to which he refers. For a woman of the middle class the choice of leisure and entertainment is very attractive compared to work and political engagement.

The heroine, Islay, falls for a Turkish colonel and he for her but they do not marry. East and West may pass on the road but do not meet. He comes, of course, from a degenerate civilization, as he rather improbably keeps reminding her, though he has perfect French and good table manners. The crisis of the book comes in the different interpretation of womanhood by the Turk and the heroine. Seeing his interest in her, the studious and unfashionable Islay has her hair dressed and buys fashionable clothes of exaggerated femininity. The colonel is disgusted; he has seen enough of coquettish women and thought Islay was different. He presents his vision of gender equality:

> strong men and women in closest sympathy working, thinking,
> together, living on the highest plane to which humanity can ever
> ascend, making a new character, a new record, and a new ideal.
> Man who forebore to deify and to exercise the old brutality they
> had called manly; women who scorned the use of beguilement
> they had come to think base.[65]

Now Islay had fallen short of this ideal, and was not going to be given a second chance.

The next novel, *Love and His Mask*, set partly in South Africa at the time of the Boer War, has a heroine who has a relationship with an officer whom she admires and respects, but has to realize that this is not enough. It may be that this was a working out of Dowie's experiences with her husband. Her three novels were about choices – characteristically wrong choices – in marriage. The beloved men in these books include one with a hereditary illness, the colonel from a 'degenerate civilisation', and the man good as a confidant on paper but not as a partner. Dowie said, 'Whoso reads my novels with a seeing eye, will find that they are studies, as faithful as I could make them, of women who made rather a grotesque little mess of trying to rearrange life.'[66]

In 1897, presumably in preparation for having a family, Norman and Dowie bought the 29-acre Kitcombe Farm in Hampshire. Dowie said to a journalist, 'In London there are so many things which one would rather a child did not see; but in the country that is not the case. The only thing to be avoided there is pig-killing.' In the short term they used the farm as a holiday home. Dowie explained, 'My husband and I have just bought a little farm, and it is our hope and intention to withdraw to it within a reasonable distance of years. We do not propose journalism and London forever.'[67] On 21 May 1897 her only child, Henry Nigel St Valéry Norman, was born. She was to write that as an infant he 'never knows what it is to lose heart over a long day, and can be found sunny of temper and eager for the coming hour, no matter how long he may have been at it, little as he is!'[68]

Henry Norman, who was forty in 1898, was scaling down his career as a newspaperman and both he and Dowie were perhaps considering their future. The *Northern Echo* for 25 February 1899 reported Norman 'has decided to give up daily journalism' and that Dowie 'has also shown an inclination towards retirement of late'. In 1899 Norman left the *Daily Chronicle* and stopped writing for the *New York Times*, for which he had been made the London correspondent in 1898. He stood as a Liberal Member of Parliament for Wolverhampton South at the election of 3 October 1900. The *Birmingham Daily Post* superciliously called him 'a brilliant if at times unduly impetuous journalist'.[69] Dowie campaigned with Norman, making platform speeches that were well received, and was said to be a considerable asset to his cause. He won the seat, but before this the series of events had been put in train that would end Dowie's career as a wife, mother and literary figure.[70]

By the end of the century Dowie seems to have become more restless and dreamy. She literally referred in an interview to dreaming while awake, not asleep. She was wishing to live 'in a dream of the maddest of impossible futures'.[71] In an article she protested:

> I never did aspire to be a traveller. There is a wide difference between a traveller and a roamer born. I was a roamer: I loved to start off in a manner unpremeditated, upon a route unsurveyed, for a destination not selected. To leave Fate a free hand, to let circumstances decide things, to strike the fetters from opportunity were the articles of my creed.[72]

As if to mark the new century, the following year she took such a leap into the unknown.

Norman, Dowie and Norman's best friend, Edward Arthur FitzGerald, all travelled to Russia together in September 1899. FitzGerald was a noted mountaineer: he had climbed the Alps from end to end, and in the Southern Alps of New Zealand he had discovered what became known as the FitzGerald Pass in 1894–5. He led an expedition in South America and wrote *The Highest Andes*, published in 1899. The trio of Dowie, Norman and FitzGerald spent a month visiting St Petersburg and Moscow. When they were in Tiflis (Tbilisi) in Georgia, Norman received a telegram that led him to go on to Central Asia. He left Dowie and FitzGerald to travel back to England together via Brussels. It was probably at this time that Dowie and FitzGerald started an affair, and in the new century her life began to unravel.

11

Evelyn Sharp and
the Last Volume

'It is family affection, not the want of it, that enslaves the man and woman in the home,' wrote Evelyn Sharp.[1] It was not considered usual 'for a middle-class girl to have any other ambition in life than to sit at home and wait for a problematic husband, performing meanwhile such ornamental household tasks as were left over when a mother, elder sisters and competent servants had all had a hand in them'.[2]

Nevertheless, she determined to leave. Her mother saw original sin in her revolt; her father might have favoured having one of four unmarried daughters off his hands, but he also disapproved. The family was in 'consternation' at her, a woman of 24, going off to make her own living. She carefully made plans, helped by a former schoolmistress who kept her interests at heart. She needed an income, however slight, so she secured a pupil who was the daughter of an architect in Bedford Square. She booked a hostel so she had somewhere to live; she borrowed £5 from her brother Llewelyn (always known as Lewen), which, added to the £5 she had saved from her dress allowance, gave her the money to venture out.

An elder brother gave her a warning of the dangers faced by a young woman living alone in town without giving any practical advice on precisely what these dangers were, so she was as ignorant of their nature when he finished his disposition as when he had started it, if more apprehensive. It felt as if she were running away, she remarked, though she 'felt anything like heroic' on a wet day when, 'oppressed by a sensation of being in disgrace', she ventured out to Aylesbury whence she took the train to London's Marylebone station to begin her new life.[3] It was January 1894 and, though she did not know it, the *Yellow Book* was being planned. There was no more propitious time to be a woman looking for writing work in London.

Evelyn Sharp was the youngest of four girls of the eleven children born to her mother, Jane Sharp (nine survived). She was born where the family lived at the time, in Denmark Hill, southeast London, a neighbourhood she suspected her father had chosen because John Ruskin lived there and could be seen riding into town and her father liked the proximity. John Sharp, a slate merchant, was only notionally a businessman. 'By taste and temperament he was an intellectual,' she wrote.[4]

Of Jane Sharp she commented, 'it has always been a matter of regret to me that I never learned to make a real friend of my mother until she was quite old and I was nearing middle age.'[5] The problem, she felt, was the large family which meant that she, as a sensitive child, could not receive the attention she required for fear of favouritism on the part of her parents; there was moreover, she notes without elaboration, her family's 'critical attitude to myself'.[6]

A kindly nurse to some extent filled the maternal gap. Sharp gave an idea of the dynamic operating among the children of the household when she noted, 'I think it is a dangerous thing for younger children to be even remotely in the power of elder brothers and sister.'[7] She complained that a large family furnishes the opportunity, 'through the accident of age, for one group of children to develop the vices of the tyrant and for the other group to develop those of the slave'.[8]

By the age of twelve the family was living in Kensington and Sharp went to Strathallen House school in Bolton Gardens. Just before she was fifteen they moved to Weston Turville near Aylesbury in Buckinghamshire, which meant she could stay on at the school as a boarder. It was her first escape from the home where she considered herself a 'misfit', and she enjoyed a 'sudden sense of freedom that exhilarated me'.[9] She pretended to be like the other girls and tried to simulate their zeal in striking off the days from the calendar as if going home were a longed-for haven. In fact, boarding school was the making of her. She said she 'began to find myself and to discover I was not the stupid person I often felt at home ... Before this, I had accepted without question the opinion of my nursery, that girls possessed neither courage nor a sense of honour.'[10]

Her emotional life was developing too; she slavishly adored the head girl (also called Evelyn) and they had literary interests in common, but 'our relationship never became unwholesome,' which suggests she was aware of other relationships that did.[11] She left school at sixteen wanting to go abroad, if only to a finishing school, as her sisters had done, and even more passionately wanting to go to college to continue her education, but for reasons she does not discuss, her parents refused. She said she had 'never managed quite to live down my resentment' at not being allowed to further her education, which would certainly have been granted had she been a boy.[12] In marked contrast to the experiences of her *Yellow Book* colleague Netta Syrett, she said:

> We did not move in those circles where advanced ideas about the education and economic independence of women had been steadily gaining ground for the last quarter of a century; and neither among the people we knew in Buckinghamshire, nor in the London set where most of our acquaintances were drawn, was it yet considered.[13]

A life of domestic tedium was alleviated when she travelled with her sisters Ethel and Mabel to Paris, but for the next eight years she was at home, attempting to educate herself. She studied alone, reading on botany, geology and entomology and writing her own stories, getting some accepted by minor magazines, though many more lay on the rejects pile on her shelf called her 'Mount of Humiliations'.

When she arrived in London she made her way to Brabazon House, a hostel in Store Street off the Tottenham Court Road. It was not unlike the women's hostel in nearby Gower Street where George Egerton had stayed a decade previously. Sharp drew on this lodging for scenes in *The Making of a Prig*, which John Lane published in 1897. It was a hostel mainly for office workers, with shorthand clerks occupying the highest rung. They worked long hours – their tea of bread and treacle was kept until 7 p.m. in time for them to return from their offices. Some women were described as too tired to do anything at the end of the day; some were reading novels, some mending stockings. It was 'a daily routine, with just enough money to support life, and not enough to buy its pleasures; enough energy to get through the toil, and not enough to enjoy its leisure'.[14] Sharp's 'cuby' or cubicle was a quarter of a dingy room that had been curtained into four compartments. There was barely room to move around the bed, and the only other furniture was a small chest of drawers on which rested a jug and basin. There was a bath in the basement, but the water had to be heated for every use so only three baths could be had per night, for which women had to put their names in a waiting-book weeks in advance.

Sharp was teaching most of the day in schools as well as coaching private pupils, and in the evenings wrote in her curtained cubicle at the hostel,

Young Evelyn Sharp, portrait from
Unfinished Adventure (1933).

using the bed for a table and a candle for a light after the gas was turned off at eleven. She sent a story to the *Yellow Book* and a novel to the Bodley Head; both were accepted (the novel on the recommendation of readers John Davidson and Richard Le Gallienne) and she came to know Harland and Lane. She later felt she had experienced incredible luck in sending her material to these places. Though her ability was clear, still she felt 'probably no other editor or publisher in London would have seen anything but immaturity in those early efforts.'[15] The first story accepted by the *Yellow Book* had been written at home. 'The End of an Episode' dealt with a novelist's blindness and the response of others, including the woman with whom he had once been in love. Eventually Sharp was to have stories in six volumes of the *Yellow Book*.

She later described her first published novel, which she had also written before she left home, as 'very immature'.[16] *At the Relton Arms* had been accepted by John Lane in a letter of 10 November 1894 offering royalties on 10 per cent with a cover price of three and sixpence.[17] It was set in a large family, not unlike the one that she had left in Weston Turville, where she examined marriage through the lives of two contrasting brothers. The

Daily Chronicle opened its review with what Sharp called 'the delightful sentence "Miss Evelyn Sharp has said the last word on the marriage question."'[18]

She accepted Lane's and the Harlands' invitations and was soon attached to the *Yellow Book* circle, remarking, 'I knew it was very heaven to be young when I came to London in the nineties.'[19] She said of the Saturday 'at homes' with the Harlands that they 'did not care much what conventional society thought of us, so long as we could succeed in pleasing our editor's fastidious taste in letters and avoid the two cardinal sins of banality and insincerity'.[20] She was a popular member of the *Yellow Book* set, forming a lasting bond with Ella D'Arcy, Netta Syrett and Mabel Dearmer; one of them gave her the nickname Becky, after Thackeray's Becky Sharp. She was also to join the newly formed Women Writers' Club, which met in Norfolk Street on Friday afternoons for women to drink tea, eat scones and discuss their profession.

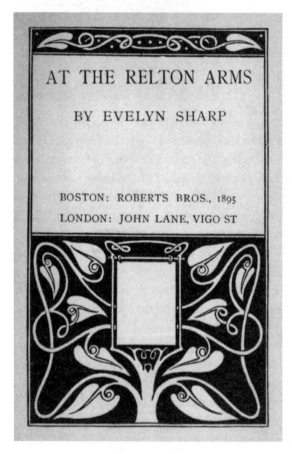

Title page of Evelyn Sharp, *At the Relton Arms* (1895).

By autumn 1896 she was close enough to John Lane to invite him for a weekend at her parents' home in Weston Turville. She wrote to 'My dear Publisher':

> Papa thinks you are '*a most intelligent man*' and likely to make your mark . . . and Mother thinks your manners are perfect and Marie has forgiven you for not going to church because you did refrain from wearing a low collar and a flannel shirt on Sunday which is her chief cause of complaint against [her brother] Lewen.[21]

Her novel *The Making of a Prig*, published by the Bodley Head in October 1897, was described by the *Daily News* as '"The Courtship of the New Girl" for its central motive is the manner in which Mr Paul Wilmot was wooed and won by Miss Katharine Austen.' Austen goes to London to make her way, living in a 'Working Ladies Home'. She visits a man she likes at his legal chambers, and through various complications they come together. The reviewer in summation says, 'It is a clever story, but it seems to want to be decadent without having the courage of its convictions,' for presenting Austen as both innocent and worldly. 'A heroine of twenty ought not to claim the immunities of an infant of ten. She is getting a big girl now.'[22]

Sharp was diversifying her efforts, noting to John Lane that she had a story accepted by *Little Folks* magazine and had sent another to *Pall Mall Magazine*. She said, 'I am teaching every morning till 2 and two afternoons as well, so I am obliged to do my writing in the evenings and I do get so sleepy.' She was writing a play, which she was finding difficult: 'I know that it must be all wrong in its stage-craft.'[23] Within a year Sharp was earning enough from her teaching and writing to move to the New Victorian Club in Sackville Street, where she was to live next door to *Yellow Book* colleague Netta Syrett when she chose to be there.

Not everyone appreciated the independent woman. On being introduced to her and hearing that Sharp was a writer and lived on her own, the painter James Whistler sneered, 'Not understood at home, I suppose? No scope for the development of your personality?' She was astonished, she said, that someone who had stood as a rebel and a pioneer 'had the most antiquated views about woman's place in the universe'.[24]

She had a friendship with Kenneth Grahame that did not develop into love, on his side, at least. She wrote of the *Yellow Book* set, 'I suppose we were as much interested in sex as young people are in all periods, but I know we did not talk eternally about it.'[25] Later in life she reflected on Grahame:

> He was very kind and courteous, but had not an ounce of humbug in him. Very sensitive but would die rather than let you think so if he could help it, and in many ways reminded one of the nicest kind of schoolboy except that he had a fine taste in literature instead of a passion for sport.[26]

She enjoyed Grahame's sense of humour and the connection he had with children, which led him to write his first great book, *The Golden Age*. They were close but not, it seemed, close enough for Evelyn. Her later lover Henry Nevinson thought she was in love with Grahame and he with her, but said Grahame was bound to honour an engagement to Elspeth Thomson that 'spoilt his life and work'.[27] However, Grahame had been writing for the *Yellow Book* and attending the Harlands' 'at homes' since 1894; he had known Sharp well for two or three years when he met his future wife. Grahame's biographer notes it likely that the acquaintance of Grahame and Elspeth Thomson dates from the second half of 1897.[28] Previously, Grahame even spent Christmas 1895 in Brussels with Sharp and the Harlands and on another occasion went to Boulogne with them. Sharp remembered, 'In my tale of adventure he counts as the perfect traveller, and those two Christmas weekends stand out in my memory as perfect holidays.'[29] There would have been ample opportunity for a romantic assignation and Sharp might well have accepted a proposal of marriage, but none came. Sharp's recollections of him suggest that Grahame, who was ten years older than her, was patronizing in a convivial way about her work, but protective about her when someone mocked her for her innocence. There was more friendship than passion in the relationship from his side.

Towards the end of 1897 she was sick at heart. She wrote to John Lane:

> I can't write anything but fairy stories just now; real things have gone so badly for me that I am too sore at heart to attempt a real story. Oh I do wish I hadn't got a heart at all. I think if you are born a woman your heart ought to be left out to put you on equality with men? How can there be equality of the sexes as long as women are given hearts?[30]

It is not possible to say whether this was related to Grahame's decline in interest in her under the influence of Elspeth Thomson, but there was no other man to whom she is recorded as being so close. One of her *Yellow Book* stories was 'In Dull Brown' in volume VIII on the difficulties of courtship for an intelligent girl, where 'The burden of her own cleverness was almost too much for her.'[31]

Stephen Gwynn was also friendly with Sharp, whom he knew via his friendship with the Dearmers. She would visit Gwynn and his wife May at their house in Chelsea. He wrote that she was

> in those days an absurdly boyish figure, but with brown eyes bigger than grow in any boy's head. She and I had this in common that we were both familiar with the life of a large family where boys predominated; but she never failed to emphasise that I had in all ways the luck of it: first that I had been a boy; next, and even more important, I had come at the tip, while she had been at the tail.

Even in adult life, therefore, she was thinking of herself in terms of her family. Gwynn continued:

> In those days we all called her Becky, but she generally spoke of herself as the 'Little Brother'. That was her attitude to life, on very many bicycling excursions and the like. I never met anybody with a jollier sense of humour, and her friends' children, but still more her friends' relations with and attitude to their children, supplied her with a deal of amusing copy.[32]

Sharp's *joie de vivre* could irritate her friends. Netta Syrett, not a morning person, disclosed that Sharp was 'never so repellent as when, especially on a wet day' she 'glowed with health'. Sharp said she felt there might be some foundation for the 'legend of the early-riser's anti-social effect on the rest of the family circle'.[33] Sharp became friends with those enthusiasts for life the Dearmers, going to Normandy with them for 'one lovely month' where May and Stephen Gwynn visited. By her friendship with the Dearmers, Sharp was unequivocally entering a socialist sphere. She said, 'we all called ourselves Christian Socialists, except Laurence Housman, who never called himself anything.'[34]

Her radicalism was no more respectful of the older generation of progressives than is usual in the young. She was invited by John Lane to write a reader's report for a collection of essays with titles like 'The Morality of Marriage' by the redoubtable Mona Caird. She reported:

> they appear to be directed towards one end – the equalisation of the sexes, politically and socially. If they had been published when some of them were written, in '92, they might have carried some weight with them. But to talk now of the slavery of woman, of her one destination being marriage, and of her physical growth being stunted and neglected, especially in such strong uncompromising terms as are employed by Mrs Caird, seems out of date if it is not absurd. It is generally a woman's own fault nowadays if she is tyrannised over by anybody, least of all by her home whether she is married or single, and it seems a pity to have written such long essays in order to tell people facts that are patent to everyone and are working out their own remedies every day.[35]

Mona Caird was obliged to find another publisher and settled for the less prestigious George Redway to produce *The Morality of Marriage and Other Essays on the Status and Destiny of Women* in 1897.

Sharp's next novel, *The Making of a Schoolgirl*, first serialized in *Atalanta* magazine in 1896 and then published by John Lane, is about a new girl going to a boarding school from a male-dominated household, as Evelyn had. She feels alienated from the forced femininity of her schoolmates, considering her failure to have been born a boy her 'greatest trouble'. It was a more successful book than Sharp's first, and was published widely internationally. Sharp was popular enough for Lane to commission a portrait of her from Edward Arthur Walton as one of the 'Bodley Heads', which was printed as the first of the art pieces in *Yellow Book* volume XII.

In writing of children she was in the same field as other *Yellow Book* writers who became known as children's authors, the most famous of them being Edith Nesbit and Kenneth Grahame, but they also included Sharp's friends Mabel Dearmer and Netta Syrett. Lane had published her first endeavours in this field, *Wymps and Other Fairy Tales*, in 1896, and its successor *All the Way to Fairyland* in 1898. 'Her fairy stories and schoolgirl tales were neither patronising nor moralistic,' writes Angela V. John, 'though they reflect her increasingly progressive views on gender, class, internationalism and peace.'[36] Her leading characters were often disabled and her fairy stories were deliberately subversive, so that the bravest boy is Kit the Coward, who understands animals and doesn't fight like other boys, while

Sharp's princess asks why the prince always has to go out into the world to find his bride: can't the princess do the finding for a change?

The Bodley Head was not a natural fit for children's literature. Stephen Gwynn, who was reading for Macmillan, brought Sharp's work to their attention, after which they published some of her children's books. It was with Macmillan that she became known for her writing about girls' boarding schools in such works as *The Youngest Girl in the School* in 1901, before her contemporary Angela Brazil did so. The theme and setting were hardly novel: books about boarding schools had started with Sarah Fielding in the eighteenth century and were still making literary success for J. K. Rowling in the twenty-first. Sharp was praised as writing books for girls that 'dared to be manly', but as Angela John remarks, she looks beyond the hockey sticks at the gender transition of her girls, moving from a home dominated by father and brothers to a female sphere in which different values pertain.[37]

Sharp lived in a flat with Ella D'Arcy in Knightsbridge for a short time in 1897, but the building was insalubrious and she moved to Marjorie Mansions in the Fulham Road.[38] Her younger brother Lancelot joined her, but it was not a happy union as a result of his drinking, and the living arrangement ceased. She moved to a flat on her own at Mount Carmel Chambers in Dukes Lane, Kensington, where she settled.

Sharp was a member of the Ottawa Skating Club, which met at the Prince's Skating Rink in Knightsbridge. It was known as a pickup place – notably for boys by homosexual men.[39] Sharp met the love of her life there in 1901 when she collided with the accomplished skater Henry Nevinson. He was a war correspondent who was also the literary editor of the *Daily Chronicle*, in which office he had corresponded with Sharp, who wrote reviews for the paper, though they had not met before. He had also contributed to the *Yellow Book*.

Perhaps Nevinson was so frequently at the rink because it gave him an opportunity to engineer encounters with impressionable young women. Sharp was certainly captivated: 'he took my hand and we skated off together as if all our life before had been a preparation for that moment,' she wrote.[40] He was a romantic figure, a man of action, but he was also depressive and unhappily married. In engaging with him, Evelyn Sharp was to find herself adding his complicated family dynamic to the baggage she already had. It was harder to escape the family than simply by running away: now she found herself crashing into another one.

MEANWHILE, THE *Yellow Book* had not outlasted the century. When volume XIII came out in spring 1897 it was the last of the series published over four years since 1894. It had often maintained a defiantly female stand under its editor's guidance. Harland had written in his whimsical way about dog and cat literature: dog literature being popular but poorly written, while cat literature was beautiful if less commercial. He wrote, 'The Cat is always a Princess, because everything nice in this world, everything fine, sensitive, distinguished, everything beautiful, everything worthwhile, is of essence Feminine, though it may be male by the accident of sex.'[41] In volume X, in which he wrote this, women outnumbered men as contributors for the first time; there were nine women out of fifteen writers and an equal number of male and female illustrators.

Vernon Lee made her only appearance in volume X but many more familiar names were to recur. Evelyn Sharp had stories in the last two volumes; Ménie Muriel Dowie in X and XII, Gabriela Cunninghame Graham in XIII, Netta Syrett in XII, Olive Custance in XI and XIII and Rosamund Marriott Watson in X, XII and XIII. Ella D'Arcy had pieces in all of the last four volumes. These women, and the males who accompanied them, were markedly from the established *Yellow Book*, Bodley Head coterie. John Lane was unwilling to spend the money to attract big names; the only notable in the last four volumes is rising poet W. B. Yeats with 'The Blessed' in XIII in April 1897.

Aline Harland, as Renée de Coutans, contributed a poem to volume X and a story to volume XII. Katharine Mix thought that Aline's devotion to Harland's interests probably kept her from becoming a writer herself. Her autobiographical work and letters show she had ability, 'but she subordinated her work to her husband's, and her output was small.'[42]

Volume XIII, due in April 1897, was late, not reaching the news-stands until May. There was no announcement that this was the last volume and it may be that no decision had been made when it went to press. The guide for future submissions went in as usual, as if anticipating continuity, but John Lane was lamenting the bad times in a letter to Arnold Bennett, saying that 'everything was in arrears.'[43] Mix quotes a director of the Bodley Head from the 1930s as saying, 'It had ceased to pay dividends.'[44] The primary objective of the *Yellow Book* had been to showcase Bodley Head writers so their other published work would sell, rather than for the quarterly to make a profit. Early issues had been a great success, however, so it was a disappointment when the revenue stream dried up. It was easy to make a financial saving of the *Yellow Book*'s costs when times were difficult.

Running the *Yellow Book* was obviously a struggle for Harland without Beardsley and D'Arcy, and having to deal with Lane's insistence on his own writers and the artists he favoured. Harland was therefore running a journal whose literary impetus was in deceleration, with reliance on a small group of writers and the unwillingness of his employer to pay for others or even to pay his editor's own invoice – Harland was forever calling on Lane to do so. His acute literary senses doubtless also told him that by volume XIII the *Yellow Book* was not getting better, even if he could not echo Ella D'Arcy's comment to John Lane, 'I'm truly sorry to find it such a poor number.'[45] Years later when asked about the demise of the *Yellow Book*, D'Arcy said, 'we were all a little tired of it.'[46] D'Arcy was one of those who lost most from its disappearance, as she had failed to diversify and had not learned to write for a market. The death of the *Yellow Book* meant the loss of a near certain place for her stories.

In literary terms, Stetz and Lasner say the *Yellow Book* had become 'increasingly self-conscious and self-reflective'; it was no longer avant-garde: 'by 1896–97, its newness was, paradoxically, turning into a matter of convention.' Other, imitative publications espousing art and literature were overcrowding the field for the *Yellow Book*. When it no longer looked like a radical departure from mainstream publishing, and had 'ceased to surprise', the *Yellow Book* had lost its *raison d'être*.[47]

Aline said Harland's health was the cause of the *Yellow Book*'s end: 'The Quarterly was to be found on every smart drawing room table in London ... The *Yellow Book* continued to be in vogue when, in January 1897, in consequence of the Literary Editor's failing health the publication ceased, having gallantly served its purpose and the needs of its day.'[48] Aline was obliged to return to New York in November 1897 because of the serious illness of her mother, who died that month; she stayed for six weeks with her father. When she returned to 'a monstrous dark and dour and sour London winter', Harland's health was poor, with his tuberculosis exacerbated by bronchitis and laryngitis.[49] They were bitterly impoverished in the bad winter of 1897–8, still at the flat in the Cromwell Road where they attempted to dodge tradesmen's bills.

This might have been the end of this couple but they took another turn. Aline and Henry Harland were received into the Roman Catholic Church in 1898. Aline does not ponder her own conversion but said of Henry's that he 'was what is called an "intellectually convinced Catholic." He had the metaphysical mind.'[50] This new departure in his life inspired a clerical note in his writing so that in 1899 Henry was writing *The Cardinal's*

Snuff-Box, the first of three novels with a Catholic atmosphere. It was a popular success, selling well in the UK and USA, which was fortunate as it funded the couple's stays in France and Italy as Harland's tuberculosis worsened. He fell ill after the last proof sheets were passed.

Evelyn Sharp visited the Harlands for a weekend at a villa they had rented for the summer outside Dieppe after the *Yellow Book* had come to an end. Sharp said it was 'one of those absurd French country houses apparently made of bits of wood nailed together and painted the colour of chocolate cream, with turrets and balconies growing out of it'.[51] Sharp remembered Harland attempting to have birds eat out of his hand and trying to identify them with the aid of coloured plates in a book.

As the century ended, Netta Syrett's relationship with the Harlands lessened; she was disappointed at the transformation that came over Harland when he and Aline converted to Catholicism. She said, 'He lost his gaiety, he became conventional, and appeared desperately afraid of shocking "respectable" people.'[52] She was not the only one who broke with the Harlands as their lives progressed. Ella D'Arcy seems to have resented Harland's success with *The Cardinal's Snuff-Box*, saying not entirely approvingly, 'it was success itself which appealed to him, for there was not a little of the woman in his nature. He developed also the desire to climb to get into the society of the duchesses and princesses whom he painted with so loving a pen.'[53] D'Arcy's unrewarded high hopes for her Roman Catholic novel may well have embittered her. She hankered after the concentrated literary thinking of the *Yellow Book* days, however, writing to Evelyn Sharp, 'P.S. How is it that there's never been any good talk – lit'ry, not "talking shop" talk – since the YB collapsed and HH joined the Roman priesthood?'[54] They were not on good terms at the end of his life. She later wrote to a well-wisher, 'It was kind of you to tell me what Henry Harland said of me, for I had been extremely fond of the Harlands, and their entire withdrawal from me during the last years of his life had been very painful.'[55]

Aline and Henry rented the Villa Solaro in San Remo on the northern Italian coast where Aline, a nurse and his mother looked after Harland. He was working on his last novel; Aline wrote of 'his physical pain and exhaustion', waiting for a remission of his disease which would again allow him to 'sit up and work, sit down and slog'.[56] He would ask her to place his manuscripts, paper and ink where he could see them, and would say, 'Tomorrow, I will begin to work. I have been lazy too long.'[57]

Aline said Harland was fully conscious on all but the last day, but so weak he could hardly speak: 'he laid his head upon my head with love, such love, and pity.'[58] He died at the villa on 20 December 1905, aged 44. Aline wrote, 'The very flesh of my heart, spiritual and physical, was torn out of it the day I left my love's room.'[59] She finished writing his last book, *The Royal End*. 'Love', he had said, 'is the Royal End . . . that shall be the last line of the book.'[60] She carried out his wishes.

Thus died the best friend a woman writer in the 1890s ever had. For the *Yellow Book* women, the new century would be a greater challenge than the one just passed.

PART TWO
Commence de Siècle

ON A DULL JANUARY MORNING a doctor entered his queen's bedroom to find her curled up in foetal position, looking towards the hand-tinted photograph of her husband that hung by the bed. In a few days Queen Victoria would be dead at the age of 82. Few people in her kingdom, and certainly none of the *Yellow Book* people, could remember a time when she was not the reigning monarch.

Her death was more than the end of a single woman's life. It marked the termination of a reign in which women had made steady, significant gains in education, property ownership, creativity, the professions and campaigning. However, the empire that made her the most powerful person in the world, male or female, was already showing signs of its dissolution when she died on 22 January 1901.

If the previous century had seen gains for women, the first half of the twentieth century would see a reassertion of the male in the exercise of that most masculine of pursuits: war. The last official matters to which Victoria had attended had been to receive reports of the Boer War, a struggle for supremacy in the southern tip of Africa where British forces had been pushed back and besieged. Some troops had surrendered, even showing the white flag, in the devastating defeats of the 'Black Week' of 10–17 December 1899.

The war was enough to rouse even Olive Custance, the least martial of writers, to write to John Lane:

> My Daddy sails for South Africa with the '3rd Norfolk' militia on Sunday, he is now colonel of it ... you know ... isn't this war sordid and horrible? Today I read that one of my favourite cousins Cecil Joliffe, had died of his wounds ... he was only twenty seven ... it is so sad ... I am pleased to hear that you like my poems ... never

mind about publishing them . . . I will write to you some more soon . . . when I feel less miserable!¹

The South African war was a shock to the complacency of empire and the harbinger of a decline in the influence of the artistic imagination as the nation entered a century during which, as it unfolded from 1899 until 1945, national effort was concentrated on fighting, preparing for or attempting to avoid three major conflicts.

The new king presided over a nation where the great question was rivalry with Germany: how many battleships could be built? Whose were the most powerful? Who had the strongest industrial economy? The new national mood was accompanied by a rhetoric of empire that was specifically anti-decadent. As George Wyndham, Under-Secretary of State for War from 1898 to 1900, said, 'The same causes which brought about the fall of the great Roman Empire are working to-day in Great Britain.'²

Enlarging this topic, Robert Baden Powell, hero of the siege of Mafeking, the relief of which occasioned one of the high points of hysterical patriotism, said:

> Remember that the Roman Empire 2000 years ago was comparatively just as great as the British Empire of today. And though it had defeated any number of attempts against it, it fell at last, chiefly because the young Romans gave up soldiering and manliness altogether . . . Don't be disgraced like the young Romans who lost the Empire of their forefathers by being wishy-washy slackers without any go or patriotism in them.³

In a literary approach Elliott Evans Mills wrote a ponderous warning in *The Decline and Fall of the British Empire* in 1905, which was supposedly a textbook written in 2005 for Japanese schoolchildren. It noted that the cause of imperial decline was the fact that the British 'had become too effete and nerve-ridden to guide the destinies of the world'. This was ascribed to 'the growth of refinement and luxury' with scorn that 'the emancipated Englishwoman of the age used her freedom for selfish rather than National ends.'⁴ In response to such jeremiads, Empire Day was first celebrated on 24 May 1902, when the empire had already entered its decline and was mustering its resources for the coming battles.⁵

There was no space for effete decadents in this picture, and little for women. One can dispute what the *Yellow Book* was, for it had many facets, but there could be common agreement that it was no vehicle for soldiering and manliness. Women did not lose anything in the early years of the twentieth century, but the onward march of progress was halted and the *Yellow Book* women were left battling in a workplace heavily weighted against them.

The First World War allowed women to take some previously male jobs but they were expected to retire back to the domestic sphere after the conflict was over. Of the cohort of 'new women' who worked for the *Yellow Book* only one, Mabel Dearmer, was to go to war. Only one, Evelyn Sharp, was an active suffragette, but others were affected by a national atmosphere that had previously found the challenging new woman thrillingly fashionable; now she was just a shrill bore. The effect of this disdain by the literary establishment was a stalling of the literary careers of almost all the *Yellow Book* women.

12

Family Battles

E ven if they were the most respectable of women, there was a limit to the amount of time a lady could stand on a public street, so for an assignation it was a good idea to be inside a building. Olive Custance was waiting in Kensington for a poet with whom she had corresponded but had not met. She was already nervous, and had written to him, 'I long very much to see you though I am shy of you and afraid you will not like me.'[1]

She was waiting, becoming increasingly frustrated, in the Victoria and Albert Museum. New building work was taking place on the museum, the foundation stone for which had been laid by Queen Victoria on 17 May 1899 in her last public appearance. Olive Custance had written to Lord Alfred Douglas in June praising his poetry. Flowers and pages of her own verse followed. They made an arrangement to meet surreptitiously at what they were still calling the South Kensington Museum. She was chaperoned by her maid – Custance always managed to involve her servants in her assignations.

She waited in increasing anger. Doubtless not wishing to appear a spurned woman in front of her maid, she had a cab called and proceeded to his address to remonstrate with him. The hansom clattered along Brompton Road, Knightsbridge and Piccadilly to Lord Alfred Douglas's rooms in Duke Street (almost opposite John Lane's rooms in the Albany), while she planned how she would deal with the uncivil gentleman.

Her anger dissipated when she came upon the handsome young man, himself in a flustered state, who had just returned from the museum. He had been there as arranged, but had gone to the wrong door, or the wrong room, perhaps because of disruption caused by building work on the new extension, or their inadequate arrangements. Anyway, they had missed each other, but now, he said, they fell in love at sight. However, Douglas wrote,

he 'did not think that I had the slightest chance of marrying her'.[2] Douglas
was at this stage still the youthful character with whom Oscar Wilde had
fallen in love. He was so juvenile in appearance he boasted he could pass
for a schoolboy up to the age of forty; he was in his thirtieth year when he
met Custance as an adult.[3]

Douglas had come into his inheritance on the death of his father in
January 1900 and was quickly spending his way through it, setting up a
racing stable in Chantilly, France, among other extravagances. They wrote
loving letters to each other, she calling him 'Prince' and he calling her 'Page'.
With her slight frame and page-boy haircut, she was a little boyish in
appearance and Douglas asked, 'Why can't you dress as a boy and come
with me?'[4] He wrote, 'You are a darling baby and you are exactly like a boy
and you know perfectly well that I love you better than anyone else, boy
or girl . . . you have everything. I used to wish you were a boy, now I am
glad you are not,' which is one of the stranger things said by a man to his
beloved.[5] They would meet in a room above the Carfax Gallery in Ryder
Street, part owned by Robert Ross, who was at that time a friend of
Douglas.

Custance's meeting with Douglas was the culmination of a habit of
writing to poets she admired, as if fishing for excitement. This time she
would certainly find it. Olive Custance was born on 7 February 1874, the
elder of two daughters of Colonel Frederick Hambledon Custance of
Weston Old Hall, Norfolk, and his wife, Eleanor Constance Joliffe. Colonel
Custance was an only son and he inherited the family estate at Weston
Longville, near Norwich, in 1892. His life was filled with the usual pursuits
of a country gentleman: he was a fisherman and trout breeder who also
shot game, often joining King Edward VII with guns at Sandringham,
Weston or other Norfolk coverts. He was anti-Catholic, which was far from
unusual at the time and is significant only because of the role of Catholicism
in his daughter's life and those of the men with whom she mixed. Olive
Custance's family background was therefore of a fine aristocratic lineage,
an estate that dated from 1558 and the best social connections.

She grew up at the family's house in Mayfair and late in her teens at
Weston (though they kept the London house). One commentator has suggested the move to the country had 'something to do with Colonel
Custance's disquiet about his eldest daughter's social habits in the city'.[6]
She had her own maid serving her in her own room in the manor house,
where she would sit at her desk and look out over the estate, which, in the
absence of any male heir, she as the eldest daughter stood to inherit.

Her diary notes cricket matches and plays she attended and her reading, which included Swinburne's verse and Pater's *Marius the Epicurean*. She would write of watching the peacocks being fed in the grounds, and of the thrill of riding out in the morning on Lady Star, one of the stable of horses: 'It was a golden morning – sunny as spring and every twig in the hedgerows was thickly jewelled with frost tears that glittered like diamonds in the soft "lemon coloured" sunlight.'[7]

All her life Custance had an obsessional interest in presenting herself to the outside world, and understanding her own feelings, to the exclusion of the feelings of others or any conception of what they might think of her, or that such a thing mattered. This is no bad stance for a poet, but it made her relationships with those around her difficult.

Her extant diaries are a disparate mix of journals and appointments diaries. They cover the period 1894, when she was twenty, until 1940, four years before her death at the age of seventy. Some years are covered in tedious detail; others go unreported so that, for example, there is no record of the 24 years between October 1913 and January 1937. Olive Custance also deleted a great deal of material, which internal evidence suggests was related to her premarital and extramarital romantic life, though sufficient remains to give a picture of a lively personality with few inhibitions.[8]

They are written in ink or pencil in Custance's extravagant handwriting, which is interspersed by exclamation marks and her personal punctuation: she had a tendency to place three dots where others would use a full stop or a comma. She did this also in her published work and was duly criticized by critics for it. Custance had been writing from an early age: nearly all the poems in her first volume, *Opals*, were written before she was seventeen.[9] She also mixed with writers from an early age, for example meeting John Gray at a party in London in 1890 when she was 16 and he 25. Gray at this time was working as a civil servant. He had been contributing prose and poetry to *The Dial* from 1889; his first volume of verse, *Silverpoints*, was published in 1893 by John Lane.

He was the first of the poets Custance pursued. She corresponded with Gray and sent him her verse, showing an early ability to negotiate the world of ambiguous sexuality characteristic of the decadents. Gray moved in Oscar Wilde's circle, was a dandy and writer of exquisite verse, and was not known to be romantically linked with any woman or man. She sent two poems from *Silverpoints*, 'The True Vine' and 'Sensation', and her own poem 'To John Gray'. This was to be published in her second book, *Rainbows* (1902), but the poem was now called 'Reminiscences'. It describes their first meeting:

I clasped your hand,
But scarcely said a word;
We stood as children stand
Whose souls are stirred
To great shy love they cannot comprehend.

Gray, on his part, was so eager to read her first book that he obtained a copy, perhaps from John Lane, before Custance had time to send him one. She wrote, 'I think it was sweet of you to be impatient for a sight of my small book . . . I must for that reason forgive you . . . though I did want to send it to you myself . . . you have given me such lovely books.'[10]

Whether there was any consideration that John Gray might be a matrimonial match for Olive is questionable. Her family were gentry and he was a self-educated civil servant who came from a very humble background. He was, however, welcomed at their London home in 1896, the year after the Wilde trials. Custance wrote in her diary:

I had sent John Gray some of my poems, and the new year brought a beautiful letter from him and the photograph I so much desired . . . and then again next morning another letter, he had read my poems and found, he said, many beautiful things in them. Oh! Prince of Poets your praise is indeed precious to me. Perhaps I shall see you in London!'[11]

From this it is clear that Gray was continuing literary friendships after the Wilde trial: he had not broken off correspondence. Custance was to see him a few days later at her family's fashionable town address in Curzon Street where she was joined by her maid 'Tanie'. Olive wrote of this meeting:

I came home from lunching with Auntie and put on my new green silk shirt (like a smock) with black skirt. The bell rang and Tanie was shown up – what happiness and I told her I had asked John Gray to tea and very soon he came and brought me 'Silverpoints' and was so kind and talked so beautifully – and looked so nice. He is my ideal poet.[12]

It is revealing that he gave her a copy of his verse: John Gray was said to have bought up copies of *Silverpoints* in the aftermath of the Wilde trials (where he had retained counsel with a watching brief to respond to any mention that might be made of him). He was said to have done this to obliterate the memory that he had ever been a decadent, yet he handed a copy to Custance the year after the trials.[13] This was, moreover, in the home of Squire Custance, who, had he known of it, would not have approved of Gray's Catholicism, his association with bohemianism, his low birth or his less than illustrious prospects: he was at this time working in the Foreign Office library. In October 1898 Gray went to Rome, to Scots College, to prepare for the priesthood and was ordained in December 1901.

Custance also made the acquaintance of Richard Le Gallienne in 1890, probably by writing to him in praise of his work. He had already seen the publication of his first book, *My Ladies' Sonnets* (1887), and a second, *Volumes in Folio* (1889). He was making his way in literary life in London from December 1888 and became a reader for John Lane in 1892. It was doubtless through her contact with him that Custance was encouraged to send some of her work to the *Yellow Book*. Her poem 'Twilight' appeared in volume III, in October 1894. It is a very 1890s piece, personifying the ending of the day and luxuriating in the 'golden gloom of dreamland' and the choirs of 'aureoled cherubim'. She was paid a guinea (one pound and one shilling) for it, which she described in Le Gallienne's phrase as 'wonderful fairy gold'.[14]

Le Gallienne had married in 1891. Custance's first diary entry, on 24 May 1894, reads: 'Dear New Journal I will unveil you today – today that is so bright and yet so sad.' The paper is damaged with age and wear, so is difficult to read continuously, but she is writing of the coming of summer in the world outside: 'outside the world is aglow', 'summer has come', '... how the birds sing! But my heart cannot go out to joyous nature today. I am very sad: this morning I heard that my dear friend Le Gallienne has lost his young [wife, Mildred] is dead.' The paper is too fragmented here but there is a lament including the words 'young husband', 'girl baby', 'that was so beautiful' and 'how can we comfort you'. 'I wandered alone in the woods, my heart felt breaking when I thought of my friends' sorrow and saw around me such a gay and glorious world. Shall send her a wreath of lilies. Alas poor little wife.' On the back of this is stuck a cutting from a newspaper: 'Writers and Readers': 'We deeply regret to announce the death from typhoid fever after a ten days illness of Mrs Richard Le Gallienne ... their little daughter was born only in December last.' Custance has added J.L. in pen, presumably the author (John Lane), who did not name the deceased except as Mrs Richard Le Gallienne. They had thus been married only three years.

Custance took to calling Le Gallienne 'Narcissus' after his 1891 work *The Book Bills of Narcissus* and the name suits him for his posing, curly dark hair and classical profile. The protagonist, a surrogate of Le Gallienne, is a bibliophile and lover of women. The promiscuous way he gathers books for which he has no means to pay mirrors his cavalier treatment of his lovers.

Her effusiveness had all been epistolary so far. She first met Le Gallienne at John Lane's home in the Albany in summer 1894, where she writes of Le Gallienne's entry: 'the moment he looked at me I felt I should love him and that he would love me!'[15] A page or pages are missing here, which is frequently the case when she went to London. The next page starts:

> ... Then we parted and went our different ways.
> 'And if you will remember
> And if you will forget.'
> And now I am back at Weston and Narcissus is far away.[16]

'Yesterday he wrote to me. He has written to me once or twice since we left London and I have written to him. But after all what are letters when one's heart is full?' 'O! to go back – to follow the river of life – wading through long pure grass in the green pastures – follow and find the flowers – be simple and glad and good once again. Follow and find love! But – King Narcissus is far away!'

After his wife's death, Le Gallienne had rooms in Chancery Lane, which were in central London but hardly as grand as the Custances' Curzon Street address. There was no secret that they saw each other. His biographer mentions that Le Gallienne took her to lunch in the period after Mildred's death.[17] For his part, Richard Le Gallienne pictured her as his muse, Nicolete, in *The Quest of the Golden Girl*, his 1896 erotic reverie. Here in a corner of her 'ancestral park' the older writer meets a young woman fishing for trout in a stream.[18] He says she

> was just soul and bloom ... As I walked by her side that May morning, I was only conscious of her voice and her exquisite girl-hood; for though she talked with the aplomb of a woman of the world, a passionate candour and simple ardour in her manner would have betrayed her, had her face not plainly declared her the incarnation of twenty.

Her talk, and something rather in her voice than her talk, soon revealed her as a curious mixture of youth and age, of dreamer and desillusionée. One soon realised that she was too young, was hoping too much from life, to spend one's days with. Yet she had just sufficiently that touch of languor which puts one at one's ease, though in deed it was rather the languor of waiting for what was going to happen than the weariness of experience gone by. She was weary, not because of the past, but because the fairy theatre of life kept its curtain down, and forced her to play over and over again the impatient overture of her dreams.[19]

They have lunch in her cottage and talk of the writers they enjoy. 'Nicolete and I were already in love with each other's brains,' he says.[20] In the novel she dresses as a boy so she can go travelling with him; they sleep in the same room where she tempts him but he manfully resists. This is the most clearly fictional part of the account; there would have been no such display of gallantry from Le Gallienne had an offer been forthcoming.

She hopes their love will end in marriage but he tells her the difference in social standing between them is too great. She is reluctant to accept this but the intervention of Nicolete's father, 'the Major-General', brings their romance to a close. With some prescience he assumes she will soon be choosing among the grooms of 'the romantic British aristocracy'; she is not the Golden Girl he seeks.[21] This was fiction, of course, but it is tempting to see Le Gallienne and Custance infatuated with each other and her father being obliged to cool the temperature. Le Gallienne's biographer Richard Whittington-Egan remarks that his fiction was usually autobiographical as the poet 'lacked the power of sustained invention, and could create convincingly neither characters nor situations'.[22] Her father certainly knew about her relationship with Le Gallienne, as she notes in her diary that she was apprehensive that her father had even seen a report in a newspaper about a Le Gallienne lecture at the Playgoers' Club. She cut out the piece which described, 'the exposition of the New Hedonism by the Religious Literary Man as Mr Richard Le Gallienne calls himself.' The title was 'The World, the Flesh and the Puritan'. Custance wrote, 'But – I am sorry about that lecture: because Daddy read about it in his morning paper!' so Le Gallienne was *persona non grata* in the Custance household.[23]

There is an undated letter from Custance with a page missing that refers to this relationship: 'he wrote that chapter called Nicolete in *The Quest of the Golden Girl* by way of revenge perhaps … though it was a pretty revenge

... I hasten to add that the story is all invention ... but Nicolete is me!'[24] 'Revenge' is an interesting expression; it may be that this letter, which seems to date from the beginning of her relationship with Alfred Douglas when such things might be discussed, refers to Le Gallienne's attempts to seduce her which she resisted (or, at least, tells Douglas she did). The Nicolete chapters are hardly vengeful.

There was no bad feeling between them, anyway. Le Gallienne in his memoirs describes 'the flower-like loveliness of Olive Custance'.[25] Two months after his marriage to Julie Norregard in 1897, Julie wrote to Olive from their home in Surrey that they could not see her in town but she was welcome to visit them there: 'Do dear young Sappho, come, and you will make us both happy – a train leaves Waterloo 11.25 and Richard would fetch you at Haslemere, you would arrive here in time for lunch.'[26]

John Lane published her first volume of verse, *Opals*, in 1897. The title came from a nickname she often used of herself. She wrote to Lane, 'I think we will call the poems Opals (you remember my ring) they are the stones of love and sorrow and they have suggested many of my songs to me.'[27] The book was produced with a blue binding with an O on each of the outer corners. Its first poem, 'Love's Firstfalls', is prefaced with a quote from Sappho. The poems tend to be ungendered – it could be a boy or girl she loves. Beauty is seen as a girl or a child or a beloved woman at her toilette:

> The white hands of my lady's maid
> Move deftly through the shining hair!

Lane had called her 'my little Sappho' and he must have kept her in mind, for when lesbian poet Natalie Barney looked in at the Bodley Head, Lane suggested she might like to buy a copy of *Opals*. She did so and was soon writing enthusiastically to Custance, sending her copies of her own works. Custance wrote to Lane, 'I had an adorable letter this morning from a beautiful American girl the author of a new volume of poems, which she sent me, called *Portraits – Sonnets de Femmes*. She had read Opals ... and fallen in love with my soul! It seems ...'[28]

'Opal responded with fire,' as Barney put it. Custance wrote a verse including the lines

> ... For I would dance to make you smile, and sing
> Of those who with some sweet mad sin have played,

And how Love walks with delicate feet afraid
    Twixt maid and maid.[29]

Natalie Barney, born in Ohio in 1876, was heiress to a fortune made in the railway business. She had a voracious sexual appetite and was not above picking up casual lovers in the toilets of Paris department stores. Barney pondered whether she should assemble a group of 'poetesses' like those who surrounded Sappho at Mytilene, for mutual inspiration. She therefore invited Custance to join her in Paris at a hotel in the rue Alphonse-de-Neuville. Custance responded that nothing would suit her more than to join such a group, and she would be in Paris in the spring.

Custance's mother, Eleanor, was meanwhile busy attempting to find a good match for her. She knew nothing of her daughter's assignations with the disgraced poet Lord Alfred Douglas and would certainly have disapproved. Olive Custance went to France to stay with her aunt Lady Anglesey, in a party with Frederick Manners-Sutton, the future Viscount Canterbury, who was a neighbour of hers. There can scarcely be any doubt that Mrs Custance thought of Manners-Sutton as a potential suitor to Olive. She was 27 in 1901; it was imperative that she marry and produce an heir. Olive let Alfred Douglas know she would be in Paris and if he wished he could meet her there. They did so, and Douglas says that for ten days they met every day. They went to lunch and dinner, wandered in the forest holding hands and visited his horses at Chantilly.[30]

She wrote passionate letters to Douglas, which he later published in his autobiography of 1929: 'I am thinking of you every moment and praying that your "luck may turn" and that things may be better soon.' 'It was so lovely to look into your clear brave eyes and talk to you.' 'Oh how I miss you ... your sweet golden head ... your small red mouth ... always it seems a little shy of my kisses ... and above all your great blue eyes ... the most beautiful eyes a boy ever had.' 'My own Bosie whom God made for me.' 'Write to me soon ... soon and tell me you love your little Page and that one day you will come back to "him".'[31] One telegram from Douglas to Olive was opened by Colonel Custance, but his daughter told him it was from Natalie Barney, whom he, in his innocence, deemed an acceptable correspondent. The dalliance between Olive and Douglas had to end, as Douglas needed to marry wealth and was preparing to visit the United States in autumn 1901, where he was expecting to find an American heiress whom he would marry for her money while she would marry him for his title.

Custance called on Natalie Barney at the rue Alphonse-de-Neuville where she was living, and later introduced Natalie to her mother and Freddy Manners-Sutton. Manners-Sutton fell for Natalie, which doubtless produced some interesting conversations that have not, alas, been recorded. They certainly remained in contact – Custance mentioned in her diary about Manners-Sutton on 9 January 1907, 'he has had *another* quarrel with Natalie.' Natalie was bewitched by Custance: she was to admire Olive's sombre and brilliant eyes, her resolute face contrasting with her breathless voice and her original ideas.[32] She was soon expressing her love, as in one letter:

> How wonderful you are . . . and how I love you for this song . . .
> more than for all your kisses – and it is I who say this! – Come my
> poet, my priestess, we will be as your soul wishes . . . Come, it is
> Tuesday night! Come to me and we will be quiet – to soften [?]
> in each others' arms . . . I only know that I so love your lips that I
> will do whatever they tell me . . . let me feel that I am all things to
> you . . . and love me . . . ah love me! . . . my beautiful white love my
> soul honours you and holds you close and is glad through its tears.[33]

Embracing Olive, she said, was like embracing the English countryside.[34] Custance was more equivocal about Barney, writing to Douglas about her:

> She is rather fascinating and clever but her life is ugly . . . and I
> cannot forgive that. She says she loves me, but some who have loved
> her tell me she does not know what love means . . . and from what
> I know of her I can well believe it . . . but because I am indifferent
> to her she has a passion for me that is almost beautiful at times . . .
> I have prayed all my life that I might meet a man I could love with
> all my soul.[35]

Custance's mother allowed Olive to leave for Venice with Natalie, being sufficiently trusting, or ignorant of the relationship, to permit it to progress. On the other hand, she was perhaps aware but felt that love between young women was a safe outlet for passions that might otherwise be expended on men to the detriment of her daughter's marriage potential. The visit to Venice was less passionate than perhaps had been intended, as both fell ill with a fever, unable to leave their twin beds.[36]

Natalie Barney returned to New York where Douglas met and liked her; they saw a good deal of each other there and in Washington. He was eager to reassure Custance he would not fall in love with Natalie. She too liked Custance's boyish figure: at Barney's request, Olive dressed 'as a pretty boy' and had her picture taken; she sent a copy to Douglas.[37] Barney had the decency to suggest she could marry Douglas (she was, after all, an American heiress, which was the only requirement). In contrast to others, she was sympathetic to Douglas in part for his connection with Oscar Wilde, who had influenced her decision to be a writer and to whom she had written while he was in prison.[38] Natalie Barney was to stay in contact with Custance; she was to be godmother to her son and they were still meeting in the 1930s.

Another member of Natalie Barney's Sapphic circle was Renée Vivien, who had been Barney's lover since 1899. She wrote as Pauline Tarn, signed herself 'Paul' and sometimes used the name 'Tess'. Initially she was jealous of Olive's relationship with Natalie and bombarded her lover with gifts including, tellingly, 'a bunch of opals vomiting on my hair from a golden dragon'.[39] Within a short time, however, she fell for Custance, whom she described as 'a little poetess whom I had admired for her colouring, as delicate as Saxe porcelain. Her short curly hair was a halo of childish grace. Her baby blue eyes opened wide as if she was enchanted by a fairy story. She seemed a young incarnation of May.'[40]

Pauline was smitten with Custance and she reciprocated, at least physically. Pauline wrote to her from 24 Hyde Park Street, London, where she was staying with her mother, 'Sweetest, how maddeningly exquisite it was to hold your fresh frail body in my arms – to clasp you and kiss you in a bewilderment of delight.' She too enjoyed sharing her memory of sensual pleasures, noting, 'I wrote to Bosie that you were like a wild rose, all faint perfumes and delicacy of colour, fresh and frail. I love you, who are the one entirely beautiful, entirely joy-giving thing in my life. You have brought me nothing but roses ... the roses of Sappho.'[41]

Pauline visited her at Weston; she wrote, 'Pauline went yesterday, we spent the day in Norwich giving each other presents.' 'She gave me an opal ring ... a "wedding ring" for me to wear when you take me out, (she says) that we may look married.'[42] Their last recorded contact is a copy of Custance's second book, *Rainbows*, inscribed 'For Tess from her devoted Olive ...', using the name Renée/Pauline sometimes used.[43]

It was typical of Custance with her self-centred existence that, overflowing with amorous excitement, she assumed Alfred Douglas would share in her joy. He was not impervious to jealousy, however, and complained when she sent him Pauline's love letters to her.[44] He emphasized she was the only girl he had ever loved, or ever looked at seriously. Douglas said he might have had the choice of 'at least three' American heiresses but he had fallen in love with her.[45] He returned to Britain anyway, unbetrothed, arriving in January 1902.

Meanwhile Custance had become engaged to be married. Douglas had been resigned to a doomed love with Custance, assuming both would marry separately, and was not shocked so much by the fact that she was affianced as he was by the man she was to marry. She had accepted a proposal from George Montagu, MP for South Huntingdon. He had attended Winchester School with Douglas and they had maintained a close friendship. Montagu broke this friendship off, however, when he stood for Parliament and was advised that his relationship with Douglas jeopardized his chances because of the Wilde scandal. Douglas was outraged at the slight, and wrote a sonnet, 'Traitor', about Montagu. Now his beloved was engaged to the man.

Custance had accepted the invitation not so much because she loved Montagu but because she had to marry someone, she liked him, he had repeatedly asked her to marry him, he was wealthy and well placed, and she knew nothing of his split with Douglas. Douglas was in Britain when he received Custance's letter telling of her engagement. He was angry and revealingly remarked, 'there was nothing against me as a husband for Olive which would not apply with at least equal force to him', which implies Montagu had also had sex with men. By the time Douglas published this in the 1920s, Montagu was the Earl of Sandwich and could easily have sued for libel, as Douglas knew as well as anyone in the kingdom. He did not because Douglas's remarks were true and, doubtless, he could prove them. From Custance's perspective Montagu was, then, another of her lovers of fluid sexuality.[46]

Douglas determined to act. He met Custance in Kettner's restaurant in Soho, affirmed his love for her, and she agreed to run away with him. It was a decision not to be taken lightly; he had no money and she was very much under her parents' control. The king had sent her family congratulations on her engagement to Montagu, so it was hardly a private matter. The weekend after they met, she was due to spend time at Lord Sandwich's country seat in Huntingdonshire to meet Montagu's family. Seeing Hinchingbrooke, the magnificent Tudor stately home she and her fiancé would inherit, might well have turned another woman's head. Montagu would inherit on the death of his uncle, the current earl, who was childless. Custance had been brought up wealthy, however, and so was not overwhelmed by grandeur; she had already shown herself more preoccupied with poetry and thoughts of romance than wealth and status.

Olive Custance, *c.* 1902, photograph by George Charles Beresford.

Douglas did not see her until the appointed time and he confessed himself uncertain as to whether she would turn up. The thrill of elopement must have countered any apprehension she had as she slipped out of the house with the assistance of her maid, saying she was going to spend a day with her friend Tanie. She arrived at St George's Church, Hanover Square, at nine o'clock on the morning of Tuesday 4 March 1902 and they were married by special licence. At Victoria station they sent a telegram to her parents at Weston Hall and took the boat train to a honeymoon in Paris.

Colonel Custance was beside himself with anger when he heard and he contacted the police, but this was no matter for them.

Douglas was clear about his genuine attraction to Olive, which fitted all the requirements for an 'exceedingly fastidious' man: she was 'well born, beautiful and outstandingly attractive . . . intellectual and appreciative of poetry and literature'.[47] This is certainly a reasonable description of Olive Custance and there is no doubt the relationship was compatible and successful for a time. The Custances were eventually reconciled to the marriage and the couple spent some time at Weston Old Hall, where Colonel Custance discussed their shared love of sports with his son-in-law and taught him fly fishing. The marriage began happily with a home at Lake Farm near Salisbury; Olive gave birth to their son Raymond on 17 November 1902. John Lane published her second book, *Rainbows*, in 1902. Her third volume of poems, *The Blue Bird*, which was dedicated to Douglas, was published in 1905. Douglas published a series of sonnets in 1907 titled *To Olive*.

Douglas is as open as one could reasonably expect a man to be about his married life in his autobiography. He is particularly concerned to deal with the canard that his marriage after a brief honeymoon period was one 'in name only', which is something he says is 'grotesquely untrue'.[48] Custance's diary gives no indication that they had anything but a normal married life. For example, after four years of marriage she describes a peaceful day: 'We spent the afternoon indoors, reading . . . Dined – and went early to bed . . .' followed by a heart in a dotted circle, which is presumably a private symbol that they had sex.[49] From written accounts it seems a marriage full of affection; one day in 1907 she wrote: 'Bosie looked very golden this evening and I kissed him so often that I bored him!!!'[50]

Douglas's statement that 'everyone is more or less bi-sexual' is more revealing of his own feelings than a universal truth.[51] It was certainly true of Custance and himself, however. He remarks that what she loved about him was his feminine side: 'she was always desperately trying to recapture the "me" that she had guessed and seen and loved.' 'Marriage', he said, 'gradually destroyed our love.'[52] He became more of a country gentleman, with his guns and fishing rods, put on weight and gradually lost his androgynous good looks. On Custance's side, childbirth rounded out the angular, boyish figure he had loved in her and she became more of a woman than his 'Page'.

The marriage was tied up with Douglas's career as an editor and what sometimes resembles a career as a full-time litigant. The story of Douglas has been frequently told, not least the manner by which he carried his gift for grievance into the courts in legal cases against people, such as Robert Ross and Freddie Manners-Sutton, who previously had been bosom friends. At the time of writing his autobiography he could quickly call to mind eight actions for libel 'which I have had to take in my life' and he was himself twice convicted of libel.[53]

Of more direct consequence to Custance, there were problems on another front. Raymond was Colonel Custance's longed-for heir and he tried every means to maintain power over the boy. Douglas's conversion to the Catholic Church in May 1911 gave the Colonel another reason to try to break up the family, under the guise of protecting Raymond from Catholic influence. Douglas had Raymond instructed and received into the Catholic Church and decided to send him to Ampleforth, the major Catholic private school.

Colonel Custance felt offended that Douglas's impecunious state meant he had to pay his daughter's bills for an extravagant lifestyle. There was no doubt that he used money to maintain control over her, about which she was well aware. She wrote in her diary, for example, 'Daddy has written one of his horrid letters and has enclosed £10 towards my doctors bill which is £40! This is what is called adding insult to injury.'[54] They were frequently hard up and Olive twice pawned a diamond ring she had been given by Douglas's mother.[55]

Eleanor Custance died on 14 November 1907, removing a restraining influence from Colonel Custance, who desperately wanted to take control of Raymond's upbringing. The Custance family property was entailed to Olive, but the Colonel persuaded her in 1911 to voluntarily relinquish her rights in return for an income of £600 a year for life. Douglas urged her to have a legal undertaking regarding the annuity signed by the Colonel at the same time that she relinquished her property rights, but he said his word was good enough and his daughter did not insist. Predictably, the Colonel then withheld the money to manipulate Olive, notably insisting that Raymond be handed over to his care.

Motherhood did not come naturally to her. When Raymond was four she wrote in her diary, 'I never seem to speak of Raymond . . . he is not very interesting to me yet . . . though I am glad to see he is looking well . . . and quite pretty.'[56] Douglas accused her of abusing the boy, saying how much she hated him and wishing he had never been born.[57] This should be viewed with some scepticism as Douglas was a master of hurtful invective and paid scant attention to the veracity of his insults, but there must be the suspicion of a grain of truth in this remark.

It is inescapable, however, that Custance was not naturally a child-rearing woman. She even had difficulty in asserting herself as an adult, which meant her fate was more than conventionally in the hands of her father and her husband, which was miserable for her when they were at loggerheads. Olive wrote in January 1913, 'I feel there is no hope for me, my life is ruined . . . Bosie is going to take away Raymond from Daddy and then my allowance will be stopped and I shall have to go and live at Weston . . . God help me!' 'I cried all last night.' 'Nothing will ever be right or happy again, I think . . .'[58]

Instead of handing Raymond over to Colonel Custance, Douglas sent the boy to live with his own mother, Lady Queensberry. The objective was clearly to make access difficult for Colonel Custance, who duly carried out his threat and stopped giving Olive the money that was hers by right and agreement. Douglas accused the Colonel of defrauding his daughter. He later said this was 'injudicious' as it 'made things very awkward for my wife by putting her in the dilemma of having to choose between supporting her husband or her father'.[59] The Colonel took an action for libel and Douglas was tried at the Old Bailey in January 1913. At the beginning of this year he was also involved in a libel trial that he had provoked Robert Ross into bringing against him and which Douglas was to lose. To compound his problems, Douglas was made bankrupt on 14 January 1913.

In the middle of the legal proceedings the pressure was too great for Olive and she went to live with her father. Douglas considered this a great betrayal and lost heart. He did not put in a defence at the trial brought by Colonel Custance and was 'bound over to come up for judgement if called on', which is a legal admonition not to repeat the offence. Also in 1913 the Colonel obtained a court order for joint custody of Raymond when he was not at school: the Chancery court decided he should spend three-fifths of his time with him and the remaining two-fifths with Douglas. By March 1913 Olive was writing: 'It would be impossible to go back and live with Bosie now . . . he always made me so unhappy . . . we were not meant to live together . . . But I still love him.'[60]

Douglas burned photographs of Olive and took up with Doris Edwards, an American fan of his work who was known to Natalie Barney, who talked to Olive about her. The conversation upset her; Olive wrote, 'I have seen Natalie who has told me about Bosie . . . Terrible things!' 'I have heard about this girl Bosie is with . . . they say she is dreadful . . . what shall I do!'[61]

Douglas says in his autobiography that he initially resisted having sex with Doris but finally succumbed. Olive was now under pressure from her father to divorce Douglas. Colonel Custance had Douglas and Doris followed by private detectives and thus produced evidence of Douglas's infidelity that would satisfy a divorce court. Instead, Olive called Douglas and, according to his account, begged him to see her. Olive's response to his infidelity was to realize how much she loved Douglas – and how she considered she owned him. The couple met and were reconciled, though they never again lived together. Doris was dismissed and returned to the USA.

Douglas wrote apologetically to Olive that he had had sex with Doris – had 'done wrong with her', as he put it – because of 'simply on my part the ache of the void of love of a woman. I had got used to you "loving" me and making a fuss of me, in the intervals of hating and abusing me, and I could not refuse love when it came to me.' He signed himself, 'Your loving boy'.[62] He was not the only one who had 'done wrong', however: he accused Olive of making a 'public exhibition' of herself with Jack Stirling, Filson Young and other men including Rupert Scott, the Earl of Clonmell.[63] It gives a flavour of their relationship that he claimed she repeatedly told him in insulting language that their marriage had been one long misery to her, though in the same letter he said he was not capable of ceasing to love her.[64] It may well be that Olive enjoyed this roller-coaster ride of emotions; it would have been easy to have had no more to do with Douglas had she felt inclined. Instead, she relished the reconciliations: for example, writing, 'All is well again ... Bosie has written me a kind letter ... I sent him some roses.'[65]

In 1915 she agreed to go to Chancery with Douglas to apply for full custody of Raymond. Colonel Custance opposed and the application was unsuccessful. The court maintained the best position was joint custody. Douglas disobeyed the order by taking Raymond to Scotland, out of the jurisdiction of the English courts. The boy was put in the care of the abbot of a Benedictine monastery at Fort Augustus. The colonel communicated with Raymond, then twelve, and arranged to have a private detective pick up the boy and bring him back to Norfolk in a motor car (a great treat for a child at the beginning of the twentieth century). Douglas and the monks were distraught at the thought that Raymond might have drowned in the loch, until they received a telegram from Olive saying the boy was back at the Custance family home at Weston. When Douglas found that Raymond had been a willing partner in the 'kidnapping' plan, he was disgusted at what he considered his son's disloyalty and washed his hands of him, not seeing him again for another ten years.

Raymond was reconciled to his father as a young man, but his life was to be an unhappy one. After Ampleforth he had a brief period in the Army, but he was declared mentally unfit. He caused his parents distress by his decision to marry 'beneath' him – to the daughter of a greengrocer. Their opposition was not merely snobbish: she was older than Raymond and had been living with another man; she was probably a gold-digger who was after Raymond's money and social position. Raymond became violent at the familial opposition and in 1927 was sent to a psychiatric home where he was diagnosed with schizophrenia. He was to live most of the rest of his life in the institution of St Andrew's Hospital, Northampton. The much fought-over heir was therefore not going to be able to fulfil his function in the Custance lineage. Olive showed mild expressions of regret over Raymond's illness, but there is no evidence of excessive hand-wringing in the diary. Colonel Custance died in 1924, removing a source of discord between Olive and her husband. Olive had converted to Catholicism in 1917, then lapsed, but seems to have returned temporarily to the Church in 1924.

Both she and Douglas were to have a number of different apartments but never lived together. She moved to Hove in 1932; Douglas had been living in the town since 1927. They visited each other almost daily and frequently took lunch together in one of the seaside town's restaurants. John Betjeman often used to dine with Douglas and Custance; he recalled, 'They got on well and he was very fond of her and was always so pleased to come and see her. She was a most amusing person – quite as witty as Bosie ... She was round-faced, plumpish, with enormous round eyes and was extremely vivacious and funny.'[66] If an unusual relationship, theirs was an affectionate one. She kept a Valentine's card he sent her in 1937 and on her 65th birthday in 1939 she was writing, 'flowers coming from kind friends. Also Bosie is having a "bedroom lunch" with me. He is staying the night.'[67]

Her diary from the late 1930s is mainly about household bills and decorating the flat, medical issues such as insomnia and throat troubles, and problems in engaging a maid who is competent and does not bore her. Her health had not been good since the 1920s: she was diagnosed with Graves' disease (a thyroid condition) in 1924. In 1927 she was complaining of a heart attack every week unless she stayed in bed or was very quiet – presumably she meant palpitations.[68] Rupert Croft-Cooke, who knew them at this time, said Custance in her last weeks was in a very weak mental state and for most of the time was incoherent or semi-conscious.[69] Douglas reported her fretting, complaining he was unkind to her and that her maid Eileen mistreated her (which he was sure was untrue).[70] She was semi-conscious on 11 February 1944 and Douglas spent several hours with her, holding her hand. The following day Eileen called him to say Olive had died in the early hours; she was four days past her seventieth birthday.

Marie Stopes, who knew Douglas perhaps better than anyone in his last years, wrote that theirs 'was a life-long devotion surviving the treacheries of others, separations and disasters. He often spoke and wrote to me of his darling Olive, revealing how their relationship has been widely misunderstood, and how precious to him was their daily association.'[71] As her Catholicism had lapsed, Douglas felt unable to arrange a funerary mass. Olive was cremated and her ashes later scattered in the water off the Brighton seafront.

13

Charlotte Mew: Love Rebuffed

A small bird-like woman appeared in a Paris street in April 1902. She had bobbed hair, arched eyebrows above penetrating eyes and a pale, oval face, and was dressed in a jacket and a shirt with a ribbon as a tie and was carrying an umbrella. A small inheritance from an aunt (a mere £20 a year) had allowed Charlotte Mew to take a trip to visit Ella D'Arcy, whom she had met at the Harlands' during the *Yellow Book* days. They had corresponded and become friends.

Mew had recently had a story published in the *Pall Mall Magazine* called 'Some Ways of Love', which carried the message that there are 'many ways of love'.[1] She may well have decided, at the age of 32, that she should seek her own way. She stayed at 26 rue de Turin, near the Place de l'Europe, in the same 8th arrondissement but still some distance away from D'Arcy's one-roomed apartment in the rue Chateaubriand. Her perpetual look of startled amazement was appropriate in the French capital, where she was stunned by the lights and traffic. 'My head was stupid and my eyes tired,' she wrote to old schoolfriend Edith Oliver; 'it is dangerous to be absent minded crossing the road as the traffic here is simply awful. The heavy two-storied steam trams and innumerable motor cars keeping one always on the qui vive.'[2] Mew was not the best traveller: she was too timid to go into a café by herself and she found her French, while perfectly adequate for reading, was not sufficiently adaptable to allow her to make herself understood, or to understand others.

She wrote of being supposed to meet Ella in the Parc Monçeau, just down the boulevard from her and easy to find, but her will failed her. 'As it was wet I did not feel inclined – and waiting for a break started off by myself in the other direction. Visited Notre Dame and prowled about the Latin Quartier [sic].'[3] This would have been a walk of many hours for her, on the other side of the city across the Seine, and so left her far longer in the rain than if she had met D'Arcy.

She wrote, 'It is a queer uncertain mind this of mine – and claims are being made upon it at the moment which I find it difficult to meet.' Her biographer Penelope Fitzgerald identified those claims as being those of the body, of her attraction to Ella D'Arcy. She was both attracted to D'Arcy and repelled by the notion of sex. She remarked, 'I found E D'A somewhat in need of someone to look after her.'[4]

D'Arcy was 45 in 1902; her hair had been ginger, but as it whitened she dyed it to a reddish orange. Mew visited her in the room where she lived with a bed and a wood fire amid her books and manuscripts. Mew found the place in a mess with no preparations made for her visit or, more importantly, for the reception of Caroline Franklin Grout, Gustave Flaubert's niece. Grout was coming later that day to discuss D'Arcy's translating her *Souvenirs Intimes*, her 1895 memoir of her uncle. Mew proceeded to tidy things up and made herself useful, going out to buy 'the little necessaries for the occasion – flowers – cakes – etc – and we arranged the room.'[5]

Mew loved Flaubert's work and would have liked to meet Grout, but her nerves got the better of her: 'As I was tired I didn't stay to see the lady but came back here – and then found myself too restless to keep quiet and went for a walk till about 5 when I dressed for dinner and started off again in pouring rain.'[6] She ate meals with D'Arcy though she liked to withhold herself, as if playing hard to get was any kind of an adult way to behave in a relationship which, in any case, was more a matter of imagination than reality. 'This afternoon I shall take it easy,' she wrote, 'and not go up to the Rue Chat perhaps till dinner though Ella will wonder where I am as I promised to turn up for déjeuner.'[7] D'Arcy perhaps did not even realize Mew's feelings for her and thought she was just being peculiar.

After a week Charlotte left the rue de Turin and had her letters forwarded to D'Arcy's address at the rue Chateaubriand. It is not obvious what happened in the following weeks, but either she stopped writing or the letters were later destroyed. Commentators have dismissed the idea that she and D'Arcy had a fling on the basis that D'Arcy had many affairs with men. Amy Dawson Scott reflected in her diary, 'Ella D'Arcy was immensely over-sexed, practically a prostitute.'[8] D'Arcy was undoubtedly a sensual woman, but being primarily heterosexual would not have precluded her from lesbian affection if it were offered, particularly when she was at a low ebb, perhaps after difficulties with men.

It is unlikely, though not impossible, that D'Arcy reciprocated Charlotte's advances, once she understood what they were. It is not inconceivable that D'Arcy should accept what physical affection she could from Charlotte, whether hugs, kisses or anything more intimate, but it is certain from knowledge of D'Arcy's personality that she would not have offered back the love that Charlotte Mew craved. She may not have been lesbian enough, but she was certainly not loving enough to take on a highly strung character like Mew.

Some degree of physical intimacy would not have been an issue for Ella D'Arcy, who prided herself on her latitude. It would have had a devastating impact on Mew, however, whose experience of intimate physical contact was close to nil, however much she may have desired it. The point is not, anyway, whether they were physically affectionate; Charlotte was looking for love and Ella was not. Though Mew's letters from later in her stay have not survived, her poetry has, and her Paris experiences were clearly emotionally charged. She writes of

> Dear Paris of the hot white hands, the scarlet lips, the scented hair
> Une jolie fille à vendre, tres chèr;[9]

She conjures the city when she writes of rooms where life has changed for her:

> I remember rooms that have had their part
> In the steady slowing down of the heart.
> The room in Paris . . .
>
> . . . Rooms where for good or for ill – things died.[10]

One of her finest works is 'Monsieur Qui Passe (Quai Voltaire)' describing events (and presumably written) almost a decade before T. S. Eliot started on 'The Love Song of J. Alfred Prufrock', which it resembles in its diction, power and imagery. The narrator encounters a woman, 'In my friend's rooms, bathed in their vile pink light'. Outside, on the Quai Voltaire, she speaks of

> 'half the kisses of the Quay –
> Youth, hope, – the whole enchanted string
> Of dreams hung on the Seine's longline of lights'

Then suddenly she stripped, the very skin
Came off her soul, – a mere girl clings
Longer to some last rag, however thin,
When she has shown you – well – all sorts of things:

In a work of great passion that speaks to a reality beneath the temporal, Mew returns to bring this ethereal character to ground with a physical description:

But she had hair! – blood dipped in gold;
And there she left me throwing back the first odd stare,
Some sort of beauty once, but turning yellow, getting old.[11]

It is unwise to attempt to distil biographical fact from creative work, but there is no question that Paris was an emotional upheaval for Mew. She was back in London in June 1902. The two women continued to correspond, and D'Arcy was complimentary about the verse that Mew had started to publish in the early twentieth century, though Mew felt D'Arcy was harsh as a critic: 'she'd always spit on everything I'd done –!'[12] She returned to 9 Gordon Street, Bloomsbury, south of the Euston Road, which had been her home since 1888. She was going back into the family nightmare.

Charlotte Mew was born on 15 November 1869, the first girl of seven children and the oldest to survive. Both her grandfathers were architects, as was her father, Frederick Mew. He was feckless and careless with money while her mother, Anna Maria Mew, was foolish and failed to engage in running the household. As they grew, her children protected her from the realities of the world, particularly economic ones. The result was genteel poverty with efforts to economize on expenses while keeping up appearances, which became increasingly desperate as their income dwindled.

Charlotte attended Gower Street School where she met its headmistress, Amy Harrison, and it was probably in this encounter that she discovered she was attracted to women. Harrison was kind about it; schoolgirl crushes were hardly new for a schoolteacher, though Mew's affection for her teacher suggested a desperation that would become apparent in later life. Harrison became overstressed and went into retirement. She took in Gower Street girls as boarders and Mew begged her parents to let her board. She was so distressed that her father made it happen and she therefore lived with Harrison for two years, taking instruction from her in English literature in the evenings. One legacy of Amy Harrison was in Mew's dress, as she took to the masculine style sported by her teacher.

At home three brothers had died in childhood. After 1885 her elder brother, Christopher, began to show signs of mania. In a few years Charlotte's sister Freda also developed mania. Poems such as 'On the Asylum Road' showed Mew's familiarity with institutions:

> Theirs is the house whose windows – every pane –
> Are made of darkly stained or clouded glass:

'Ken' strongly conveyed the feelings of observing another's mental incapacity:

> If in His image God made men,
> Some other must have made poor Ken –
> But for his eyes which looked at you
> As two red, wounded stars might do . . .

A friend said that the 'sad condition' of her siblings 'was a constant torment to Charlotte'.[13] As well as the emotional misery of having unwell family members, the strained family finances now had to bear the cost of private institutional care (it would have been unthinkable to have them in a public institution). Charlotte had already lived in layers of deceit: that her mother was in charge of the household and that the family had enough to live on as a middle-class household. Now she also had to conceal madness in the family while suppressing her own sexual feelings, perhaps fearing they were a sign of incipient insanity. Her siblings had been stricken with *dementia praecox*, the mania of the young, which usually manifests in the under-25s. Now known as schizophrenia, it was defined only in 1893 by Emil Kraepelin. It was considered to be hereditary, which led Charlotte and her younger sister Anne to decide together never to have children. This meant the route to financial security of marrying a man who could keep them was closed; they would have to struggle on their own means.

The death of Fred Mew in 1898 was a shock, though he had not been much of a breadwinner for several years. What money the family had was invested in an annuity for Anne Marie, bringing in a reasonable sum of £300 a year. The thinking of older relatives and advisors was that Charlotte and Anne would find husbands to support them. The sisters therefore remained with their demanding mother at the dark and gaunt 9 Gordon Square with its narrow rooms and passages lined with drawings and plans of Fred Mew's work.

They let the top floor of the Gordon Street house to lodgers, although they were ashamed of this decline into the class of urban landladies and would never refer to it. Alida Monro, a friend who visited, said she was unaware of the existence of the lodgers, commenting: 'The sudden drop in her financial circumstances had a most damaging psychological effect. Charlotte Mew inherited from her mother a view of life that was very prevalent during the last century, namely that appearances must be kept up at all cost.'[14]

Anne studied at the nearby Royal Female School of Art and became adept at painting birds and flowers with which she decorated furniture commercially. Unfortunately she was too much of a lady to ask for a reasonable rate for her work and she was always underpaid.

Charlotte Mew
as a teenager.

Charlotte had been unsuccessfully writing stories for publication when she had 'Passed' accepted in the *Yellow Book* and then, fearing scandal, submitted work to the more staid *Temple Bar*, which was to take twelve of her pieces between 1899 and 1905. She wrote of people with limited backgrounds who were unable to make moral choices and often just let the situation drift or returned to what was expected of them.

Her first piece of published verse was 'Requiescat' in *The Nation* in 1909, followed in the same publication by 'The Farmer's Bride' on 3 February 1912. In a form of dramatic monologue made popular by Browning, the narrator describes how his young wife tried to run away, was caught and was currently imprisoned in the home, and how he yearns for the love she still withholds from him. Mew's unique voice, control of material and understanding of her subject gave her immediate attention among those who understood poetry. Among them was Harold Monro, who was setting up the Poetry Bookshop at 35 Devonshire Street, Bloomsbury, at the end of 1912. It was to be a place for the sale, publication and general encouragement of poetry, which meant they were actively looking out for the poets of the future. Monro's friend (later his wife) Alida Klementaski, who worked in the Poetry Bookshop, loved 'The Farmer's Bride' and they wrote to Charlotte Mew 'asking whether or not she had other poems, or a number of poems that could be got together to form a book'.[15] Mew responded very kindly to the tentative suggestion, but with her characteristic lack of confidence declared that no one would want to read them if they were published. She sent another poem, 'The Changeling'. Alida said she would read it at the bookshop and asked if Mew would like to be there on one Tuesday evening in November 1915. The meeting room was a 12-foot-square room off Theobald's Road in Bloomsbury, a converted gold-beaters' studio up a steep flight of stairs. When she came into the shop she was asked, 'Are you Charlotte Mew?' and her reply, delivered characteristically with a slight smile of amusement, was, 'I am sorry to say I am.' Monro described her as

> very small, only about four feet ten inches, very slight, with square shoulders and tiny hands and feet. She always wore a long double-breasted top-coat of tweed with a velvet collar inset. She usually carried a horn-handled umbrella, unrolled, under her arm, as if it were psychologically necessary to her, a weapon against the world. She had very fine white hair that showed traces of once having been a warm brown. Her eyes were a very dark grey, bright with

black lashes and highly arched dark eyebrows. Her face was a fine oval, and she always wore a little hard felt pork-pie hat put on very straight. The whole time she was speaking she kept her head cocked at a defiant angle.[16]

She had at last found a community of people who, if not like-minded, were at least accepting of her eccentricities. The last time she had enjoyed such an atmosphere was two decades earlier with the *Yellow Book*.

She would visit Alida in her seven-and-sixpenny a week bedsit in Red Lion Square, where they would lay a length of sacking over the coal box for a seat and smoke and talk into the night. Alida said Charlotte was 'a great teller of stories and always had new ones, never failed to see the humour in any situation, and never went on a visit anywhere without coming back with a riotous account of what had taken place'.[17] She said Mew lost her self-deprecatory manner as she became accustomed to a person. She was evidently a friend who was even poorer than the Mews, so Charlotte was prepared to invite her to Gordon Square, where Charlotte would some-times take a paper from one of two trunks she had and roll it into spills to light her cigarettes, or give it to her ill-natured parrot to chew. She said she couldn't think what else to do with her manuscripts. This was perhaps one of her jokes, or perhaps it was not. She always smoked her own handmade cigarettes in a long holder. She would stand beside the fire, one hand on the mantelpiece, one tiny foot on the fire bars, 'shaking her head towards her left shoulder, and swinging a signet ring which she wore on her right-hand little finger round and round in a most fascinating manner by moving her third finger against it'.[18] Her tendency to swear – unusual in a lady – was one way in which her inner personality expressed itself through the shell of gentility. Her swearing tended to be words such as 'blighter' and 'damn' rather than anything stronger.

Monro offered to print Mew's poems and asked to see more: she offered seventeen. These were published in 1915, despite wartime paper shortages, under the title *The Farmer's Bride*. They sold but not spectacularly well, nor were they widely reviewed, but their intensity and originality were appre-ciated by the poetry avant-garde. Virginia Woolf called Mew 'the greatest living poetess'.[19] An enlarged edition of *The Farmer's Bride* was published in 1921; in the USA it came out under the title *Saturday Market*. The compilers of the volumes of *Georgian Poetry* felt they should bring themselves up to date and include a woman in their next book. Monro proposed Mew but her entry was blocked by Walter de la Mare, who was not happy about the metre of 'The Farmer's Bride', so Mew did not appear in these prestigious and best-selling anthologies. On the other hand, Ezra Pound, acting Literary Editor of *The Egoist*, appreciated her value and took her long poem 'Fête'.

The war reached the poetry bookshop when Monro was called up in 1916, leaving Alida to run the place alone. War had truly arrived in this haven of literature: even the shop cat Pinknose was wounded, blinded in one eye in an incendiary raid. Mew did her bit by volunteering to visit war widows and pensioners as a representative of the War Pensions Committee.

Another literary circle to which Charlotte Mew gained entry was that of Amy Dawson Scott, known as Sappho, a great organizer of the Victorian and Edwardian period and friend to such *Yellow Book* characters as Netta Syrett. She wrote to Mew in what was probably rather a high-handed approach from her position as a literary grandee. Mew remarked to Alida, 'Mrs Dawson Scott asked me to go down last Saturday and recite the poem to some literary friends and in my brightest way I replied that she had mistaken me for Little Titch or Margaret Cooper at the piano and politely declined.'[20] Dawson Scott finally prevailed and she first met Mew on 30 May 1912, describing her as 'an Imp with brains' and inviting her to tea.[21]

Charlotte Mew,
1922 or 1923.

Soon she had Mew doing readings in her house in Southall with a little table before her and on it her papers and cigarettes, as she smoked all the time. She was slow to start the recital but when she did she seemed possessed 'and seemed not so much to be acting or reciting as a medium's body taken over by a distinct personality. She made slight gestures and used strange intonations at times, tones that were not in her usual speaking range.'[22] She would finish with a characteristic toss of the head. Evelyn Underhill, an Imagist poet, wrote, 'an hour with Miss Mew is like having whiskey with one's tea – my feet were clean off the floor! Heavens, what a tempest she produced – the most truly creative person I have ever come near.'[23] Mew's poems were like nothing many of them had ever heard.

Dawson Scott wrote:

Have seen a good deal of Charlotte Mew and admire her verse very much. She is tiny, like a French Marquise, uses amazing slang, and has ungainly movements – a queer mixture. Has a wonderful young soul, neither quite boy nor quite girl. Under this curious husk is a peculiarly sweet, humble nature.[24]

She became a family friend, taking Dawson Scott's children on outings. In 1913 Dawson Scott also introduced Mew to May Sinclair, who became the last failed love of Mew's life. Sinclair was a successful novelist and suffrage activist who took a keen interest in the work of Freud and the other psychoanalysts. Sinclair had a close relationship with Mew but seemed not to realize that her friend read much more into it than she did, which was surprising given Sinclair's supposedly brilliant psychological insights.

They corresponded frequently. On 4 July 1913 Sinclair apologized for not having more time to give her at the annual Women Writers Club dinner. Two weeks later she wrote, 'I don't know any living writer (with, possibly, the exception of D. H. Lawrence) who is writing things with such profound vitality in them. And you have qualities of tenderness and subtlety that he has not.'[25] She had her typist make copies of Mew's poems to send to influential people, so she was using her contacts to further Mew's career and paying the copying bill.

They saw a great deal of each other, in a relationship full of misunderstandings. When Sinclair dispatched herself to Yorkshire to finish a book, Mew considered it was a way of getting away from her because of the intensity of the relationship (an intensity that was probably mainly in Mew's imagination). When Sinclair wanted to move because of noisy neighbours,

Mew took it as an instruction to exhaust herself in house-hunting. Mew wanted to imbue every utterance of Sinclair's with romantic significance in a way that baffled her friend. May was hardly unequivocal, however; she wrote a poem after Verlaine that she shared with Mew, who might well have thought that such phrases as 'your little body, so tender' and 'your wicked little heart' referred to her.[26]

Finally the misunderstandings came to a head in a scene in summer 1914 in which Mew begged Sinclair for love and was rebuffed. According to Sinclair, Mew pursued her to a bedroom and attempted to grab her until she reprimanded her friend with, 'My good woman, you are simply wasting your perfectly good passion.'[27] Mew never saw her again.

Dawson Scott later had tea with May Sinclair and wrote about it in her diary, 'Charlotte has been bothering and annoying May . . . Charlotte is evidently a pervert. Are all geniuses perverts?'[28] Her daughter Marjorie, who called Dawson Scott 'sexually inhibited and naïve', asked why Charlotte did not come round anymore and later said, 'my mother told me the detailed story.'[29]

How Sinclair embellished the scene for further entertainment is shown in a letter from Gladys Bronwyn Stern, the novelist known familiarly as Peter. She described an anecdote told by May Sinclair to herself and Rebecca West: 'she was telling us in her neat precise voice how a lesbian poetess named Charlotte M had once in a fit of passion chased her upstairs into her bedroom – "And I assure you, Peter, I assure you Rebecca, I had to leap the bed five times!"'[30] Sinclair was playing up the scene for comic effect, and doubtless covering her embarrassment at the implications of an advance that she might otherwise have been considered to have encouraged.

From Charlotte Mew's point of view, Sinclair had not only rejected her, which was painful enough, but had committed the unforgivable sin of talking about it. Alida Monro wrote that Mew 'had a strict moral code in respect of other people's conduct, particularly in regard to their sex relationships, and absolutely cut out from her friendship anyone on whom a breath of scandal blew'.[31]

Mew had other literary contacts to console her. She sent a copy of her book to Sydney Cockerell, director of the Fitzwilliam Museum, who immediately fell in love with her verse and, among many other kindnesses, himself sent a copy to Thomas Hardy. This led to a three-day visit to Hardy's house, Max Gate, near Dorchester, in December 1918, where they read their verse to each other. It was a great honour as the elderly poet and novelist saw few visitors by this time in his life. He was to describe her as 'far and away the best living woman poet, who will be read when others are forgotten'.[32]

At Gower Street the family had been reduced to the basement by the end of the war – all the upper floors were let. Anne Mew struggled on decorating furniture in a studio in Bloomsbury. The family decline was slow but relentless; the lease was up on the house in 1922 and they moved to 86 Delancey Street, near Regent's Park, which was beyond their means. 'Ma' suffered a fall and died on 22 May 1923. Charlotte took the death very hard, despite her friends considering it a merciful release both for Anna Mew and for her two daughters, who were now free. They were, however, even poorer as Anna's annuity had died with her.

Kind-hearted Sydney Cockerell lobbied for a civil list pension for Charlotte. This was achieved by one of the male old-boys' networks. Cockerell went to see the prime minister Stanley Baldwin, who was well connected in artistic circles as the nephew of Edward Burne-Jones and cousin of Rudyard Kipling. Cockerell successfully sought the endorsement of John Masefield, Walter de la Mare and Thomas Hardy. At the end of 1923 Mew was told she was receiving a pension of £75 a year.

Anne fell ill in 1926 and the sisters put their furniture in storage and moved to Chichester for her to recuperate; early in 1927 she was diagnosed with liver cancer. They moved to Charlotte Street – Anne to live above the Etoile restaurant, Charlotte to sleep in Anne's studio, which was nearby. Anne died on 18 June 1927; her gravestone, soon to be that of Mew as well, bore the legend 'cast down the seeds of weeping and attend' from Dante's *Purgatorio*.

It was also a blow that Hardy died on 11 January 1928. Sydney Cockerell, as his executor, found in his papers that Hardy had copied out Mew's poem 'Fin de Fête', starting

Sweetheart, for such a day
One mustn't grudge the score;
Here, then, it's all to pay,
It's Good-night at the door[33]

He gave the manuscript to Mew, for whom it was a most treasured possession.

Mew became relatively wealthy in January 1928, on the death of her uncle, who bequeathed her some £8,000. She may well have thought it was all too late. She began to have obsessive thoughts or, rather (as she had always had them), allowed them to overwhelm her. She berated herself for not having had her sister's main artery cut to ensure she was not prematurely buried; her sister might have been buried alive. She became preoccupied with the notion that the black spots of soot around the studio were in fact disease-bearing organisms that had caused Anne's death.[34] She still lived in the clutter of the studio where everything was a reminder of her dead sister. Her family had gone, down even to the pet: their ancient and beloved parrot Wek died in 1921.

Mew rejected medical advice to go to an asylum, but was prepared to enter a nursing home, so on 15 February 1928 she checked in to 37 Beaumont Street, close to Madame Tussaud's waxworks and Baker Street station. She was supposedly being treated for 'neurasthenia', nervous debility, but even given the wide range of options this diagnosis afforded, she seems to have received no treatment. Her friends visited her in this dismal place and found her depressed, which was unsurprising. She suffered from a lack of sleep. Alida last saw her there when Charlotte complained about the view – a grey wall – and gave Alida the copy of 'Fin de Fête' that had been copied out by Thomas Hardy. As she had so cared for the artefact, it should have been obvious this was a goodbye gift.

Charlotte left Beaumont Street on 24 March 1928 to buy a bottle of Lysol, a common antiseptic and abrasive, usually used diluted. She poured herself a glass, drank it and lay down on her bed. Her doctor called that afternoon on a routine visit and found her in pain, foaming at the mouth and talking to herself. Her last words were to him, 'Don't keep me, let me go.'[35] Suicide by drinking phenol (the active ingredient in Lysol at this time) was common in the early twentieth century. As soon as the dose was swallowed there would have been a burning pain from mouth to stomach with corrosion of the lips, mouth and tongue. 'The pain, however, is not usually great,' wrote pathologist Sydney Smith, 'owing to the local anaesthetic action of the substance.'[36] Charlotte Mew would have experienced weakness and giddiness, passing into insensibility, coma and death. The coroner ruled 'suicide whilst of unsound mind'.[37]

Sydney Cockerell wrote an obituary column in *The Times* that was published under the headline 'A poet of rare quality', noting simply that she had 'died suddenly' but giving those accustomed to reading between the lines of such reports the information: 'her whole life was a courageous battle with sorrows and adversities that have at last proved too much for her.'[38] He speculated how much she had destroyed of her work, for 'her fastidious self-criticism proved fatal to much work that was really good and

... the printed poems are far less than a tithe of what she composed.' The manuscripts had been kept in two trunks, one of which was bequeathed to Alida Monro. It was her last experience of Charlotte Mew's sense of humour: the trunk was empty.

14

Ella D'Arcy: 'Not dead yet'

Regardless of whether her experiences with Charlotte Mew were a joy or a conundrum, or both, in the early years of the century Ella D'Arcy was enjoying Paris. 'Life is but thought,' she wrote to the Anglo-American writer William H. Rideing, quoting the American poet Sara Teasdale,

> and so at the present moment I choose to think it is very agreeable to be in Paris, where I experience all the pleasure of great heat and great solitude without having to go to the Sahara to get them. I also have a gem of a femme de ménage. She is 26, has a crumpled-up little face, and plaits her hair Scandinavian fashion in a lump over either ear. She reads Nietsche [*sic*] in German (she is French) and discusses his philosophy with me between cleaning my books and emptying the dust box. She is ambitious to lend me the works of Diderot! She has written a book on Feminism, which she assures me will, when it appears, entirely change the whole aspect of the woman question in Europe. (How glad poor Mr Asquith would be to know that!)[1]

Her mention of the prime minister and his problems with women's issue shows she was to some extent following stories of suffragette militancy, even though she did not subscribe to English newspapers and had no money to make frequent return trips. Her political stance was more anarchic than socialist or even feminist. She later wrote to Evelyn Sharp, obviously after hearing of the Labour Party's first election victory, which took place on 22 January 1924,

> to tell you of my delight that Labour is 'in'. Equally delightful are the letters I receive from the 'classes', bewailing the fate of 'dear old

England' rushing to the dogs with socialists in the saddle. No, really, the 'bourgeois' is too funny, and were he wiped out the laughter of nations would be hard hit. But he will never be wiped out . . . the last man on earth will be a silk hatted bourgeois, just as the soi-disant first man was a bourgeois aproned with fig leaves.[2]

She knew the aristocrats of expatriate Bohemians in Paris, frequently visiting Gertrude Stein and her brother Leo when they lived at the rue de Fleurus. She lived in the same street herself at this time, and writes as if they could just drop in. 'Dear Miss Stein, I've been round twice in the last few days to see you without success! Will not you and M. Stein come up tonight to see me? You may meet a friend or two and you will certainly give me much pleasure.'[3]

They bonded over art, D'Arcy's first love, with her saying, 'I shall hope to see a great deal more of you, and to pursue my education in Picasso.'[4] Another time she 'came round with M. Lucien Delpon de Vissec who would very much like to see the pictures' and was said to be 'a buyer.'[5] She may not have been entirely candid about her attitude to Stein's collection when she was enjoying Stein's hospitality. She saw *Yellow Book* colleague C. Lewis Hind in 1910, who said she 'was so eloquent in describing her disgust at the pictures by Matisse and others that she had seen at Madame Stein's that I went to Paris the next week and was so impressed and entertained that I began there and then to write in praise of Post Impressionism'.[6]

She was devoted to the memory of the symbolist poet Arthur Rimbaud, whose verse she translated and whose biography she wrote. She defended him from his detractors with extravagant praise: 'That he is by far the greatest of poets, of any age of any country, says nothing to them. He was a rebel, a communist, which is enough to ensure their contempt.' She eventually set her work aside: 'It is no good running one's head against a stone wall is it? There was not a publisher, nor an editor in London, who could hear his name without turning purple from hair-roots to shirt-collar.'[7] Her work, written so close to his death at the age of 37 in 1891, probably contained priceless information about Rimbaud from people in Paris who knew him. Its loss is a literary tragedy.

The notion that the end of the *Yellow Book* was the end of D'Arcy's career is erroneous, but she struggled to have a long book accepted and was always more successful with short stories. Her most significant contribution at the end of the century was 'Our Lady of Antibes' in the *Century Magazine*, which examined the role of domestic violence in relationships.

Young Jeanne, daughter of a violent man, rejects her doting lover until her indifference angers him and she falls in love with his anger.

She made four contributions to the *English Review* in 1909–10 with more tales of unhappy marriages, uncertain religious vocations and compromised artistic integrity. One of them, 'An Enchanted Princess', describes an old woman who is kind to children and who they imagine is an enchanted princess waiting for the prince to come and free her from the spell she is under. She lets on that she had been loved, but had not run away with him; she was 'terribly sorry, but then it was too late'.[8] Finally D'Arcy despaired of fiction, writing to an enquirer, 'I have published various stories [in] various magazines, but no other books, as I could find no publisher willing to take them, and finally I was reduced to burning them.'[9]

Her idleness was an enemy of promise, but she was also very easily discouraged. Arnold Bennett, for example, wrote on 12 December 1910, 'called on Ella D'Arcy, and I made her promise to bring me the novel she had written some years ago, and then left in a drawer because one publisher, John Murray, had refused it.'[10] This may have been her Shelley novel, and the rejecting publisher not Murray but John Lane. Her familiarity with the subject was valuable to her, however, as Lane remembered her when he wanted to publish a translation of André Maurois' novelistic biography *Ariel*, which appeared as *Ariel: The Life of Shelley* in 1924.

She received £30 for the translation with no royalties, later saying, 'In fact I was informed that my translation would not be accepted in America. A different translation would be necessary there. I have learned since that it *is* my translation naturally, and no other.'[11] Relations with John Lane, however, were amicable. She wrote to him, ''Tis whispered in heaven and muttered in hell that Ariel will appear on the 8th,' and asked for the reviews, 'in particular the abusive ones'.[12] The translation was such a success that it was used as one of the first Penguin paperbacks ever published, when the imprint launched in 1935.[13]

In the 1930s Katherine Lyon Mix, a young American, began collecting material for a PhD thesis on the *Yellow Book* and made contact with as many of its contributors as she could find. She visited Paris and met D'Arcy, who she said 'had dyed her hair a dreadful red orange' and spent her days 'at the Café des Deux Magots, drinking bock and watching the young Bohemians stroll by'. Mix found her 'a bright and witty talker with sharp comments about life', when she met her in London and in Paris; D'Arcy supplied much of the colour in Mix's work *A Study in Yellow*.[14] D'Arcy was pleased to have Mix's interest, but wrote:

I am so very tired of Paris, although I enjoy an excellent bed here which I may not find elsewhere ... We made a mistake you and I in our choice of a subject. The YB is abhorrent to our Jix-ridden [*sic*] crowd ... The YB has always from the beginning excited their fury ... Rebels once, perhaps, as men get on in years, they become tax payers, fathers of families, take tea on Sundays with Mrs Grundy, and expiate the courage of their youth by trying to exterminate all free thought in the young people of today.[15]

When she was in her seventh decade A.J.A. Symons wrote asking for biographical information. She replied, 'I cannot think of anything of interest to tell you. But to save you the trouble I can repeat the information I gave *Who's Who* half a century since Published "Monochromes" "Modern Instances" and "The Bishop's Dilemma" with John Lane in 1895 and 1897.' She added, characteristically, 'Marie Corelli rounded off her own very copious biography in the same volume with "not married yet". Today I should be inclined to add, "Not dead yet" as being my surest claim to fame.'[16]

Ella D'Arcy's last years were spent going out to the café from her single room in the rue Jacob; she suffered a stroke in 1937 and was taken to England. Presumably in default of anyone to pay her medical bills, she was taken to the infirmary of the St Pancras Workhouse at Highgate. She was among the 256 females housed in a total of eight long 32-bed wards, with communal bathrooms and lavatories at one end.

She died there on 5 September 1937, 'fulfilling the gloomy prophecy she had made in a letter to M. P. Shiel some 40 years earlier'. It would not have been at all out of character for D'Arcy in 1897 to have said she would probably die in a workhouse.[17] The cause of death was given as senile dementia; she was eighty years old and described as a 'spinster and authoress'. She was buried in the Roman Catholic section of Brookwood Cemetery.

Blanche Crawford, her sister, wrote to John Lewis May on 27 September 1937 thanking him for his 'generous praise and appreciation of my sister Ella D'Arcy's work' in his recently published *John Lane and the Nineties*, and informing him of her death. She added, 'She left a great deal of MSS, which I believe should be of value and interest.'[18] These have not come to light.

15

Netta Syrett's Drama Curtailed

Schoolteacher Netta Syrett entered her class to teach at a girls' school in Ealing on the mild Monday of 21 October 1901 and her thirty or forty pupils burst into applause. Syrett had no idea of the reason for this enthusiastic reception; she discovered that they had learned from a newspaper that she had beaten four hundred other contestants to win a high-profile literary prize. Going home for lunch to her sisters at Morpeth Terrace, she found that several newspaper reporters had already called and she was a minor literary sensation.

Syrett had received a letter that morning saying she had won the Playgoers' Prize, but had no idea that her success would be attended by such publicity and was 'bewildered by all the fuss'.[1] It came about because one of her sisters had suggested she enter a competition for a new play, which had been proposed when Herbert Beerbohm Tree and George Alexander, both later to be knighted as actor-managers, were challenged at a Playgoers' Club dinner. They were criticized for taking their plays from the same small group of playwrights, meaning that no new talent could emerge. In response the club initiated a competition to find a new play that would be acted by Beerbohm Tree and Alexander for one matinee performance.

Syrett had already written a four-act play, *A Modern Love-Story*, which she submitted for the competition.[2] The play has not been published, except for Act 1, and there is only one copy extant, which is in the Lord Chamberlain's (censor's) files. The main character is 26-year-old Nancy Thistleton, who tires of her work as a type-writer (the term 'typist' was not in current use) and of life in her dreary lodgings in Granley Street Chambers, where her landlady freely offers her opinion that Nancy should have a husband. Nancy smokes cigarettes, though they are 'an expensive luxury', as she tells her friend Isabel Ferris, who is an art teacher.[3] The cigarettes have been given to her by a man, Mr Fielding. 'I am 26. I have two or three remaining years of youth. I don't want to waste them,' she says; 'do we, and thousands of women like us, live at all?' She describes her existence:

> Take any day – they are all alike. In the morning I walk to the office, I work till one. At one I go to the nearest ABC [Aerated Bread Company shop] for lunch. Back again at two. Click, click, till five. Then tea, then more work till the walk home. A meal of sorts, then the evening is before me.[4]

She rages at the monotony and loneliness of her life: 'The world is full of women who have waited ... There's one thing that always comes to those who wait long enough. Indifference – apathy.' She doesn't want to be 'cheated by hope'; should she not take a chance at the *joie de vivre*? She feels her frustration is very much related to her class and the necessity for respectability;

> If I were a shop-girl, I could meet the shop-walker round the corner; if I were a duchess that would account for many little eccentricities. But for the modern young woman who works for a living wage, and has the misfortune to be a lady, there is no chance of any kind.[5]

William Fielding, her lover, is a married drama critic who is unsatisfied because his wife is an alcoholic (a 'dipsomaniac', in the terms of the time) and has been committed to an asylum. He understands Nancy's predicament: 'girls who work as you do, who live in a groove as you must, don't marry. How many men for instance have you spoken to within the last six months?' 'Not one.'[6] At the culmination of the first act, she decides to go off with him, even though she does not love him – she is fond of him and they are entertained by each other.

A less successful second act takes place in a hotel on the Riviera where Nancy has taken up with a Captain Egerton. Violet Stuart, an affluent and calculating young woman, suggests in a conversation about how Nancy manages to dress so well: 'There are more ways than one. Perhaps *she* doesn't pay her dressmaker.'[7] In fact Nancy has come into an inheritance and managed to move into her own flat, been able to meet people and go out more, and then met Egerton and left London alone to winter on the Riviera with Egerton following her. Fielding also follows her but realizes Nancy does not love him, 'In a decadent age like this, intuitions are no longer feminine.'[8]

They have had a relationship for four years after which she has tired of him, ironically after his wife has died and he has proposed marriage. Nancy refuses him.

In Act 3 Egerton confides in Fielding, not knowing that he was Nancy's lover, that he is worried about Nancy's past – does he really want to marry a woman with a past? Fielding is to marry the calculating Violet, who knows he wants her only because her father is influential politically. 'It isn't my idea of a brilliant match, but it will do,' she says; 'I'm going to marry Will Fielding because I don't see my way to anything better, and he's going to marry me because of papa's influence.'[9] Violet receives a telegram from Monte Carlo, where Fielding had gone, saying a man has shot himself. Nancy's distress at the supposed death of Fielding gives her away as being in love with him, but it is quickly revealed that the telegram is a mistake; it has been wrongly delivered and the dead man is not Fielding. Act 4 opens back in Granley Street Chambers. Egerton enters – still chasing Nancy for an answer to his proposal, which she rejects. She realizes she has acted fool-ishly, and it is Fielding she really loves. He arrives, having been thrown over by Violet, and they are reunited.

The play is full of insights into the situation of women at the turn of the century, such as the landlady's urging that she should take any man just in order to be married. Nancy's friend Isabel says, 'Nothing ever happens to me, nothing ever will happen!' She wishes she had done what Nancy did and taken a lover. 'Do not regret anything,' she tells Nancy, 'At least you have lived. I wish to heaven I had had your chance!' Thus the woman who did what was expected of her and looked after a sick relative laments her respectability. The scheming Violet is an example of the sort of woman who achieves a 'good' marriage to a man with money regardless of personal affection. A matronly woman advises Nancy, 'one can't be comfortable with-out being bored,' and suggests marrying a man who could give her 'tea, muffins and the fireside'. Egerton suggests Nancy is not a New Woman, to which she replies: 'The same old woman under new conditions, that's all.'[10]

The previous experience Netta Syrett had enjoyed on the literary scene had involved the Harlands' drawing room and tea parties at Lane's. Now she was to encounter the business end of the literary world in an atmosphere that was anything but welcoming to women, or newcomers, and she was both. The first troubling event was a meeting connected with the Playgoers' Club, where she was persuaded to take the chair though she disliked public speaking. The event was a talk by Norreys Connell (Conal O'Riordan) on the subject 'Can novelists write plays?' As soon as she entered the room she realized the hostility rising silently from the audience, most of which, she gleaned, comprised unsuccessful competitors for the Playgoers' Prize and their supporters. 'The wave of enmity that reached me was like a blast from some furnace,' said Syrett.[11] A further disappointment was that Beerbohm Tree and Alexander resented being held to account to act in the play, a promise they had made after a good dinner. The great men of the theatre could not back out, but they minimized their contribution by taking the two smallest men's parts: Beerbohm Tree as a waiter with two words and Alexander as a man with one line. 'It was not playing the game,' as Syrett said, and she considered it was done deliberately to 'wreck the play by making it farcical'.[12]

Syrett was thrown into the top level of a West End production ignorant even of theatre jargon. She was given the choice of actresses for the female parts, at which Lilian Braithwaite came to her flat and begged for the main role. Syrett said she was 'so pretty and charming as well as so desperately anxious for my consent, that my sisters, even less worldly wise than I, fell upon me after she had left with my promise to consider the matter, declaring that I ought to have given her the part at once!'[13]

Syrett found Alexander a good producer, calm and focused, though his manner to Syrett was 'far from encouraging'. He played to his expectations of her, thinking the stage work would need considerable technical fixing, and was surprised to find that, novice though Syrett was, the play performed smoothly. He also wanted changes in lines on the basis that a respectable actress, careful of her reputation, could not mouth the sort of gossip expressed in Syrett's script by the scheming Violet. Syrett wondered what actresses were for if they couldn't say the playwright's lines, but she said, 'Mabel Beardsley would probably be glad to do so.' 'Very well,' said Alexander, 'get Mabel Beardsley,' which Syrett did, and was happy to have a friend in the theatre (and repay the boon that Mabel had granted by introducing Netta to the *Yellow Book* set).[14]

She was now to receive a lesson in literary life that should not have surprised her quite so much had she appreciated the underlying current of animosity that motivated reaction to the fall of Oscar Wilde. The law had punished him according to its lights and that should have been an end to the matter. The backlash, however, was against all the decadents and everything associated with them, and that included women with a tendency to be explicit in sexual matters. As Syrett said of this play, 'certain gentlemen on and off the stage affected to be so deeply shocked and outraged that one might have considered chastity to be their outstanding virtue!' Syrett remarked that over the rehearsal period she 'felt too miserable and depressed to repel suggestions that it was immoral'.[15]

Another challenge was the title, which stated that a play about adultery was in fact about love. The play was daring in that it dwelt frankly with extramarital relationships, as had work by Ibsen, Shaw and Wilde, but that was in the previous century. It needed to be softened, and shown to be not about modern love but about the progress towards respectability of one lost woman. It is not recorded whether Syrett fought the change, but the *Penny Illustrated Paper* noted on 19 April, 'The title has been altered to "The Finding of Nancy"'.[16]

There was to be one performance at St James's Theatre on the afternoon of 8 May 1902. The theatre was packed, the publicity having attracted a huge audience. Netta Syrett attended with Sissie Welch, whose actor husband James Welch was on tour in Yorkshire. Sissie turned to her at the end of the first act and said: 'It's all right, Netta! You've got the house!' Beerbohm Tree sent flowers to her box during the performance, presumably in the interval, with a note of congratulation: 'How well it is going.' It was one of the happiest days of her life. Syrett's old friend Max Beerbohm in the *Morning Post* confirmed the positive response of the audience: 'The play was met with an enthusiastic, almost a frenzied reception, and Miss Syrett had to appear not once or twice.'[17] Syrett went to Sissie Welch's flat in Gray's Inn for supper where Sissie, after the meal, put her on the sofa and forbade her to talk, and she 'listened to the others going over details of the afternoon's triumph'.[18]

The press was in the most part fair and even generous. The critic of the *Penny Illustrated Paper*, for example, applauded the matinee and its 'capital cast' and said, 'No doubt we shall hear more of Miss Netta Syrett the fair author who has already made her mark in some bright and clever works of fiction.'[19] The *Times* reviewer considered himself sceptical of the rapturous welcome for a play produced under such peculiar conditions, but acceded that some of the applause 'was clearly won by the play on its merits. We have seen many worse plays than "The Finding of Nancy" produced by managers of their own free will and not in fulfilment of a rash after-dinner pledge.'

Clement Scott in the *Daily Telegraph* felt Syrett 'surveys some problems with acute and penetrating glance'. He noted

> a first act which is so fresh and at the same time so absolutely torn
> out of the bosom of living experience, that it takes the house by

storm. It is clearly not true that average theatrical audiences are content with the conventional and the familiar, as managers are so fond of believing. Sometimes, when the unconventional strikes home, because it is real and because 'it has been lived', they respond as quickly and as sympathetically as the preachers of the new dramatic evangel have always declared they would, whenever the chance was offered to them.

Later he called it a 'brilliant first act'. After this, however, 'we are in the hands of a dramatist who, with all the advantages of her sex, could paint the problem from the women's side and enlist our sympathy . . . the audience was interested, excited, expectant, anxious for what was to come.' After this, though, he says the plot 'lost itself' and he did not like the resolution. He too remarked on the 'boisterous applause which greeted Miss Netta Syrett at the close'.[20]

Syrett accused this review of 'ludicrous and hypocritical invective', which is a rather extreme reaction.[21] She took Scott's remark about lived experience to imply that he thought the play autobiographical and that Syrett's own morals were as loose as those of Nancy. Nevertheless, Syrett's friends assured her that she was a star, her fortune was made and the play would be a spectacular success. Sure enough, George Alexander summoned her to the St James's Theatre by telegram the day after the newspaper notices appeared. She saw Alexander in his private room, already dressed and made up as the Tyrant of Rimini for his role in the matinee performance that day. She expected him to announce that he intended to put the play on for a run, but Alexander proceeded only to repeat the praise he had previously given her. After she had thanked him again, there was nothing more to be said. She got up and left; the theatre run was not discussed.

She later heard that he had intended to put the play on for a run of after-noon performances but had been dissuaded, fearful of the moral reputation of the theatre. She was convinced Clement Scott was her principal enemy. Critics such as Scott certainly had an influence in the imposition of a moral code. His belief that drama was a new 'religion of the people' required priests to police it. Alexander listened to him: Scott's intervention in 1892 had led to the replotting of Wilde's *Lady Windermere's Fan.*[22]

Syrett should not have gone into a meeting with a powerful man without knowing what she hoped to get out of it; she should have raised the question of a run herself, and should have mobilized her friends to attack Scott in print if she were so convinced of his pernicious influence. Not at this time in her life nor at any other did she show the fighting spirit that such actions required.

Losing a West End run was of course serious, but it was the loss of something she had never had. A harder blow was to come when she was sent for by her headmistress, a personal friend who was 'kind, affectionate but, I must add, not a very courageous woman'.[23] In tears the headmistress told Syrett she must dismiss her as she had received a letter from the mother of a girl in Syrett's class which said that this teacher must surely be a bad influence. The suggestion was that the play had been immoral and so, therefore, was Syrett. It is worth noting, in the context of women's lives, that everyone here was female: Syrett herself, the headmistress, the letter writer and the girl she sought to protect. If there was patriarchal control evidenced here, it was entirely within the hands of women to pull against it. This is doubtless what Syrett meant when she had one of her characters saying, 'It's beastly to be a girl, because women are so silly!'[24] The excitement of the play and its aftermath left Syrett emotionally drained and unwell. Her father came to the rescue and gave her and Nell Syrett a holiday in France, after which Nell returned home and Syrett went to see Ella D'Arcy in Menton.

The Syrett sisters lived together in their flat until 'matrimony began to break out among the sisterhood'.[25] When three of the five girls had married, the flat was given up. Their father died in February 1906, which meant Syrett no longer had a financial fallback. Now such uncertain ventures as writing further plays had to be set aside to leave time for the tested work of writing novels for which she knew she had a market.

Syrett's efforts in the theatre were abortive, notwithstanding her evident talent. Her story shows the difficulties women faced in getting into the theatre business in the late nineteenth and early twentieth centuries, whatever their abilities. Despite this feeling that the theatre could not bring in an income, she did make another foray into the medium in 1909 with *Might Is Right* at the Haymarket, on the controversial subject of suffragette militancy. In this one-act comedy a secret suffrage society captures a young bachelor prime minister and holds him hostage until he promises to bring in a government Bill extending the franchise to women. He falls in love with the secretary of the society, who makes her acceptance of his proposal of marriage conditional on the suffrage Bill. The play was directed by Herbert Trench, artistic director of the Haymarket, and ran for eighteen performances.[26] Syrett refers resentfully in her memoirs to miscasting and the cuts made in her text, so it was clearly a disappointment to her. Her memoirs omit mention of her 1929 book about a suffragette, *Portrait of a*

Rebel, and its film adaptation, *A Woman Rebels* (1936, dir. Mark Sandrich) starring Katharine Hepburn. This was the only film made of a Syrett book, so her reluctance to mention it suggests a distasteful experience, perhaps a disagreement over artistic interpretation.

Her sister Nell married Peter Thorp, who, as 'T', became drama critic of *Punch*. After their marriage Netta shared a flat with them in Prince of Wales Mansions, Battersea Park; she described the window boxes brimming over with flowers and coloured awnings above the balconies leading from roomy flats.[27] She had introduced the couple when she was working on an anthology for children, *The Dream Garden*, for which Nell did three illustrations. Thorp was working as a printer on the book, which included a number of authors Syrett had encountered via the *Yellow Book*, including Fiona Macleod, Edith Nesbit, Nora Chesson and Evelyn Sharp. Though she eventually introduced Nell to Thorp, she had attempted to keep them apart. She wrote that she had thought, 'If Nell sees this attractive young man she'll fall in love with him. She shall not see him.' Her concern was his lack of money and worldly prospects. When they did meet Nell said, 'What a beautiful young man! Why didn't you tell me about him?'[28] Thorp did some reading for Elkin Matthews, including, he said, 'discovering' Ezra Pound, 'a fact which that disdainful poet, when I hesitatingly mentioned the matter to him at one of my sister-in-law's, Netta Syrett's, literary routs seemed somehow to resent'.[29] Obviously, from this comment, Syrett knew Pound well enough to have him as a guest, presumably when he was in London from 1908 to 1920.

Somerset Maugham also became her friend in 1902, and they were close for the next four decades. It was rumoured that Maugham had an affair with Syrett's brother Jerrard (known as Jack), who was another creative talent among the Syrett siblings but suffered from 'nervous trouble', which, with its extremes of creativity and depression, would probably be diagnosed in the twenty-first century as bipolar disorder. He lived most of his life in Italy, where Syrett visited him for extended periods.

She wrote every morning and produced a novel a year. She admitted the quality was not always there: 'circumstances have forced me to write too much . . . though I have always wished to write as well as I could.'[30] She wrote about women in sexless marriages, women in adulterous relationships, and those who bore children out of wedlock. In this way she introduced a variety of models of women to her reading public and questioned the viability of marriage. Jill Shefrin noted her 'striving to combine personal aspirations with romance and domesticity'.[31]

Syrett wrote children's stories at the same time as she was writing adult novels. She and her friend and fellow *Yellow Book* contributor Mabel Dearmer wanted to stage plays for children, so acquired the Royal Court Theatre for the month of the Christmas holidays in 1913. They were to perform *The Cockyolly Bird* by Dearmer and three short plays by Syrett. Unfortunately the expenses of the theatre swallowed up any chance of profit they might have had. The performance was chiefly notable, on reflection, for an early appearance of Noël Coward in the opening ceremony where, dressed as a pierrot, he 'sang clever little verses about animals (words and music composed by himself).'[32] The enterprise received applause from fellow *Yellow Book* writer Ella Hepworth Dixon for these 'two clever ladies' in a piece called 'The Woman's Progress', noting these theatrical producers alongside the achievements of women mayors, aviators, heads of colleges and masters of foxhounds.[33]

Syrett rented a flat in Paris in 1905 in the rue Victor Considrant, near the Luxembourg Gardens, while its owner was abroad and invited Ella D'Arcy to stay. She wrote a piece for the *Daily Mail* describing eating *en plein air*: 'tonight, here in Paris, in the Latin Quarter, we dine in the street.'[34] D'Arcy introduced Syrett to her friend Arnold Bennett, whom Syrett did not like, finding him too 'touchy'. She writes of her men friends, 'I knew a great many with whom I often dined, and either went on to some play or to a dance.' She would 'part with' these man friends if they got married. Syrett herself has no recorded romantic attachments.[35]

Her sister Elsie had an illegitimate child, Robinetta, by a Canadian airman in 1918. It is a testament to Netta Syrett's open-mindedness that she did not cut off her sister and her child but helped with her education.[36] Syrett wrote frankly about sex, but neither her autobiography, such as it is, nor her personal comments say how she found this material. It may have been that she was just a very good listener and picked her friends carefully. She seems to have had a curiosity about sexual feeling in others rather than feeling any desire herself. She may have been lesbian, as Netta Murray Goldsmith suggests, but as Goldsmith concedes, there is scant evidence for this excepting Syrett's many female friendships, including, from 1913, sharing rooms in Soho Square with Molly Clugston, one of the first female accountants.[37]

Netta Syrett was a visible presence at literary gatherings and was one of the vice-chairs of a circle of 96 women writers dining at the Criterion in June 1904, 'undiverted by the fascinating presence of men', as a report had it.[38] Among her many friendships with successful writers was one with the novelist and playwright Constance Smedley, who held Syrett in high regard and invited her to help form a club early in the twentieth century. Smedley wrote that she had 'a perpetual hunger to write and discuss writing problems with fellow writers . . . I cast about to make some sort of literary circle from the people I knew.' She invited Syrett, Jerome K. Jerome, W. K. Locke, Violet Hunt and Ella D'Arcy to discuss a literary club that was to be called the Society of the Golden Key:

> But when these good people arrived to hear more of the 'Golden Key' it began to stick in the keyhole most uncomfortably: my dreams of a united and sympathetic group withered beneath the extreme unsentimentality of their scepticism. It was plain they did not feel any of us could help anyone else.[39]

Soon another club was being set up with Syrett's involvement. The Lyceum was the first women's club to venture into the male-controlled

for we have always been assured incapable of any excellence in th painting. Moreover, ladies—disc selves in black velvet

MISS NETTA SYRETT : PRODUCER OF A TRIPLE BILL AT THE CHILDREN'S THEATRE.

Miss Netta Syrett, who joined Mrs. Percy Dearmer in the scheme of The Children's Theatre, produced a triple bill— "The Fairy Doll," "The Strange Boy," and "The Enchanted Garden "—at the Court Theatre. The proceeds of this enterprise are to be devoted to the establishment of a "Children's

MRS. PERCY DEARMER : MANAGER, WITH MISS NETTA SYRETT, OF THE CHILDREN'S THEATRE.

Mrs. Percy Dearmer has written a play entitled "The Cockyolly Bird," which is now running at the Court Theatre. The scheme of The Children's Theatre was for the production of simple plays to be acted by children for children.

Photograph by Kate Pragnell.

desire took her, and suddenly

Netta Syrett and Mabel Dearmer celebrated by *Yellow Book* colleague
Ella Hepworth Dixon in *Ladies' Supplement to the Illustrated London News*,
17 January 1914.

clubland of Piccadilly, taking over premises that previously housed the Imperial Services Club. The Lyceum, which opened on 20 June 1909, was intended for ladies working in literature, journalism, art, science and medicine, and had a library, an art gallery and 35 rooms. Netta Syrett was on the provisional committee on literature along with fellow *Yellow Book* writers Nora Chesson, Pearl Craigie and Ella Hepworth Dixon. Their role was to evaluate the eligibility of proposed members, of whom 1,200 were rejected 'on account of insufficient qualification'. Smedley said women with university degrees were admitted, and 'wives and daughters of distinguished men'. The reason for this was that 'The wives and daughters of men of letters and artists and eminent professors would belong to interesting circles, and would keep the club in contact with men in the professions. It would not be so exclusively a feminine affair.'[40]

Syrett was on the committee of the Femina Vie Heureuse Prize, which was an award to a British novelist along the lines of the French literary prize of the same name. The prize committee met from 1920 to 1940 and had anything but a happy life. Syrett repeatedly stood for president and vice president, generally receiving only one or two votes, only becoming vice president in 1932.[41] The minutes show her comments on contemporary fiction: 'I thought it was good and unusual, and no sex business which was such a relief.' 'I don't want to read about hateful and cruel people.'[42] Her opinions were not universally shared. She resigned on 13 April 1938, writing from 10 Editha Mansions, Edith Grove, Chelsea SW: 'The lack of courtesy with which certain of its members have intimated their disregard of my opinion when books are discussed makes it seem unnecessary for me to expose myself to further unpleasantness by attending the meetings, especially as it has always meant a physical effort to do so.'[43]

Like Charlotte Mew, she was a friend of 'Sappho' Scott (Catherine Amy Dawson Scott), who founded the international authors' society PEN in 1921; Syrett was one of the earliest members. She said of 'Sappho', 'I was always exceedingly fond of her, though I saw very clearly why she offended as many as she attracted.' She shared Syrett's late-developing interest in 'the branch of science known as Psychical Research' and such manifestations of it as precognitive dreams.[44] Attempts to engage Syrett more fully in the life of PEN foundered on her resistance to speaking in public. She wrote to the secretary:

No, no, no my dear Mr Hermon Ould! The thought of saying even two words in public gives me cold shivers down my spine

– and I might just as well enjoy my dinner! Especially as there are so many people who simply adore hearing their own voices. Do give one of them a chance.[45]

At the beginning of the First World War Syrett, now around fifty years old, tried to get a job teaching in order to free a male teacher to go abroad to fight, but was told she did not have the required certificate (though the Cambridge Certificate she did have was higher than the basic one they asked for). She described the cost of the war to women like her:

In 1914 we felt young, full of energy, as ready for exertion and almost as unmindful of it as we were at twenty-five. By 1918, even for those of us who like me led a quiet existence and suffered no bereavement through the war, much of the spirit of youth had fled, and I fancy this was largely due to a prosaic physical cause – undernourishment.[46]

She published her memoir *The Sheltering Tree* in 1939, with its epigraph from Coleridge that friendship is a sheltering tree. In a positive review in the *Times Literary Supplement* Marjorie Hessell Tiltman wrote, 'Her own emotional reactions to life she has deliberately chosen to withhold . . . There is a finesse, a dignity in Miss Syrett's rejection of one set of values in favour of another that is more often associated with the old-fashioned term of gentlewoman than with that of writer.'[47]

The book received little attention, perhaps because the date of its publication on the eve of war meant minds were occupied elsewhere. Throughout her life, as well as the 38 novels, Syrett produced twenty children's books. In this she was like Evelyn Sharp, also from a big family, who similarly interspersed writing children's with adult books and had no children herself. If Netta Syrett had a role model for artistic work it was the men of the *Yellow Book* set. She wrote, 'if these men married at all it was late in life, but most of them remained bachelors, with just enough money to make life pleasant and comfortable for themselves and none to spare for a wife and possible children.'[48] To have married and had children would have encroached on Syrett's always-prized independence to an unacceptable degree.

Her last novel, *Gemini*, of 1940, had a psychic theme, as did many of her later works. Her output was unstinting; in the last ten years of her working life she produced fifteen full-length books. They show women coming of age and discovering a world of variously bohemianism, art, socialism and

84, EBURY STREET,
S.W.1.

Oct 7ʰ 1928.

Dear Mr. Roberts, I wrote to you
making an appointment on
my return to town, but my letter
was sent back with an intimation
that you had left England.
I was a young and rather shy
girl when the Yellow Book was
started, so although I often
went to the Harlands' "Evenings"
I didn't become really intimate
with any of the Yellow Book set,
though when he was in a good
mood I enjoyed nonsensical
talks with Mr Harland, who
could be delightful... but was
sometimes difficult. He struck

Netta Syrett's letter to Donald Roberts, 7 October 1928.

psychic phenomena, and thus give a picture of an intelligent woman's influences at the end of the nineteenth century and the first decades of the twentieth. At the end of *The Sheltering Tree* she says that her work will die as newcomers will write new books and theirs will in turn be superseded by new young writers. She asks for no long-term recognition: 'The interest and excitement of writing – with any luck, will sustain these newcomers for their lifetime, and no sensible person should ask of our transitory existence more than this.'[49]

She may have felt the approach of death in 1940 as it was in that year that she wrote a will, which included instructions that all her personal papers were to be recovered from where she had them in storage at Clapham Junction: 'Before the furniture is sold I request that whoever superintends the sale shall cause all papers and letters contained in two bureaus (and in one or two cardboard boxes) to be burnt unread.' She made specific bequests of jewellery to her great-nieces and bequeathed 'some keepsake' to a number of other women, and to Somerset Maugham. In most cases she did not specify what the keepsake was, but to her old friend Molly Clugston she left four volumes of Keats.

Netta Syrett spent her last years in a Woking nursing home where family members were amused at her reply when a member of staff wished her, 'Good morning, Miss Syrett': 'Yes, I am "Miss", but I am not a virgin.'[50] She died on 15 December 1943 at the age of 78 with her sister Georgiana Buttar present. In a brief note *The Times* remarked that 'her work always bore the stamp of a woman of education and intelligence.'[51]

16

Mabel's War

'If anyone had told me I should have got to this stage without doing something great, I should not have believed them,' said Mabel Dearmer early in 1914.[1] In the first years of the century she had set about making a name for herself by writing serious literature, as she did not want to write books only for and about children. Stephen Gwynn said, 'the need for self-expression was with her a driving force; and she had much to say that could not be said within that limited range,' so she set to writing novels.[2]

She wrote six between 1902 and 1909, some of them derived from her early experiences of marriage and child-rearing. Others involved protagonists who struggle to live ethically in a compromised world and have been described as 'topical Anglican potboilers'.[3] They were books like *The Alien Sisters*, which is about illegitimacy, and *Gervase*, which turns on the prohibition of marriage with a deceased wife's sister. They were well, if not enthusiastically, received, a reviewer commenting on the 'passionate earnestness of Mrs Dearmer ... the fire of her emotion burns on every page.'[4]

In 1909 she had a dramatic presentation of her 1905 novel *The Difficult Way* produced at the Royal Court, under the title *Nan Pilgrim*, with Lilian Braithwaite playing the title role. It included the song 'Tranquility', a translation she had made from Verlaine set to music by Ralph Vaughan Williams, who was working with her husband on his *English Hymnal*.

Dearmer had been producing plays for children in her husband's church hall; her first adult venture was producing W. B. Yeats's *The Hour-Glass*, a morality play, in January 1909. This started a new direction in her life; she went to see the Passion Play at Oberammergau in 1910 and was inspired to found the Morality Play Society, which was run from the vicarage. As Nan Dearmer (then Nan Knowles) recalled, 'nothing seemed to tire Mabel, she was quite inexhaustible ... drawing-room, dining-room, schoolroom, bed-rooms were all full of people typing, addressing envelopes, fitting and sewing costumes. One would even find women sitting sewing on the stairs. Mabel was in her element, directing it all.'[5]

Percy Dearmer's mother died in 1911 and left them somewhat better off, and with a motor car, a Renault. This became the transport of the Morality Play Society, carrying people and props all over London. Stephen Gwynn advised Mabel in 1911 to write plays and not bother with administration. She said, 'I have written plays, I can write no better; and they cannot be produced. My business is to make myself a position in which I can produce them.'[6] Her play *Don Quixote*, according to Gwynn the best thing she ever wrote, was never produced.[7]

Her first play for the Morality Play Society was *The Soul of the World*, a life of Jesus in three acts: Bethlehem, Gethsemane and Calvary. She had it performed in the Great Hall of London University at the Imperial Institute and was delighted to receive a positive review from George Bernard Shaw. He said to her, 'You are one of the few people living who can write plays.'[8] She wrote to him:

> I was exceedingly delighted with what you said about my play in the Daily Telegraph. I had suffered much at the hands of the half-penny papers, who talked about 'indifferent verse' and 'missing the mark' and so on. Still, you might have liked it without saying so, and it is for that I am most grateful.[9]

She asked his advice on an offer she had had to put the play on in New York, which in the end came to nothing.

She came up against theatre censorship, which, as well as prohibiting performances that offended against strict codes of sexual morality, forbade those featuring characters from the Bible or representations of living people. The university authorities were threatened with prosecution for allowing her play to be performed and so the run ended.

Undaunted, she explored the dramatic possibilities of the Old Testament story of Joseph and wrote *The Dreamer* in 1912. Again, she could not have it performed legitimately and wrote to *The Times* on censorship and religious plays in her role as Director of Plays for the Morality Play Society: 'Why is the censor bound to exclude every play which bases itself upon a Bible story? ... Had there been a Censorship in Greece with the rules of our Censorship surely the world would be the poorer; for the Greek tragedies drew their very being from the religion of the Greek.'[10] She eventually had it performed in December 1912 at the King's Hall in King Street, Covent Garden. A *Times Literary Supplement* reviewer of her collected plays said it was, 'if not dramatic, a plainly constructed and thoughtful exposition which lent itself to stately spectacular effects.'[11] Again, the hall was threatened with prosecution, and there were no more productions.

It had also proved very costly to produce, so Dearmer gave readings to maintain the society's finances. Finally she took to producing children's plays with Netta Syrett under the title The Children's Theatre. Their productions were critically acclaimed even if they never developed the knack of making money from theatre production. She had built up such a store of theatrical costumes that she was able to lease them to other theatre companies at a profit, sending off a dozen Roman soldiers' uniforms or a score of angels' haloes on demand, all of which kept her theatrical enterprises afloat but ate further into the time she might have used for writing.

One of her problems was her tendency to move on to other challenges once she had overcome the ones she faced, as Gwynn recounted: 'when the difficulties were surmounted and the road lay clear, her interest seemed to flag. What kept her working at the stage with such fury was less the desire to succeed as the will to achieve what she had attempted.'[12]

Borne down by the pressure of theatre production, battles with the law and arguments over copyright, she felt the need to get away in spring 1914. She was offered a lease on Gurner's Farm in Oakridge Lynch in the Cotswolds, which was a cottage and farm buildings that had been used as a home and studio by the ceramics painters Alfred and Louise Powell.[13] She went on a day out with Stephen Gwynn to look at it in spring 1914 and fell in love with the place. The cottage had a thatched roof on a building of warm Cotswold stone with mullioned windows. She was to spend the summer there, with Stephen Gwynn often living in a barn in the grounds that had been converted to a studio. He later said that their 'comradeship' of nineteen years had never been closer than in the months before and after the outbreak of war.[14] Other friends visited and Percy Dearmer came and went as his work allowed. Mabel learned to cook, which delighted her, and made jam from the plums in the orchard, 'happier, I believe, than ever in all her life', according to Gwynn.[15] She was busy with the plum harvest in summer 1914 and had no time for newspapers. 'From the early dawn, when, from my outdoor bed, I watched the sun rise through the tangle of flowers overtopped by gigantic hollyhocks to full midday, I was busy,' she wrote.[16]

She was on her own in early August when she received a letter from Stephen Gwynn posted from the House of Commons, saying, 'There is a war and we are in it.'[17] The war began to take over everything, even the harvest, when her friends did not want to join her from London to help, for fear of missing war developments. She could not enter their excitement. 'I did not hate the enemy,' she wrote; 'I hated the spirit that made war possible.'[18] Then came a letter from her twenty-year-old son, Christopher, who was a fine linguist and had been intending to take a degree in languages. He had been in France and wrote, 'I am coming home to enlist.'[19] He urged on her the justice of the war but she explained to him, 'I can't hate my enemy. I have spent my whole life trying to learn a different lesson.'[20] Her eldest son, Geoffrey, then enlisted, and Stephen Gwynn told her he too was joining up.

Mabel returned to London and worked with the Belgian Refugee Committee. She was rehearsing a play to raise funds for refugees, but made time to attend a Church League for Women's Suffrage service at St Martin-in-the-Fields on 26 March 1915. This was to be conducted by her husband for a team of nursing volunteers headed out to Serbia. The women of the unit, organized by Mabel Stobart, wore grey uniforms and round black hats, looking very keen and business-like. Mabel wondered how many would return; then she became aware of Percy Dearmer's address, 'I myself am to accompany you to Serbia.' He had that morning been appointed chaplain to the British units there.

Mabel sat in her pew, 'with my nose and eyes getting rather swollen and very red and dropping tears on my hymn-book.'[21] She thought of being alone with no great work to do in the empty cottage with its flowers and sunshine. 'During the singing of the last hymn an idea struck me. Here was the work for which I had waited. I had no doubt and no hesitation.'[22]

Mabel, dressed up in her green silk dress and fur coat as the vicar's wife, approached the severe Mabel Stobart, who recalled:

> Mrs Dearmer with tears on her face, came up to me. 'This is the first I have heard of my husband going to Serbia; Mrs Stobart, you must take me with you – as an orderly. My sons are both at the front, and now my husband is going, I must go too.'[23]

Mrs Stobart had led teams in the Balkans in the 1912–13 war and had recently returned from Belgium:

I'm afraid I was brutal. I pointed at her earrings and pretty chiffons. 'This kind of thing isn't suitable,' I said.

'I will leave them all behind, and wear – well, your uniform!' as she looked bravely at my dull grey clothes.[24]

Mabel's own account of this meeting was less realistic about what she would encounter:

'What can you do? What are you trained for?'

'Nothing, but I am an ordinary sensible woman and can learn quickly.'[25]

Stobart feared for Dearmer's physical health, that she was insufficiently robust to face the challenge, and that she would have to accept discipline. Dearmer resisted all arguments and insisted on volunteering; she was told that she could go as a hospital orderly.

When Mabel finally caught up with Percy Dearmer, he apologized for not having had time to tell her earlier that he was going. She said she was going too. He said, 'What fun!' and hailed a taxi to get them home. She said they were going to endure great hardships and had better get used to them, so they should take the Tube.[26]

On Easter Sunday, 4 April 1915, they left the vicarage to be shipped out to Serbia via France, Percy in khaki and Mabel in her new grey uniform with a black hat. As they waited for their train, Christopher came rushing on to the platform to say goodbye for the last time.

When the unit arrived in Paris, Mabel attended a lecture by a doctor who had been with an American relief unit. He was the only one of the medical staff who had survived: all the other doctors and nurses had died. Dearmer wrote, 'We shall not be a Field hospital at all but a fever unit – the people are dying in thousands from starvation as much as anything.' Despite this grim prognostication, she was pleased to be on her mission and said in the same letter to Gwynn, 'I am ever so happy.'[27] In Malta she was able to see her son Geoffrey, who took a boat out to her troopship and took her ashore for dinner.

They travelled via Piraeus and Thessalonika to Kragujevac, then the capital of Serbia, where they set up a tented hospital encampment and a chain of emergency dispensaries. Mabel shared a tent with three other orderlies. Percy Dearmer was also based in the camp but with his own responsibilities and a higher status: at meals he would sit with the doctors and Mrs Stobart, while Mabel sat with the other orderlies. In letters addressed from the Stobart Field Hospital she wrote of inoculations, of paraffin and 'vermigel' treatments against parasites, temperatures taken every morning and then Swedish drill. She was soon fixed into the routine, which started at 4.30 a.m. with bedtime at 8 p.m., waiting for new arrivals of wounded in a camp that was always full, watching the death cart carry off the day's tally.

She was put in charge of the linen tent for the whole camp of 62 tents, so was responsible for the entire hospital's bedding and clothing supply for patients and orderlies. After rain the linen tent was 'a sea of thick mud on the floor with rough packing cases and crates on their sides all round – filled with things that are nearly always wet'.[28] She wrote that she had not sat on a chair for seven weeks, and 'My walk to the store house is ankle-deep in sticky mud and there are ponds and lakes everywhere – but no words can describe the beauty of the mountains in the clean air.'[29] As for disease, she said, 'the word typhus is greeted by shrieks of derisive laughter in spite of the doctors assuring us there will be lots more opportunities of dying uncomfortably.'[30]

She was to find war bizarre: 'Everything is so curiously mixed up. We are friends and enemies all together – half our wounded are Austrian.'[31] The camp narrowly escaped bombs when Austrians attacked nearby military targets. She recalled, 'one aeroplane was so low that it seemed to emerge from two clouds of bursting bombs . . . When it was over we went to breakfast which was only a quarter of an hour late.'[32] She wrote on 3 June 1915, 'They shelled the town here for practice today and I was so tired I slept through the whole thing.'[33] In the same letter she reported that typhus had come to the camp. She reassured Gwynn, 'If I get it, will you always remember that I am *very* strong with a terrific constitution, and most tremendously alive from my life in the open,' though on the other hand, 'one has to stop someday, and personally I would rather "stop" here, doing this work, than anywhere else in the world.'[34]

When she became ill she was keen to stay working, so said she 'made myself scarce when temperatures were taken, and kept on'. She notes illness had 'made me quite thin, and when I stand up, I feel as if I hadn't got a stomach at all.'[35] On 12 June she reported that enteric fever had hit the camp with eleven people down. Fever began to overcome her; on 14 June she was writing in her copy of the New Testament, 'Burning hell – out of the deep.'[36]

Her fever broke and she rallied, though exhausted; her husband was able to write 'out of danger' and 'recovering steadily' at the end of the month.[37] She had recovered enough to laugh and read the papers, but then relapsed

Oakridge Lynch War Memorial: Mabel Dearmer's monument.

and there was another week of high fever. Mabel Dearmer, Henry Harland's 'Helen of Troy', died on 11 July 1915. Gwynn took comfort in his belief that she had reached a contentment in life that had previously been denied her. From Serbia she wrote that 'the storms were over' and she was at last 'gliding down a smooth stream of life'.[38]

Her death at least spared her from the pain of her son Christopher's death from wounds at Suvla Bay, Gallipoli, only three months later on 6 October. Her elder son, Geoffrey, became a celebrated war poet. He wrote the verse on a war memorial erected in Oakridge Lynch that commemorates his mother and brother.[39]

Proud of the war all glorious went the son.
Loathing the war all mournful went the mother.
Each had the same wage when the day was done.
Tell me was either braver than the other.[40]

The memorial, a fountain designed and constructed by Alfred Powell, who had leased her the cottage, is remarkable in being one of very few war memorials to a woman, and also because it was unveiled in 1917, almost a year before the war ended. Stephen Gwynn was present, though not Percy Dearmer, who had already moved on and was by now in India with a new wife.[41]

17

Unresting Dragonfly

Ménie Muriel Dowie's husband Henry Norman finally rejoined his wife in England in 1900, after he had left her in Tbilisi with his best friend Edward FitzGerald. He was disconcerted to find she no longer wanted to have sex with him. This was not the best way to conceal an affair – but she said there was no other man involved, he believed her, and they did not split up immediately. By January 1901, at least a year after her affair with Edward FitzGerald began, Norman had found out about her adultery and they separated. In June she wrote a letter asking him to try to fix the marriage, quoting a friend who 'said you would forgive me, and you would not be the first man who had forgiven his wife'.[1] She had recently been ill, and Henry had been kind to her, she noted, and she promised to be faithful in the future and to concentrate on her writing. He was unable to forgive, however, or she was unable to keep away from FitzGerald.

A private detective followed Dowie and provided evidence for Norman to petition for divorce for adultery between 15 and 17 January 1902 at the Lord Warden Hotel in Dover, where she and FitzGerald were 'passing as husband and wife'. It is likely that this was a set-up by all the parties involved, with the objective of ensuring a divorce. At this time a court required proof by one party that the other party had committed an act incompatible with the marriage. A woman's adultery alone (though not a man's, in the absence of aggravating factors) was grounds for divorce. An industry of private detective agencies grew up who would gather evidence of adultery from a couple who had agreed with their estranged partners to be complicit in the enterprise. The case was heard in the Probate, Divorce and Admiralty division of the High Court; it was not defended, though Dowie and FitzGerald were both represented.

Justice Gorell Barnes gave Norman custody of the child, but in a man-oeuvre presumably designed to punish her for her transgression, she was forbidden access. This does not seem to have been part of the court pro-ceedings (it is not mentioned in the report in *The Times*). With the child Norman's responsibility alone, he could decide who should have access and he denied it to Dowie. She later told her niece Rosamond Lehmann that Norman had been 'a cruel man' over the divorce but the record is not littered with her complaints; presumably she recognized the futility of pursuing the matter in these circumstances.[2] Norman's brief diary of events merely notes for 1902, 'I divorced my wife (see 1891)', and in 1891 notes that he got married '(see 1902)'. The decree absolute came through on 10 August 1903.[3]

Dowie said her separation from her son was 'a grief which I never con-templated or was asked to contemplate as remotely possible'.[4] She sometimes went to see him play sport at Winchester, where he was at school, but did not speak with Nigel again until he was a university student. She had no other children. Norman destroyed all papers relating to her and refused to hear her name mentioned. There must have been some correspondence as Dowie referred to Norman sending her a picture of Nigel when he was eight.[5]

Norman was knighted in 1906. He married again, in 1907, to 'Fay' McLaren, who was 27 years younger than himself and the daughter of a wealthy industrialist. In May 1910 Lady Norman received a letter from Dowie that said, 'I am using all my courage to write to you and make a request,' and asked Lady Norman to see her:

> I can only beg you to imagine how much a talk with you about Nigel would mean to me. If you have met people who know me, you can never have doubted how devoted I am to him and nothing that could ever happen would make that otherwise... You cannot possibly know what the horror of being cut off from him has meant.[6]

It is not known whether any meeting with Lady Norman took place, but Dowie did not meet her son as a child or teenager. The double standard of sexual morality for men and women was reflected in the harsh treatment she suffered. It contrasts baldly with the way Norman and Dowie's *Daily Chronicle* and *Yellow Book* colleague Henry Nevinson was treated, despite his marital transgressions with various women including Evelyn Sharp: he ended his life the recipient of honorary degrees and celebratory banquets.[7]

Ménie Muriel Dowie portrait from *The Sketch*, 22 January 1896.

Dowie seems to have written nothing for publication after her divorce. *Things About Our Neighbourhood*, published in 1903 by Grant Richards, was a compilation of her *Country Life* pieces. Her one published piece of verse, dating from this time, gives an indication of her state of mind and hints at the difficulty she had with relationships. 'The Thrall Song', printed in the *Pall Mall Magazine*, juxtapositions a queen and her servant:

In the kingdom which is ours
Free from any laws at all,
Here's how we'll divide the pow'r:
You'll be Queen – and I'll be thrall.

The queen on her pedestal with the trappings of grandeur seems to have the best of the deal, but she commands only one man while he is more than satisfied '*With a whole Queen to himself.*'[8] The implication of the verse is that the queen realizes too late the nature of the relationship.

Dowie and FitzGerald married on 13 August 1903 and devoted much of the next fifteen years to travelling abroad in Europe, North Africa and Asia. When in England they lived at 38 Green Street, Park Lane, London. In 1918 she and FitzGerald purchased Marsden Manor, near Cirencester. In a working out of her eugenic ideas she began to breed cattle. The farm was particularly noted for its Red Poll, which were milk and beef animals; she also bred polo ponies and sheep. She was literally hands-on in the farm; as her friend Berta Ruck said, 'Delicate hands! They looked as though a powder-puff was the heaviest thing they could handle. All the same, I have seen them competently help to deliver a baby-calf.'[9]

Ruck was a prolific writer of novels with titles such as *Shopping for a Husband*, *The Unkissed Bride* and *The Girl Who Was Too Good-Looking*. She met Dowie at a women writers' dinner at the Savoy in the early 1920s, where Ruck described her as 'what was then called a "very society" woman of means'. She recounted their conversation:

> The first words she spoke to me were a reproof because I had refused salad. 'English people eat far too little fresh green food,' she said in a clear, convinced voice, 'You should always take plenty of salad.'
>
> To look at, Ménie was incarnate elegance. Tall, unbelievably slim. Imagine a female skeleton, exquisitely put together. Over this, a covering of just enough delicate flesh, not to let the bones show through. Skin fine as the finest crepe de Chine. A mere soupçon of expertly put on make-up. White floss silk hair, cut short, brushed back to follow the beautiful shape of her head. Dress? Always Paris where she went to her dressmakers every spring and autumn. There too she bought accessories to harmonise. From the latest hat, set at the right angle to the hand-made shoes on her narrow high-instepped feet, everything was immaculate. This finish was not a matter of money. Richer women can display atrocious taste![10]

Dowie's return to a settled home in England corresponded with her renewed relationship with Nigel. He turned 21 in May 1918 and as an adult could make his own decisions about who he would see. Rosamond Lehmann,

Dowie's niece (who was four years younger than Nigel), was at Cambridge at the same time as Nigel and the Lehmanns were instrumental in effecting a meeting between Nigel and his mother. 'He had been brought up by his father and stepmother to consider her a wicked, loose woman,' said Lehmann. She questioned whether trust was ever fully built between Dowie and Nigel.[11] She gave an impression of Dowie: 'She was fascinating, brilliant, an actress, a liar – there was something wicked in her, though there was generosity and tenderness as well.'[12]

Lehmann depicted Dowie in the character of Mrs Jardine in *The Ballad and the Source*, which was published in 1944 (after Dowie's death). Jardine is a sophisticated, damaged woman in poor health whose marital transgressions are in the past, but her corrupted relationships continue. The bulk of the fiction takes place when the narrator is a child (presumably the way Lehmann saw Dowie), who notes, 'I did not realise then what poisons from what far-back brews went on corroding her.'[13] Much later, in 1976 when Lehmann herself was an old woman, she returned to Dowie's story in *A Sea-Grape Tree* where the same narrator from *The Ballad and the Source*, now an adult, converses about infidelity with the spirit of the dead Mrs Jardine. 'I lived for beauty – what I sowed I reap,' the wraith says.[14]

One picture that seems accurate from the book is of Harry, Mrs Jardine's husband, who has the shaking hands and distant air of the elderly alcoholic. This may well have been an accurate childhood reflection of Lehmann's, as Edward FitzGerald became alcohol-dependent; he would begin each day with a glass of champagne and a digestive biscuit, and continue in the same vein.[15]

Dowie's relationship with her son developed as he grew older. Nigel Norman became a businessman and an air commodore in the Auxiliary Air Force, a civilian corps that supported and reinforced the Royal Air Force from the mid-1920s. He designed and built several airports in England with his company, Airwork Limited. Dowie and FitzGerald bought Nigel an Avro biplane and in 1928 hosted a flying weekend party at Marsden Manor for Nigel and his friends. Guests arrived by air to find a huge white M made out of tablecloths laid out on the field.

By the end of 1928 Dowie had finally had enough of her husband, and set out without him to travel to Austria and on to Egypt. While in Cairo in January 1929 she fell seriously ill, possibly with malaria. Her son flew to meet her, expecting to find her dying, but she recovered after a long convalescence in Venice and Vienna. Her health had often been poor, and even as a young woman had spoken of having 'a delicate chest'.[16]

When Nigel returned to the UK, Ruck joined her in Cairo early in 1929. Doubtless it was felt that the still invalid Dowie needed a companion for her journey to Austria. This was far from unusual, as Ruck wrote, 'Often she would send an itinerary, expenses, and an invitation for a friend to join her. Just like that! The summons came to me at Windsor to join her in Cairo. Enclosed was my route. I should have to wait two days in Athens.'[17] Ruck described the experience of travelling with Dowie:

> She could make any impersonally sumptuous suite in the Ritz, Crillon or Ruhl into her own characteristically perfect boudoir, and bedroom. They would be immediately pervaded by her aura: her special blend of scents, soaps, cosmetics. Filled with her unique possessions! The first thing she would order to be unpacked was her travelling door-stop, the immense frog in green porcelain, a gift from her son. The frog-Prince gave an air to any place in which he squatted on the thick carpet beside the door to her bath-room. Ménie always travelled with her own small down-filled face-pillows. Without these on her bed she would have been as restless as the princess on the crumpled rose-leaf. She did not sleep well, in any case. She was often over-tired by these long motor trips. She never admitted it. She would at once begin to draw up the next day's schedule, what she wanted to show me, where and on what spécialité de la maison we should have lunch, and at what time she would order her car. She had a long, black glossy pencil-slim Rolls. She had everything. Except the one thing that would keep me from any wish to exchange my life for hers, even for a day – good health.[18]

Those reflective remarks were written for Ruck's memoirs after Dowie's death. A more immediate picture is given in her journal for the trip:

> Ménie is all this time getting stronger, but the moment she acquires a little strength she again fritters it, expending energy on totally unnecessary things. It is like being with an ailing but unresting dragonfly for a companion! She sends me for a taxi, then darts across the road to get it herself. Rushes into, or at, every shop that takes her fancy. Never ceases to comment. Nothing could be more exhausting! Must she? She says, 'If I sit a moment quiet, I start to concentrate on the failure I have made of my life.' Impossible to

consider it thus with her brilliant and handsome son, and already one grandson?[19]

Even a sister novelist and traveller, therefore, saw Dowie's achievement not in terms of the books she had written, or even the adventures she had had, but the men she had borne, even down to the second generation. Her son Nigel had married Patricia Moyra Annesley in Paris in 1926; they were to have three sons.

In October 1929 Dowie took legal steps to separate her finances from those of Edward FitzGerald. A little more than a year later he died at the

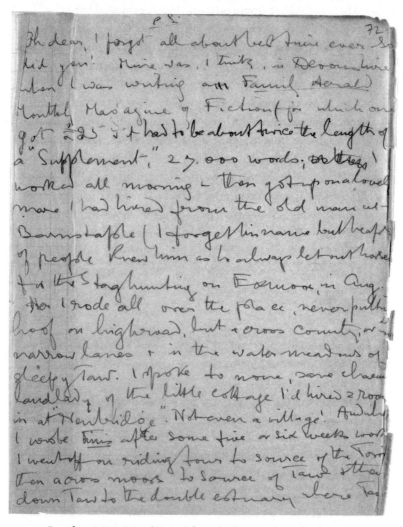

Page from Ménie Muriel Dowie's letter to Berta Ruck, no date but 1933.

age of 59 on 2 January 1931. It was later found that he had mismanaged their finances, or had failed to keep an eye on them: £400,000 was lost in the Wall Street Crash of 1929; some money had perhaps been embezzled and there was a wrangle with his secretary, but the money was never recovered. FitzGerald's estate at death was £52,560, and Dowie had to sell the farm.

Dowie settled in a house in Shepherd's Crown, near Winchester, close to her son and grandsons, who spent time there. Dowie would winter abroad in the 1930s, when as Ruck said, 'health forbade her to winter on "this bleak rock in the north sea" as she called England. Before the first fogs descended on our island, she, with car and personal maid, would be off to Monte Carlo, Nice and Cannes.'[20] She always had many men friends, but none seem particularly noteworthy. Ruck said she 'collected' people, 'army, foreign office, and "well knowns" in the medical, legal, political worlds'.[21]

Dowie emigrated to the USA in 1941, partly because a dry, desert climate was more comfortable for her asthma. She bought a plot of land in Tucson, Arizona, and had a bungalow built with thick walls in case the family needed to come over when Britain lost the war – as she believed it would – and she could build another storey.

Nigel Norman became an air commodore and took part in the Battle of Britain. He died on active service on 19 May 1943 on his way to North Africa to help organize the Sicily landings, a few days short of his 46th birthday. The port engine of the Lockheed Hudson in which he and others were travelling failed; he was preoccupied with telling other passengers to enter the brace position in preparation for the crash and did not protect himself.

His son, Dowie's eleven-year-old grandson Torquil Norman, was evacuated to the USA during the war and went to live with her. He had not recalled knowing her in England before the war and it was an unusual relationship for both of them. It might be thought that, having missed out on her own son's childhood, she would enjoy having a boy around the house, but she seemed too old now to rise to the challenge of motherhood. Torquil felt he must have behaved badly, but he was probably only a high-spirited child and she was old and unwell. He remembered, 'she had a little machine she used to pump up and she'd put a mask on to calm her asthma.' Dowie had a humped back in her later years, with a strong face and thin grey hair cut short and pulled back.

He remembered his grandmother's passion for wildlife and her pride in her Mannlicher-Schönauer rifle, which impressed him no end; she said it never jammed. She lived with Martha, a companion in her thirties who looked after her and drove the car. 'In her old age she got fond of the gin bottle,' Torquil Norman said; he once dropped a bottle of gin while they were out shopping: 'it was the first time I saw her really angry.'[22]

By now she gives the impression of being a brooding, unhappy woman. 'These closing scenes are very badly arranged,' she remarked on the end of her life, taking a literary metaphor though she had written nothing for publication for more than forty years.[23] She died in Tucson on 25 March 1945, her death remarked on in the British press as having 'broken an interesting link with the literary world of the nineties . . . an unusual personality, combining great personal attraction and sparkling wit'.[24]

18

George Egerton:
'This life is dry rot'

Chavelita sailed off to Norway in autumn 1899 to her next adventure. This was to be with Ole, a Norwegian student fifteen years her junior, with whom she began a passionate affair. From comments in the letters she later wrote him, it seems they met in a boarding house where both were resident. This would fit with her customary method of finding lovers that did not involve any great expense of forethought. Ole signed himself O.C.B., which is all that is known about his identity, except that he was depressive, frequently threatened suicide and was under the control of his parents who had plans for him. Chavelita went on a mission to save the gloomy student: 'to gladden, to inspirit one morbidly inclined mind, to kindle an unquenchable beacon light in the gloom of one soul which I found in darkness'.[1] She quickly fell into her usual relationship with men: of paying for everything and converting her experiences into literature. 'Hitherto *man* has been the master lover, the chronicles of woman's love have been but tales of sacrifice,' she wrote.[2]

When she returned to England early in 1900 she began writing to him, starting with a letter from Kiel railway station in Germany, where she sat at 5.30 a.m. She was driven to write of their parting and begged the railway porter for some paper so she could express herself. She writes:

> My own dear Love, my darling Boy . . . I cannot forget your face, your white, strained face, and the misery in your eyes . . . I have kept my watch at your time, I know what you are doing, I went to you last night at the hour I knew you would try to sleep, I felt how you stretched out your arms, how you called on me and how you suffered at the silence and the void.[3]

She comforted him for what reads like a childhood of emotional neglect and describes their intimacies: 'I bend to give you my mouth and say my dear, dear love I am all your very own; every inch of my body, every secret cranny of the soul of me.'[4] The letters start in positive mood: 'MY OWN, MY VERY, VERY OWN, You joy-bringer! You maker of spring in my heart!'[5] Ole is not always so effusive and seems to have been trying to express his failing confidence in the relationship, at which Chavelita wrote, 'Into what strange place of misconception have you strayed? I am miserable, heart-sick over your last letter . . . surely you are not gone back to all the old doubts, the old tortured self-questionings.'[6] Her letters then reassumed their enthusiastic tone, and she visited her lawyer to put her affairs in order before leaving England to join Ole for the rest of their lives together.

Doubtless with the memory of Knut Hamsun's having burned her letters to him, this time she kept copies and was therefore in a position to publish them. She created a flimsy structure that the letters were given by the woman in love, signing herself R.A., to George Egerton. The introduction of *Rosa Amorosa* has 'George Egerton' writing of sitting by the fire with 'the little soul who wrote them' and discussing books. She says, 'I should not mind if I had a crystal disc in my forehead, so that all I have ever thought might be seen through it, a *camera lucida* for all men.'[7] She offered it to Grant Richards, who had published her *Wheel of God*.

Chavelita returned to Christiania in March 1901 to find Ole still wavering, and distant with her. He was unable to tell his parents about her and unwilling to marry without their consent. It was the end. She returned, irritated, but at least she had got a book out of the relationship. It was published in May 1901 to less than critical acclaim. The reviewer in *The Times* said there may be people who like this kind of thing, 'But they would probably be neither healthy people nor pleasant people. A mixture of flabby sentimentalism and raging self-consciousness – that is what the writer of these letters has produced.'[8]

Their sexual compatibility had been satisfying, but now Chavelita was ready for something else. Perhaps surprisingly for a 42-year-old woman, she had another man, also fifteen years her junior, also vying for her affections. Reginald Golding Bright and Chavelita were introduced in 1899 by a mutual friend, the actress Annie Russell. They corresponded, with Chavelita's maternal attitude patronizing his romantic one in letters where Bright responded to her worldly-wise flirtation. Bright's ardour seems to have been piqued by Chavelita's passion for Ole, about which she wrote to him, 'I found him in the earth call that is myself.'[9] He need not wait till the publication of

Rosa Amorosa to hear of their passion; she was giving him an event by event account of it. Whatever effect she thought this would have on a man who had been sending her flowers and books is uncertain. 'I am grateful to you, boy, for much dear thought of me,' she wrote; 'you care for me in a strange beautiful way, a way I greatly care to have.' She signed herself 'your little Mother'.[10] When she went to Norway on her ill-fated last visit to Ole in March 1901, Bright accompanied her to Harwich.

She wrote to Golding Bright as 'My dearest Boy', 'Good little son' and 'boy', which is similar to her form of address to Ole.[11] She also called her son 'boy', though when he became an older teenager she addressed him as 'My dear old Son'.[12] She continued her correspondence with Bright from Norway and wrote to him of the breakdown in her and Ole's relationship, on receipt of which he sailed across the North Sea to propose. She accepted, though not immediately, and they married on 11 July 1901.

Bright was a journalist, a drama critic who was working towards becoming a theatrical agent. Some six months after marriage he joined the American agent Bessie Marbury's London office, of which he became chief in 1906. He became the agent of Somerset Maugham, Hall Caine, J. M. Barrie and George Bernard Shaw. Here was, at last in her life, a change from the feckless men Chavelita had bonded with previously. Bright had a job, ambition, ability and a home. He was also prepared to take on her son, so both Chavelita and George moved into his apartment at 2 South Square, Gray's Inn. It was a generous arrangement from Bright's side, as her dependents were not only her six-year-old son, whose education would have to be considered, but Chavelita's father, who was unwell.

Chavelita had been disappointed by her later lack of success at fiction and determined on a career as a playwright. This was not by chance, nor solely stimulated by her relationship with Bright. She had long thought of writing a play and knew many people in the theatre world, such as James Welch and Annie Russell, as well as those introduced by her new husband. It was also propitious that at the same time as there was a decline in interest in novels about troubled women, there was a rise of drama influenced by Ibsen with its focus on sexual hypocrisy and personal dilemmas. Through her husband's work she came into close contact with Shaw, who was a leading member of those bringing the theatre of social problems to the Edwardian stage; it was a fertile field for a writer of problem women, such as Chavelita.

Shaw was generous with his advice, if harsh. He had been advising her on a play in 1904, suggesting extensive rewrites. After she had completed them, he said the work 'clamours for production', and then suggested some more revisions. Chavelita was notoriously touchy about her work and had the successful autodidact's resistance to rewrites, as if she had needed no traditional assistance to get thus far, so she scorned such offers now. In the same letter in which he encouraged the play's production at the Royal Court Theatre, he gave such advice as 'you must increase its impetus by coming down ruthlessly on all discursiveness into little momentary inventions towards the end.'[13] She may have refused to revise further or there may have been some difficulty with other requirements of the theatre or the Stage Society, which performed works at the Royal Court, but the play was never performed.

There was no irremediable breach with Shaw, however, as she sent her next play, *His Wife's Family*, to him for a review, which was not positive. 'It is of no commercial use,' he explained, 'You have not got the proper quality of dramatic dialogue: and you will write a practicable commercial play as soon as you condescend to study the market and the materials you have to work with.'[14] Her characters were all Irish and there were not enough Irish actors, nor was the subject-matter of interest either in England or Ireland, he explained. He advised, 'Try an English comedy and accept the limitations of our existing theatres.'[15]

While they had enjoyed an early friendship, in later life Chavelita never spoke kindly of Shaw. He returned the compliment, writing to Terence de Vere White, who had requested biographical information:

> She was so intolerably loquacious that she talked herself off the stage after she had won her way to the centre of it by her literary talent. It was incessant gabble, gabble, gabble, without any grace of address or charm of speech. Many sought to meet her once, but not twice.[16]

Shaw showed a marked preference for people who shut up and let him talk. De Vere White recalled she actively boasted of her scraps with him, 'I used to wonder at her when she told me of verbal knock-outs given, without provocation, to such as Shaw, who, it seemed to me, was worth preserving as a friend.'[17]

Shaw may have been correct about London and Dublin rejecting her Irish stereotypes, but there was elsewhere an Irish community eager to hear their native voices and representation of their culture on stage. Chavelita sent her play to Arnold Daly in New York, where it was staged in October 1908 at the Wallack's Theatre. The *New York Times* critic enjoyed the wit of a play about an Irishwoman who marries a sober Englishman who finds he has taken on her bankrupt family; the critic noted its 'many charming and appealing qualities', which 'make the more regrettable the fact that it lacks any real dramatic quality'.[18] She blamed the play's failure on Daly, writing to him, 'You had no right to take a property of mine and destroy it by hurried and inadequate rehearsal and less right to cut out sixty minutes of the acting and one whole part.'[19]

The play did impress theatre producer George Tyler, who bought the rights to perform her next play, *The Backsliders*. In 1910 she sailed to New York to supervise the rehearsals, determined that this time she would keep control of the production, which was an attack on Fabian socialists, feminists, vegetarians and other such 'progressives'. Her supervision was to no avail; the play was no better received than the last and failed to find an audience in New York, where it opened in January 1911.

Her play showed how out of step Chavelita was with advanced women. While one *Yellow Book* colleague, Netta Syrett, was writing *Might Is Right* and another, Evelyn Sharp, was engaging in suffragette militancy and writing tales of the militants, Chavelita was explicitly rejecting any sympathy with women's political aspirations. She considered that the women's rights movements produced 'an atrophied animal, with degenerate leanings towards hybridism'.[20]

Chavelita corresponded with Ellen Key, the leading Swedish writer on women, who admired *Rosa Amorosa* as a guidebook to 'the great mystery of love'.[21] Key, author of *The Woman Movement* and biographies of many famous women, shared Chavelita's preoccupation with woman as 'an enigma' who is psychologically and spiritually different from men. Neither Key nor Chavelita was so much concerned with gender equality as with emphasizing what they saw as valuable female characteristics. Chavelita wrote enthusiastically:

> What an indomitable fighter of a woman you are! How have you kept your vitality? How have you kept the flame of your spirit burning so brightly? I am often so weary that I just flicker, and only turn up the light when someone wants to read a line or two by the light of me, and when they are gone, I turn it down again and sit in the half gloom.[22]

Key must have asked Chavelita about the women's movement because she replied, 'I know little of the "woman movement" here, I am not in

George Egerton (Mary Chavelita Dunne), early 1930s, photograph by Walter Benington.

sympathy with the Labour Party and I dislike all the advanced women I have met over here. I should hate the average English woman to have suffrage.'[23] The next month she was asking for an exclusive right to translate Key, which was presumably refused as nothing further was heard of this project.

Chavelita's father suffered a stroke in 1902 and, partially paralysed, needed a nurse to care for him for the rest of his life until he died on 5 February 1910 at the age of 72. She had written in 'The Captain's Story' of a man who had always talked of the great work he was to produce, which eventually came to nothing. She had no great patience with children and was irritable with her son George as a young child, but after his early teenage years she began to warm to him, writing chatty letters with advice on life and love, as if he were one of her young men admirers. He attended the progressive Bedales School, which took a non-denominational approach to religion and was popular with Fabians and intellectuals. Chavelita's sprightly letters show that the interest in fishing she had taken from her father had been passed on to her son: 'Do tell me about fishing. Catch any eels? Want a fly or two? What about [a] hat? Remember how your old Mother watches the post.'[24]

He was good at sports and aspired to be an actor, which was encouraged by Bright. When summer 1914 approached, George, at nineteen, was preparing to go to Clare College, Cambridge. Chavelita seemed stimulated by the heightening international crisis. She went to Trafalgar Square after war had been declared and described

> girls lost to all decency screaming and waving flags to every drunken lout … I wish in some ways they could share the slaughter – I could do with less of them. An odd idea came to me today. It wouldn't be half bad patriotism for every girl to "lie with her lover," to use the old term, and chance the begetting of a man to replace him.[25]

George returned home to discuss what he should do. Chavelita was more in favour of George's volunteering to fight than was Bright, who perhaps understood the dangers better than she did. Bright was 'negative, makes it very difficult', she wrote.[26] George wrote to the War Office offering his services on 10 August, and was at home with Chavelita when he received a telegram the following day telling him to report to a military board, where he was selected for Sandhurst to train as a machine-gun officer. He died on 26 September 1915 on the second day of the Battle of Loos, the biggest British attack of the year. He was holding a captured German trench, almost exactly two months before his twentieth birthday.

On 5 October Chavelita received a letter from his commanding officer, who spoke, as is customary in these cases, of George's fearless bravery, his splendid qualities as an officer and the great loss to the regiment, and assured her that his death was instantaneous. As Bright wrote, 'her grief is heartrending.'[27] Ella D'Arcy now had the task, as she once had of congratulating Chavelita on George's birth, of commiserating her on the boy's death. She wrote, 'I shall not attempt to say anything consoling, for I know there is no consolation possible and nothing to be said.'[28] Chavelita wrote to John Lane, 'My boy's death broke the main-spring. I ended then, as far as ambition and desires are in question.'[29]

She may have lost ambition, though she did continue to write. The end of her theatre career was her last play, *Camilla States Her Case*, which opened at the Globe Theatre, Shaftesbury Avenue, on 7 January 1925. In it an ill-matched couple present their disagreements on stage. In order to provide evidence for a divorce, Camilla takes a woman friend who is a male imper-sonator to a hotel for a weekend. In common with her other works, there was a strong female lead expressing opinions not distant from those of Chavelita herself. By contrast *The Times* said the lead male was 'incredible, a poor dummy over whose shoulder Camilla shoots her sentiments at the gallery', but nevertheless called the play 'amusing'.[30] The glittering, witty Camilla's husband was presented as a 'pompous old bore', which may have, given Chavelita's tendency to put herself in her fiction, been a reflection of her opinion of Bright, who was indeed no conversationalist.[31] It closed on 14 February, which meant it had a respectable run, if not a great one.

In later life Chavelita became interested in her Irish genealogy, perhaps to gain from an imagined aristocratic lineage some of the ascendancy she had lost when she ceased to be such a famous writer. She made contact with distant members of her family, including the de Vere Whites, who were in fact her first cousins, though she referred to the son of the family, Terence, as her nephew. He was fourteen when he first met her and wrote, 'I remem-ber only that she talked in monologue and was very observant of our numerous failings . . . she complained of the low intellectual level of our parents' friends and this, indeed, if discouraging, was well-founded.' He remembered her as 'the neatest of women', who in this case wore a grey dress with white lace at the neck and sleeves.[32] Whatever she thought of the rest of her relatives, she formed a bond with young Terence and began a corre-spondence with him. As he grew older he became, while still affectionate, alert to her wiles and was suspicious at her perennial illnesses, when 'I found her always spry when I came to London, indefatigable in her talk and ready to go out to theatre or supper.'[33]

He was to witness 'the change in her husband's attitude to her genius – from worship to boredom; the failure of her plays; the absence of anyone who took an interest in her as a writer.'[34] She continued to write without success, noting in 1931 that her last book was 'rejected by 13 publishers.'[35] She and Bright led a comfortable life at Ridgmount Gardens, Bloomsbury, which had been their home since the 1920s (they moved flats within the development from 59 to 44 in 1937). They attended the theatre and dined at the Savoy Grill, often joined by clients of Golding Bright's, such as J. M. Barrie. Chavelita did not feel sufficiently stimulated, however, saying, 'Life is a lonely business for intelligent old women like myself.'[36] She wrote to M. P. Shiel in 1935:

> I keep brain alert with genealogy and languages . . . I may get memoirs done, I care so little, seems all so futile, had my son not crossed over at Loos, might have done, he was interested in me. A strangely beautiful person . . . I shall be 75 the end of the year and yet I find nothing new in the youth I meet.[37]

Golding Bright's business went with the start of the war in 1939 as the theatres were ordered to close. He fell ill in 1940; his sight failed and he tended to drowsiness, both of which were probably complications of diabetes. The couple remained in London during the Blitz despite an invitation from a correspondent for her to stay with them in the provinces, on which she wrote, 'Death by bombing infinitely preferable.'[38] In October 1940 they suffered an enemy attack. She wrote, 'Bomb dropped through shaft of lift at back next to us. Six casualties. A moaning man carried out, seven ambulances . . . at 2am we went home to wade through glass on stairs and passage.'[39] All their windows were blown out and for a time their flat had no water, gas or telephone.

Reginald Golding Bright died on 14 April 1941 with his head on Chavelita's shoulder. Bright had very much handled the business side of the marriage. With him gone, it was clear Chavelita's finances were uncertain as her investments were in Norway, currently under Nazi control, and Bright's share of his theatrical agency was now worth little. She sold Bright's shares, many of her books and much of her furniture. She went to live in boarding houses but was not popular as 'she could not refrain from lecturing her elderly and duller-witted companions,' De Vere White wrote; 'they did not always appreciate her dialectical manner.'[40]

The publisher Martin Secker enquired in 1945 about the chance that she might write her memoirs. She was positive and remarked, 'There is material for more than one book – I can recall 1864.'[41] She later wrote from the Inverness Court Hotel, Inverness Terrace W2, suggesting she write about the men she knew (not mentioning any women):

Have you ever had a book of pss to other people's biographies? They crowd in on me G. Moore, Le Gallienne, Stevenson and many others. Ibsen among the outsiders. Began with Keynotes, might end with Footnotes. My plans depend on whether I settle down to write or not. This life is dry rot.[42]

She suffered a minor stroke in summer 1945 and went to a nursing home at Ifield Park in Crawley, Sussex, where she died two months later on 12 August 1945 after a fall, at the age of 85. At the height of her fame she had written to John Lane:

I have good books perhaps great books in me yet and I am going to write them as I think best – and then find readers somewhere. We are getting off the rails Johnny, it is for you to keep on. I can go to County Infirmary if necessary, live on cheese and bread and spring water whilst I wait for tide to turn, but I won't trot the line of London so-called literary set, or even the best publisher in the world. I have always known how to live, I expect when it comes I'll know how to die.[43]

19

Suffragette Warrior

Evelyn Sharp would later think of the time when she crashed into Henry Nevinson in the Prince's Skating Rink on 30 December 1901 as the most momentous event of her personal life. Her professional career was on an even keel; she was keeping herself as a teacher but was also writing children's books, stories and journalism. She had previously corresponded with Nevinson, who was the literary editor of the *Daily Chronicle*, as she wrote reviews for the paper, though they had not met before. He had also contributed to the *Yellow Book*.

Nevinson had been a professional journalist since 1897 and had most recently been a correspondent reporting from the Boer War. Sharp's incipient relationship with him was paused when, at the end of April 1902, he sailed back to South Africa to report on the end of the war. When he returned, their friendship resumed in meetings at the skating rink in Montpelier Square; Sharp invited him to a tea party at her flat at nearby Mount Carmel Chambers in Dukes Lane, Kensington.

He described the evening on 19 September 1903 when he cycled over from his home in Hampstead to a literary gathering at her flat. Netta Syrett was there talking about plays, Nevinson recorded, but his main attention was on Evelyn, who was 'both pretty and wise – exquisite in every way she seemed, with eyes singularly brilliant'. He remained with her after the other guests had left. He notes he stayed 'unwittingly', so it was not his calculated intention to be alone with Evelyn Sharp, but she was not averse to his company. She told him, 'The first time I saw you I knew you wanted something you have never got.'[1] This was not, he must have surmised, the statement of a person who was endeavouring to resist intimacy. He said he left suddenly and later regretted it, so what happened specifically is uncertain, but they were to date their relationship from 1903 so presumably this was the year in which they first had sex, even if not on that day. He certainly brought her joy: 'Oh I am so glad I love someone who could never make me feel ashamed of what I have given him so freely,' she wrote to him, words preserved because he carefully transcribed them into his diary.[2] She described him as 'the man who made me a woman. But for you I should never have discovered the meaning of womanhood.'[3]

Soon after this encounter, Evelyn Sharp's life as a single, independent woman was interrupted when her father died in November 1903 and the 34-year-old spinster was expected to go and live with her mother. She sublet her flat and for most of 1904 lived in Brook Green, Hammersmith. She may well have felt, as did a character in one of her stories, 'the daughter has gone on, and the home hasn't.'[4] The story 'The Daughter who Stays at Home' describes the resistance to change in an all-woman household of an aged mother with an educated daughter, a cook and a maid. In response to her now home-bound existence, Sharp gave up her teaching posts and decided to rely on journalism for an income. She had already been writing short sketches and light factual articles for the *Daily Chronicle*, *Westminster Gazette*, *Pall Mall Gazette* and some of the weeklies and monthlies. Nevinson put her in contact with R. H. Gretton, London editor of the *Manchester Guardian*, to which she contributed for thirty years. It was a considerable sacrifice of independence to live with her mother, but she was not tied to the family as she had been as a child. In spring 1904 she visited Venice with fellow *Yellow Book* writer Lena Milman. Her meetings with Nevinson were necessarily restricted, but they maintained a voluminous correspondence.

Nevinson had his own family entanglements. He had married Margaret Wynne Jones on 1 April 1884. She was 26 and pregnant; he was 27. It seems to have been an unhappy marriage almost from the start, despite a shared outlook in radical politics. Margaret almost died in childbirth and did not adapt easily to motherhood. 'It is a terrible thing to be a mother, and in comparison, all other work and other vocations are as child's play,' she wrote.[5]

Nevinson wrote in his diary about his wife:

a fairly energetic woman, little suited to me, being by nature a traditional Catholic and conservative, always inclined to contradict me on every point and all occasions: eloquent, always on the melancholic and unhopeful side, but often humorous and full of observant stories ... My absences in wars were indifferent or pleasing to her and she never welcomed me back or cared to hear of my journeys: felt jealous of any success espec. in writing, for her chief ambition was to write.[6]

What Margaret thought of the situation is not known, except by omission, as in her autobiography *Life's Fitful Fever* (1926) she scarcely mentions Nevinson in the text and he is absent from the index. She had been a rent collector for a charity in the early years of their marriage, was to be elected a Poor Law Guardian in 1904, and later in her public career was to become the first woman Justice of the Peace to adjudicate at Criminal Petty Sessions. Her Anglo-Catholic beliefs probably precluded divorce, even after her children were grown up and no longer needed family support.

Evelyn Sharp can hardly have been ignorant of Nevinson's married state. What she was probably unaware of until quite far into their relationship was that she was not his only girlfriend, or even his favourite one. Nevinson had fallen in love with another radical woman, Irish nationalist Nannie Dryhurst. She was the same age as Nevinson and had married another Hampstead intellectual the same year in which he had married. Nevinson met her on 1 February 1892; he was in love with her for twenty years and probably after that also. In 1913 he was still calling his relationship with Nannie 'the event of my life'.[7] As he had by then been with Evelyn for ten years, this is hardly a ringing endorsement of their union.

During the time when Evelyn Sharp was living with her mother in 1904, Nevinson conceived a passion for Jane Brailsford, the wife of his radical journalist colleague Noel Brailsford. Nevinson had first met her in Macedonia the previous year. He was again on his travels in 1904–5, this time exposing the evils of slavery in Angola, and he dutifully wrote to 'The three' – Evelyn Sharp, Nannie Dryhurst and Jane Brailsford. They were all, like his wife, attractive, intelligent, politically committed women. How much Sharp knew of his promiscuous affections in 1904 cannot be said, but she certainly went through his diaries at one time, perhaps after his death when she may have been thinking of a biography.[8]

A life of challenging journalistic work for both of them was interspersed with outdoor activity. Sharp and Nevinson were members of a walking club of writers and artists who explored the country around London on Saturdays until, as Sharp wrote, 'a political cause and a world war' were to 'murder leisure'.[9] The first of these to consume Evelyn Sharp's life was the issue of votes for women, which was being invigorated by Emmeline Pankhurst and her family. Sharp was already a member of the conservative

London Society for Women's Suffrage when she encountered the 'fiery spirits' of the Women's Social and Political Union and had to decide 'whether to throw in my lot with them or to turn my back on the whole disturbing question'.[10] Her awakening to militancy came in autumn 1906 when she was at Tunbridge Wells reporting for the *Manchester Guardian* on the annual conference of the National Union of Women Workers.

The event took place on the day when several leading suffrage campaigners appeared in court in connection with a protest at the House of Commons. When the issue was discussed, the actress and novelist Elizabeth Robins took the platform and made a stirring speech whose effect on Evelyn Sharp was intensified by the fact that she had admired the actress often in her roles in Ibsen plays. Robins said she had come straight from the police court to give the conference an eyewitness account of the arrested women. The romance of rebellion mingled with the seduction of celebrity and Sharp's natural passion for justice. She was claimed. The effect on her life, Sharp said, 'was disastrous. From that moment I was not to know again for twelve years, if indeed ever again, what it meant to cease from mental strife; and I came to see with a horrible clarity why I had always hitherto shunned causes.'[11]

She was to join the WSPU, which had been founded in 1903, but it was not until 1906 that they were given the appellation 'suffragettes'. They embraced the term as radical activists with a taste for eye-catching spectacle. Their policy was the same as that of the law-abiding suffragists: votes for women with a property qualification, on the same basis that men were enfranchised. Their methods were different because they were angry at the slow progress towards women's suffrage despite repeated promises from parliamentarians. Evelyn Sharp associated her impatience for women to obtain the vote with her social concerns for the housing, education and nutrition of the poor, not doubting that women would use their votes for the betterment of society. She made her first speech in a meeting at Fulham Town Hall, sharing a stage with Christabel Pankhurst, and made a creditable showing. She later addressed every kind of meeting, indoor and outdoor, but never lost her distaste for the platform or the stomach cramps that accompanied public speaking for her.

Her mother was shocked by her new commitment and obliged Sharp to make a promise never to undertake actions that risked imprisonment. Her acceptance of this limitation meant she volunteered for 'every other disagreeable kind of service to the cause', many of them conducted on the street or on public platforms in rough areas.[12] This work gave her material for stories that went into the *Manchester Guardian* and *Daily Chronicle* and were collected in her book *Rebel Women*.

There was a militancy truce throughout most of 1910, when the book was published, when high hopes were placed on a 'Conciliation Bill' that would grant limited women's suffrage. At the end of the year militancy was back on the table when the government failed to find time for this Bill. The book was therefore written in the first stage of militancy, involving demonstrations, throwing stones at government buildings, imprisonment and hunger strikes. The destruction of private property, arson and bombings belong to a later phase of suffragette activity, from 1912 to 1914.

Rebel Women is perhaps the best representation of the life of suffragette foot soldiers, featuring scenes from everyday life such as 'The Women at the Gate', about a woman travelling on a bus to a suffragette demonstration, and 'To Prison While the Sun Shines', about a visit to the police court. Most, if not all, the stories are drawn from Sharp's own experience, such as 'Filling the War Chest', which is a first-person account of collecting for funds in the street outside a Tube station along with a lame newsboy and a wretched flower seller.

'Patrolling the Gutter' indicates how much of the suffragette work was conducted literally on the streets, in engaging with the public by marching with placards, running the suffragette shop or carrying a hoarding advertising a meeting along the roadway. Not all was without danger: in 'The Black

Evelyn Sharp (holding placard) outside Votes for Women shop, 1910.
The woman in black by the door is May Sinclair.

Spot of the Constituency' suffragettes talk about the missiles that have been hurled at them at public meetings, including banana skins, mud, chestnuts and fish. Sharp may well have been expressing her own thoughts when in 'At a Street Corner' the central character is giving a speech in the street and 'thinking regretfully of a happy past in which the chief aim of a well-ordered life had been to avoid doing anything that would attract attention'.[13]

Sharp developed the intolerance of the zealot in the early years and via the medium of her autobiography she was to apologize for 'my irritating conduct throughout these years', remarking on 'my dreadful fanaticism'.[14] A suggestion of this is given by her old friend Stephen Gwynn, who from 1906 was serving as a Member of Parliament. His positive recollection of her was shadowed by

> memories of Evelyn Sharp the suffragette, coming to me as a member of Parliament, to try to get what she considered fair play for some friend who had been run in by the police – and her big eyes blazing with indignation, and her voice trembling with resentment that she should have so far demeaned herself to ask of the enemy (for we were all that) even fair play for a friend.[15]

She had been bound by the pledge to her mother not to risk imprisonment, but Jane Sharp wrote absolving her of the promise at the end of 1910. Relieved of her pledge, on 11 November 1911 she duly became prisoner number 11528 at Holloway for smashing the windows of the War Office during a protest at the failure of the Conciliation Bill, in the company of some three hundred other women. She was again arrested in 1913 and this time went on hunger strike. She recounted not the horrors of hunger, but 'the feeling of being utterly deserted and left to die alone, which assailed me in the long hours as I lay there, a prey to apprehensions I could not define'.[16] When her mother received visits from friends offering condolences at her daughter's imprisonment, she 'reduced them to stupefaction' by her endorsement of her daughter and her cause.[17] Sharp was soon released unconditionally.

Margaret Nevinson was treasurer of the Women Writers' Suffrage League, of which Evelyn Sharp was vice president, so there were doubtless a few frosty encounters, perhaps when they and Henry Nevinson all attended an 'at home' for the League at the Waldorf Hotel on 4 May 1909.[18] It might be thought less than sororal behaviour to be having sex with the husband of another suffragette, but if Sharp, or Margaret Nevinson, had any comment to make on their situation it is not recorded. All three wrote autobiographies, showing the usual lie by omission of such forms. In none is the question of this affair addressed; Evelyn Sharp is notably coy about Nevinson and never refers to Margaret. The lack of recognition is reciprocated in Margaret Nevinson's autobiography, which does not mention Sharp. Nevinson's three-volume autobiography mentions both women, but Evelyn many more times than Margaret.[19]

Sharp and other suffragettes physically put themselves into the political machine by interrupting the meetings of government ministers and storming Parliament, where they were literally manhandled by stewards or policemen. 'Little details like the tearing of a lace cuff or the rending of gathers in a skirt – our unpractical pre-war clothes added considerably to the indignation of ejection – seemed often to matter more than real injuries, which in most cases were not discovered until later.'[20] Nevinson recorded finding her after one action 'bruised and bleeding'.[21] He expressed his admiration for her to Sidney Webb:

> She has one of the most beautiful minds I know – always going full gallop, as you see from her eyes, but very often in regions beyond the moon, when it takes a few seconds to return. At times she is the very best speaker among the suffragettes, and Holloway knows her, for savage rage tears her heart.[22]

Her time was rarely clear enough for her to write books, and she mainly occupied herself with journalism and with suffragette activism. She described for Elizabeth Robins, who was now a friend, a march from Kingsway to Holloway when the police let the suffragettes proceed without an escort, 'they evidently hoped the crowd would break us up,' but the public cheered them the whole way.

> Today we shall be fighting again for free speech, in Trafalgar Square and Hyde Park. Who am I to be doing all these ugly things when I only long for solitude and a fairy tale to write? I don't know, I don't know. I only know I shall go on till I drop, and so will hundreds of others whose names will not be known.[23]

Evelyn Sharp played a leading role in the drama of the WSPU when police arrived at their Clements Inn headquarters at 9.30 p.m. on 5 March 1912. They had come to arrest prominent suffragette campaigners Emmeline and Frederick Pethick-Lawrence, together with Christabel Pankhurst, who had until recently been living at Clements Inn but was doing so no longer and so escaped seizure. Frederick realized Sharp was fully capable of taking over their newspaper, *Votes for Women*, and he left it in her hands the day before that week's issue went to press.

Immediately after the Pethick-Lawrences had been taken into custody, Sharp went straight to Christabel Pankhurst's flat to warn her. Christabel disguised herself as a nurse and escaped to Paris. Evelyn Sharp took a cheque signed by Christabel transferring all the WSPU's funds so they could not be seized by the state. The money was deposited into the account of the physicist Hertha Ayrton and then transferred abroad.

Now the WSPU was safe and Sharp was the editor of *Votes for Women*, which was owned by the Pethick-Lawrences. They served time in prison, hunger-struck and were forcibly fed, but after they were released there was no thanks for their sacrifice. They were expelled from the WSPU for arguing that the policy of destruction of private property was both immoral and strategically counterproductive. 'A kind of grim and fanatical bitterness had crept into the struggle,' Sharp commented in her autobiography.[24] She neglects to detail this fissure between the leaders of the movement, but there is little doubt of her sympathies as she continued editing *Votes for Women* and maintained her association with the Pethick-Lawrences after they split from the Pankhursts.

Along with Nevinson and other long-time campaigners, Sharp was to found the United Suffragists early in 1914; the Pethick-Lawrences soon joined. The new organization attempted to heal divisions by being open to both men and women, militant and non-militant suffragists. In August 1914, however, both the militant suffragettes and constitutional suffragists downed banners and suspended all activity in support of the war effort.

Sharp, working through the medium of the United Suffragists and *Votes for Women*, was prepared to continue the campaign, albeit low key, through the war years. As part of her continued resistance she refused to pay income tax, saying, 'a war fought to save democracy did not seem to me to provide the best reason for supporting the principle of taxation without representation.'[25] She consequently came home one day in 1917 to find a bailiff in her flat. All her possessions, excepting her clothes and her bed, were then taken away, her mail was intercepted, her telephone was cut off and her gas and electricity were discontinued, though both supply companies allowed these to be restored under a friend's guarantee. Friends also clubbed together to buy back her furniture when it went up for sale.

She was proved correct in maintaining suffrage activity during the war. Far from being postponed because of the war, a limited franchise for women was achieved during it, as part of the Representation of the People Act 1918, which also guaranteed universal manhood suffrage. Sharp felt it was the happiest moment of her life to walk up Whitehall with Nevinson on the evening of 6 February 1918 when the Royal Assent was given. She had lived 'to see the triumph of a "lost" cause for which we had suffered much and would have sacrificed everything'.[26]

Her mother's increasing understanding of Evelyn Sharp's role in the suffrage campaign meant they had a better relationship nearing the end of her life than at any other time. They had little time to enjoy it, however. Jane Sharp died after a stroke in February 1915. Evelyn's elder brother Lewen, an architect, had died in October 1914. The death of older family members left her now more at the behest of importunate siblings. Her father had died leaving Evelyn and her sister Ethel's husband as trustees of a complicated trust fund. The fund was unequally divided so that Algernon was discriminated against because he had become a Roman Catholic. This might not have been such a problem had he been financially viable, but he was bankrupt and called upon Evelyn and Nevinson to pay off money lenders and pay his rent. Her younger brother Lancelot, back to drinking after a period of sobriety, also expected his sister to subsidize him. Lancelot later threatened to sue her for mismanagement of the family trust, in which action he was supported by her sister Ethel. She spoke of being able to trace 'all the bitterness of my own soul' to being born in the 'wrong family'.[27] Nevinson, whose home was hardly a model of domestic bliss, spoke of her 'hopeless family'.[28]

As a journalist, she had her great times in the 1920s when she was on the staff of the *Daily Herald*. She reported on the chaos of Ireland in the desperate last years of British rule in 1920–21. She would not stay with radicals lest she put them in danger, kept no diary or notes and carried essential information in her shoes. She described the raids, looting and burnings committed by the specially recruited British force, the 'Black and Tans'. She noted that they persuaded even those who had not previously supported Sinn Féin to do so. Peace, she argued, was not being restored; government excesses were producing precisely the opposite effect from that intended.

Similarly, she argued that the harsh treatment of Germany after the Great War would not cow the population but would foment another war. Sharp had become increasingly pacifist during the war and afterwards visited the previous foes, working for the Society of Friends (Quakers), whose fairness and commitment to peace had long impressed her. She went to Germany as part of the Quaker mission to alleviate hunger caused by the blockade, wartime disruption and the influenza pandemic. She returned in 1923 with Nevinson, she writing for the *Daily Herald*, he for the *Manchester Guardian*, both of them reporting on conditions in the Ruhr region following the French and Belgian occupation.

Sharp was one of those 'thrilled at the news of the Russian revolution' in November 1917 and became a founder member of the '1917 Club', where politics, modern art and literature were discussed.[29] She felt communism was no more than basic Christianity but would not join the Communist Party because it would not embrace pacifism. She visited the Soviet Union in January 1922 with the Friends Relief Committee, going to the Volga region where the civil war and harvest failures had reduced large parts of the country to starvation. She wrote movingly of the starving or malnourished children she encountered, and back home she toured to lecture on her adventures to raise money for famine relief.

She turned her experiences into utopian fiction in *Somewhere in Christendom: A Fantasy*, published in 1919. It describes the war-ravaged nation of Ethuria where the nation is inspired by a female prophet, who puts childbirth and the family at the centre of a revolutionary nation in which there are no armed forces or clergy and vegetarianism is the norm. It did not sell well; as she wrote to Stanley Unwin, 'I am sorry the book has been such a complete failure, as individuals are so curiously enthusiastic about it; and it is a very serious thing for me to have a book out, after all these years, that is not a success.'[30] She had confidence in the material, however, which she later worked into a play, *But Why Not?* She gave a reading of it in October 1923 that Ella D'Arcy attended, so at least that one of her *Yellow Book* friendships survived the stage of militancy that had alienated others.[31]

From May 1922 she contributed to the daily feature in the *Manchester Guardian* 'on subjects which are of special interest to women' that became the Women's Page.[32] This celebration of women's journalism seems progressive, but Sharp was a woman who had been writing journalism since the beginning of the century, including her challenging foreign reporting. Now her work, by virtue of her gender, was to be relegated to a specialist column which, to add injury, was shorter and therefore less well paid than non-women's page pieces. This did not seem like progress.

She was asked by her friend Bertha Ayrton to write a biography of her mother, Hertha Ayrton, in whose house on Norfolk Square in Paddington she had recuperated after being imprisoned. She wrote in December 1924

Evelyn Sharp, 1933, pencil drawing by William Rothenstein.

to Chatto & Windus, who seemingly gave encouragement as she was later writing about length and illustrations.[33] The work was completed by the following November but she wrote:

> I am naturally very disappointed that you feel you cannot make me an offer for the publication of my biography of Mrs Hertha Ayrton. As I have spent a year in writing it, I wonder if you could give me some idea as to why you think it would not repay publication. It

would help me very much to know what you feel is wrong with it, before I send it elsewhere.[34]

It was published in March 1926 by Edward Arnold at 15 shillings for three hundred pages. It had been a struggle for Sharp, and probably more a duty than a labour of love.

More appropriately to her abilities, she wrote *The London Child* in 1927, a study expanding on her commitment to child welfare and her interest in child psychology. The *Times Literary Supplement* reviewer praised its accuracy but urged that she 'lecture us with less enthusiastic sweetness'.[35] She also wrote *Here We Go Round: The Story of the Dance* about the country dance revival that was being promoted by her brother Cecil Sharp. Both she and Nevinson became members of the English Folk Dance Society national committee, becoming particularly active after her brother's death in 1924. To Evelyn's distress, Nevinson used dance as an occasion for meeting younger women. In 1930 he was 74, and she was 61. Evelyn suspected Nevinson was having a relationship with Maud Karpeles, formerly Cecil Sharp's companion in dance and folk music research, who was in her forties. Nevinson took time out after a work trip to America to travel to Canada with Karpeles and others who were on a folk dancing tour of the country.

Margaret Nevinson became ill in the late 1920s. A period of physical ill health was followed by mental illness in which she believed there was a plot to murder her. At one time she attempted suicide in a bath. It was a miserable, protracted end to an unhappy marriage; she was to die at home in Hampstead on 8 June 1932. Within two weeks Sharp and Nevinson were discussing their future and were seen out and about looking happy together, which was commented on as being in somewhat bad taste.

They married at Hampstead Register Office on 18 January 1933, after politely refusing Prime Minister Ramsay MacDonald's offer to be best man, out of both their wish to have a private ceremony (when his appearance would have made it a very public one) and suspicion of his current politics. Sharp moved into Nevinson's home at 4 Downside Crescent, Hampstead, and worked on her memoir, *Unfinished Adventure*, whose narrative ends on 18 January 1933, noting that her latest adventure would be marriage. 'I shall not sail alone,' she wrote.[36]

Even with Margaret dead, however, Evelyn had not entered a cheery family. Nevinson did not get on with his musical daughter, Philippa, and his artist son, Richard (famous as C.R.W. Nevinson), did not get on with anyone. Within a year Nevinson's health had failed; he had diabetes and a hernia. They stayed activists, however – they were at the inaugural meeting of the National Council for Civil Liberties in 1934. Both were also active in the international writers' movement English PEN.

With a decline in paid work, the income of the Nevinsons fell but Evelyn still showed the ability to embark on new creative directions. At 67 she was writing the libretto for Ralph Vaughan Williams's *The Poisoned Kiss*, which was performed in Cambridge on 1 May 1936 and then transferred to Sadler's Wells. They stayed at home during the Blitz of 1940 with blacked-out windows and a sheltered room on the ground floor so they did not have to rush to Belsize Park and take shelter with hundreds of others. No precautions could withstand a direct hit, however. Three bombs fell nearby on 8 September, the second day of the Blitz, damaging windows and a ceiling; another exploded close by a month later. They were directly hit on 13 October at 7.30 p.m. when a bomb in a nearby garden blew out all their windows and the base of a bomb hit their roof. Minutes later three houses were blown up on the adjoining street, Haverstock Hill. Evelyn Sharp, Nevinson and their maid Marguerite Scott were in the kitchen amid the dust, splintered glass and acrid smoke. They had wished to stay in London during the war, but with holes in the roof and gas and water supplies cut they had to move.

They moved in with folk-dancing friends in the country, then to Chipping Campden in the Cotswolds. Evelyn was used to village life but her husband chafed at the quietness of the countryside after the activity of London. His days of action, however, were over. He had grown thin and Evelyn pushed him around in a bath chair. She wrote, 'I know he could never be happy again, a hopeless invalid when he loathed being dependent, in a continuous war in which he could take no part.'[37] He suffered several falls that sent him to bed, after which he would rally and rise, only to fall again.

Finally, on Saturday 8 November 1941, ill with diabetes and uraemia, he was losing consciousness and becoming delirious. Evelyn stayed by his side. 'But on Sunday he went into a semi-conscious state,' she wrote,

> knowing me but that was all. Sunday morning, Armistice Sunday the 9th, he just spoke to me in the early morning and smiled and corrected me in a whisper when I purposely misquoted a stanza of the 'Ancient Mariner' (an old joke between us) and that was the last time he spoke or noticed anything. He just slept quietly all day, and at 6.15, with his hand in mine, he stopped breathing.[38]

She wrote to friends, 'I tell myself it was better he should go, still mentally alert, with an article half-finished and two books just out. But oh, I am desolate! Our friendship lasted forty years, and we were married just 8½ of it. But it is the long friendship that I miss.'[39] There were more than 330 letters from friends and admirers of Nevinson, and obituaries in all the main newspapers, though *The Times* had dusted off a previously written one that mentioned his wife Margaret, but not Evelyn.

She returned to Hampstead to stay with neighbours in Downside Crescent while she sorted out her stricken house. It was a miserable time but, as she said with her typical grasp of perspective, 'When the world is behaving so horribly what does it matter if one person has stopped being happy?'[40] She kept enough furniture and books for her own use and in December 1941 took them to a first-floor flat in Young Street, Kensington. The house was sold for £650, divided between Evelyn and Nevinson's two children.

She worked on organizing Nevinson's papers, editing a last book of his work, and wrote reviews, obituaries and features. On 26 June 1942 she was invited to broadcast about Ibsen on the BBC Home Service.

She suffered a bout of flu in 1943 and then a breakdown in health, a result of the stress of the previous years as well as the continuing misery of being a committed pacifist in a world war. In her mid-seventies she was still working, but her sight was failing. She stayed with friends, then alone and then in nursing homes for the final seven years of her life. She died on 17 June 1955 aged 85, at the Methuen Nursing Home in Gunnersbury Avenue, Ealing, having outlived most of her friends and all the *Yellow Book* women.

Her *Times* obituary, under the heading 'Miss Evelyn Sharp', lauded an 'author, journalist and crusader for a variety of social and humane causes'.[41] It mentioned her time with the *Yellow Book*, women's suffrage and her travels as a journalist. It failed to celebrate her real achievement: Evelyn Sharp had the resilience of a survivor, which saw her through from the young woman who left home to seek her fortune in 1894 to the imprisoned suffragette and the reporter from famine regions, and her long, long wait for the complete attention of the man she loved.

20

The Ship with Black Sails

At the beginning of the new century Ethel Colburn Mayne prepared for her second venture to London. This time, she determined, she would plan her way and it would not end in humiliation. On one of her visits to the capital, probably staying with Violet Hunt, she was introduced to Charles Francis Cazenove of the Literary Agency of London, who offered to represent her. Agents were relatively new on the literary scene, dating from the last quarter of the nineteenth century. As befits a youthful profession, Cazenove was himself 33 in 1903, which was five years younger than Mayne, and he was eager to push new talent.

Charles Mayne's pension was adequate to support his small family, but Ethel was still obliged, despite her maturity, to ask her father for money. Gaining an agent was a step towards independence, and an adult understanding of the marketplace of literature. She wrote to Cazenove from Cork to suggest outlets for her work, putting forward foreign books that deserved to be translated and asking whether there were jobs she could do to make money. She attempted to break into the lucrative market for plays in 1904 by collaborating on one play and writing two others. None found a producer and she returned to fiction.

In May 1905 she returned to South Kensington to rent a flat at 11 Cecil Court, Hollywood Road, with her sister Violet, who was ten years younger than her. It was within walking distance of Cromwell Road, the former home of the Harlands. The whole family was to move to London: the 1911 census enumerator found retired magistrate Charles Mayne with his family – Ethel, who was 46, and son Edward, 42 – living at 11 Holland Road, Kensington, with their 22-year-old servant, Eileen Carroll from Tipperary. Violet had married and moved to Bedford, so Ethel was filling the role of the spinster daughter who ran the household for her 71-year-old father.

Her letters to Cazenove indicate the work of an agent included some very practical administration, at least as far as Mayne was concerned. A postcard said she had corrected all the manuscripts: '*Do* hurry up the typist. I want to have it done and finished and paid for!! ... must I correct *all three* typescripts?' She was therefore relying on another person to type the material and was impatient of the technical details of her work.[1]

Mayne treated him as a friend; on 14 November 1907 she was asking Cazenove to buy her two 10s 6*d* tickets for a Covent Garden performance.[2] In another letter she was chatting about the problem of managing servants and inviting him to tea with Violet Hunt. Sometimes she unburdened herself to him: 'I have lost heart about myself absolutely. Perhaps it will prove to be only a phase – but the phase is in full force at present. I always told you I should be the worst client you ever had – and you see that I am.'[3]

In 1906 and 1907 she translated from the German *The Confessions of a Princess*, an anonymous 'sensational' work, and from the French *The Diary of a Lost One* by Margarete Boehme. In neither case did she want her name on the title page. Both three-hundred-page novels sold well and went into several editions, but she received a flat fee of less than £50 each.[4] She chatted with Cazenove about the German translation:

> I am glad that the translation need not be verbatim. Indeed, it could not have been, for the charming lady is quite unprintable (in English) at moments! ... I think I know what is possible and what isn't; you know I have no excess of prudery in these matters; but one has to remember the British Public – and indeed the whole of the book is very 'Gallic' to put it flatteringly, for German has a grossness that French nearly always escapes. But it is most amusing.[5]

A correspondence with him about another translation shows her business mind: 'I would undertake it for 10/- a thousand words ... this would make it about £60 ... it seems very long for a novel, 119,427 words – only 500 off 120,000. But I would do it for £55 if they paid for the typing! Which comes to exactly £5! At 10*d* a thousand.'[6] Further down the chain, it appears, another woman was getting paid less than a shilling per thousand words for typing Maynes's not markedly legible cursive script.

Hack work was hopefully behind Mayne after 1908 when Cazenove obtained a three-novel deal for her with Chapman and Hall, whose managing director was her old *Yellow Book* colleague Arthur Waugh. He had looked at a book she called 'Miss', which he eventually published in May 1908 as

The Fourth Ship. This is a complex work dealing with the lives of women from the 1850s to the '90s, seen from the point of view of Josie Lawrence, an Irish provincial girl. She yearns for some kind of independence but is never sure exactly what this entails, though she wants to earn her own living. The first third of the novel is devoted to her, the second to Millicent North, a brilliant pianist who is frustrated in her attempt to become a music teacher and instead settles for marriage to Philip Maryon, a young police officer. Part three is devoted to the lives of the three daughters of this union, notably of Christabel, whose attitudes and name, which she shares with that of the suffragette leader, suggest her life will be directed under her own agency. The characteristic Mayne touch of 'the dark underside of motherhood' in this book comes from the self-hating Millicent's emotional blackmail of her daughters, and her undermining of them to their friends.[7] The novel carries the epigraph: 'There are three ships that we all watch for – the golden-sailed *Love*; the ship with white sails called *The Little Child*; the *Success* with rosy sails. For some of us all come home; for some one or the other, for some,

Cover of Ethel Colburn
Mayne, *The Fourth Ship*
(1908).

again, none of these comes home.' It was the best received of Mayne's novels and was praised by the serious reviewers.

Two years later Chapman and Hall published her second collection of stories, *Things That No One Tells*, its title being an apt description of the contents of the stories. In 'Madeline Annesley', for example, in what is perhaps a suicide note, certainly one read by her lover after the eponymous heroine is dead, she ponders feminine virtue: 'I suppose a man never quite believes how much less cold and – shall I say "good"? a woman is than all her lessons of repression have made her seem. You say that you "ruined" me: I say that you made me . . . I would lose anything rather than that memory.'[8]

Mayne's enduring reputation was based on her stories, of which she produced four more volumes between 1917 and 1925: *Come In, Blindman, Nine of Hearts* and *Inner Circle*. There were two other novels but these long works show a structural weakness that is not evident in the stories. She recognized her limitations and wrote:

> I always feel that once the latest is finished, I shall never write another!! But in my mind is a plot for one all the same – I can hardly say 'a plot' for plots refuse to come to me, it is always a character which lures me to write about it – and 'the things that no one sees' always seem to me the dramatic things![9]

Mayne's characterization is strong and her insights superb, but her characters never inhabit situations worthy of them – an apt description of her life. She was at the height of her powers, but though translation and biographical work poured in, the ship of success with its rosy sails eluded her.

Away from her gloomy and unfulfilled fictional characters, Mayne wrote romantic biography with notable early success with *Enchanters of Men*, a study of mistresses, courtesans and actresses in earlier centuries. At last seeing a market, she began writing factual work on Regency themes, which reached a high point with her two-volume life of Byron in 1912, which *The Times*, in the following decade, called 'one of the most brilliant biographies of our age'.[10]

It was followed in 1929 by *The Life of Lady Byron*, which definitively interpreted Byron's relationship with Augusta Leigh, his half-sister, as being sexual and therefore incestuous, and the reason why Byron's separation from his wife was irrevocable. Reviewers noted, 'Miss Mayne has not only vindicated Lady Bryon in this book; she has made it impossible for anyone not to vindicate her in the future . . . brilliantly intuitive and sublimely fair,' and 'Lady Byron will be viewed for ever after as Miss Mayne has seen her.'[11]

A Shelley descendant, Richard Edgcumbe, who himself had edited a family diary, felt moved to give her a telling off:

> I assure you that the documents published by Lord Lovelace are by no means 'unassailable'. You should not, I think, pass judgement upon a matter of which you have only heard scrappy evidence (on both sides) without a far deeper (I mean more prolonged) study than it is possible that you have given to it. I have been at it for forty years, and have still much to learn.[12]

Mayne had learned how to turn a literary spat into publicity for her work, and sent the letters on to the literary journalist Clement Shorter, knowing of his interest in the subject and with the hope that 'if you should think of writing about it in the *Sphere* or the *Sketch*, and were at all inclined to give it space, the Press Picture Agency at Westminster have some very nice photographs of me. Forgive my presumption . . .'[13]

Her old rival Ella D'Arcy had been unsuccessfully trying to get her book on Shelley published before translating Maurois' *Ariel* in 1924, something of which Mayne cannot have been unaware. However much Mayne knew, no comment is recorded. Ella D'Arcy's stories appeared in the *English Review*, over which Mayne had some influence via her friendship with its editor Ford Maddox Hueffer (later Ford) and with Douglas Goldring, who worked on the journal. Mayne was clearly not so spiteful as to blackball her erstwhile enemy, presuming she had the power to do so.

The work she put into the two-volume Byron biography meant she used up her financial resources, as she wrote to Cazenove, 'I want some quickly done and quickly *paid* work most *horribly*! Really and truly, I am hard-up to the last degree, and will work more than I have done for ages. You see I have had such a long time on Byron, and that of course leaves me short of cash.'[14]

A contributory problem was the appearance of a tranche of previously private letters from Lady Lovelace late in the book's development. This required alterations that were so late in the process Mayne had to pay for them from money owing on delivery of the manuscript. She was paid the residue of her advance but Cazenove took his 10 per cent fee from the full amount. She wrote to him that she was considering whether I can any longer afford myself the luxury of relationship with the agency . . . I received £1.19.0 from Methuen from the balance owing to me of £10; and from that sum, you, taking 'fee ten per cent commission' for the agency deduct £1.0.0. You will answer, of course that it is from the whole sum that you deduct this commission.[15]

Their relationship was at an end: he waived the six months' notice; if she wanted to go, he would not stop her. She was resigned to the parting, if regretfully, writing, 'It is most unhappy, and I regret it from the bottom of my heart. Right or wrong, that is the way I feel, and so, an end.'[16] She was later represented by A. P. Watt, but her fiction was always a challenge to sell. Arthur Waugh wrote to Watt in 1922 expressing his 'regret' at being unable to take on a new volume of stories, but 'the very delicacy and restraint of her work has stood in the way of its making a popular appeal. She has never been what the Americans call a really paying proposition, and now that the cost of production has increased so seriously, her last book made rather a heavy loss.'[17]

She stayed close to Violet Hunt and often visited South Lodge, where it was said that Hunt's 'real heart was with the novelists, who flocked around her,' referencing May Sinclair and Ethel Colburn Mayne among others.[18] Ford Madox Ford lived with Hunt from 1910 to 1918 (in the early part of the period as Hueffer). Mayne was close enough to be brought into their shabby personal arrangements. She and another friend (and *Yellow Book* contributor) Dollie Radford consulted a lawyer to see whether Ford's ploy of divorcing his wife under German law would leave him free to marry Hunt. In fact, they discovered, such a marriage might well be legal in Germany but would probably be bigamous in England.[19]

After enlisting as a lieutenant in the Welsh Regiment, Ford gave a going away party on 16 August 1915 at South Lodge on the eve of leaving for France. Various guests including Ethel Colburn Mayne, Wyndham Lewis, Ezra Pound, W. L. George and May Sinclair kept Ford and Violet from quarrelling, at least until it was time for them to leave. When he finally deserted Hunt, according to her biographer, 'he made arrangements for her close friend Ethel Colburn Mayne to present her with a *fait accompli* once he had left London.'[20]

Mayne's solid reputation and skill in French led to her being invited to serve in the 1920s and '30s on the English Committee of the Femina Vie Heureuse Prize, along with *Yellow Book* colleagues Netta Syrett and

Ella Hepworth Dixon. During 1924–5 she was president of meetings at the Institut Français. The minutes record common-sense literary views. Of a book that Netta Syrett favoured, Mayne said: 'I thought it was well written but I don't think it is a book for us to send to France. It is common-place and the end is quite unbelievable.'[21]

She was involved in the selection of some important works including E. M. Forster's *A Passage to India*, Virginia Woolf's *To the Lighthouse*, Richard Hughes's *A High Wind in Jamaica* and Stella Gibbons's *Cold Comfort Farm*. She was more acerbic, not to say tetchy, in her pronouncements as time went on, saying of Robert Graves's *Count Belisarius* in 1939, 'I shan't read it,' and at the next meeting: 'I haven't read it and I never shall.'[22] It was, nevertheless, selected.

Her works were included in three volumes of *Georgian Stories*, the representative anthology edited by Arthur Waugh. In 1922 her 'Lovell's Meeting' was published alongside stories by Violet Hunt, E. M. Forster, Algernon Blackwood, Katherine Mansfield, D. H. Lawrence, May Sinclair and Mayne's friend Mary Butts. Butts, a story writer and poet who may have been introduced to Mayne by Violet Hunt, was 25 years her junior. They knew each other well at least from 1918 when Mayne was one of the witnesses to Butts's marriage to the poet John Rodker. The relationship was warm, with Mayne writing to her as 'Darling Mary' with 'all my love, dearest', and noting, 'I think of you always, even though I mightn't say so. Ethel.'[23] The affection was not one-sided; Butts wrote in her journal of dinner with Ethel, 'not only the argument and the voice, but all of her, the impact of her love and wit and imagination'.[24]

Despite the restraint of her work, Mayne was no prude: she had no apparent criticism of Butts leaving her husband to take up with a painter, Cecil Maitland, with whom she explored opium and mysticism in the circles of Aleister Crowley. The depth of their friendship and her keen insight into her own plight is shown in a letter to Butts:

Oh, Mary, I wish you were here to let me weep on your breast for my lost self!! I cannot see myself ever writing anything of my own again and it kills me. It's not because I am too old, too out of the movement (such as it is) – no, it's that my experience has not been rich enough, it has only been of what I may not now write of – the emotional life, the life of the sense and the spirit. It's not enough. When I think of a theme, only some variant of that presents itself; I have a book in my mind now on the differences between such women as you, for instance, and myself – so akin in everything that signifies, and yet so outwardly different. But I don't find the way to frame it; I am so analytical and there are so many things to be done besides analysis. Do you think I ever shall find the frame or do you think that, in that sense, I am too old? I mean for the sustained effort? Is that why I shrink?[25]

She tried to help her friend, not always to great effect, complaining that 'the fools on the Femina committee' had voted Butts's book *The Death of Felicity Taverner* off the final list, despite Mayne's and Hunt's urging 'that they were making a hideous mistake'. She wrote to Butts, 'I had set my heart on at least sending Felicity to France.'[26]

She always described herself as Irish but had no apparent interest in politics and did not write about the conflicts that raged in her country for almost the whole of her life. Part of the family income came from an Irish estate that was so mortgaged as to be virtually valueless and which, after the founding of the Irish Free State in 1922, was compulsorily purchased. The family was left with a hope of compensation at some time in the future.

Charles Mayne's death on 8 January 1927 was a double blow as it also meant the loss of his pension. After her father's death she moved from fashionable Holland Road, Kensington, to various Richmond and Twickenham addresses. In the middle of January 1931 she ran out of headed paper and was presumably too poor to have more printed for her current address, 8 Spring Terrace, Sheen Road, Richmond, so she took to using cheap, lined letter paper. Her brother-in-law died in 1934 and her sister, Violet Cotter, and Violet's son Terence, who had been born in 1911, were living with her in the late 1930s.

Mayne was saved from penury by the poet Sylvia Lynd (incidentally, the daughter of Nannie Dryhurst, Evelyn Sharp's rival for Nevinson's love). Lynd applied to the Royal Literary Fund on 11 January 1927, showing detailed knowledge of Mayne's condition:

I know that for many years Miss Mayne has viewed her future with anxiety . . . now solely dependent on literary work and she is neither young nor strong. She began her literary career as a contributor to the *Yellow Book* in 1895, since then she has published several novels and books of short stories, all of which have added to her reputation (many critics consider her, since Katherine Mansfield's death, the best English short story writer); but she was not written a 'best seller' and unless a book is a best seller ... it brings its author very little money even if admired and quite 'successful'.

She gave Mayne's average literary earnings as about £27 per year. Another submission estimated she would receive about £45 from her father's estate, which suggests considerably lowered circumstances at the end of his life.[27]

The prime minister, Stanley Baldwin, asked for a couple of specimens of her work, notably the life of Byron. An award of £85 a year was offered on 16 March 1927 for 'services to literature'. Twenty years later she was still waiting for the sum from the compulsorily purchased Irish estate and she wrote to the Royal Literary Fund, which awarded her a grant of £150 in two annual instalments in May 1939. It was 'less than a farm labourer's pre-war wage', as a friend commented.[28]

As she became older her confidence, never her strong suit, dwindled. At the age of 75 in 1940 she offered a book to Macmillan:

> Would you at all care to consider a volume of short stories from me? I used to be thought a good hand at them! ... I don't greatly hope for an encouraging answer in these days, but as I feel that the stories are really good, and as I've had them ready for some time, I take a chance.[29]

Harold Macmillan himself wrote the rejection letter: 'the difficulties of wartime publishing added to the hard time short story collections have recently had presenting too big an obstacle for us to overcome. I am sorry for your work has a distinction which we should have been glad to associate with our list.'[30] The only book of hers they did publish, *A Regency Chapter: Lady Bessborough and Her Friendships* of 1939, recovered only half the advance to her of £150.[31]

Her literary output dried up stream by stream: fiction ran out first, then the biographical history; her last translation had been in 1932. Her friends too began to fall away: Mary Butts died in March 1937 from a ruptured appendix; Violet Hunt went into a decline. Norah Hoult, a young Irish writer who knew both Mayne and Hunt, wrote a thinly veiled book about Hunt's final years and descent into dementia, *There Were No Windows*. In it, Mayne, in the character of 'Edith', takes a long bus journey to visit Hunt in South Lodge, where they had enjoyed such witty conversations in the early years of the century. She dreads the ordeal of Sunday lunch, and the state to which her friend has fallen: 'to think of her becoming such a bore, and such a dreary lachrymose bore!'[32] Her old friend's repetitions infuriate her, as do her paranoid suspicions about the sex life of the single servant she has looking after her. She is no longer the vivacious literary hostess, but 'a drooling, not too clean, semi-deranged old woman.'[33]

The Mayne character fears air raids: not that they might kill her, but that death by bombing would be 'an ill-conditioned, inelegant affair.'[34] Mayne and her invalid sister had already packed to make a quick escape if the bombs were to fall on Welby House, 25 The Avenue, Twickenham, where they had been living since 1937. On 30 September 1940, in the fourth week of the London Blitz, a nearby property to theirs was hit by a high-explosive shell and 25 The Avenue suffered category B damage – so serious it would have to be demolished. Ethel and Violet, now 75 and 65, were brought out by emergency workers and admitted to the West Middlesex Hospital at 5 a.m.[35] After a six-week stay in hospital for Mayne (two weeks for Violet) they moved to a nursing home in Torquay, near to where their two brothers lived. Ethel Colburn Mayne finally saw the fourth ship, the ship with black sails, on 30 April 1941 at the age of 76 at the Trinity nursing home when she died of heart failure.

Obituarists recognized her primarily as a short story writer, the *Times Literary Supplement* writer noting that her last story collections were 'masterpieces of an austere art which rejects everything but the essence of the psychological situation.'[36] *The Times* remarked on 'her intense sympathy with and understanding of humanity.'[37]

Her own elegy, and a striking reminder of the way the view from the *Yellow Book* permeated her life in art, came in a piece for Ezra Pound's *Little Review*, a journal which carried the strapline, 'Making no compromise with the public taste'. She wrote:

> You found yourself in the enchanted place and never knew how you got there. Was it better than the 'real' place? You often thought it was, and people told you you were decadent, that that was decadence – to find the words about it better than the thing itself. You said you didn't care; if this were decadence you were glad to be a decadent. It was a time, believe me, worth the living in.[38]

APPENDIX:
LIST OF ALL WOMEN WRITERS
FOR THE *YELLOW BOOK*

The purpose of *Decadent Women* is to give life and voice to some of the forgotten women writers in the *Yellow Book*. The criterion was that they should be writers of undoubted quality, that they should not have had a biography written about them before the project started, and there should be sufficient surviving documents or testimonies to allow their authentic voices to be heard. Charlotte Mew was not originally included as one of the principal characters because of the 1984 biography of her by Penelope Fitzgerald, but she refused to stay out.

The first list is of women who have a significant role in *Decadent Women: Yellow Book Lives*, by their most commonly used writing name.

Gabriela Cunninghame Graham (1859–1906), née Caroline Horsfall, aka
    Gabrielle de la Balmondière
Olive Custance (1874–1944), married name Lady Alfred Douglas
Ella D'Arcy (1856/7–1937)
Mabel Dearmer (1872–1915), née Jessica Mabel White, as an illustrator in the
    Yellow Book
Ménie Muriel Dowie (1867–1945), married names Norman and FitzGerald
George Egerton (1859–1945), née Mary Chavelita Dunne, married names
    Clairmonte and Bright, 'Mrs Melville'
Leila Macdonald (1871–1944), married name Crackanthorpe
Ethel Colburn Mayne (1865–1941), aka Frances E. Huntley
Charlotte Mew (1869–1928)
Evelyn Sharp (1869–1955), married name Nevinson
Netta Syrett (1865–1943)

Other women writers in the *Yellow Book*

Laurence Alma-Tadema (1865–1940)
Marie Clothilde Balfour (1862–1931)
Susan Christian (1866–1958), married name Susan Hicks-Beach
Ellen M. Clerke (1840–1906)

Constance Cotterell (1864–1947)
Victoria Cross (1868–1952), née Annie Sophie Cory, aka V. C. Griffin
Ella Hepworth Dixon (1857–1932), aka Margaret Wynman
Marion Hepworth Dixon (1856–1936)
Jennie A. Eustace (1865–1936)
Constance Finch (1871–1950)
Eva Gore-Booth (1870–1926)
Aline Harland (1860–1939), née Aline Meriam, aka Renée de Coutans
Mrs Murray Hickson (1859–1922), née Mabel Greenhow, second married name
    Mabel Kitcat
Elsie Higginbotham (1868–1931)
John Oliver Hobbes (1867–1906), née Pearl Richards, married name Craigie
Nora Hopper (1871–1906), married name Chesson
Mary Howarth (1858–1939), married name Nall
Mrs J.E.H. Gordon (1850/51–1929), née Alice Brandreth, second married name
    Alice Mary Brandreth Butcher, Lady Butcher
K. Douglas King (1865–1901), married name Burr
Vernon Lee (1856–1935), pseudonym of Violet Paget
Ada Leverson (1862–1933), née Beddingon
Annie Macdonell (1874–1964), married name Lee, aka Amice Lee
Rosamund Marriott Watson (1860–1911), née Rosamund Ball, married names
    Tomson, Armytage, took name of partner H. B. Marriott Watson
Katharine de Mattos (1851–1939), née Stevenson, aka Theodor Hertz-Garten
Dora Greenwell McChesney (1871–1912)
Lena Milman (1862–1914), Angeline Frances Milman, married name Clarke
Edith Nesbit (1858–1924), married name Bland
Frances Nicholson [?]
Julie Norregard (1863–1942), married name Le Gallienne
Ada Radford (1860?–1934)
Dollie Radford (1858–1920), née Caroline Maitland
Hermione Ramsden (1867–1955)
Alma Strettel (1853–1939), married name Harrison
Lily Thicknesse (1863–1952), née Haynes
Rose Haig Thomas (1853–1942), née Rose Haig
Dolf Wyllarde (1871–1950), pseudonym of Dorothy Margarette Selby Lowndes

Men with editorial control over the *Yellow Book*

Aubrey Beardsley (1872–1898)
Henry Harland (1861–1905), aka Sydney Luska
John Lane (1854–1925)

REFERENCES

Abbreviations

Beinecke	Beinecke Rare Book and Manuscript Library, Yale University, New Haven, Connecticut
Berg	Henry W. and Albert Berg Collection of English and American Literature at the New York Public Library, Astor, Lenox and Tilden Foundations
BL	British Library, London
Bodleian	Department of Special Collections and Western Manuscripts, Bodleian Library, University of Oxford
Brotherton	Brotherton Library, University of Leeds
Butler	Butler Library, Columbia University, New York
Cambridge	Manuscripts Reading Room, Cambridge University Library
Clark	William Andrews Clark Memorial Library, University of California, Los Angeles
DLB	*Dictionary of Literary Biography*
Lilly	Lilly Library, Indiana University Bloomington Libraries
MSL	Mark Samuels Lasner Collection, University of Delaware Library, Museums and Press, Newark
NLI	National Library of Ireland, Dublin
NLS	National Library of Scotland, Edinburgh
NLW	National Library of Wales, Aberystwyth
ODNB	*Oxford Dictionary of National Biography*, www.oxforddnb.com
O'Connell	O'Connell Collection, Rare Books and Special Collections, Princeton University Library, Princeton, New Jersey
PRO	Public Records Office, Kew (now National Archives)
Ransom	Harry Ransom Center, University of Texas at Austin
Reading	Reading University Library
Rutgers	Special Collections and University Archives, Rutgers University Libraries, New Brunswick, New Jersey
YB	*Yellow Book*

Part One: *Fin de Siècle*

1 Bernard Muddiman, *The Men of the Nineties* (London, 1920); Osbert Burdett, *The Beardsley Period* (London, 1925). The neglect of women writers in the books about the 1890s in the early decades of the twentieth century is covered in Jad Adams, 'The 1890s Woman', in *The Edinburgh Companion to Fin-de-Siècle Literature, Culture and the Arts*, ed. Josephine M. Guy (Edinburgh, 2018).

2 Jad Adams, *Madder Music, Stronger Wine: The Life of Ernest Dowson* (London, 2000).

3 Heather Marcovitch has written a helpful resumé of critical commentary on the *Yellow Book* itself in 'The *Yellow Book*: Reshaping the *Fin de Siècle*', *Literature Compass*, XIII/2 (2016), pp. 79–87.

1 The Launch

1 Waugh to Gosse, 17 April 1894, Gosse Correspondence, Brotherton, Leeds.

2 Elizabeth Robins Pennell, *Nights: Rome, Venice, London, Paris* (London, 1916), p. 185.

3 Berta Ruck, MS of 'A Smile for the Past', fols 6–11, NLW MS 23307 E.

4 Elizabeth Robins Pennell, *The Life and Letters of Joseph Pennell*, vol. I (Boston, MA, 1929), p. 274, and Pennell, *Nights*, p. 186.

5 C. Lewis Hind, *Naphtali: Being Influences and Adventures While Earning a Living by Writing* (London, 1926), p. 90.

6 Joseph Hone, *The Life of George Moore* (London, 1936), p. 158.

7 Ella Hepworth Dixon, *'As I Knew Them': Sketches of People I Have Met on the Way* (London, 1930), p. 55.

8 Pennell, *Nights*, p. 186.

9 Netta Syrett, letter to Donald A. Roberts, 7 October 1928, MS in MSL.

10 Waugh to Gosse.

11 Pennell, *Nights*, p. 187.

12 J. Lewis May, *John Lane and the Nineties* (London, 1936), p. 74.

13 Pennell, *Nights*, p. 187.

14 Michael Field, *Michael Field, the Poet: Published and Manuscript Materials*, ed. Marion Thain and Ana Parejo Vadillo (Peterborough, ON, 2009), p. 261.

15 Ibid., p. 262.

16 J. W. Lambert, *The Bodley Head, 1887–1987* (London, 1987), p. 85.

17 John Gawsworth, *Ten Contemporaries: Notes Toward Their Definitive Bibliography* (London, 1932), p. 58.

18 May, *John Lane*, pp. 128–9.

19 Gawsworth, *Ten Contemporaries*, p. 59.

20 Linda K. Hughes, 'Women Poets and Contested Spaces in *The Yellow Book*', *Studies in English Literature, 1500–1900*, XLIV/4 (2004), p. 861.

21 Margaret Stetz and Mark Samuels Lasner, *The Yellow Book: A Centenary Exhibition* (Cambridge, MA, 1994), pp. 12–14, and Barbara Schmidt, 'Henry Harland', *Yellow Nineties 2.0*, www.1890s.ca.

22 Albert Parry, 'Henry Harland: Expatriate', *The Bookman*, LXXVI (January 1933), pp. 7–8.

23 Ella D'Arcy, 'Yellow Book Celebrities', *English Literature in Transition, 1880–1920*, XXXVII/1 (1994), p. 33.

24 Ethel Colburn Mayne, 'Reminiscences of Henry Harland' (1929), MS, MSL.

25 G. Glastonbury [Aline Harland], 'The Life and Writings of Henry Harland', *Irish Monthly* (April 1911), p. 214.

26 Netta Syrett, *The Sheltering Tree* (London, 1939), p. 80.

27 Joseph Pennell, letter to Henry Harland, 1894, MSL.

28 Karl Beckson, *Henry Harland: His Life and Work* (London, 1978), p. 56.

29 Arthur Waugh, *One Man's Road: Being a Picture of Life in a Passing Generation* (London, 1931), p. 251.

30 Ibid., pp. 252–3.

31 Katherine Lyon Mix, *A Study in Yellow* (Lawrence, KS, 1960), p. 77.

32 'New Books and New Editions', *The Times,* 9 April 1894, p. 8.

33 Pennell, *Life and Letters of Joseph Pennell*, vol. I, p. 273.

34 John Spalding Gatton, '"Much talk of the Y. B.": Henry Harland and the Debut of the *Yellow Book*', *Victorian Periodicals Review*, XIII/4 (Winter 1980), pp. 132–4.

35 'Yellow Dwarf' [Harland], 'A Birthday Letter', *YB*, IX (1896), p. 20.

36 Evelyn Sharp, note on letter of 10 November 1894, Evelyn Sharp Nevinson Papers, Bodleian.

37 Evelyn Sharp, letter to R. A. Walker, 14 April 1919. MS, MSL.

38 May, *John Lane*, pp. 208–9, gives a partial list of the attendees.

39 Harland to Le Gallienne, Beinecke, ZA Letter file Box H; dated 'Saturday', no other date but obviously spring 1894, before April.

40 C.M.P. Taylor, 'D'Arcy, Constance Eleanor Mary Byrne', *ODNB*.

41 D'Arcy, 'Yellow Book Celebrities', p. 33.

42 Anne M. Windholz, 'Ella D'Arcy', *British Short Fiction Writers, 1880–1914: The Realist Tradition*, DLB 135, ed. William B. Thesing (Detroit, MI, and London, 1993), p. 94.

43 The *ODNB* entry for D'Arcy records her studying art in 1875 and 1877.

44 D'Arcy, 'Yellow Book Celebrities', p. 33.

45 May, *John Lane*, p. 76.

46 Mix, *A Study in Yellow*, p. 190.

47 Beckson, *Henry Harland*, p. 60.

48 May, *John Lane*, p. 38.

49 Mayne, 'Reminiscences'.

50 Glastonbury [Aline Harland], 'Life and Writings of Henry Harland', p. 218.

51 Stetz and Lasner, *Yellow Book*, pp. 21–3.

52 Henry James, 'The Death of the Lion', *YB*, I (April 1894), p. 20.

53 Ibid., p. 19.

54 Ibid., p. 44.

55 Max Beerbohm, 'A Defence of Cosmetics', *YB*, I, p. 78.

56 Ibid., p. 70.

57 Ella D'Arcy, 'Irremediable', *YB*, I, p. 88.

58 Ibid., p. 104.

59 Arthur Waugh, 'Reticence in Literature', *YB*, I, p. 218.

60 Hubert Crackanthorpe, 'A Modern Melodrama', *YB*, I, pp. 229–30.

61 Hubert Crackanthorpe, 'Reticence in Literature', *YB*, II (July 1894), p. 265.

62 'A Yellow Melancholy' in 'Current Literature', *New Review* (June 1894), p. 503.

63 'The Yellow Book, an Illustrated Quarterly', *The Times*, 20 April 1894, p. 3.

64 'The Yellow Book', *National Observer*, 21 April 1894, p. 588. With similar racial disdain, *The Spectator*'s critic noted the 'slant eyes and blubber lips' of a character in the first volume; 'The Yellow Book', *The Spectator* (19 May 1894), p. 695.

65 J. W. Lambert and Michael Ratcliffe, *The Bodley Head, 1887–1987* (London, 1987), p. 64.

66 Eliza Lynn Linton, 'The Wild Women, No. 1: As Politicians', *Nineteenth Century* (July 1891), p. 79.

67 Ethel Colburn Mayne, 'Herb of Grace', *The Clearer Vision* (London, 1898), pp. 17 and 20.

68 Waugh, 'Reticence', p. 212.

69 Frederick Wedmore, 'The Yellow Book', *Academy* (April 1894), p. 257.

70 Richard Le Gallienne, 'Four Prose Fancies, III: The Arbitrary Classification of Sex', *YB*, VI (July 1895), p. 320.

71 'A Yellow Melancholy', *New Review*, p. 503.

72 *Punch*, 24 November 1894, p. 249.

73 Linda Dowling, 'The Decadent and the New Woman in the 1890s', in *Reading Fin-de-Siècle Fictions*, ed. Lyn Pykett (London, 1996), p. 50.

74 *Academy*, 28 April 1894, p. 339.

2 Gabriela's Deceptions

1 Robert Cunnninghame Graham, letter to Grace Stevenson, 8 September 1932 from Port of Menteith; NLS Acc 11335, Bundle 142.

2 Obituary and report of funeral, *The Herald*, 20 September 1906; *Sterling Sentinel*, 25 September 1906.

3 Katherine Lyon Mix, *A Study in Yellow* (Lawrence, KS, 1960), p. 259. Mix sets the event in Spain; she had probably received the story orally, perhaps from her chief informant Ella D'Arcy.

4 A. F. Tschiffely, *Don Roberto: Being the Account of the Life and Works of R. B. Cunninghame Graham, 1852–1935* (London, 1937), p. 138.

5 A. F. Tschiffely, *Tornado Cavalier: A Biography of R. B. Cunninghame Graham* (London, 1955), p. 70. This is an abbreviated version of the 1936 biography.

6 Cedric Watts and Laurence Davies, *Cunninghame Graham: A Critical Biography* (Cambridge, 1979), p. 42, quoting a letter of condolence with no date but probably September 1906, of course referring to a much earlier meeting with Gabriela.

7 Tschiffely, *Don Roberto*, p. 139.

8 George Stevenson, *Benjy* (London, 1919), p. 31.

9 Ibid., p. 137.

10 Ibid., p. 70.

11 Ibid., p. 84.

12 'Aunt Madge', letter to Grace Stevenson, 3 December 1954, NLS, bundle 142. She was six when Gabriela ran away.

13 Marthe Stevenson, account sent to Lady Polwarth, 1985, NLS, bundle 142. Marthe was usually known as Peggy.

14 Tschiffely, *Tornado*, p. 70.

15 Herbert Faulkner West, *A Modern Conquistador: Robert Bontine Cunninghame Graham, His Life and Works* (London, 1932), p. 40.

16 Robert Bontine Cunninghame Graham, 'Miss Christian Jean', in *His People* (London, 1906), pp. 214–15.

17 C. T. Watts, *Joseph Conrad's Letters to R. B. Cunninghame Graham* (Cambridge, 1969), p. 145. The novel was not published, not even after her death when Cunninghame Graham collected her unpublished works. Edward Garnett advised against, perhaps out of respect for the feelings of his friend Anne Elizabeth Bontine, who outlived Gabriela by nineteen years, dying in 1925.

18 Watts and Davies, *Cunninghame Graham*, p. 41.

19 Anne Taylor, *The People's Laird* (Easingwold, Yorks, 2005), p. 86.

20 Gabriela Cunninghame Graham, Diary, NLS 135.

21 Lady Polwarth, 'Introduction', in Alexander Maitland, *Robert and Gabriela Cunninghame Graham* (Edinburgh, 1983), p. ix.

22 Tschiffely, *Tornado*, p. 71.

23 Gabriela Cunninghame Graham, 'The Waggon Train', in *Christ of Toro and Other Stories* (London, 1908), p. 77.

24 Ibid., p. 83.

25 Taylor, *People's Laird*, p. 99; she dates it as 2 or 20 August 1880.

26 Ibid., p. 100.

27 Will at NLS, SRO SC65/36/5, 22 January 1906. The clerk had trouble with the unfamiliar name and rendered it as 'Chidcock.'

28 Letter, Gabriela to Robert Bontine Cunninghame Graham, 18 March 1904. Maitland, *Robert and Gabriela*, p. 154.

29 Letter, Gabriela to Robert Bontine Cunninghame Graham from Hotel del Commercio, Salamanca, 3 June or July 1889 [indistinct], NLS 55.

30 Taylor, *People's Laird*, p. 113.

31 Tschiffely, *Don Roberto*, p. 269.

32 Taylor, *People's Laird*, p. 133.

33 Marthe Stevenson, account sent to Lady Polwarth, 1985.

34 'Aunt Madge', letter to Grace Stevenson, 3 December 1954.

35 W. B. Yeats, letter to Katharine Tynan, *The Letters of W. B. Yeats*, ed. Alan Wade (London, 1954), p. 64.

36 Gabriela Cunninghame Graham, Diary, NLS bundle 135. The record of expenses may not relate to the year 1888.

37 Maryellen Bieder, 'Emilia Pardo Bazán and Gabriela Cunninghame Graham: A Literary and Personal Friendship', *Bulletin of Spanish Studies*, XCIX/5 (2012), p. 732. The Women's Franchise League was founded by Emmeline Pankhurst and others in July 1889.

38 Keir Hardie, letter to Gabriela Cunninghame Graham, 24 December 1887, NLS bundle 141.

39 Walter Crane, letter to Gabriela Cunninghame Graham, 1 July 1889, NLS bundle 141; Oscar Wilde, letter to Gabriela Cunninghame Graham, c. late June 1889, NLS bundle 141.

40 'The Trafalgar Square Riots', *The Times*, 1 December 1887, p. 13.

41 'Mrs Cunninghame Graham on Her Husband's Imprisonment', *Airdrie Advertiser*, 19 January 1888, p. 3.

42 'Police Brutality Towards Mr Graham', *Airdrie Advertiser*, 19 January 1888, p. 3.

43 Gabrielle [sic] Cunninghame Graham, 'Mr Graham's Arrest', *The Times*, 15 November 1887, p. 8, and 17 November 1887, p. 5

44 'Mrs Cunninghame Graham on Her Husband's Imprisonment'.

45 Walter Crane, *An Artist's Reminiscences* (London, 1907), p. 268.

46 'The Trafalgar Square Demonstration', *Airdrie Advertiser*, 19 November 1887, p. 3.

47 'Mrs Cunninghame Graham and the Kilsyth Miners', *Glasgow Herald*, 3 February 1888, p. 10.

48 Taylor, *People's Laird*, p. 187, quoting Stead papers, Churchill College, Cambridge.

49 Gabriela Cunninghame Graham, letter to John Burns, 29 February 1888, BL, 46284 f5.

50 Richard Bontine Cunninghame Graham, letter to Mr Smith, 14 December 1888, quoted in Taylor, *People's Laird*, p. 206.

51 'Mr Cunninghame Graham', *The Times*, 13 May 1891, p. 5.

52 'Latest Intelligence', *The Times*, 2 May 1891, p. 7.

53 Friedrich Engels, letter to Paul and Laura Lafrague, 3 May 1892, *Correspondence* (Paris, 1959), vol. III, p. 179.

54 Taylor, *People's Laird*, p. 224.

55 Tschiffely, *Don Roberto*, p. 139.

56 'Mrs Cunninghame Graham on Ireland', *Glasgow Evening News*, 4 July 1892, p. 4; 'Remarkable Speech by Mrs Cunninghame Graham' [to the Glasgow Branch of the Irish National League], *Glasgow Herald*, 4 July 1892, p. 10.

57 Gabriela Cunninghame Graham, *Santa Teresa, Being Some Account of Her Life and Times* (London, 1894), pp. 365 and 75.

58 Gabriela Cunninghame Graham, *Santa Teresa*, preface by R. B. Cunninghame Graham, 2nd edn (London, 1907), p. vi.

59 G. and R. B. Cunningham Graham, 'The Batuecas', in *Father Archangel of Scotland and Other Essays* (London, 1896), pp. 198–9. In this Gabriela wrote four out of thirteen essays: 'A Will', 'Yuste', 'The Batuecas' and 'La Vera de Plasencia'.

60 Mrs Cunninghame Graham, 'Spain', in *National Life and Thought of the Various Nations Throughout the World: A Series of Addresses*, ed. South Place Ethical Society (London, 1891), pp. 157–80; address delivered at the South Place Institute, 1889–90.

61 Letter of 7 April 1890, quoted in Taylor, *People's Laird*, p. 239.

62 Letter n.d., quoted ibid., p. 281.

63 Gabriela to Cunninghame Graham, 21 September [?1900], in Watts and Davies, *Cunninghame Graham*, p. 258.

64 'Books of the Week', *The Times*, 6 April 1894, p. 13.

65 'Santa Teresa', *Morning Post*, 3 July 1894, p. 3.

66 J. Lewis May, *John Lane and the Nineties* (London, 1936), p. 210.

67 Mix, *A Study in Yellow*, p. 259, probably informed from Tschiffely, *Don Roberto*, p. 264, where he gets the decade wrong, as 1887, or perhaps the publication said to have rejected a piece from Cunninghame Graham on grounds that it was 'immoral' was not the *Yellow Book* at all, and the date is correct but the journal wrongly identified.

68 Robert Bontine Cunninghame Graham, letter to John Lane, 19 November 1906, Ransom, Lane papers, indicating that very soon after Gabriela's death her husband was collecting her work for publication.

69 Mrs Cunninghame Graham, *The Science of To-morrow and Mediaeval Mysticism*, published lecture in NLS, no publisher, no date, p. 5.

70 'Farewell to Gartmore', *Glasgow Herald*, 22 November 1900, p. 11.
71 Gabriela Cunninghame Graham, letter to Mrs Bontine, 4 December 1900, NLS bundle 137.
72 'Don Juan's Last Wager at the Prince of Wales's', *Reynolds's Newspaper*, 4 March 1900, p. 8.
73 'Prince of Wales's Theatre', *Saturday Review*, 10 March 1900, p. 295.
74 Letter of 29 March 1900, quoted in Watts and Davies, *Cunninghame Graham*, p. 184.
75 Robert Bontine Cunninghame Graham, letter to Miss [Mary?] Horsfall, 13 September 1906, NLS bundle 142.
76 Mary Horsfall, letter to her sister [it is not clear which one], 6 September 1906, NLS.
77 Death certificate, NLS bundle 142.
78 Gabriela Cunninghame Graham, 'The Promise', *Rhymes from a World Unknown* (London, 1908), p. 14.
79 Cedric Watts, 'Robert Cunninghame Graham', *ODNB*.
80 Marthe Stevenson, account sent to Lady Polwarth, 1985.
81 'Aunt Madge', letter to Grace Stevenson, 3 December 1954.
82 Marthe Stevenson, account sent to Lady Polwarth, 1985.
83 Jean Cunninghame Graham, *Gaucho Laird: The Life of R. B. 'Don Roberto' Cunninghame Grahame* (Glasgow, 2004), pp. 189–90.
84 Maitland, *Robert and Gabriela*, p. 23.
85 Marthe Stevenson, account sent to Lady Polwarth, 1985.
86 Faulkner West, *A Modern Conquistador*, p. 40; Tschiffely, *Don Roberto*, p. 138.
87 Mix, *A Study in Yellow*, p. 259.
88 Ibid., p. 144.
89 Watts and Davies, *Cunninghame Graham*, p. 296.
90 Ibid. p. 33.
91 Paul Bloomfield, preface to *The Essential R. B. Cunninghame Graham* (London, 1952), p. 17.
92 *Labour Elector*, 22 June 1889, quoted in Taylor, *People's Laird*, p. 219.

3 The Forerunner

1 J. Lewis May, *John Lane and the Nineties* (London, 1936), p. 128.
2 George Egerton, *The Wheel of God* (London, 1898), p. 9.
3 Ibid., p. 47.
4 George Egerton, *A Leaf from the Yellow Book: The Correspondence of George Egerton*, ed. Terence de Vere White (London, 1958), p. 13.
5 Margaret Stetz, 'George Egerton: Woman and Writer of the Eighteen Nineties', PhD thesis, Harvard University, 1982, p. 5.
6 Egerton, *Wheel of God*, p. 77.
7 George Egerton, letter to John Lane, 29 November 1895, Clark, Box 7 f 80.
8 Egerton, *Wheel of God*, p. 127.
9 Ibid., p. 185.
10 Ibid., pp. 93–4.
11 Stetz, 'George Egerton', p. 11.
12 Egerton, *Wheel of God*, p. 96.
13 Ibid., p. 97.

14 Ibid., p. 163.

15 Ibid., p. 136. The original for 'Aston House' may well have been Warwickshire House, which had a main entrance on Gower Street; my thanks to Emily Gee of Historic England for this information.

16 Ibid., p. 187.

17 Ibid., pp. 146–7. This story is omitted from the U.S. edition of the book by Putnam's in 1898.

18 Higginson is referred to as such in this account for reasons of simplicity, but it seems that after marriage to Whyte-Melville he took her name rather than she taking his. This was doubtless less from feminist gallantry than a desire to confound any pursuing creditors.

19 Ibid., pp. 187, 188 and 190.

20 George Egerton, 'A Shadow's Slant', *Keynotes* (London, 1894), p. 144.

21 Egerton, *Leaf from the Yellow Book*, p. 16.

22 Stetz, 'George Egerton', p. 12, cites anonymous contemporary testimony in the National Library of Ireland.

23 Egerton, *Wheel of God*, p. 206.

24 Ibid., p. 219.

25 Egerton, 'Empty Frame', *Keynotes*, p. 118.

26 Egerton, 'Under Northern Sky', *Keynotes*, pp. 124 and 126.

27 Stetz, 'George Egerton', p. 14.

28 Egerton, *Wheel of God*, p. 202.

29 George Egerton, *Discords* (London, 1894), p. 168.

30 George Egerton, letter to Captain Dunne, 15 March 1891, quoted in Egerton, *Leaf from the Yellow Book*, p. 10.

31 Egerton, 'Now Spring Has Come', *Keynotes*, pp. 39–40.

32 Ibid.

33 Ibid., pp. 44 and 46.

34 Ibid., pp. 54, 55 and 62.

35 Ibid., pp. 58, 60 and 61.

36 Ibid., pp. 62 and 63.

37 George Egerton, 'A Keynote to Keynotes', in *Ten Contemporaries: Notes Toward Their Definitive Bibliography* (London, 1932), p. 57.

38 Letter to Captain Dunne, 4 January 1893, quoted in Stetz, 'George Egerton', p. 26.

39 Egerton, 'Keynote to Keynotes', pp. 57–8.

40 Ibid.

41 Thomas P. Gill, letter to George Egerton, quoted in *Leaf from the Yellow Book*, p. 26.

42 Bodley Head contract 2, box 5, University of Reading archives. James G. Nelson, *The Early Nineties: A View from the Bodley Head* (Cambridge, MA, 1971), p. 100. There were two sixpences to the shilling and twenty shillings to the pound, so Chavelita would have to sell 40 books to make £1. Margaret Stetz has worked out that by the end of 1894 she had made £175 from *Keynotes*.

43 George Egerton, letter to Clement K. Shorter, 21 March 1894, MSL.

44 Camilla Prince, 'The Missing Modernist Link: George Egerton's Pioneering Use of Literary Impressionism', *George Egerton and the Fin-de-Siecle*, Loughborough University, 7–8 April 2017.

45 Egerton, 'A Cross Line', *Keynotes*, p. 22.

46 Hugh E. M. Stutfield, 'The Psychology of Feminism', *Blackwood's Magazine*, 161 (January 1897), pp. 104–17.

47 Margaret Stetz, 'Keynotes: A New Woman, Her Publisher and Her Material', *Studies in the Literary Imagination*, XXX/1 (Spring 1997), p. 99.

48 Egerton, 'A Cross Line', *Keynotes*, pp. 17–18.

49 'Borgia Smudgiton' [perhaps Owen Seaman or Ada Leverson], 'She-notes', *Punch*, 17 March 1894, p. 129.

50 Anonymous, 'Donna Quixote', *Punch*, 28 April 1894, p.195; the illustration on p. 194 is by Linley Sambourne.

51 John Davidson, *Yellow Book* writer and friend of Chavelita, was the first to mention Nietzsche in non-fiction; he translated some, in *The Speaker* ('The New Sophist', 28 November 1891), and later in the *Glasgow Herald* on 18 March 1893.

52 Laura Marholm Hansson, *Six Modern Women: An English Rendering of Laura Marholm Hansson's 'Das Buch der Frauen'*, trans. Hermione Ramsden (London, 1896), p. 61.

53 Ibid., p. 62.

54 Egerton, *Leaf from the Yellow Book*, p. 51.

55 Egerton, 'Keynote to Keynotes', p. 59.

56 Ibid.

57 George Egerton, letter to Clement Shorter, 20 January 1894, O'Connell.

58 George Egerton, letter to Clement Shorter, 14 August 1894, O'Connell.

59 George Egerton, letter to Captain Dunne, 19 October 1893, O'Connell.

60 George Egerton, letter to Clement Shorter, 7 July 1894, O'Connell, quoted in Stetz, 'George Egerton', pp. 31–2.

61 Egerton, *Leaf from the Yellow Book*, p. 50.

62 George Egerton, letter to Richard Le Gallienne, 5 February 1895, in Egerton, *Leaf from the Yellow Book*, p. 48.

63 Discovered by Margaret Stetz while curating the Richard Le Gallienne exhibition at Liverpool Central Library, 2016.

64 Harold Child, *A Poor Player* (Cambridge, 1939), p. 80.

65 Egerton, *Leaf from the Yellow Book*, pp. 55–6.

66 W. B. Yeats, letter to George Egerton, 19 June 1896, in W. B. Yeats, *Collected Letters*, ed. Warwick Gould, John Kelly and Deirdre Toomey (Oxford, 1997), p. 39.

67 George Egerton, letter to Clement Shorter, 7 July 1894, O'Connell.

68 George Egerton, 'Virgin Soil', *Discords* (London, 1894) p. 153.

69 Ibid., p. 155.

70 Ibid., p. 162.

71 Anon., 'The Fiction of the Year', *Leeds Mercury*, 26 December 1896, p. 4.

72 Egerton, 'An Empty Frame', *Keynotes*, p. 123.

73 Egerton, *Wheel of God*, pp. 231–2.

74 Ibid., pp. 263–4.

75 George Egerton, letter to John Lane, 4 October 1894, Clark, Box 7 f 34.

76 Stetz, 'George Egerton', p. 74, quoting a letter to Golding Bright of 2 April 1901.

77 Ibid., p. 76.

78 Ibid., p. 74.

79 Ella D'Arcy, letter to George Egerton, 24 November 1895, O'Connell, C0105, Box 1 (Bright).

80 Egerton, 'Keynote to Keynotes', p. 59.

81 Egerton, *Leaf from the Yellow Book*, pp. 41–2.

82 Egerton, *Wheel of God*, p. 234.

83 George Egerton, letter to John Lane, 10 July 1897, Ransom, Lane archive.

84 George Egerton, letter to Frederic Chapman, 17 July 1897, Ransom, Lane archive.

85 George Egerton, letter to Frederic Chapman, 20 August 1897, Ransom, Lane archive. She had good reason to complain, as there was already a volume of short stories titled *Fantasies*, by Mabel Nembhard, that came out in 1896 and with which *Fantasias* was likely to be confused.

86 Stetz, 'George Egerton', p. 78.

87 Egerton, 'Keynote to Keynotes', p. 59.

88 James G. Nelson, *Publisher to the Decadents: Leonard Smithers in the Careers of Beardsley, Wilde and Dowson* (High Wycombe, 2000).

89 George Egerton, letter to Grant Richards, 1 August 1897, quoted in Stetz, 'George Egerton', p. 115.

90 Egerton, *Wheel of God*, p. 322.

91 'Books of the Day', *Morning Post*, 16 June 1898, p. 2.

92 Grant Richards, *Author Hunting: Memoirs of Years Spent Mainly in Publishing* [1934] (London, 1960), p. 94.

93 Grant Richards, letter to George Egerton, 4 November 1899, O'Connell, cited in Stetz, 'George Egerton', p. 133.

94 George Egerton, letter to Bram Stoker, 27 September 1898, Brotherton.

95 George Egerton, letter to Bram Stoker, 4 May 1898, Brotherton.

4 *Yellow Book* Types

1 Evelyn Sharp, 'A Group of the Nineties', *Manchester Guardian*, 19 January 1924, p. 7.

2 William Locke, letter to Donald A. Roberts, 24 November 1927, MSL.

3 C. Lewis Hind, *Naphtali: Being Influences and Adventures While Earning a Living by Writing* (London, 1926), pp. 89–90.

4 Ella D'Arcy, 'Yellow Book Celebrities', *English Literature in Transition, 1880–1920*, XXXVII/1 (1994), p. 33.

5 Netta Syrett, *The Sheltering Tree* (London, 1939), p. 114.

6 D'Arcy, 'Yellow Book Celebrities', p. 35.

7 Jill Telford Owens, 'Charlotte Mew', *British Short Fiction Writers, 1880–1914: The Realist Tradition*, DLB 135, ed. William B. Thesing (Detroit, MI, and London, 1993), p. 219.

8 Sharp, 'Group of the Nineties'.

9 Locke, letter to Roberts, 24 November 1927.

10 Katherine Lyon Mix, *A Study in Yellow* (Lawrence, KS, 1960), p. 232. Mix also mentions Stephen Gwynn as being frequently present, which may mean his wife May also was.

11 Fr Rolfe [Baron Corvo], *Nicholas Crabbe or The One and the Many: A Romance* [1903–4] (London, 1960), p. 42.

12 Ethel Colburn Mayne, 'Reminiscences of Henry Harland', 1929, MS MSL.

13 Sharp, 'Group of the Nineties'.

14 Syrett said in a letter to Roberts, written from 84 Ebury Street, SW1: 'Do
you by any chance know my novel *The Victorians*? In it I have drawn a little
sketch of the *Yellow Book* set making Henry Harland (under another name
of course) the publisher and not the editor of the magazine which I have
called the *Purple Wonder*.' In fact she called it *The Puce Quarterly*, MS letter,
7 October 1928, in MSL. No page numbers. Hereafter: Roberts letter from
Syrett, *The Victorians* (London, 2015), p. 299.

15 Netta Syrett, *Strange Marriage* (London, 1930), p. 101.

16 Evelyn Sharp, *Unfinished Adventure: Selected Reminiscences from an
Englishwoman's Life* (London, 1933), p. 58.

17 Patrick R. Chalmers, *Kenneth Grahame: Life, Letters and Unpublished Work*
(London, 1933), p. 66.

18 Syrett, *The Victorians*, p. 319.

19 Syrett, *Sheltering Tree*, p. 78.

20 Syrett, *Strange Marriage*, p. 129.

21 Sharp, *Unfinished Adventure*, p. 69.

22 Sharp, 'Group of the Nineties'.

23 Ibid.

24 Syrett, letter to Roberts, 7 October 1928.

25 Rolfe, *Nicholas Crabbe*, p. 31.

26 Ibid., p. 61 fn.

27 Ibid., p. 42; Sharp, *Unfinished Adventure*, pp. 63–4.

28 Rolfe, *Nicholas Crabbe*, p. 43.

29 Syrett, *Sheltering Tree*, p.77.

30 Locke, letter to Roberts, 24 November 1927.

31 Ella D'Arcy, Clark, Box 14 folder 3. Identified as Sunday October 1896 (no
day) in *Some Letters to John Lane*, ed. Alan Anderson (Edinburgh, 1990),
p. 27.

32 Syrett, *Sheltering Tree*, p. 105.

33 Rolfe, *Nicholas Crabbe*, p. 34.

34 J. Lewis May, *The Path Through the Wood* (London, 1930), p. 147.

35 J. Lewis May, *John Lane and the Nineties* (London, 1936), p. 40.

36 Ibid., p. 35.

37 May, *Path Through the Wood*, p. 179.

38 James G. Nelson, *The Early Nineties: A View from the Bodley Head*
(Cambridge, MA, 1971), p. 271.

39 May, *Path Through the Wood*, p. 179.

40 May, *John Lane*, p. 150.

41 Henry Harland, letter to John Lane, 12 June 1894, cited in Lorraine Janzen
Kooistra and Dennis Denisoff, 'Critical Introduction to *The Yellow Book*
Volume 2 (July 1894)', *Yellow Nineties 2.0*, www.1890s.ca.

42 Margaret Stetz, 'Sex, Lies, and Printed Cloth: Bookselling at the Bodley Head
in the Eighteen-Nineties', *Victorian Studies*, XXXV/1 (Autumn 1991), p. 71.

43 Grant Richards, *Memories of a Misspent Youth, 1872–1896* (London, 1932),
pp. 210–11.

44 May, *Path Through the Wood*, p. 152.

45 J.M.B. [Bulloch], 'The Bower of Sappho', *The Sketch*, 4 December 1895,
quoted in May, *John Lane*, p. 151.

46 May, *John Lane*, p. 207.

47 Clark, correspondence, box 4 folder 13, repr. in Ella D'Arcy, *Some Letters to John Lane*, ed. Alan Anderson (Edinburgh, 1990), p. 20.

48 Published in the *Westminster Gazette*, repr. in May, *John Lane*, p. 212.

49 Olive Custance, diary, Berg; this entry is undated and there are pages missing before it. The previous date is 24 June 1894.

50 Custance, diary for 1894, dated 'December Friday', Berg. Her misspelling of Walter 'Stieket' has been corrected.

51 Henry Harland, letter to Olive Custance, n.d. [January 1896], Berg.

52 Custance, diary, 4 January 1894, Berg.

53 Henry Harland, two letters to Olive Custance, undated but January 1896.

54 Henry Harland, letter to Olive Custance, 26 February 1896, Berg.

55 Henry Maas, J. L. Duncan and W. G. Good, ed., *The Letters of Aubrey Beardsley* (London, 1971), 7 January 1897 and 11 February 1897, p. 240.

56 Ibid., 3 March 1897, p. 264.

57 Ibid., 5 March 1897, p. 267.

58 *YB*, III (October 1894), p. 12.

59 'IV. Sexes, Ages, and Condition as to Marriage', *Census of 1891: Preliminary Report*, 30 June 1891, available at www.visionofbritain.org.uk.

60 Richard Davenport-Hines, *Sex, Death and Punishment* (London, 1990), p. 134. Gladstone resigned on 2 March 1894.

61 George Egerton, letter to John Lane, 5 May 1895, 'As to the jury it is a farce to call a nonconformist churchgoer, or a methodist cheesemonger the Peer of a literary man like Oscar. We all know that a jury composed of say Rosebery, Leighton, the late Walter Pater or John Addington Symonds would look at a question of the kind from a different standpoint.' Clark, Wilde MS Box 7 Folder 63.

62 Syrett, letter to Roberts, 7 Octber 1928.

63 Arthur Waugh, *One Man's Road: Being a Picture of Life in a Passing Generation* (London, 1931), p. 251.

64 Owen Seaman, 'A Ballad of a Bun', *The World*, 13 March 1895, p. 74.

65 Arthur Symons, *The Symbolist Movement in Literature* (London, 1899), p. 4.

66 Sharp, 'Group of the Nineties'.

67 Hugh E. M. Stutfield, 'Tommyrotics', *Blackwood's Magazine*, 157 (June 1895), pp. 833–45.

68 Hubert Crackanthorpe, 'Reticence in Literature', *YB*, II (July 1894), p. 266.

69 Blanche Crackanthorpe, letter to John Lane, n.d. [1895], Ransom, John Lane Collection 10.4.

70 B. A. Crackanthorpe, 'The Revolt of the Daughters', *Nineteenth Century*, 35 (January 1894), pp. 23–31.

71 Linda K. Hughes, 'Rosamund Marriott Watson', *Late 19th and Early 20th Century British Women Poets*, *DLB* 240, ed. William B. Thesing (Farmington Hills, MI, 2005), p. 309.

72 Ibid., p. 316.

73 Linda Dowling, 'The Decadent and the New Woman in the 1890s', in *Reading Fin de Siècle Fictions*, ed. Lyn Pykett (Harlow, 1996), p. 48.

74 Lyn Pykett, *Engendering Fictions: The English Novel in the Early Twentieth Century* (London, 1995), p. 20.

75 Jerusha McCormack, *John Gray: Poet, Dandy and Priest* (Hanover, NH, 1991), p. 108.

76 Elaine Showalter, *Daughters of Decadence: Women Writers of the Fin-de-Siècle* (London, 1993), p. ix.

77 Ibid., p. x.

78 Mostyn Turtle Pigott, 'The New Girl and the Decadent', *The World*, 30 October 1895, p. 26.

79 Sharp, 'Group of the Nineties'.

80 David Weir, *Decadence: A Very Short Introduction* (Oxford, 2018), p. 3.

5 'Hast thou slain the Yallerbock?'

1 Katherine Lyon Mix, *A Study in Yellow* (Lawrence, KS, 1960), p. 190.

2 Ella D'Arcy, letter to John Lane, 20 April 1895, Clark, OW Collection, correspondence box 4, folder 13.

3 Ibid.

4 James G. Nelson, 'Sir William Watson', ODNB.

5 The New York papers the *Evening Post*, *The World* and *New York Telegraph* covered the arrest on the day it happened, 5 April 1895.

6 John Lane speaking in 1922, quoted in Margaret D. Stetz and Mark Samuels Lasner, *The Yellow Book: A Centenary Exhibition* (Cambridge, MA, 1994), p. 32.

7 For example, 'Bail for Wilde refused', *New York Tribune*, 7 April 1895, p. 4.

8 'Oscar Wilde in Jail', *Daily Inter-Ocean*, 6 April 1895, p. 3. The same agency copy is printed in the *Trenton Evening Times*, and doubtless many other newspapers. The British newspapers, despite their abundance of detail about the arrest, omit this reference. There is a persistent story that there was a riot outside the Bodley Head office in Vigo Street stimulated by outrage over the Wilde trial. The source is J. Lewis May, *John Lane and the Nineties* (London, 1936), p. 80: 'The public ... engaged in quite a passable little riot in Vigo Street. They threw stones at John Lane's windows and clamoured for the head of Bodley on a charger.' May does not appear to have witnessed it and neither did anyone else apparently, despite the plethora of memoirs about these times. Neither is it mentioned in any of the national newspapers of the time, London's evening newspapers nor weekly local newspapers of the area (though two of these could not be viewed as they are too fragile and had not been digitized or microfilmed at time of research). The fact that something was not reported in a newspaper does not, of course, mean it did not happen, but in the absence of any corroborative evidence, the single account of J. Lewis May is best treated with scepticism.

9 *Illustrated Police Budget*, 13 April 1895, p. 1.

10 'Bow Street Proceedings Today', *Westminster Gazette*, 11 April 1895, p. 5.

11 John Sutherland, *Mrs Humphry Ward: Eminent Victorian, Pre-eminent Edwardian* (Oxford, 1990), p. 191.

12 Evelyn Sharp, *Unfinished Adventure: Selected Reminiscences from an Englishwoman's Life* (London, 1933), p. 75.

13 Jean Moorcroft Wilson, *I Was an English Poet: A Critical Biography of Sir William Watson* (London, 1981), p. 125.

14 Ibid.

15 Haldane Macfall, *Aubrey Beardsley: The Man and His Work* (London, 1928), pp. 62–3.

16 Stetz and Lasner, *Yellow Book*, p. 31.

17 D'Arcy, letter to Lane, 20 April 1895.
18 Ibid.
19 Ibid.
20 Ibid.
21 Anne M. Windholz, 'The Woman Who Would be Editor: Ella D'Arcy and the *Yellow Book*', *Victorian Periodicals Review*, XXIX/2 (Summer 1996), p. 119.
22 Mix, *Study in Yellow*, p. 145.
23 John Lane, letter to George Egerton, 21 April 1895, quoted in George Egerton, *A Leaf from the Yellow Book: The Correspondence of George Egerton*, ed. Terence de Vere White (London, 1958), p. 38.
24 'Young London Writers: A Talk with John Lane, Publisher of the *Yellow Book*', *New York Times*, 12 April 1895, p. 2.
25 Sharp, *Unfinished Adventure*, p. 57.
26 Ella Hepworth Dixon, *My Flirtations* (London, 1892), p. 28.
27 W. V. Harris, 'John Lane's Keynote Series and the Fiction of the 1890's', *PMLA*, LXXXIII/5 (1968), p. 1412.
28 George Egerton, letter to her father, *c.* spring 1895, quoted in Margaret Stetz, 'George Egerton: Woman and Writer of the Eighteen Nineties', PhD thesis, Harvard University, 1982, p. 89.
29 George Egerton, letter to John Lane, 5 May 1895, from The Cottage, Chesham, Bucks, Clark, Box 7 folder 63.
30 Margaret Stetz, 'The Love that Dared Not Speak *His* Name: Literary Responses to the Wilde Trials', in *Bound for the 1890s: Essays on Writing and Publishing in Honor of James G. Nelson*, ed. Jonathan Allison (High Wycombe, 2006), p. 57.
31 George Egerton, *Fantasias* (London, 1898), pp. 140 and 142.
32 Maryellen Bieder, 'Emilia Pardo Bazán and Gabriela Cunninghame Graham: A Literary and Personal Friendship', *Bulletin of Spanish Studies*, LXXXIX/5 (2012), p. 745.
33 Stetz, 'The Love that Dared Not Speak *His* Name'.
34 Ella D'Arcy, 'The Death Mask', *YB*, X (July 1896), p. 270.
35 Ibid., p. 274.
36 Linda K. Hughes, 'Women Poets and Contested Spaces in the *Yellow Book*', *Studies in English Literature, 1500–1900*, XLIV/4 (Autumn 2004), p. 859.
37 Penelope Fitzgerald, *Charlotte Mew and Her Friends* (London, 1984), p. 63.
38 Ibid., p. 67.
39 Richard Le Gallienne, 'The Arbitrary Classification of Sex', *YB*, VI (July 1895), p. 318.
40 Mix, *Study in Yellow*, p. 189.
41 Hughes, 'Contested Spaces', p. 851.
42 Mix, *Study in Yellow*, p. 263.
43 Mabel Kitcat, 'Henry Harland in London', *The Bookman* [New York], XXIV/6 (August 1909), p. 609.
44 'The *Yellow Book* 7', *Bookman* (January 1896), pp. 372–3.
45 Ella D'Arcy, 'The Web of Maya', *YB*, VII (October 1895), p. 300.
46 Evelyn Sharp, 'In Dull Brown', *YB*, VIII (January 1896), p. 187.
47 'The Desert of Sahara', *Pall Mall Gazette*, 6 May 1895, p. 4.
48 'Mr William Watson in the Yellow Book', *Leeds Mercury*, 11 May 1895, p. 7.
49 'The Evergreen', *Glasgow Herald*, 27 May 1895, p. 11.

50 Testudo [Mostyn Pigott], 'The Second Coming of Arthur', *The World*, 8 May 1895, p. 29.

51 Stetz and Lasner, *Yellow Book*, p. 33.

52 Ella D'Arcy, letter to John Lane, dated 'Wednesday morning', 1894, Clark, ow Collection, correspondence box 4, folder 13; repr. in D'Arcy, *Some Letters to John Lane*, ed. Alan Anderson (Edinburgh, 1990), p. 14.

53 Ella D'Arcy, letter to John Lane, 11 April 1896, Clark, ow Collection, correspondence box 4, folder 13, headed paper: 'Office of the Yellow Book'.

54 Ella D'Arcy, letter to John Lane, 16 May 1894, Clark, ow Collection, correspondence box 4, folder 13.

55 Ella D'Arcy, letter to John Lane, 'Wednesday morning' [probably winter 1894], Clark, ow Collection, correspondence box 4, folder 13.

56 Ella D'Arcy, letter to John Lane, n.d., from 57 Marloes Road, Clark, ow Collection, correspondence box 4, folder 13.

57 Ella D'Arcy, letter to John Lane, 11 April 1896, from 'Office of the Yellow Book', Clark, ow Collection, correspondence box 4, folder 13.

58 Ella D'Arcy, letter to John Lane, dated 'Friday' (identified in D'Arcy, *Some Letters to John Lane*, ed. Alan Anderson (Edinburgh, 1990) as January 1895), from chez Monsieur le Conte d'Alcantara, Juan-les-Pins. Clark, ow Collection, correspondence box 4, folder 13.

59 D'Arcy, *Some Letters to John Lane*, p. 6; A. Reynolds Morse, *The Works of M. P. Shiel* (Los Angeles, CA, 1948), p. 21.

60 Fr Rolfe [Baron Corvo], *Nicholas Crabbe or The One and the Many: A Romance* [1903–4] (London, 1960), p. 31.

61 Ella D'Arcy, letter to John Lane, 11 April 1896, from 'Office of the Yellow Book', Clark, ow Collection, correspondence box 4, folder 13.

62 Ibid.

63 Ella D'Arcy, letter to John Lane, 30 December 1896, Clark, ow Collection, correspondence box 4, folder 13.

64 'The Yellow Book', *The Spectator*, 19 May 1894, p. 695.

65 'Books of the Day', *Morning Post*, 13 June 1895, p. 6.

66 *Pall Mall Magazine*, quoted at the back of Ella D'Arcy, *The Bishop's Dilemma* (London, 1898).

67 'Monochromes', *The Graphic*, 13 July 1895, p. 58.

68 *Saturday Review*, quoted at the back of *The Bishop's Dilemma*.

69 Ella D'Arcy, letter to John Lane, 25 July 1895, Clark, ow Collection, correspondence box 4, folder 13.

70 'Two Keynotes', *Pall Mall Gazette*, 21 June 1895, p. 4.

71 '"Our" Academy of Letters', *Pall Mall Gazette*, 3 December 1897, p. 10.

72 Evelyn Sharp, 'A Group of the Nineties', *Manchester Guardian*, 19 January 1924, p. 7.

73 Netta Syrett, *The Sheltering Tree* (London, 1939), p. 98.

74 Ibid., p. 99.

6 Office Wars

1 Norah Hoult, *There Were No Windows* (London, 1944), p. 59.

2 Frances E. Huntley [Ethel Colburn Mayne], 'A Pen-and-Ink Effect', *YB*, VI (July 1895), p. 289.

3 Ethel Colburn Mayne, 'Another Criticism', *English Review* (August 1920), p. 46.

4 Ethel Colburn Mayne, 'Reminiscences of Henry Harland', in *Bound for the 1890s: Essays on Writing and Publishing in Honor of James G. Nelson*, ed. Jonathan Allison (High Wycombe, 2006), p. 18.

5 Ethel Colburn Mayne, 'Reader and Writers', *New Age*, 17 October 1918, p. 397.

6 Frances E. Huntley [Ethel Colburn Mayne], 'Two Stories', *YB*, VIII (January 1896), p. 51.

7 Mayne, 'Reminiscences', p. 18.

8 Ibid.

9 Ibid., p. 19.

10 Mayne, 'Reader and Writers', p. 397.

11 Mayne, 'Another Criticism', p. 46.

12 Mayne, 'Readers and Writers', p. 397.

13 Mayne, 'Reminiscences', p. 22.

14 Ethel Colburn Mayne, *Browning's Heroines* (London, 1913), pp. viii and ix.

15 Mayne, 'Reminiscences', p. 20.

16 Ibid., p. 21.

17 Ibid., p. 23.

18 Ibid., p. 20.

19 Ella D'Arcy, letter to John Lane, 22 December 1895, Clark, OW Collection, correspondence box 4, folder 13.

20 Mayne, 'Reminiscences', p. 23.

21 Mayne's *The Romance of Monaco and Its Rulers* (1910) was published in the United States by John Lane, perhaps as a separate deal by Mayne's agent, or perhaps the rights were sold by Hutchinson, who were her UK publishers.

22 Ella D'Arcy, letter to John Lane, 11 April 1896, from 'Office of the Yellow Book', Clark, OW Collection, correspondence box 4, folder 13.

23 Ibid.

24 Ibid.

25 Ella D'Arcy, letter to John Lane, 23 April 1896, Clark, OW Collection, correspondence box 4, folder 13.

26 Ibid.

27 Mayne, 'Reminiscences', p. 23.

28 Ibid., p. 24.

29 Susan Winslow Waterman, 'Ethel Colburn Mayne', in *Late-Victorian and Edwardian British Novelists, Second Series*, DLB 197, ed. George M. Johnson (Detroit, MI, 1999), pp. 191–2.

30 Ethel Colman Mayne, 'One Near One', in *The Clearer Vision* (London, 1898), p. 178.

31 Ibid., p. 188.

32 Ethel Colburn Mayne, 'The Lost Leader', in *The Clearer Vision*, p. 121.

33 Violet Hunt, 'Recent Literature', *Daily Telegraph*, 5 October 1898, p. 11.

34 Ethel Colburn Mayne, *Jessie Vandeleur* (London, 1902), pp. 48 and 67.

35 Ibid., p. 75.

36 Ibid., p. 213.

37 Anne M. Windholz, 'The Woman Who Would be Editor: Ella D'Arcy and the *Yellow Book*', *Victorian Periodicals Review*, XXIX/2 (Summer 1996), p. 127.

38 Susan Winslow Waterman, 'Ethel Colburn Mayne: Unheralded Pioneer of Modernism', MA thesis, Georgetown University, Washington, DC, 1995, p. 16.

39 Ibid., p. 45.

40 Ella D'Arcy, letter to John Lane, undated except 'Monday' [presumably April 1897], from Nelson Villa, Hythe, Kent, Clark, OW Collection, correspondence box 4, folder 13; Queen Victoria's Diamond Jubilee was on 22 June 1897.

41 Ella D'Arcy, letter to John Lane, 13 April 1897, Clark, OW Collection, correspondence box 4, folder 13.

42 Katherine Lyon Mix, *A Study in Yellow* (Lawrence, KS, 1960), p. 183.

43 Constance Smedley, *Crusaders: The Reminiscences of Constance Smedley (Mrs Maxwell Armfield)* (London, 1929), p. 56.

44 Netta Syrett, letter to John Lane, 7 July 1895, Ransom, John Lane Collection 47.5.

45 Smedley, *Crusaders*, p. 55.

46 Ella D'Arcy, letter to John Lane, Sunday (October 1896), Clark, OW Collection, correspondence box 4, folder 13.

47 Ella D'Arcy, letter to John Lane, 11 April 1896, Clark, OW Collection, correspondence box 4, folder 13.

48 Wages of domestic servants, Board of Trade (Labour department), HMSO 1899. It is important to recognize, however, that domestic servants in a large house would receive bed and board. Note also W. Roberts, 'Life on a Guinea a Week', *Nineteenth Century* (March 1888), pp. 464–7.

49 Ella D'Arcy, letter to John Lane, 13 April 1897, Clark, OW Collection, correspondence box 4, folder 13.

50 'The Bran Pie of Current Literature', *Pall Mall Gazette*, 30 July 1898, p. 3.

51 Ella D'Arcy, 'A Marriage', *Modern Instances* (London, 1898), p. 75.

52 Evelyn Sharp, letter to John Lane, 4 August 1898, Bodleian file 71.

53 'I only heard accidentally from Mr Chapman on Tuesday of your engagement.' George Egerton, letter to John Lane, 26 August 1897, Clark, OW Collection, correspondence box 7, folder 100.

54 J. Lewis May, *John Lane and the Nineties* (London, 1936), p. 166.

55 Ibid., p. 167.

56 Margaret Stetz, '"Mrs John Lane" of the Bodley Head: The Business of Domesticity in a New Century', *Journal of the 1890s Society*, 28 (2001), p. 22.

57 Mix, *Study in Yellow*, p. 254.

58 Lena Milman, 'A Few Notes Upon Mr James', *YB*, VII (October 1895), p. 71.

59 William C. Frierson, *The English Novel in Transition, 1885–1940* (Norman, OK, 1942), p. 51.

60 Ella D'Arcy, letter to John Lane, 11 April 1896, from 'Office of the Yellow Book', Clark, OW Collection, correspondence box 4, folder 13.

61 Ella D'Arcy, letter to John Lane, 13 April 1897, Clark, OW Collection, correspondence box 4, folder 13.

62 Ella D'Arcy, letter to John Lane, undated except 'Monday' [presumably April 1897], Clark, OW Collection, correspondence box 4, folder 13.

63 'The Bishop's Dilemma', *Belfast News-Letter*, 27 May 1898, p. 6.

64 Benjamin Fisher, 'Ella D'Arcy, First Lady of the Decadents', *University of Mississippi Studies in English*, X (1992), p. 242.

65 Ella D'Arcy, letter to John Lane, 10 March [probably 1897], Clark, OW Collection, correspondence box 4, folder 13.

66 Ella D'Arcy, letter to John Lane, 13 March [probably 1897], Clark, OW Collection, correspondence box 4, folder 13.

67 Evelyn Sharp, letter to John Lane, n.d. [doubtless 1897], Bodleian, Lane Letters 44.

68 Evelyn Sharp, letter to John Lane, 12 June 1898, Bodleian, Lane Letters 69. The mention of pigs and Irish is a casual racial slur (the Irish supposedly lived with their pigs).

69 Ella D'Arcy, letter to Arthur Stedman, 31 October [probably 1899], Butler.

70 Ella D'Arcy, letter to John Lane, Friday (?), January 1895, Clark, OW Collection, correspondence box 4, folder 13.

71 Ella D'Arcy, letter to Frederick Chapman, 9 May 1898 (?), Ransom, John Lane Collection.

72 Ella D'Arcy, letter to John Lane, 31 May 1898 (?), Ransom, John Lane Collection.

73 Ella D'Arcy, letter to John Lane, n.d. [but after 1 June 1898], Ransom, John Lane Collection.

74 Ella D'Arcy, letter to John Lane, 11 September 1898 (?), Ransom, John Lane Collection.

75 Ella D'Arcy, letter to Arthur Stedman, 15 April 1899, Butler.

76 Ella D'Arcy, letter to Richard Watson Gilder, 29 July 1899, New York Public Library Century Collection.

77 Ella D'Arcy, letter to Richard Watson Gilder, 8 September 1899, New York Public Library Century Collection

78 Ella D'Arcy, letter to Richard Watson Gilder, 22 December 1899, New York Public Library Century Collection.

79 Karl Beckson, *Henry Harland: His Life and Work* (London, 1978), p. 61.

80 Netta Syrett, *The Sheltering Tree* (London, 1939), p. 100.

81 Ibid., p. 98.

82 William Locke, letter to Roberts, 24 November 1927, MSL.

7 A Paris Mystery

1 Henry Maas, J. L. Duncan and W. G. Good, ed., *The Letters of Aubrey Beardsley* (London, 1971), p. 223.

2 'A Mystery of Paris', *Daily Chronicle*, 12 December 1896, p. 7.

3 Last Will and Testament of Anne Eliza Macdonald, probate 10 March 1896, Courts Service, Principal Registry of the Family Division.

4 Blanche Crackanthorpe, dedication to Hubert Crackanthorpe, *Last Studies* (London, 1897). William C. Frierson notes that Crackanthorpe went to Cambridge for one term but was sent down for some misdemeanour, but in the absence of any more authoritative source, this is discarded.

5 David Crackanthorpe, *Hubert Crackanthorpe and English Realism in the 1890s* (Columbia, MO, 1977), pp. 58, 136.

6 Blanche Crackanthorpe, 'A Last Word on the Revolt', *Nineteenth Century*, 35 (1894), p. 428.

7 Ibid.

8 From verses by Francis Jammes quoted in D. Crackanthorpe, *Hubert Crackanthorpe*, p. 59.

9 Francis Jammes, 'Hommage à Hubert Crackanthorpe', *Association Francis Jammes, Bulletin*, 14 (December 1990), p. 31.

10 Roger Fry, letter to R. C. Trevelyan, 15 March 1896, in *Letters of Roger Fry*, ed. Denys Sutton, vol. I (London, 1972), p. 165.

11 D. Crackanthorpe, *Hubert Crackanthorpe*, p. 122.

12 Ibid., p. 80.

13 Ibid., p. 79. Will dated 16 December 1893.

14 Hubert Crackanthorpe, letter to Mrs Heywood, 28 September 1893, Cumbrian archives. The strike lasted fifteen weeks and ended in mid-November 1893. Crackanthorpe had given trade unionist Ben Tillett a space to write on 'Labour Questions' in the first volume of the *Albemarle* in January 1892.

15 Katherine Lyon Mix, *A Study in Yellow* (Lawrence, KS, 1960), p. 183.

16 Linda Hughes, 'Women Poets and Contested Spaces in the *Yellow Book*', *Studies in English Literature, 1500–1900*, XLIV/4 (Autumn 2004), pp. 849–72; and Sally Ledger, 'Wilde Women and the *Yellow Book*', *English Literature in Transition, 1880–1920*, V/1 (2007), pp. 5–26.

17 Leila Crackanthorpe, letter to John Lane, 11 October 1895, from Hotel Quisisana, Wiesbaden, Germany, Ransom, John Lane Collection 10.4. This was not the great ophthalmologist Alexander Pagenstecher (1828–1879) but his brother Hermann (1844–1932), who took over directorship of the ophthalmology hospital after his death.

18 Crackanthorpe, letter to Selwyn Image, 1895, quoted in D. Crackanthorpe, *Hubert Crackanthorpe*, p. 105.

19 Crackanthorpe, *Hubert Crackanthorpe*, p. 81.

20 Hubert Crackanthorpe and Henry Harland, *The Light Sovereign: A Farcical Comedy in Three Acts* (London, 1917), p. 25.

21 *YB*, V (April 1895), p. 137.

22 Ibid., p. 145.

23 Harold Child, *A Poor Player* (Cambridge, 1939), p. 78.

24 Constance Smedley, *Crusaders: The Reminiscences of Constance Smedley (Mrs Maxwell Armfield)* (London, 1929), p. 34.

25 Ibid.

26 Grant Richards, *Memories of a Misspent Youth, 1872–1896* (London, 1932), p. 236.

27 Smedley, *Crusaders*, p. 33.

28 Child, *Poor Player*, p. 80.

29 Ibid., p. 82.

30 D. Crackanthorpe, *Hubert Crackanthorpe*, p. 123.

31 Lesley A. Hall, '"The Great Scourge": Syphilis as a medical problem and moral metaphor, 1880–1916', www.lesleyahall.net, accessed 12 November 2022, and correspondence with Dr Hall.

32 Personal information from Richard Whittington-Egan, 22 March 2006; his informant was Hesper Le Gallienne.

33 Major Haldane Macfall, letter to Vincent Starrett, 1 December 1923, Lilly, Starrett MSS.

34 Ella D'Arcy, letter to John Lane, 11 April 1896, Clark, OW Collection, correspondence box 4, folder 13.

35 Richard Whittington-Egan and Geoffrey Smerdon, *The Quest of the Golden Boy: The Life and Letters of Richard Le Gallienne* (London, 1960), p. 302.

36 D. Crackanthorpe, *Hubert Crackanthorpe*, pp. 123 and 135.

37 Hubert Crackanthorpe, letters to Grant Richards, 6 October and 18 October 1896, O'Connell.

38 Hubert Crackanthorpe, letter to Grant Richards, 18 October 1896, Donohue Rare Book Room, University of California at San Francisco.

39 D. Crackanthorpe, *Hubert Crackanthorpe*, p. 128.

40 'The Fate of Mr Crackanthorpe', *Pall Mall Gazette*, 26 December 1896, p. 5.

41 D. Crackanthorpe, *Hubert Crackanthorpe*, p. 135.

42 Ibid., p. 136.

43 Ibid.

44 Leila Crackanthorpe, letter to John Lane, 'Sunday evening' [either 9 or (more likely) 15 November 1896], Ransom, John Lane Collection 10.4.

45 D. Crackanthorpe, *Hubert Crackanthorpe*, p. 137.

46 Leila Crackanthorpe, letter to John Lane, 17 November 1896, Ransom, John Lane Collection 10.4.

47 Leila Crackanthorpe, letter to John Lane, n.d. [probably 16 November 1896], Ransom, John Lane Collection 10.4.

48 *Kelly's Post Office Directory* for London, 1897.

49 Leila Crackanthorpe, letter to John Lane, Tuesday 17 November [1896], Ransom, John Lane Collection 10.4.

50 Whittington-Egan and Smerdon, *Quest of the Golden Boy*, p. 306.

51 'Death of Mr H. Crackanthorpe', *The Times*, 25 December 1896, p. 3.

52 'English Author's Disappearance: A Paris Mystery', *Leeds Mercury*, 15 December 1896, p. 7.

53 'Lost in Paris', *Daily News*, 15 December 1896, p. 5.

54 D. Crackanthorpe, *Hubert Crackanthorpe*, p. 137.

55 'Mr Crackanthorpe's Death', *Northern Echo*, 26 December 1896, p. 5.

56 D. Crackanthorpe, *Hubert Crackanthorpe*, p. 20.

57 Dayrell Crackanthorpe, letter to John Lane, 27 December 1896, Ransom, John Lane Collection 10.4.

58 Richard Le Gallienne, 'Hubert Crackanthorpe: In Memoriam', *The Star*, 2 January 1897, p. 1.

59 'The Late Mr Hubert Crackanthorpe', *Daily News*, 28 December 1896, p. 5.

60 'Court Circular', *The Times*, 2 January 1897, p. 6.

61 Ella D'Arcy, letter to John Lane, 30 December 1896, Clark, OW Collection, correspondence box 4, folder 13.

62 Macfall, letter to Starrett, 1 December 1923.

63 Hubert Crackanthorpe, *Collected Stories, 1893–1897* (Gainesville, FL, 1969), p. 249.

64 David Crackanthorpe to Jad Adams, 24 January 2007, personal communication.

65 William Rothenstein, *Men and Memories, 1872–1900*, vol. I (London, 1931), p. 208.

66 Macfall, letter to Starrett, 1 December 1923.

67 Benjamin F. Fisher, 'Hubert Crackanthorpe', *British Short Fiction Writers, 1880–1914: The Realist Tradition*, DLB 135, ed. William B. Thesing (Detroit, MI, and London, 1993), p. 67.

68 Leila MacDonald, letter to Aline Harland, 27 May 1907, MSL.

8 Mabel's Urge for Fame

1 Birth, marriage and death certificates rely on statements to the registrar, which may be lies. If two people say they are married, and want to take

responsibility for a child they have produced together, there is no reason for a registrar to ask difficult questions.

2 It is hard to be certain in tracking certificates of people with very common names such as 'White'. No marriage certificate has been located for Selina Prichard and William White, which may mean they were married abroad, or there was a failure in the records, or that they were not married, notwithstanding that they had the same address and he acknowledged parenthood of his daughter.

3 Mabel Dearmer, *Letters from a Field Hospital with a Memoir by Stephen Gwynn* (London, 1915), p. 4.

4 Ibid., p. 5.

5 Ibid. Dearmer's biography has suffered from a lack of specificity caused by her premature death in time of war, when minds were on things other than the biographical details; the hagiographic account by Stephen Gwynn, who loved her; and the sketchy account by her husband's second wife, who did not.

6 Anne Collyer, 'Interview with Mrs Percy Dearmer', *The Poster: An Illustrated Monthly Chronicle*, II (January 1899), p. 19.

7 Dearmer, *Letters from a Field Hospital*, p. 5.

8 Ibid.

9 E. W. Walters, *Heroines of the World War* (London, 1916), p. 110.

10 Dearmer, *Letters from a Field Hospital*, p. 31.

11 J. Saxon Mills, *Life and Letters of Sir Hubert Herkomer* (London, 1923), pp. 223–4.

12 Ibid.

13 Nan Dearmer, *The Life of Percy Dearmer* (London, 1940), p. 36.

14 Ibid.

15 Dearmer, *Letters from a Field Hospital*, p. 6.

16 Percy Dearmer, letter to Lord Beaucham, 7 November 1891, quoted in Nan Dearmer, *Life of Percy Dearmer*, pp. 76–7.

17 Ibid., p. 87.

18 Ibid.

19 Ibid., p. 88.

20 Mabel Dearmer, *The Difficult Way* (London, 1905), p. 44.

21 Ibid., p. 82.

22 Jill Shefrin, '"Dearmerist Mrs Dearmer": A Lecture', Friends of the Osborne and Lilian H. Smith Collections (Toronto, 1999), p. 12.

23 Nan Dearmer, *Life of Percy Dearmer*, p. 144.

24 Collyer, 'Interview with Mrs Percy Dearmer', p. 20.

25 Stephen Gwynn, *Experiences of a Literary Man* (London, 1926), p. 140.

26 Fr Rolfe [Baron Corvo], *Nicholas Crabbe or The One and the Many: A Romance* [1903–4] (London, 1960), p. 57.

27 Dearmer, *Letters from a Field Hospital*, p. 12.

28 Evelyn Sharp, *Unfinished Adventure: Selected Reminiscences from an Englishwoman's Life* (London, 1933), p. 78.

29 Collyer, 'Interview with Mrs Percy Dearmer', p. 20.

30 Diana Maltz, 'Mabel Dearmer', *Yellow Nineties 2.0*, www.1890s.ca.

31 Collyer, 'Interview with Mrs Percy Dearmer', p. 20.

32 'Christmas Books', *The Graphic*, 18 December 1897, p. 202.

33 Collyer, 'Interview with Mrs Percy Dearmer', p. 19.

34 Nan Dearmer, *Life of Percy Dearmer*, p. 105.
35 Laurence Housman, *The Unexpected Years* (London, 1937), p. 129.

9 Netta Syrett and the Flat of Girls

1 Dennis Denisoff and Lorraine Janzen Kooistra, 'Critical Introduction to *The Yellow Book* Volume 13 (April 1897)', *Yellow Nineties 2.0*, www.1890s.ca.
2 Linda Gertner Zatlin, *Aubrey Beardsley: A Catalogue Raisonné* (New Haven, CT, 2016), vol. I, p. 516.
3 Netta Syrett, *The Sheltering Tree* (London, 1939), p. 6.
4 Syrett wrote to James Lewis May on 23 October 1936 about his book on Lane, 'I think you have captured the atmosphere of the nineties admirably. What an amusing and stirring time it was! I am interested to find myself "the niece of Grant Allen"! A very distant connection is all I can claim by way of relationship – but it doesn't matter! I knew him & his wife very well and often stayed with them when I was a girl.' Clark, Box 66 Folder 4.
5 Syrett, *Sheltering Tree*, p. 40.
6 Elizabeth Coutts, 'Frances Buss', ODNB.
7 Netta Syrett, *The Victorians* (London, 1915), pp. 82, 99, 103 and 94.
8 Coutts, 'Frances Buss'.
9 Syrett, *Sheltering Tree*, p. 14.
10 Syrett, *Victorians*, pp. 122 and 179.
11 Ibid., p. 135.
12 Ibid., p. 234.
13 Netta Syrett, *Nobody's Fault* (London, 1896), p. 74.
14 Jill Tedford Jones, 'Netta Syrett', in *Late-Victorian and Edwardian British Novelists, Second Series*, DLB 197, ed. George M. Johnson (Detroit, MI, 1999), p. 283.
15 Syrett, *Sheltering Tree*, p. 14.
16 Ibid., p. 31.
17 Ibid., p. 33.
18 Grant Allen in *My First Book*, ed. Walter Besant (London, 1894), p. 43.
19 Syrett, *Sheltering Tree*, p. 44.
20 Ibid., pp. 47 and 48.
21 Grant Allen, 'The New Hedonism', *Fortnightly Review*, 55 (March 1894), p. 384.
22 Bonnie J. Robinson, 'Netta Syrett', in *British Short Fiction Writers, 1880–1914: The Realist Tradition*, DLB 135, ed. William B. Thesing (Detroit, MI, and London, 1993), p. 357.
23 Netta Syrett, *Strange Marriage* (London, 1930), p. 48.
24 Syrett, *Sheltering Tree*, p. 38.
25 Ibid., p. 40.
26 Netta Syrett, 'The Failure of the University Woman', *Daily Mail*, 26 February 1902, p. 6.
27 Netta Syrett, *Nobody's Fault* (London, 1896), p. 101.
28 Syrett, *Sheltering Tree*, p. 55.
29 Ibid., p. 34.
30 Ibid., p. 56.
31 Ibid., p. 54.
32 Netta Syrett, 'That Dance at the Robsons', *Longman's Magazine*, 1 April 1890, pp. 639–40.

33 Syrett, *Sheltering Tree*, p. 63.
34 Ibid., p. 66.
35 Ibid., p. 65.
36 Ibid., p. 158.
37 Ibid., p. 90.
38 Ibid., p. 68.
39 Matthew Sturgis, *Aubrey Beardsley: A Biography* (London, 1998), pp. 144 and 153.
40 Syrett, *Sheltering Tree*, p. 72.
41 Ibid., pp. 95 and 73.
42 According to Sturgis, *Aubrey Beardsley*, p. 144, it was orange, not yellow, that was considered 'the very hue of decadence'.
43 Syrett, *Strange Marriage*, p. 101.
44 Syrett, *Victorians*, p. 173.
45 Syrett, *Strange Marriage*, p. 18.
46 Syrett, *Sheltering Tree*, p. 76.
47 Syrett, *Victorians*, p. 174.
48 Syrett, *Sheltering Tree*, pp. 73–4.
49 Ibid., pp. 76 and 79.
50 Patrick R. Chalmers, *Kenneth Grahame: Life, Letters and Unpublished Work* (London, 1933), p. 67.
51 Syrett, *Sheltering Tree*, p. 76.
52 Roberts letter in which she also asks that, 'if quoted, I should prefer my name to be unmentioned', MS letter from Netta Syrett to Donald A. Roberts, 7 October 1928, in MSL. No page numbers, no date.
53 'Wives and Daughters', *Nottinghamshire Guardian*, 27 June 1896, p. 8.
54 J. Lewis May, *John Lane and the Nineties* (London, 1936), p. 210.
55 Syrett, *Nobody's Fault*, p. 80.
56 Ibid., pp. 144 and 183.
57 'Recent Novels', *The Times*, 26 May 1896, p. 5.
58 Readers' report on Syrett's book *The Tree of Life*, Ransom, John Lane Collection 64.5.
59 Arthur Waugh, 'London Letter', *The Critic* [New York], 2 January 1897, p. 11.

9 Ménie Muriel Dowie's Celebrity

1 Ethel M. Heddle, 'Celebrated Lady Travellers, 1. Menie Muriel Dowie', *Good Words* (London, 1901), p. 15.
2 '"The Girl in the Karpathians": A Talk with Mrs Henry Norman (Ménie Muriel Dowie)', *Young Woman*, 54 (March 1897), p. 208.
3 Helen Small, 'Ménie Muriel Dowie', ODNB.
4 '"The Girl in the Karpathians"', p. 209.
5 Ibid., p. 208.
6 Ménie Muriel Dowie, 'For Dear Love's Sake', *Monthly Magazine of Fiction*, XVI/81 (January 1892), p. 7.
7 Heddle, 'Celebrated Lady Travellers', p. 16.
8 *The Times*, 20 June 1891, p. 1. Stalls seats were seven shillings and sixpence, so this was a select audience. Liza Lehmann was the daughter of Dowie's aunt Amelia, née Chambers.

9 '"The Girl in the Karpathians"', pp. 209–10. The title was probably the *People's Journal for Fife and Kinross*, as this was where Dowie lived; the first number of the *Dundee, Perth and Forfar People's Journal* was published in 1858, but quickly spawned regional editions.

10 Ethel F. Heddle, *Three Girls in a Flat* (London, 1896); G. Krishnamurti, *Women Writers of the 1890s* (London, 1991), p. 57.

11 Heddle, *Three Girls in a Flat*, p. 4.

12 Ibid., p. 7.

13 Heddle, 'Celebrated Lady Travellers', p. 16. If Heddle is referring to Amelia Lehmann she has the wrong name for her husband, a painter who was named Wilhelm Augustus, but known as Rudolf Lehmann.

14 *Dundee Courier and Argus*, 15 January 1889, p. 4.

15 Ménie Muriel Dowie, letter to Berta Ruck, no precise date or address, NLW MS 23716D Ff 72–3 1933. The magazine was published by William Stevens, 421 The Strand.

16 Cover of *Monthly Magazine of Fiction*, XVI/81 (January 1892), which contained Ménie Muriel Dowie's 'For Dear Love's Sake'.

17 This brief memoir was sent to Berta Ruck in 1933 when Dowie was in her sixties, NLW MS 23716D Ff 72–3 1933.

18 Heddle, 'Celebrated Lady Travellers', p. 19. 'Lucy' was Annie Lucy Chambers Dowie (b. 1862).

19 Ibid., p. 16.

20 Ménie Muriel Dowie, 'In Ruthenia', *Fortnightly Review*, 48 (October 1890), pp. 520–21.

21 Ménie Muriel Dowie, *A Girl in the Karpathians* (London, 1891), p. 11.

22 'The British Association Meeting in Leeds', *Yorkshire Herald*, 10 September 1890, p. 5. All the other speakers were men, some distinguished.

23 'Science Notes', *Liverpool Mercury*, 18 September 1890, p. 5.

24 'London Gossip', *Birmingham Daily Post*, 10 October 1890, p. 7.

25 'All Sorts and Conditions', *Dundee Courier and Argus*, 6 October 1890, p. 3.

26 'Earlier Closing of Liverpool Shops', *Liverpool Mercury*, 21 October 1890, p. 7.

27 'The Half Holiday Bill', *Daily News*, 12 February 1891, p. 6.

28 Heddle, 'Celebrated Lady Travellers', p. 18.

29 Advertisement in *Northern Echo*, 15 January 1991, p. 1. She gave a number of such lectures, for example in Leeds on 5 February and Liverpool on 8 February 1891.

30 Helen Small, notes to Menie Muriel Dowie, *Gallia* (London, 1995), p. x; advertisement in *Pall Mall Gazette*, 29 May 1891.

31 Dowie, *A Girl in the Karpathians*, 3rd edn (1891), p. vii.

32 Ibid., p. 5.

33 'Theatrical Gossip', *The Era*, 4 July 1891, p. 8.

34 'Our London Correspondence', *Glasgow Herald*, 25 April 1891, p. 7.

35 'Round the Dundee Studios', *Dundee Courier and Argus*, 19 April 1895, p. 2.

36 *Northern Echo*, 27 June 1891, p. 3.

37 Eliza Lynn Linton, 'The Wild Women as Social Insurgents', *Nineteenth Century*, 30 (October 1891), p. 597.

38 Eliza Lynn Linton, 'The Partisans of the Wild Women', *Nineteenth Century*, 31 (April 1892), p. 460.

39 'Marriage of Miss Muriel Dowie', *Pall Mall Gazette*, 5 September 1891, p. 5.

40 Henry Norman (1858–1939), MP for Wolverhampton South (1900–1910) and Blackburn (1910–23). Knighted in 1906 and created a baronet 1915.

41 'Our London Correspondence', *Liverpool Mercury*, 5 September 1891, p. 5.

42 Heddle, 'Celebrated Lady Travellers', p. 16.

43 'Miss Menie Muriel Dowie', *The Queen, the Lady's Newspaper and Court Chronicle*, 3 June 1893, p. 924.

44 Heddle, 'Celebrated Lady Travellers', p. 17.

45 'A Journey Through the Balkans: A Chat with Mr and Mrs Henry Norman', *The Sketch*, 22 January 1896, p. 72.

46 '"The Girl in the Karpathians"', p. 213.

47 Marie Belloc Lowndes, *The Merry Wives of Westminster* (London, 1946), p. 23.

48 Dowie, 'Wladlislaw's Advent', *YB*, IV (January 1895), pp. 90–115, and 'An Idyll in Millinery', *YB*, X (July 1896), pp. 24–53.

49 Dowie, 'My Note-Book in the Weald', *YB*, xii (January 1897), pp. 39–64.

50 Quoted in introduction by Helen Small to Dowie, *Gallia*, p. xxv.

51 'Books of the Day', *Morning Post*, 28 March 1895, p. 3.

52 'Recent Novels', *The Times*, 16 April 1895, p. 8.

53 Dowie, *Gallia*, p. 41.

54 Ibid., p. 109.

55 Ibid., p. 113.

56 Ibid., pp. 114–15.

57 Ibid., p. 167.

58 Ibid., p. 200.

59 Ibid., p. 192.

60 Gail Cunningham, '"He-Notes": Reconstructing Masculinity', in *The New Woman in Fiction and in Fact: Fin-de-Siècle Feminisms*, ed. Angelique Richardson and Chris Willis (London, 2002), p. 96.

61 David Rubinstein, *Before the Suffragettes: Women's Emancipation in the 1890s* (Brighton, 1986), p. 223.

62 'The New Vagabonds' Club', *Pall Mall Gazette*, 7 June 1895, p. 7.

63 'Court Circular', *Morning Post*, 23 February 1898, p. 5.

64 Ménie Muriel Dowie, *The Crook of the Bough* (London, 1898), pp. 98–9.

65 Ibid., p. 280.

66 Heddle, 'Celebrated Lady Travellers', p. 18.

67 '"The Girl in the Karpathians"', p. 208.

68 Heddle, 'Celebrated Lady Travellers', p. 18.

69 *Birmingham Daily Post*, 26 September 1900, p. 46.

70 He lost the Wolverhampton seat in 1910 but was returned as MP for Blackburn in the second election of that year, a position he held until 1923.

71 Heddle, 'Celebrated Lady Travellers', p. 19.

72 Ménie Muriel Dowie, 'Among Karpathian Peaks,' *Nottinghamshire Guardian*, 2 September 1899, p. 6.

11 Evelyn Sharp and the Last Volume

1 Evelyn Sharp, *Unfinished Adventure: Selected Reminiscences from an Englishwoman's Life* (London, 1933), p. 54.

2 Ibid., p. 52.

3 Ibid., p. 54.

4 Ibid., p. 11.
5 Ibid., p. 29.
6 Ibid., p. 38.
7 Ibid., p. 30.
8 Ibid., p. 29.
9 Ibid., p. 31.
10 Ibid., pp. 34 and 35.
11 Ibid., p. 33.
12 Ibid., p. 40.
13 Ibid., p. 52.
14 Evelyn Sharp, *The Making of a Prig* (London, 1897), p. 100.
15 Sharp, *Unfinished Adventure*, p. 56.
16 Ibid., p. 55.
17 John Lane, letter to Evelyn Sharp, 10 November 1894, Bodleian, MS Eng Lett d 276 3.
18 Sharp, *Unfinished Adventure*, p. 73.
19 Ibid., p. 56.
20 Ibid., p. 58.
21 Evelyn Sharp, letter to John Lane, 10 September 1896, Bodleian, MS Eng Lett d 276 8.
22 'Some New Novels', *Daily News*, 6 November 1897, p. 6.
23 Evelyn Sharp, letter to John Lane, n.d. [after October 1897], Bodleian, MS Eng Lett d 276 40.
24 Sharp, *Unfinished Adventure*, pp. 52–3.
25 Ibid., p. 58.
26 Peter Green, *Kenneth Grahame: His Life and Times* (London, 1959), p. 152.
27 Henry Nevinson's diary of 1932, quoted in Angela V. John, *Evelyn Sharp: Rebel Woman* (Manchester, 2009), p. 18.
28 Green, *Kenneth Grahame*, p. 205.
29 Sharp, *Unfinished Adventure*, p. 65.
30 Evelyn Sharp, letter to John Lane, n.d. [after October 1897], Bodleian, MS Eng Lett d 276 40.
31 Evelyn Sharp, 'In Dull Brown', *YB*, VIII (January 1896), p. 198.
32 Stephen Gwynn, *Experiences of a Literary Man* (London, 1926), p. 137.
33 Sharp, *Unfinished Adventure*, p. 82.
34 Ibid.
35 Readers' reports, 1894–9, Ransom, John Lane Collection 64.5.
36 Angela V. John, 'Evelyn Sharp', *ODNB*.
37 Ibid.
38 John, *Evelyn Sharp: Rebel Woman*, p. 19.
39 Matthew Sturgis, *Oscar* (London, 2018), p. 460.
40 John, *Evelyn Sharp: Rebel Woman*, p. 36.
41 'The Yellow Dwarf' [Henry Harland], 'Dogs, Cats, Books, and the Average Man', *YB*, X (July 1896), p. 12.
42 Katherine Lyon Mix, *A Study in Yellow* (Lawrence, KS, 1960), p. 230.
43 Ibid., p. 273, quoting *The Journal of Arnold Bennett*.
44 Ibid., p. 274.
45 Ella D'Arcy, letter to John Lane, undated except 'Monday' [presumably April 1897], Clark, OW Collection, correspondence box 4, folder 13.

46 Mix, *Study in Yellow*, p. 274.
47 Margaret D. Stetz and Mark Samuels Lasner, *The Yellow Book: A Centenary Exhibition* (Cambridge, MA, 1994), p. 39.
48 G. Glastonbury [Aline Harland], 'The Life and Writings of Henry Harland', *Irish Monthly* (April 1911), p. 215; originally written for the *Redwood*, an amateur magazine published by students of Santa Clara College, California.
49 Ibid., p. 215.
50 Ibid., p. 216.
51 Sharp, *Unfinished Adventure*, p. 68.
52 Netta Syrett, letter to Roberts, 7 December 1928, MSL.
53 Ella D'Arcy, '*Yellow Book* Celebrities', *English Literature in Transition, 1880– 1920*, XXXVII/1 (1994), p. 35.
54 Ella d'Arcy, letter to Evelyn Sharp, 3 February 1924, Bodleian, MS Eng Lett c.277.
55 Ella D'Arcy, letter to Mr Rideing, n.d. [after 1905, perhaps long after], O'Connell.
56 Glastonbury [Aline Harland], 'Life and Writings of Henry Harland', pp. 218–19.
57 Ibid., p. 219.
58 Karl Beckson, *Henry Harland: His Life and Work* (London, 1978), p. 131.
59 Ibid., p. 132.
60 Glastonbury [Aline Harland], 'Life and Writings of Henry Harland', p. 218.

Part Two: *Commence de Siècle*

1 Olive Custance to John Lane dated 'Friday' – probably 1900, Berg.
2 Robert Baden Powell, *Scouting for Boys: The Original 1908 Edition*, ed. Elleke Boehmer (Oxford, 2004), p. 295.
3 Ibid., p. 277.
4 Elliott Evans Mills, *The Decline and Fall of the British Empire* (Oxford, 1905), pp. 2, 12 and 16.
5 The British Empire in land mass was larger during the 1919–39 period than at any previous time, but it was being undermined by nationalist movements leading to the loss of Ireland in 1922 and increasing Indian independence agitation from 1919. It was further corroded by the growing realization that maintaining overseas territories cost more than it was worth to the UK, a point that had probably been reached in the 1890s (depending on how the value of colonies is calculated).

12 Family Battles

1 Olive Custance, letter to Lord Alfred Douglas, summer 1901, BL Eccles Bequest, Add MS 81703.
2 Lord Alfred Douglas, *Autobiography* (London, 1931), p. 188.
3 Ibid., p. 24.
4 H. Montgomery Hyde, *Lord Alfred Douglas: A Biography* (London, 1984), p. 136.
5 Douglas Murray, *Bosie: A Biography of Lord Alfred Douglas* (London, 2000), p. 127.
6 Edwin James King, 'New Biographical Work on Custance', 12 December 2017, www.olivecustance.org, accessed 13 November 2022.

7 Olive Custance, diary, 19 November 1894, Berg.

8 Publication of part is in Caspar Wintermans, *I Desire the Moon: The Diary of Lady Alfred Douglas (Olive Custance), 1905–1910* (Woubrugge, 2004).

9 Ibid., p. 10.

10 Patricio Gannon, *John Gray: The Prince of Dreams* (Aylesford, 1963), p. 2.

11 Custance, diary, 4 January 1896.

12 Custance, diary, 8 January 1896. In fact she says 'Monday 8' but this is impossible as the entry describes what she did on Monday and Tuesday.

13 Jerusha Hull McCormack, *The Man Who Was Dorian Gray* (Basingstoke, 2001), p. 300: 'From the mid-nineties onwards, John Gray began to buy up copies of *Silverpoints* in order to "immobilise" or destroy them.'

14 Custance, diary, 21 November 1894.

15 This entry is undated and pages are missing before it; the previous date is 24 June 1894.

16 She is quoting from Christina Rossetti's 'When I am dead, My dearest', which in fact runs: 'And if thou wilt, remember, And if thou wilt, forget.'

17 Richard Whittington-Egan and Geoffrey Smerdon, *The Quest of the Golden Boy: The Life and Letters of Richard Le Gallienne* (London, 1960), p. 323.

18 Ibid., p. 124.

19 Ibid., pp. 121–2.

20 Ibid., p. 131.

21 Ibid., p. 122.

22 Ibid., p. 126.

23 Custance, diary, December 1894.

24 Olive Custance to Alfred Douglas, n.d. [1901 or 1902], BL Eccles Bequest, Add MS 81703.

25 Richard Le Gallienne, *The Romantic Nineties* (London, 1993), p. 97.

26 Julie Norgaard, letter to Olive Custance, 20 April 1897, Berg.

27 Olive Custance, letter to John Lane, n.d. [1897 or 1896], Berg.

28 Olive Custance, letter to John Lane, 30 December 1900, MSL.

29 Natalie Barney, *Souvenirs Indiscrets* (Paris, 1960), p. 51.

30 Douglas, *Autobiography*, p. 189.

31 Ibid., pp. 204–7.

32 Barney, *Souvenirs Indiscrets*, p. 59.

33 Natalie Barney, letter to Olive Custance, n.d., Berg.

34 Barney, *Souvenirs Indiscrets*, p. 58.

35 Custance, letter to Douglas, n.d., 1901, Berg.

36 Barney, *Souvenirs Indiscrets*, p. 61.

37 Custance, letter to Douglas, n.d., 1901. She sent him a photo of herself, saying it was taken in Paris to please Natalie Barney. BL Eccles Bequest, Add MS 81703.

38 Diana Souhami, *Wild Girls: Paris, Sappho and Art; The Lives and Loves of Natalie Barney and Romaine Brooks* (London, 2004), p. 40.

39 Barney, *Souvenirs Indiscrets*, p. 53.

40 Renée Vivien, *Une Femme m'apparut* (Paris, 1977), p. 122.

41 Renée Vivien, letter to Olive Custance, 31 October 1901, Berg.

42 Custance, letter to Douglas, 31 October [presumably 1901], BL Eccles Bequest, Add MS 81703.

43 My thanks for this information to Philip Cohen, who owns this book.

44 Douglas, letter to Custance, September 1901, Berg.
45 Douglas, *Autobiography*, p. 188.
46 Ibid., p. 196.
47 Ibid., p. 212.
48 Ibid., p. 200.
49 Custance, diary, 29 April 1906. It occurs in several places.
50 Custance, diary, 13 May 1907.
51 Douglas, *Autobiography*, p. 212.
52 Ibid., p. 216.
53 Ibid., p. 238.
54 Custance, diary, 10 October 1906.
55 Montgomery Hyde, *Douglas*, p. 151.
56 Custance, diary, 26 April 1906.
57 Murray, *Bosie*, p. 196.
58 Olive Custance's diary is for 1912, being used for 1913 and the page dates may not reflect the dates of writing. The entries certainly give a flavour of the turmoil at this time; the dates under which the entries quoted are written are 18 January 1913, 19 January, 31 January and 2 February.
59 Douglas, *Autobiography*, p. 240.
60 Custance, diary, 25 March 1913.
61 Custance, diary, 20 May and 21 May. It is notable also that Douglas was still in contact with Barney in 1930: Caspar Wintermans notes a letter from him to Barney, which is in the Bibliothèque Doucet in Paris (Wintermans, *Douglas*, p. 201). Barney was very much a part of their lives; see, for example, Olive's urging Douglas, who was going to Paris, to see Natalie and give her Olive's love in a letter of Wednesday, n.d., but from Inglenook, Bembridge, where she was in 1928. BL Eccles Bequest, Add MS 81703. Doris Edwards later became Doris Carlyle (Murray, *Bosie*, p. 346).
62 Douglas, letter to Custance, 3 June 1913, quoted in Hyde, *Douglas*, pp. 192–3.
63 Douglas, letters to Custance, 19 September 1913 and 14 August 1915, quoted in Hyde, *Douglas*, pp. 196 and 200.
64 Murray, *Bosie*, p. 213.
65 Custance, diary, 3 October 2013.
66 Rupert Croft-Cooke, *Bosie: The Story of Lord Alfred Douglas, His Friends and Enemies* (Indianapolis, IN, 1963), p. 352.
67 Valentine card, an adaptation of a Victorian card by Douglas that is in the Custance archive in the Berg. Custance, *Diary*, 7 February 1939.
68 Olive Custance, letter to Alfred Douglas, 14 February 1927, BL Eccles Bequest, Add MS 81703.
69 Croft-Cooke, *Bosie*, p. 380.
70 Hyde, *Douglas*, p. 327.
71 Marie Carmichael Stopes, *Lord Alfred Douglas: His Poetry and His Personality* (London, 1949), p. 21.

13 Charlotte Mew: Love Rebuffed

1 Charlotte Mew, 'Some Ways of Love', *Pall Mall Magazine*, 24 (July 1901), pp. 301–10.
2 Charlotte Mew, letter to Edith Oliver, n.d. [April 1902], University at Buffalo, New York, Special Manuscripts Collection B703F56.

3 Ibid.

4 Ibid.; Penelope Fitzgerald, *Charlotte Mew and Her Friends* (London, 1992), p. 82.

5 Charlotte Mew, letter to Edith Oliver, n.d. [April 1902].

6 Ibid.

7 Ibid.

8 Marjorie Watts, *Mrs Sappho: The Life of C. A. Dawson Scott* (London, 1987), p. 58. This may be an old-fashioned usage of the word prostitute to mean someone who displays themselves sexually; or Dawson Scott believed prostitutes do the work they do because they are oversexed; or she is implying D'Arcy was not above trading sex for favours.

9 Charlotte Mew, 'Le Sacré-Coeur', *Collected Poems of Charlotte Mew* (London, 1953), p. 40.

10 Mew, 'Rooms', ibid., p. 65.

11 Mew, 'Monsieur Qui Passe (Quai Voltaire)', ibid., p. 41.

12 Fitzgerald, *Charlotte Mew*, p. 96.

13 Alida Monro, 'Charlotte Mew: A Memoir', in *Collected Poems of Charlotte Mew*, p. ix.

14 Ibid.

15 Ibid., p. vii.

16 Ibid., p. viii.

17 Ibid., p. x.

18 Ibid., p. xiv.

19 Sibyl Severance, 'Charlotte Mew', in *British Poets, 1880–1914*, DLB 19, ed. Donald E. Stamford (Detroit, MI, 1983), p. 311.

20 Monro, 'Charlotte Mew: A Memoir', p. xviii.

21 Marjorie Watts, 'Memories of Charlotte Mew', PEN *Broadsheet*, 13 (Autumn 1982), p. 12.

22 Fitzgerald, *Charlotte Mew*, p. 111.

23 Watts, 'Memories of Charlotte Mew', p. 12.

24 Ibid.

25 T.E.M. Boll, 'The Mystery of Charlotte Mew and May Sinclair: An Inquiry', *Bulletin of the New York Public Library*, 74 (September 1970), p. 447.

26 'Du petit corps si tendre . . . Du petit coeur malin'; repr. in Fitzgerald, *Charlotte Mew*, p. 136.

27 Watts, 'Memories of Charlotte Mew', p. 12.

28 Ibid., p. 13. In her biography of her mother, Watts quotes this passage slightly differently: 'All the geniuses I have ever met have been sexually unsound . . . Charlotte is evidently a pervert. Is then genius merely one form of sex?' Watts, *Mrs Sappho*, p. 58.

29 Watts, 'Memories of Charlotte Mew', p. 13.

30 Boll, 'Mystery of Charlotte Mew', p. 453.

31 Monro, 'Charlotte Mew: A Memoir', p. xii.

32 Jill Tedford Owens, 'Charlotte Mew', in *British Short Fiction Writers, 1880–1914: The Realist Tradition*, DLB 135, ed. William B. Thesing (Detroit, MI, and London, 1993), p. 224.

33 Mew, *Collected Poems of Charlotte Mew*, p. 55.

34 Monro, 'Charlotte Mew: A Memoir', p. xi.

35 Ibid., p. xii.

36 Sydney Smith, *Forensic Medicine: A Text-Book for Students and Practitioners* (London, 1934), p. 438.
37 Monro, 'Charlotte Mew: A Memoir', p. xviii.
38 S.C.C. [Sydney Cockerell], 'Obituary Miss Charlotte Mew', *The Times*, 28 March 1928, p. 21.

14 Ella D'Arcy: 'Not dead yet'

1 Ella D'Arcy, letter to William H. Rideing, 22 August [1909 or 1910], from Paris, rue de Fleurus, O'Connell.
2 Ella D'Arcy, letter to Evelyn Sharp, 'Sunday' 26 January 1924 [D'Arcy has the day wrong, 26 January 1924 was a Saturday], Bodleian, F 55 MS Eng Lett c.277.
3 Ella D'Arcy, letter to Gertrude Stein, 1910, Beinecke, YCAL MSS 76, Gertrude Stein and Alice B Toklas papers, Box 103 2011.
4 Ella D'Arcy, letter to Gertrude Stein, 22 March 1910, Beinecke.
5 Ella D'Arcy, letter to Gertrude Stein, n.d. ('Sunday'), Beinecke.
6 C. Lewis Hind, *Naphtali: Being Influences and Adventures while Earning a Living by Writing* (London, 1926), p. 94.
7 Ella D'Arcy, letter to Katherine Mix, 14 February 1930, Ransom, Penelope Fitzgerald Collection.
8 Ella D'Arcy, 'An Enchanted Princess', *Century Magazine* (December 1910), p. 13.
9 Ella D'Arcy, letter to A.J.A. Symons, 10 April 1925, MSL.
10 Arnold Bennett, *The Journal of Arnold Bennett, 1896–1910* (London, 1932), 12 December 1910.
11 D'Arcy, letter to A.J.A. Symons, 10 April 1925.
12 Ella D'Arcy, letter to John Lane, 3 February 1924, Ransom, John Lane Collection.
13 Bevis Hillier, 'Antiques', *The Times*, 10 May 1975, p. 9.
14 Katherine Lyon Mix, *A Study in Yellow* (Lawrence, KS, 1960), p. 236; Penelope Fitzgerald, *Charlotte Mew and Her Friends* (London, 1992), p. 27.
15 Ella D'Arcy, letter to Katherine Mix, 30 June 1930, Ransom, Penelope Fitzgerald Collection.
16 Ella D'Arcy, letter to A.J.A. Symons, 30 October 1925, Butler.
17 Ella D'Arcy, *Some Letters to John Lane*, ed. Alan Anderson (Edinburgh, 1990), p. 9. I have not seen this letter and do not know its whereabouts.
18 Blanche Crawford, letter to John Lewis May, Clark, JLM Collection, box 42 f 2. She lived at 27 Stanhope Gardens, SW7.

15 Netta Syrett's Drama Curtailed

1 Neta Syrett, *The Sheltering Tree* (London, 1939), p. 117.
2 'The Competition for Playwrights', *The Times*, 21 October 1901, p. 12.
3 Netta Syrett, *The Finding of Nancy*, BL, Lord Chamberlain's Office papers. Licensed 28 April 1902 with an address of 3 Morpeth Terrace, Ashley Place SW4. Act 1 may be found in *Thousands of Noras: Short Plays by Women, 1875–1920*, ed. Sherry Engle and Susan Croft (Bloomington, IN, 2015).
4 Ibid., pp. 5–6.
5 Ibid., pp. 7–8.
6 Ibid., p. 11.
7 Ibid., p. 18.
8 Ibid., p. 27.

9 Ibid., p. 41.
10 Ibid., pp. 25, 50 and 21.
11 Syrett, *Sheltering Tree*, p. 118.
12 Ibid.
13 Ibid., p. 119.
14 Ibid., p. 121.
15 Ibid., pp. 120 and 119.
16 *Penny Illustrated Paper*, 19 April 1902, p. 245.
17 *Morning Post*, 9 May 1902, p. 5.
18 Syrett, *Sheltering Tree*, p. 124.
19 'PIP Playgoer', *Penny Illustrated Paper*, 10 May 1902, p. 293.
20 *Daily Telegraph*, 9 May 1902, p. 10.
21 Syrett, *Sheltering Tree*, p. 124.
22 Victor Emeljanow, 'Clement Scott', *ODNB*.
23 Syrett, *Sheltering Tree*, p. 125.
24 Netta Syrett, *The Victorians* (London, 1915), p. 113.
25 Syrett, *Sheltering Tree*, p. 92.
26 P. J. Wearing, *The London Stage, 1900–1909: A Calendar of Performers and Personnel* (Lanham, MD, 2014), p. 495. There were reviews in the *Era*, *Illustrated London News*, *Sketch*, *Stage* and *World*.
27 Syrett, *Sheltering Tree*, p. 94.
28 Ibid., p. 148.
29 Peter Thorp, *Friends and Memories* (London, 1931), p. 72.
30 Bonnie J. Robinson, 'Netta Syrett' in *Late-Victorian and Edwardian British Novelists, First Series, DLB* 153, ed. George M. Johnson (Detroit, MI, 1994), p. 358.
31 Jill Shefrin, 'Netta Syrett', *ODNB*.
32 Syrett, *Sheltering Tree*, pp. 216–17. Syrett's plays were *The Fairy Doll*, *The Strange Boy* and *The Enchanted Garden*.
33 Ella Hepworth Dixon, 'The Woman's Progress', *Ladies' Supplement to the Illustrated London News*, 17 January 1914, p. 2.
34 Netta Syrett, 'A Paris Evening', *Daily Mail*, 4 September 1905, p. 4.
35 Syrett, *Sheltering Tree*, p. 114.
36 Family information. Robinetta, always known as Robin (1918–1995), lived with her mother; neither married.
37 Netta Murray Goldsmith, 'Netta Syrett's Lesbian Heroine', *Women's History Review*, XIII/4 (2004), pp. 541–57.
38 'Social', *Sheffield Evening Telegraph*, 22 June 1904, p. 2.
39 Constance Smedley, *Crusaders: The Reminiscences of Constance Smedley (Mrs Maxwell Armfield)* (London, 1929), p. 46.
40 Ibid., pp. 67 and 61.
41 'Femina Vie Heureuse and Northcliffe Prize Committee', *Daily Mail*, 17 October 1932, p. 19.
42 Femina Vie Heureuse Prize, English Committee: Minutes and Papers, MS Add. 8900 1/2/16, 1/2/32, Cambridge.
43 Minutes 1929–32, Add. 8900 1/2/1–1/2/19, Cambridge.
44 Syrett, *Sheltering Tree*, pp. 197 and 280.
45 Netta Syrett, 'Monday Night', n.d. [after December 1926 when Ould became secretary], Ransom, PEN Collection correspondence.
46 Syrett, *Sheltering Tree*, p. 231.

47 Marjorie Hessell Tiltman, 'Novelist's Memoirs', *Times Literary Supplement*, 4 February 1939, p. 76.
48 Syrett, *Sheltering Tree*, p. 93.
49 Ibid., p. 218.
50 Goldsmith, 'Netta Syrett's Lesbian Heroine', p. 552.
51 'Netta Syrett', *The Times*, 18 December 1943, p. 6.

16 Mabel's War

1 Mabel Dearmer, *Letters from a Field Hospital* (London, 1915), p. 30.
2 Ibid., p. 10.
3 Jill Shefrin, '"Dearmerist Mrs Dearmer": A Lecture', Friends of the Osborne and Lilian H. Smith Collections (Toronto, 1999), p. 36.
4 'The Alien Sisters', *Times Literary Supplement*, 20 August 1908, p. 6.
5 Nan Dearmer, *The Life of Percy Dearmer* (London, 1940), p. 155.
6 Dearmer, *Letters from a Field Hospital*, p. 33.
7 Ibid., p. 18.
8 Ibid., p. 24.
9 Mabel Dearmer to G. B. Shaw, 5 December 1911, BL, Bernard Shaw letters, Add 50516 f104.
10 Mabel Dearmer, 'On Censorship and Religious Plays', *The Times*, 5 April 1912, p. 2.
11 'Mrs Dearmer's Plays', *Times Literary Supplement*, 22 February 1917, p. 89.
12 Dearmer, *Letters from a Field Hospital*, p. 31.
13 My thanks to John Loosley of the Oakridge History Society for information about Oakridge Lynch.
14 Dearmer, *Letters from a Field Hospital*, p. 3.
15 Ibid., p. 43.
16 Ibid., p. 45.
17 Ibid., p. 46.
18 Ibid., p. 47.
19 Ibid., p. 48.
20 Ibid., p. 50.
21 Ibid., p. 61.
22 Ibid., p. 62.
23 M. A. Stobart, *The Flaming Sword in Serbia* (London, 1916), p. 52.
24 Ibid.
25 Dearmer, *Letters from a Field Hospital*, p. 62.
26 Ibid., p. 65.
27 Ibid., p. 79.
28 Ibid., p. 153.
29 Ibid., p. 146.
30 Ibid., p. 157.
31 Ibid., p. 134.
32 Ibid., p. 162.
33 Ibid., p. 149.
34 Ibid., pp. 150–51.
35 Ibid., pp. 155 and 156.
36 Ibid., p. 174.
37 Nan Dearmer, *Life of Percy Dearmer*, p. 195.

38 Dearmer, *Letters from a Field Hospital*, p. 177.
39 Geoffrey Dearmer lived to be 103; he died in 1996.
40 Inscription on Oakridge Lynch war memorial, unveiled 1 December 1917.
41 He married Nan Knowles, daughter of a family friend, in August 1916. She gave few details: 'I had known him from the time that I was a child and as I grew up we had become friends.' Nan Dearmer, *Life of Percy Dearmer*, p. 204.

17 Unresting Dragonfly

1 All references to the divorce case are based on *The Times* Law Report, 30 January 1903, p. 9.
2 Patrick French, *The Life of Henry Norman* (London, 1995), p. 140.
3 Henry Norman, 'Diary Dates 1858–1939', a list of events year by year made up by Norman when he planned to wrote an autobiography. Norman archive, Ramster Hall, Chiddingfold.
4 French, *Life of Henry Norman*, p. 93.
5 Ibid.
6 Ibid., pp. 92–3.
7 Honorary degrees from the University of Liverpool in 1935 and University of Dublin in 1936, for example. H. N. Brailsford, 'Henry Woodd Nevinson', *ODNB*.
8 Ménie Muriel Dowie, 'The Thrall Song', *Pall Mall Magazine* (July 1903), p. 393.
9 Berta Ruck, MS of *A Smile for the Past*, NLW, MS 23307 E, ff6–11.
10 Ibid.
11 French, *Life of Henry Norman*, p. 141.
12 Janet Watts, introduction to Rosamond Lehmann, *The Ballad and the Source* (London, 1982), p. x.
13 Rosamond Lehmann, *The Ballad and the Source* (London, 1944), p. 42.
14 Rosamond Lehmann, *A Sea-Grape Tree* (London, 1982), p. 87.
15 French, *Life of Henry Norman*, p. 93.
16 Ethel M. Heddle, 'Celebrated Lady Travellers, 1. Menie Muriel Dowie', *Good Words* (London, 1901), p. 17.
17 Berta Ruck, *A Smile for the Past* (London, 1959), p. 152.
18 Ibid., p. 157.
19 Berta Ruck, 'Notes 1928 1929 Journey with Ménie, Summer in Austria', Entry of 14 May 1929. Travel Journals no. 362 Box 2 Journal 2, University of Delaware special collections.
20 Ruck, *Smile*, p. 152.
21 Ruck, MS of *A Smile for the Past*.
22 Author interview with Sir Torquil Norman, 11 February 2011.
23 Berta Ruck, note F 1, 5 May 1945, NLW, MS 23744D.
24 'Mrs E. FitzGerald Author and Traveller', *The Times*, 2 April 1945, p. 6. The *New York Times* incorrectly referred to her as 'the former Lady Norman of England' and did not mention her literary achievements or the name Dowie, 'Mrs Edward FitzGerald', *New York Times*, 27 March 1945, p. 19.

18 George Egerton: 'This life is dry rot'

1 George Egerton, *Rosa Amorosa: The Love Letters of a Woman* (London, 1901), p. 10.
2 Ibid., p. 16.

3 Ibid., pp. 18 and 19.

4 Ibid., p. 23.

5 Ibid., p. 26.

6 Ibid., p. 186.

7 Ibid., p. 9.

8 'Notes on Books', *The Times*, 29 May 1901, p. 9.

9 Letter of 29 March 1901, quoted in Margaret Stetz, 'George Egerton: Woman and Writer of the Eighteen Nineties', PhD thesis, Harvard University, 1982, p. 85.

10 George Egerton, *A Leaf from the Yellow Book: The Correspondence of George Egerton*, ed. Terence de Vere White (London, 1958), p. 58.

11 Egerton, *Rosa Amorosa*, pp. 70, 58, 62 and 19.

12 Egerton, *Leaf from the Yellow Book*, p. 58.

13 G. B. Shaw, letter to George Egerton, 2 December 1904, ibid., p. 64.

14 G. B. Shaw, letter to George Egerton, 25 May 1907, ibid., p. 65.

15 Ibid., p. 67.

16 Egerton, *Leaf from the Yellow Book*, p. 102.

17 Ibid., p. 178.

18 'Humorous Types in "His Wife's Family"', *New York Times*, 7 October 1908, p. 7.

19 Egerton, *Leaf from the Yellow Book*, p. 67. Her translations of French plays were more successful than her other excursions in the theatre, seeing performances in London and New York from 1912 to 1915.

20 George Egerton, *The Wheel of God* (London, 1898), p. 349.

21 Stetz, 'George Egerton', p. 172.

22 George Egerton, letter to Ellen Key, 13 September 1906, National Library of Sweden SE S-HS L41:58.

23 Ibid.

24 Egerton, *Leaf from the Yellow Book*, p. 80.

25 George Egerton, diary, 6 August 1914, quoted ibid., p. 86.

26 Ibid., p. 88.

27 Ibid., p. 89.

28 Ella D'Arcy, letter to George Egerton, 15 October 1915, Princeton University Library, CO105 Box 1 (Bright).

29 Egerton, *Leaf from the Yellow Book*, p. 99.

30 'Globe Theatre', *The Times*, 8 January 1925, p. 10.

31 'The Passing Shows', *Tatler and Bystander*, 21 January 1925, p. 112.

32 Egerton, *Leaf from the Yellow Book*, p. 91.

33 Ibid.

34 Ibid., p. 101.

35 George Egerton, journal, 6 January 1931, quoted ibid., p. 112.

36 George Egerton, letter to Terence de Vere White, 19 May 1939, quoted ibid., p. 166.

37 George Egerton, letter to M. P. Shiel, 31 June 1935, Ransom, John Lane Collection, Armstrong T.I.F. file.

38 Egerton, *Leaf from the Yellow Book*, p. 96.

39 George Egerton, letter to Terence de Vere White, 20 October 1940, quoted ibid., p. 172.

40 Ibid., p. 176.

41 George Egerton, letter to Martin Secker, 30 April 1945, Lilly, Secker MSS LMC 2203-2.

42 George Egerton, letter to Martin Secker, 19 May 1945, ibid.

43 George Egerton, letter to John Lane, 27 June 1895, Clark, Box 7 folder 68.

19 Suffragette Warrior

1 Angela V. John, *War, Journalism and the Shaping of the Twentieth Century: The Life and Times of Henry W. Nevinson* (London, 2006), p. 99.

2 Henry Nevinson, diary, 19 May 1906, quoted in Angela V. John, *Evelyn Sharp: Rebel Woman* (Manchester, 2009), p. 45.

3 Ibid.

4 Evelyn Sharp, *Rebel Women* (London, 1910), p. 110.

5 Margaret Wynne Nevinson, *Life's Fitful Fever: A Volume of Memories* (London, 1926), p. 113.

6 Henry Nevinson, diary, 8 June 1932, quoted in Michael J. K. Walsh, *Hanging a Rebel: The Life of C.R.W. Nevinson* (Cambridge, 2008), p. 238.

7 John, *Evelyn Sharp: Rebel Woman*, p. 41.

8 An entry for long before she knew him, 23 March 1893, for example, has some remarks in her hand in the third person about his finding a new love. Bodleian, Nevinson Diaries 43973 e.610/1 (1893).

9 Evelyn Sharp, *Unfinished Adventure: Selected Reminiscences from an Englishwoman's Life* (London, 1933), p. 92.

10 Ibid., p. 129.

11 Ibid., p. 130.

12 Ibid., p. 137.

13 Sharp, *Rebel Women*, p. 60.

14 Sharp, *Unfinished Adventure*, pp. 135 and 134.

15 Stephen Gwynn, *Experiences of a Literary Man* (London, 1926), p. 138.

16 Sharp, *Unfinished Adventure*, p. 147.

17 Ibid., p. 139.

18 John, *Evelyn Sharp: Rebel Woman*, p. 43.

19 In the single-volume version of *Fire of Life* he produced in 1935, when married to Sharp, Margaret Nevinson is mentioned once, Evelyn Sharp eight times, some very complimentary: for example, 'brilliant mind and dogged resolution' (p. 265), 'humorous and indignant spirit' (p. 120), 'ready with her penetrating simplicity, her sympathetic wit and her indignant pathos' (p. 85).

20 Sharp, *Unfinished Adventure*, p. 138.

21 John, *Evelyn Sharp: Rebel Woman*, p. 58.

22 Elizabeth Crawford, *The Women's Suffrage Movement: A Reference Guide, 1866–1928* (London, 1999), p. 629.

23 Evelyn Sharp, letter to Elizabeth Robins, 3 May 1913, Ransom, Elizabeth Robins collection.

24 Sharp, *Unfinished Adventure*, p. 145.

25 Ibid., p. 164.

26 Ibid., p. 169.

27 John, *Evelyn Sharp: Rebel Woman*, p. 46.

28 Ibid., p. 47.

29 Sharp, *Unfinished Adventure*, p. 231.
30 Evelyn Sharp, letter to Stanley Unwin about *Somewhere in Christendom*, 12 February 1920, Reading, AVC 5/25.
31 John, *Evelyn Sharp: Rebel Woman*, p. 126.
32 Announcement in *Manchester Guardian*, 19 May 1922, p. 7.
33 Evelyn Sharp, letter to Chatto & Windus, 29 December 1924, Reading, C&W Archive.
34 Evelyn Sharp, letter to Chatto & Windus, 24 November 1925, Reading, C&W Archive.
35 'The London Child', *Times Literary Supplement*, 7 April 1927, p. 243.
36 Sharp, *Unfinished Adventure*, p. 306.
37 Evelyn Sharp, 'Henry Nevinson's last days', 14 December 1941, Ransom, Lane papers.
38 Ibid.
39 Ibid.
40 John, *Evelyn Sharp: Rebel Woman*, p. 201.
41 'Miss Evelyn Sharp', *The Times*, 21 June 1955, p. 13.

20 The Ship with Black Sails

1 Ethel Colburn Mayne, letter to C. F. Cazenove, 22 April 1907, Lilly, LMC1727 Mayne MSS.
2 Ethel Colburn Mayne, letter to C. F. Cazenove, 14 November 1907, ibid.
3 Ethel Colburn Mayne, letter to C. F. Cazenove, Monday 2 August [no year, presumably 1909 if Monday August 2 is correct], Ransom, Mayne Collection MS-2745.
4 Susan Winslow Waterman, 'Ethel Colburn Mayne', in *Late-Victorian and Edwardian British Novelists, Second Series*, DLB 197, ed. George M. Johnson (Detroit, MI, 1999), p. 194. She later translated Boheme's *The Department Store* (1912) and was credited as the translator.
5 Ethel Colburn Mayne, letter to C. F. Cazenove, n.d., Ransom, Mayne collection.
6 Ethel Colburn Mayne, letter to C. F. Cazenove, 20 April 1911, Lilly, LMC1727 Mayne MSS. There were twelve pennies to a shilling and twenty shillings to a pound. A typist at this rate would have to type 24,000 words to earn a pound.
7 Waterman, 'Ethel Colburn Mayne', p. 195.
8 Ethel Colburn Mayne, 'Madeline Annesley', *Things That No One Tells* (London, 1910), p. 188.
9 Ethel Colburn Mayne, letter to Miss Welch, 7 June [probably 1908], MSL.
10 'Lady Byron', *The Times*, 28 June 1929, p. 23.
11 *Time and Tide*, 19 July 1929, pp. 882–3; *The Spectator*, 29 June 1929, p. 1017.
12 Richard Edgcumbe, letter to Ethel Colburn Mayne, 16 November 1912, Brotherton.
13 Ethel Colburn Mayne, letter to Clement Shorter, 21 November 1912, Brotherton.
14 Ethel Colburn Mayne, letter to C. F. Cazenove, 17 September 1912, Lilly, LMC1727 Mayne MSS.
15 Ethel Colburn Mayne, letter to C. F. Cazenove, 11 November 1912, ibid.
16 Ethel Colburn Mayne, letter to C. F. Cazenove, 22 November 1912, ibid.

17 Arthur Waugh, letter to A. P. Watt, 4 May 1922, Wilson Library, University of North Carolina, A. P. Watt & Co records. Constable published *Nine of Hearts* and *Inner Circle*.

18 Joan Hardwick, *An Immodest Violet* (London, 1990), p. 69.

19 Ibid., p. 94.

20 Ibid., p. 152.

21 Femina Vie Heureuse Prize, English Committee: Minutes and Papers, MS Add. 8900 Minutes 1/2/35, Cambridge. The book was *They Knew Mr Knight* by Dorothy Whipple.

22 MS Add 8900 Minutes 1/2/32, Cambridge.

23 Ethel Colburn Mayne, letters to Mary Butts, 22 December 1931 and 6 March 1932, Bienecke, Gen Mss 487, Mary Butts papers, Box 1 folder 32.

24 Mary Butts, *Journals of Mary Butts*, ed. Nathalie Blondel (New Haven, CT, 2002), 18 November 1931, p. 374.

25 Ethel Colburn Mayne, letter to Mary Butts, 14 June 1932, Bienecke, Gen Mss 487 Mary Butts papers, Box 1 folder 32.

26 Ethel Colburn Mayne, letter to Mary Butts, 18 November 1933, ibid.

27 Public Record Office, PRO – PREM 5/268 Ethel Colburne Mayne.

28 Norah Hoult, *There Were No Windows* (London, 1944), p. 59.

29 Ethel Colburn Mayne, letter to Lovat Dixon, 13 March 1940, Reading, Macmillan letterbooks 196/62.

30 Harold Macmillan, letter to Ethel Colburn Mayne, 11 April 1940, Reading, Macmillan letterbooks 969.

31 From Macmillan to Ouvry & Co., administrators, 21 May 1941, '*Regency Chapter* was the only book we published by Miss Mayne. The terms were a royalty of 10% on the first 2,000 copies … £150 was paid on account of these royalties. Unfortunately the sale of the book was very small, and the advance was not earned. Indeed, there is an unearned balance of over £74.' Reading, Macmillan letterbooks 471 and 472.

32 Hoult, *There Were No Windows*, p. 59.

33 Ibid., p. 60.

34 Ibid., p. 74.

35 Register of Incidents, Register of Casualties, War Damage Incident Book, London Borough of Richmond upon Thames.

36 'Obituary Ethel Colburn Mayne', *Times Literary Supplement*, 10 May 1941, p. 230.

37 'Miss Ethel Colburn Mayne', *The Times*, 2 May 1941, p. 7.

38 Ethel Colburn Mayne, 'Henry James as seen from the *Yellow Book*', *Little Review*, v/4 (August 1918), p. 2.

SELECT BIBLIOGRAPHY

Ardis, Ann, *New Women, New Novels: Feminism and Early Modernism*
(New Brunswick, NJ, 1989)

Beckson, Karl, *Henry Harland: His Life and Work* (London, 1978)

Guy, Josephine M., *The Edinburgh Companion to Fin-de-Siècle Literature, Culture
and the Arts* (Edinburgh, 2018)

Heilmann, Ann, *New Woman Fiction: Women Writing First-Wave Feminism*
(Basingstoke, 2000)

Lambert, J. W., and M. Ratcliffe, *The Bodley Head, 1887–1987* (London, 1987)

Le Gallienne, Richard, *The Romantic '90s* [1925] (London, 1993)

May, J. Lewis, *John Lane and the Nineties* (London, 1936)

Mix, Katherine Lyon, *A Study in Yellow* (Lawrence, KS, 1960)

Pykett, Lyn, *Reading Fin-de-Siècle Fictions* (London, 1996)

Richardson, Angelique, and Chris Willis, eds, *The New Woman in Fiction and in
Fact: Fin-de-Siècle Feminisms* (London, 2002)

Rubinstein, David, *Before the Suffragettes: Women's Emancipation in the 1890s*
(Brighton, 1986)

Schaffer, Talia, *The Forgotten Female Aesthetes: Literary Culture in Late-Victorian
England* (Charlottesville, VA, 2000)

Sharp, Evelyn, *Unfinished Adventure: Selected Reminiscences from an
Englishwoman's Life* (London, 1933)

Showalter, Elaine, *Daughters of Decadence: Women Writers of the Fin-de-Siècle*
(London, 1993)

Stetz, Margaret D., and Mark Samuels Lasner, *England in the 1890s: Literary
Publishing at the Bodley Head* (Washington, DC, 1990)

Syrett, Netta, *The Sheltering Tree: An Autobiography* (Edinburgh, 1939)

Thompson, N. D., ed., *Women Writers and the Woman Question*
(Cambridge, 2012)

Toronto Metropolitan University (formerly Ryerson University), *Yellow Nineties
2.0*, www.1890s.ca

Waugh, Arthur, *One Man's Road: Being a Picture of Life in a Passing Generation*
(London, 1931)

Weir, David, *Decadence: A Very Short Introduction* (Oxford, 2018)

ACKNOWLEDGEMENTS

So many people have helped me in researching and writing this book that I am sure I will omit some, for which I apologize in advance. Initial travel to U.S. archives for this book was supported by a grant from the British Academy for which I am most grateful; the Authors' Society gave a grant allowing me to concentrate exclusively on finishing the book in the last months of composition. The Scouloudi Foundation also supported financially as did the Institute of English Studies for conference travel.

This project really took off when Warwick Gould invited me to apply for a research fellowship at the Institute of English Studies, School of Advanced Study, University of London. His support in applications and other technical matters has been invaluable. Over the years I have received support from other staff and colleagues at the IES, most recently enthusiastic encouragement from Clare Lees.

It is impossible to thank Mark Samuels Lasner and Margaret Stetz sufficiently for their friendship and encouragement. Mark generously allowed the use of work in his collection including visual material. Margaret shared her extensive knowledge of the 1890s, in particular of George Egerton. Other scholars who were so kind as to share were Susan Winslow Waterman, who generously shared with me her research on Ethel Colburn Mayne, and Jill Shefrin, who gave me her work on Mabel Dearmer.

Robert Langenfeld as editor of *English Literature in Transition, 1880–1920* gave me a home for essays on some of the characters in *Decadent Women*. Some of the text of *Decadent Women* has previously appeared in the journal, relating to Gabriela Cunninghame Graham, Leila Macdonald, Ménie Muriel Dowie, Olive Custance and Netta Syrett. Those essays are more extensive and academic than the accounts in this book. They are: 'Gabriela Cunninghame Graham: Deception and Achievement in the 1890s', L/3 (2007), pp. 251–68; 'The Drowning of Hubert Crackanthorpe and the Persecution of Leila Macdonald', LII/1 (2009), pp. 6–34; 'Ménie Muriel Dowie: The "Modern Woman of Choices"', LVIII/3 (2015), pp. 313–40; 'Olive Custance: A Poet Crossing Boundaries', LXI/1 (2018), pp. 35–65; 'Netta Syrett: A *Yellow Book* Survivor', LXII/2 (2019), pp. 206–43.

I was grateful for guidance and publication from Petra Dierkes-Thrun as editor of *The Latchkey: Journal of New Woman Studies*, and from R.K.R. Thornton for advice and research materials. Elizabeth Crawford made available her invaluable research skills when I was stuck. A consistent resource has been the *Yellow Nineties* online website: may it continue to grow and thanks to Lorraine Janzen Kooistra for encouragement.

I am grateful to have received assistance and encouragement from (in no particular order): Patricia Pulham, Sarah Parker, Catherine Maxwell, Marion Thain, Laurel Brake, Benjamin Fisher, Philip K. Cohen, Jane Desmarais, Jessica Gossling, Alice Condé, Lesley Hall, Marie Mulvey Roberts, Anthony Cummins, Caspar Wintermans, Richard Whittington-Egan, Esther Dedieu, Philip K. Cohen, Merlin Holland, Leo McKinstry, Benjamin Fisher, Rebecka Klette, Camilla Prince, Kirsten Macleod, Anna Vaninskaya, Dúnlaith Bird, Marianna Muravyeva and Sasha Dovzhyk.

Some family members of people who feature in *Decadent Women* have generously given time to talk or write about their relatives, including the 12th Marquess of Queensberry, David Crackanthorpe, Merlin Holland, François Chapon, Miranda Gunn and Juliet Woollcombe. I must also thank Jean, Lady Polwarth for many kindnesses and correspondence; and Sir Torquil Norman, the only person I have met who actually knew one of my characters.

Staff at the following libraries and archive centres have given advice and answers to my sometimes recondite requests: Michael Bott at the Reading University Library; Philippa Jones at the Brotherton Library, University of Leeds; Oliver House at the Bodleian Library, University of Oxford; Sheila Mackenzie and Laura MacPherson at the National Library of Scotland; Godfrey Waller at Cambridge University Library; Maggie Macdonald at the Clan Donald library; Alice Grayson at Kendal Record Office; staff at the National Library of Wales, the British Library, Public Records Office and the National Library of Sweden.

In the USA: Patrice S. Fox at the Harry Ransom Humanities Research Centre; Nina M. Schneider at the William Andrews Clark Memorial Library; Meg Rich at the Princeton University Archive; Alison Fraser at the University at Buffalo; staff at the Library of Congress; the Van Pelt-Dietrich Library at the University of Pennsylvania; the Butler Library at Columbia University; University of Delaware Library and the Mark Samuels Lasner Library; the Lilly Library, University of Indiana; Beinecke Rare Book and Manuscript Library, Yale University; Albert C. King Manuscript Centre, Rutgers University Libraries; Henry W. and Albert Berg Collection of English and American Literature at the New York Public Library, Astor, Lenox and Tilden Foundations.

During work on this book I have presented papers relating to subjects covered at conferences in St Petersburg, Oxford, Edinburgh and frequently in London. I have benefited from the comments made by colleagues and by informal conversations.

Bevis Hillier kindly read the manuscript, gave me the benefit of his stylistic advice and saved me from many solecisms. My companion in research and work, as in life, is Julie Peakman, who has been endlessly supportive and has been with me on many travels. No one could wish for a better companion.

PHOTO ACKNOWLEDGEMENTS

The author and publishers wish to express their thanks to the sources listed below for illustrative material and/or permission to reproduce it. Some locations of works are also given below, in the interest of brevity:

Photos Jad Adams: pp. 12 (*right*), 292; © The British Library Board: p. 151; collection of the author: pp. 21, 70, 199, 329; David O. McKay Library, Brigham Young University–Idaho, Rexburg: pp. 94, 101, 102, 117, 157, 176; from Ménie Muriel Dowie, *A Girl in the Karpathians* (London, 1891), photo collection of the author: p. 206; London School of Economics and Political Science Library: p. 317; Mark Samuels Lasner Collection, University of Delaware Library, Museums and Press, Newark: pp. 52, 60, 89, 100, 111, 173, 184, 284; from J. Lewis May, *John Lane and the Nineties* (London, 1936), photo collection of the author: p. 92; from Charlotte Mew, *The Rambling Sailor* (London, 1929), photo collection of the author: p. 262; National Library of Wales, Aberystwyth (MS 23716D, fol. 72): p. 300; National Portrait Gallery, London: pp. 308, 323; Philadelphia Museum of Art, Library and Archives, PA: p. 160; Robarts Library, University of Toronto: p. 222; Toronto Metropolitan University Libraries and *Yellow Nineties 2.0*: p. 28; Toronto Public Library, Osborne Collection of Early Children's Books: p. 190; from H. D. Traill, *From Cairo to the Soudan Frontier* (London and Chicago, 1896), photo Harold B. Lee Library, Brigham Young University, Provo, UT: p. 12 (*left*); University of California Libraries, Los Angeles: p. 129; Victoria and Albert Museum, London: p. 33; William Andrews Clark Memorial Library, University of California, Los Angeles: p. 116; courtesy of Juliet Woollcombe: p. 178.

INDEX